The Visionary Mode

The Visionary Mode

~ BIBLICAL PROPHECY,
HERMENEUTICS,
AND CULTURAL CHANGE

Michael Lieb

Cornell University Press
ITHACA AND LONDON

Copyright © 1991 by Cornell University

First published 1991 by Cornell University Press.

International Standard Book Number 0–8014–2273–6
Library of Congress Catalog Card Number 91–9439
Printed in the United States of America
Librarians: Library of Congress cataloging information appears on the last page of the book.

⊗ The paper in this book meets the minimum requirements of the American National Standard for Information Sciences—Permanence of Paper for Printed Library Materials.   ANSI Z39.48-1984.

For Mark and Larry,
the sources of my pride

Contents

Acknowledgments   ix
Introduction   1

Part I. BIBLICAL AND JUDAIC CONTEXTS

One   The Etiology of Vision   15
Two   The Phenomenology of Vision   42
Three The Hermeneutics of Vision   85
Four   The Esoterics of Vision   127

Part II. THE CHRISTOCENTRIC FRAME

Five   The Gnosis of Vision   173
Six   The Spirituality of Vision   216
Seven The Theosis of Vision   263
Eight The Poetics of Vision   306

         Conclusion   351
         Index   355

Acknowledgments

During the long period of writing this book, I have incurred many debts both personal and institutional. I wish first to acknowledge the assistance of those individuals who devoted numerous hours to the evaluation of my book in its entirety. These are the readers for Cornell University Press, Joseph Anthony Wittreich, Jr., and Jason P. Rosenblatt, who read *The Visionary Mode* in its initial stages and in its final form. As the result of their scrutiny, criticism, and suggestions, my work has benefited immensely. For their wise and judicious comments, as well as for their careful reading, I extend my heartfelt thanks. I am likewise extremely grateful to Bernhard Kendler of Cornell University Press for his counsel, encouragement, and support, and for helping me see my book through to completion.

Other individuals have similarly had a share in this undertaking. These include Michael Masi, who read the manuscript and offered very helpful suggestions and Antonio C. Mastrobuono, who provided learned counsel and commentary on the Dante chapter. Bernard McGinn and Jon D. Levenson kindly responded to a published article that would eventually serve as the basis of the Ezekiel chapter, and, with continuing interest, Professor McGinn suggested additional texts that I should explore. During a wonderful year of liberation from academic responsibilities, Clark Hulse and I had long talks over lunch about the progress of our mutual enterprises. It is a time that I shall long remember.

At one point or another, portions of the study benefited from the assembled wisdom of various gatherings, most notably those that occurred at the Newberry Library and at the University of Illinois at Chicago Institute for the Humanities, very early in the career of this book. Mary Beth Rose, John Tedeschi, Paul Gehl, and Richard H. Brown, in particular, will no doubt recall the fiery lessons that this study afforded. I am indebted to them for their good humor and support. I also thank my graduate students, whose lively interest and discussion helped me to acquire a greater sense of what I was attempting to accomplish. If the teacher thanks his students, the student also thanks his teachers. Accordingly, I extend my appreciation to Rachel Z. Dulin and Walter L. Michel, whose patience during long periods of instruction under the auspices of the Spertus College of Judaica has meant a great deal to me.

Funding to undertake the research and writing involved in *The Visionary Mode* has come from a number of sources. A six-month Newberry Library Senior National Endowment for the Humanities Fellowship and a six-month University of Illinois at Chicago Institute for the Humanities Fellowship during the initial stages of the project were immensely helpful in supporting the basic research. Grants-in-aid from the American Council of Learned Societies and the American Philosophical Society on two separate occasions provided the opportunity for continued research and writing, as well as travel to collections. In the later stages of the project a full-year fellowship from the John Simon Guggenheim Memorial Foundation allowed me to bring years of research into focus and to complete the writing of large portions of the book. Finally, the recent bestowal of an Alan M. Hallene Senior University Scholar award from the University of Illinois is a signal instance representing my own institution's faith in my work.

Research for my project was undertaken at a number of institutions, including the Newberry Library, the Regenstein Library of the University of Chicago, the Asher Library of the Spertus College of Judaica, the Krauss Library of the Lutheran School of Theology at Chicago, the libraries at the University of Illinois at Chicago and Urbana-Champaign, Loyola University of Chicago, Northwestern University, the University of California at Los Angeles, Cambridge University, Hebrew University, and the British Library. I deeply appreciate the many courtesies shown me by the directors and librarians of these institutions.

Appearing in revised form, the first chapter was originally published as an article titled "Ezekiel's Inaugural Vision as a Literary Event" in *Cithara* 24 (1985): 22–39. Permission to use this article as part of the present study is gratefully acknowledged.

My final gesture of thanks and affection goes to my family. The care, understanding, and assurances of my wife, Roslyn, have meant everything. Her faith in my work has sustained me during years of research and writing. Those sources of my pride, the two young men to whom this book is dedicated, will remember a similar dedication over a decade ago in an earlier volume. With the publication of the present volume, I once again have the opportunity to acknowledge how much my sons mean to me.

MICHAEL LIEB

Chicago, Illinois

The Visionary Mode

Introduction

In his discussion of the foundations of religious thought, Michael Fishbane maintains that "religions often first produce concrete expressions or objectifications of their deepest religious intentions" by means of core images and that "these intentions recur in spiritualized or interiorized forms" in the later traditions. Referring to such core images as manifestations of what he calls "pure" Yahwism, Fishbane maintains that one of the most arresting occurrences of "pure, concrete Yahwism" is to be found in the vision that inaugurates the prophecy of Ezekiel. "While this theophanic vision is a complex blend of anthropomorphic, theriomorphic, and volcanic imagery," he writes, "there is nevertheless conveyed, through distancing similes and exalted expressions, a depiction of the most transcendent god, YHWH." In the vision of Ezekiel, "the ontological distance between God and man-world is portrayed in all its awesome enormity. The vision confronts Ezekiel with thunderous otherness." As a result of this "otherness," Fishbane concludes, later traditions of religious thought build on the "symbolic structures" implicit in Ezekiel's *visio Dei*.[1]

Adopting that *visio Dei* as the basis of my investigations, I seek in this book to trace the history of the traditions through which Ezekiel's vision found expression from the point of its inauguration in biblical prophecy to its delineation as a poetic event in the later Middle Ages. In doing so, I aim to explore the "thunderous otherness" of the *visio Dei* as a reflection of what might be called the visionary mode. A fundamental manifestation of the religious experience, the visionary mode constitutes the underlying premise upon which the argument of this book is founded. In order to establish a theoretical context for the study as a whole,

---

1. Michael Fishbane, *The Garments of Torah: Essays in Biblical Hermeneutics* (Bloomington: Indiana University Press, 1989), pp. 60–61.

I shall at this juncture suggest how the visionary mode is to be defined, what constitutes it, and the way it is to be distinguished from other modes of apperception.

Because the visionary has its roots in the experiential, perhaps the most appropriate point of departure lies in an exploration of the psychological dimensions of the visionary mode. From this perspective, the person who will provide the most illuminating analysis is Carl Gustav Jung.[2] His discourses on the visionary establish an ideal context for coming to terms with the nature of the visionary mode, a phrase that he in fact coined. What he says about the visionary mode is particularly germane not only because of the acuity with which he delineates the experience from a psychological point of view but because of his insistence on associating that experience with those issues that are of paramount importance here: literary texts and the interpretations they elicit.

These issues are at the forefront of Jung's "Psychology and Literature," an essay first published in 1930.[3] According to Jung there are two modes of artistic creation: the psychological and the visionary.[4] The psychological mode makes use of materials characteristic of the conscious life of the individual, including "crucial experiences, powerful emotions, suffering, passion, [and] the stuff of human fate in general." Drawing on these materials, the poet raises them from the commonplace to the level of poetic experience, which bestows upon them a universality of conviction and significance. "The raw stuff [*Urstoff*] of this kind of creation is derived from the contents of man's consciousness [*Sphäre des Menschen*], from his eternally repeated joys and sorrows, but clarified and transfigured by the poet."[5] As engaging as this form of

2. References are to *The Collected Works of Carl Gustav Jung*, ed. Sir Herbert Read et al., 20 vols., Bollingen Series 20, 2d ed. (New York: Pantheon, 1953–1979), hereafter cited as *CW*, followed by volume and page number. References to the German are to the *Gesammelte Werke*, ed. Dieter Baumann et al., 19 vols. (Olten: Walter-Verlag, 1971–1983), hereafter cited as *GW*, followed by volume and page number.

3. Entitled "Psychologie und Dichtung" in the original, the essay appeared in *Philosophie der Literaturwissenschaft* (1930) and thereafter in expanded and revised form in *Gestaltungen des Unbewussten* (1950). See also Jung, *The Vision Seminars*, ed. Mary Foote, 2 vols. (Zurich: Spring Publications, 1976).

4. According to Read et al., *psychological* as a designation is a bit confusing, because the "visionary" mode also deals with psychological material. As a synonym for *psychological*, the term *personalistic* is suggested (*CW*, XV, 89, n. 2). In the course of its development Jung's discussion, however, does make the distinction clear enough.

5. According to Jung, "countless literary products belong to this class: all the novels

artistic creation might be, its "contents always derive from the sphere of conscious human experience—from the psychic fore-ground of life [*dem seelischen Vordergrund stärkster Erlebnisse*]." For that reason, Jung calls this mode of creation "psychological": its domain is that of the "psychologically intelligible" (*CW*, XV, 89–90; *GW*, XV, 102–103).

In stark contrast to the psychological mode is the visionary mode ("*visionären Erlebnis*"). Here, all is reversed and unfamiliar, indeed, most strange. Deriving its existence from the "hinterland of man's mind [*hintergründiger Natur*]," it appears to emerge "from the abyss of prehuman ages, or from a superhuman world of contrasting light and darkness." It is "a primordial experience [*Urerlebnis*]" that transcends human understanding. Sublime and mysterious in its immensity and shattering impact, "it bursts asunder our human standards of value and aesthetic form." Our response to its presence is that of being dumfounded: "we are astonished, confused, bewildered, put on our guard, or even repelled; we demand commentaries and explanations [*Man verlangt Kommentare und Erklärungen*]." Despite our need to understand, the *Urerlebnis* finally defies all attempts at explanation, for it is "a revelation whose heights and depth are beyond our fathoming." Its effect is to "rend from top to bottom the curtain upon which is painted the picture of an ordered world, and allow a glimpse into the unfathomable abyss of the unborn and of things yet to be [*eröffnet ein Blick in unbegreifliche Tiefen des Ungewordenen*]." So conceived, its nature is fundamentally transformative. Constantly in a state of flux, it distinguishes itself by virtue of its propensity to change. Underlying its formation is a dynamism through which it is for-ever defining and redefining itself both as an originary event and as a subject of discourse.

Thus Jung celebrates it: "Formation, transformation, / Eternal Mind's eternal recreation [*Gestaltung, Umgestaltung, / Des ewigen Sinnes ewige Unterhaltung*]" (*CW*, XV, 90–91; *GW*, XV, 104–105). Drawn from the scene of the *Finstere Galerie* in the first act of the second part of Goethe's *Faust*, the lines commemorate Faust's de-scent to the other-worldly and perilous realm of *die Mütter*, those

---

dealing with love, the family milieu, crime and society, together with didactic poetry, the greater number of lyrics, and drama, both tragic and comic" (*CW*, XV, 88–89; *GW*, XV, 89).

supernal entities capable of assuming a multitude of forms ("*Um-schwebt von Bildern aller Kreatur*").[6] The allusion is apposite not only because it suggests a specific literary context for the visionary mode but because it provides a verbal formulation through which the visionary may be concretized. The verbal playfulness implicit in the German original reinforces the sense of divine play that underlies Jung's understanding of the visionary itself. The visionary for Jung is as much a play of senses and meanings as it is a play of psychological states. Form (*Gestaltung*) as visionary enterprise never remains static: it is always on the verge of transformation (*Umgestaltung*), of replicating itself in a manner that at once embodies its original identity, its *Gestaltung*, and of forging a new identity, its *Umgestaltung*. This is the eternal recreation, the ludic dance, of the eternal mind. To fix that mind, to presume to know it in any absolute sense, is to violate the transformative nature of its very being.

At its core the visionary is, of course, unknowable and unfixable. It can be transmitted only through the offices of those empowered to make its presence known. For Jung, such individuals are the seers and prophets. Through them, the visionary assumes what amounts to poetic form. As seers and prophets, they are poets of the highest order. Having access to the visionary, they feel "the secret quickening of human fate by a suprahuman design" and are imbued with "a presentiment of incomprehensible happenings in the pleroma." Such individuals, Jung observes, are able to catch a glimpse of "the psychic world that terrifies the primitive and is at the same time his greatest hope" (*CW*, XV, 95–96; *GW*, XV, 109–110). Exploring the creative process by which the works of such seers and prophets are enunciated, Jung maintains that, although the "primordial experience" is the source of their creativity, this experience is "is so dark and amorphous that it requires a related mythological imagery to give it form." Wordless and imageless in itself, this *Urerlebnis* is essentially "a tremendous intuition striving for expression." As such, "it is like a whirlwind [*Windwirbel*] that seizes everything within reach and assumes visible form as it swirls upward." Because the revelation of the vision can never replicate the *Urerlebnis* in its originary content, the seer

6. Johann Wolfgang von Goethe, *Faust, der Tragödie (Zweiter Teil)* (Leipzig: Philipp Reclam, 1982). I am indebted to my colleagues Leroy Shaw and Gloria Flaherty for the source of this allusion.

as poet must have recourse to "a huge store of material if he is to communicate even a fraction of what he has glimpsed, and must make use of difficult and contradictory images in order to express the strange paradoxes of his vision [*unheimliche Paradoxie der Vision*]" (*CW*, XV, 96–97; *GW*, XV, 110–111).

As examples of the kinds of mythological paraphernalia that the visionary draws upon to express the *unheimliche Paradoxie der Vision*, Jung offers the heaven, purgatory, and hell of Dante's *Commedia*, the underworld of Goethe's *Faust*, and the poetry of Blake. Along with these, Jung invokes the phantasmagoric world of India, the Old Testament, and the Apocalypse. The depth psychologist who analyzes this variegated spectacle, according to Jung, is in a position to provide comparative data and a terminology commensurate with the visionary content that is portrayed. From the psychological point of view, the rendering of the vision in mythopoeic terms is seen to be a manifestation of the collective unconscious, a phenomenon with its own inborn structure and phylogenetic law. Conceived in this manner, the psychic structure reveals "traces of the earlier stages of evolution it has passed through." These traces are a reflection of the metamorphic nature of the visionary mode as it is constantly transforming itself from its point of origin in the collective unconscious to its point of actualization in the world of forms. These forms, in turn, often exhibit a decidedly esoteric quality: they become "fragments of esoteric doctrines [*Fragmente alter Geheimlehren*]" (*CW*, XV, 96–97; *GW*, XV, 109–110).

The transformative dimension of the visionary mode with its manifestation in *Fragmente alter Geheimlehren* particularly interests Jung, both as depth psychologist and as cultural historian. From the very beginnings of human society, he observes, one finds traces of humanity's attempt to formulate the ineffable in esoteric terms. "Even in the Rhodesian rock-drawings of the Stone Age," says Jung, "there appears, side by side with amazingly lifelike pictures of animals, an abstact pattern—a double cross contained in a circle." This image has appeared in practically every culture, and in the modern world it is found not only in Christian churches but in Tibetan monasteries. This is the so-called sun-wheel (*Sonnenrad*). "Since it dates from a time when the wheel had not been invented," Jung observes, "it cannot have had its origin in any experience of the external world. It is rather a symbol for some inner experience." Assuming the significance of archetypes, such

symbols are characteristic of every culture, which adopts them
and makes them part of its lore and at times even systematizes
them into a body of secret teaching ("*System der Geheim- und Weisheitslehre*") concerning the things that lie beyond earthly existence
(*CW*, XV, 96; *GW*, XV, 110).

Such is the nature of the cultural mythology the visionary mode
generates. Accordingly, the visionary is seen not only as a psychological phenomenon but as a cultural event, one through which
the need to conceptualize and indeed systematize the ineffable in
symbolic terms is made known. At the center of both the psychological and the cultural dimensions that distinguish the visionary
mode is an awareness of the transformative quality of the *Urerlebnis* at the very core of its being. This quality is crucial to any
consideration of the visionary as a fundamental manifestation of
the religious experience.

That fact assumes paramount importance not only to such theo-
reticians as Carl Gustav Jung but to all those who have attempted
to assess the nature of the visionary. Addressing this phenomenon
as a specifically apocalyptic event, Amos Wilder, for example,
demonstrates how verbal and nonverbal expression, including
prophecy, art, and poetry, are fed by "buried hierophanies" that
rise to the surface in the form of "apocalyptic encounter and
utterance," there to "find their own archetypal voice."[7] As a result
of this breaking forth of the visionary, "momentous hierophanies
are historicized and receive innumerable ad hoc revisions and
interpretations." Both in the ancient world and beyond, we are
confronted with "kaleidoscopic rearrangements of a numinous
repertoire" (pp. 437–438). In those rearrangements later writers
both appropriate earlier hierophanies and transform them in visionary terms (p. 441). As a result of such transformations a process of acculturation occurs: we behold what Wilder calls "the
progressive culturizing of the initial vision" (p. 447).

Like Jung, Wilder locates that "culturizing" both historically and
hermeneutically. Most notably, it assumes the form of "esoteric
disclosures of higher wisdom," particularly as "proto-scientific lore
about man, nature, and the cosmos." It manifests itself in other
forms as well, including "the phenomenonology of ecstatic accla-

---

7. Amos Wilder, "The Rhetoric of Ancient and Modern Apocalyptic," *Interpretation: A
Journal of Bible and Theology* 25 (1971): 437. Parenthetical references in my text are to this
essay.

mation" and various forms of mystical *praxis*. In all such cases
there is an attempt either to reformulate the unknowable, to bestow "meaning" upon it and to provide it with a discernible identity, or to incorporate it into a framework consonant with the idea
of reenacting the experience from which it emerged in the first
place. This latter perspective reflects a "concern for the esoterics
of revelation and interpretation." Here, one finds an elaborate
development having to do with what Wilder calls the "machinery"
of visions, one that reflects a "fascination with the processes and
media of *knowing*, with words and numerals and signs" (pp. 441–
442, 445–447).

As Jung, on the one hand, and Wilder, on the other, make
clear, then, the visionary is a phenomenon of immense complexity
and range. Essentially transformative, it elicits commentaries and
explanations that are themselves in effect reformulations of what
is constantly in a process of change. These reformulations are the
means by which the visionary is acculturated in a complex act of
transmission. Underlying this act is a hermeneutics in which the
propensity of the *Urerlebnis* to undergo transformation at every
stage is realized in the very act of implementing it in "knowable"
form. Whether as a hermeneutics or as a poetics, that form is itself
a reenactment of the vision, one that says as much about how the
reenactment occurs as it does about the vision it seeks to elucidate.
With its source in the utterances of seers and prophets, the visionary reveals itself as a phenomenon of immense fascination
and richness. In the terms through which Rudolf Otto describes
it in his own phenomenological vocabulary, it is a manifestation
of *das Heilige* (the holy) itself, that *mysterium tremendum* which is
ganz andere (wholly other) and which overpowers with its awesomeness.[8] Encountering this phenomenon, hermeneuts of all
persuasions generate the kaleidoscopic rearrangements of their
own numinous repertoire. What results are the complex traditions
of exegesis that distinguish the visionary mode as a focus of interpretive discourse and reenactment.

It is the nature of this discourse and reenactment to produce
texts that are as rich and multifaceted in their own way as the text
of the originary event whose mysteries they seek to illuminate. In

8. Rudolf Otto, *Das Heilige: Über das Irrationale und der Idee des Götlichen und sein Verhältnis
zum Rationalen* (Breslau: Trewendt and Granier, 1922), passim. Translated by John W.
Harvey as *The Idea of the Holy: An Inquiry into the Non-Rational Factor in the Idea of the Divine
and Its Relation to the Rational* (London: Oxford University Press, 1931).

attempting to disclose the secrets of that event, the hermeneut generates a new text with its own claims to authority. From the perspective of the visionary mode, this idea gains particular cogency, for the exegete of the visionary is not only the purveyor of interpretive strategies but, in effect, the means by which those strategies find renewed authority within the hermeneutical milieu that the new interpretation provides for them. In the encounter with the primal text through which the vision announces its presence, the hermeneut authorizes the visionary event anew. His interpretation becomes the new text of that event; he the seer through whom the visionary mode undergoes its transformation. In the seer are fulfilled the terms of the dictum: *"Gestaltung, Umgestaltung, / Des ewigen Sinnes ewige Unterhaltung."* Bestowing upon the event a renewed authority, the hermeneut devises a version of the text as compelling in its disclosures as the primal text that is the putative source of the interpretation. The new text, the new reading, is in effect the source not only of a new awareness but of a reenvisioning of the originary event.

As the result of this reenvisioning, the event assumes the aura of a new legitimacy, a new code with its own set of interpretive laws. Achieving that status, it takes its place in what Joseph Anthony Wittreich, Jr., aptly calls "the line of vision." Within that line the visionary experience becomes at once "a way of seeing" and "a way of writing."[9] Each comments upon the other, and each is dependent upon the other. In that mutual commentary and interdependence, there arises a visionary hermeneutics that is both self-perpetuating and self-authorizing. This process of self-authorization distinguishes the line of vision as a phenomenon of utmost interest and fascination, for in the act of reenvisioning, that is, in writing the vision anew, the hermeneut is able to claim an interpretive authority tantamount to that which promulgated the visionary experience at its most primal level.

Because of the theological implications that such an idea entails, the adoption of this outlook runs the risk of subjecting one to charges of being guilty of something like interpretive heresy. Such

9. *Milton and the Line of Vision*, ed. Joseph Anthony Wittreich, Jr. (Madison: University of Wisconsin Press, 1975), pp. xv–xvi. Although the volume focuses upon Milton, Wittreich's observations are relevant to the entire "line of vision" addressed in the present study. See also Wittreich's *Visionary Poetics: Milton's Tradition and His Legacy* (San Marino, Calif.: Henry E. Huntington Library, 1979), which will be addressed in the later discussion of the poetics of vision.

is particularly true considering that the basis of the visionary delineated here is that category of otherness called "God." The source of interpretation, after all, is the *visio Dei*, or at least the text in which that vision is portrayed. If one arrogates to oneself an authority tantamount to that medium through whom the vision is originally transmitted, such an act bestows upon the hermeneut a status as authoritative as the one who enunciated the *visio Dei* in the first place. Dealing in sacred matters and appropriating them to his own use, the interpreter becomes heretic, one whose understanding of the visionary causes the event to assume a form potentially at odds with those who devised laws determining the propriety or impropriety of coming to terms with its original conception.

Both the idea of such a heresy and how it operates in the highest realms are a mainstay of that most profound source of interpretive discourse, the Talmud. There, the whole issue is given what amounts to a rabbinical legitimacy in a classic debate over the nature of authority. The debate in question appears in a famous ʾ*aggadah* from the tractate *Baba Meziʾa* (59a–59b). According to the ʾ*aggadah*, the rabbinical authorities found themselves engaged in a disagreement concerning the subject of ritual purity. The focus of the disagreement was the so-called *Tanur shel ʿAknai*, or the ʿAknai Oven. As the text suggests, this was an appropriate name for the oven, since the rabbis encompassed the subject with arguments like a "snake," a meaning implicit in the term ʿ*Aknai*. As they debated the subject of ritual purity, the great sage Rabbi Eliezer brought forth every imaginable argument on behalf of his cause, but the other sages continued to disagree, as each expounded his own point of view.

In order to demonstrate that his interpretation was not only correct but divinely ordained, Rabbi Eliezer effected a series of miracles. He saw to it that a carob tree was torn from its roots, that a stream of water was made to flow backward, and that the walls of the schoolhouse were inclined to fall inward upon themselves—all to show that *halakhah* was in agreement with him. When he realized that these miracles proved unconvincing to the other sages, who continued to maintain the authority of their own interpretations, he called upon the authority of Heaven itself: "If the *halakhah* agrees with me," he proclaimed, "let it be proved from Heaven!" At that point the Heavenly Voice (*bat kol*) cried out: "Why do ye dispute with R. Eliezer, seeing that in all matters the *halakhah* agrees with him!" In response to this declaration, Rabbi Joshua arose and exclaimed: "It is not in heaven [*lo' bashamaim hiy'*]."[10] As the authorities interpreted Rabbi Joshua's response, they agreed that once the Torah had been proclaimed from Sinai, it was left to the sages alone to determine the proper interpretation of *halakhah*. Under those circumstances, even so profound an authority as the *bat kol* proved insufficient to countermand the interpretive claims of those empowered to perform their own reading of divine matters.

What is true of the rabbinical sages is likewise true of those who seek to bestow a new hermeneutical authority on the formative content of the visionary event from one generation to the next: that event is created and recreated in the succeeding milieus through which it assumes an authority all its own. There is no *bat kol*, no voice from heaven, to be called upon to authorize or authenticate it. Its *halakhah* is that which arises within the context of those whose interpretations authorize and revitalize it in the traditions of exegesis it inspires and by means of which it is constantly transformed. These are the traditions that I undertake to explore here.

To that end, the book is divided into two parts, the first of which addresses the biblical and Judaic dimensions of the visionary mode; the second, the Christocentric dimensions. Beginning with an exploration of the etiology of the visionary, I locate the source of that phenomenon in the *visio Dei* that inaugurates the prophecy of Ezekiel. This event, more than any other, is looked upon as the ultimate well-spring of visionary enactment. In Jungian terms, it is seen to be the truly archetypal *Urerlebnis* against which all others are to be placed.[11] From it arise the hermeneutical traditions that are also a line of vision through which the *Urerlebnis* becomes at once a way of seeing and a way of writing and by means of which we behold the progressive acculturation of the initial vision as it undergoes a series of transformations from one

10. References are to the *Hebrew-English Edition of the Babylonian Talmud*, trans. Salis Daiches and H. Freedman, ed. I. Epstein, 30 vols. (London: Soncino Press, 1960–1990). For recent commentary on this text, see Eliezer Berkovits, *Not in Heaven: The Nature and Function of Halakha* (New York: Ktav, 1983), esp. pp. 47–50.

11. For a discussion of Jung's incorporation of these elements into his own work as a means of exploring the psychological basis of Ezekiel's vision, see my "Ezekiel's Inaugural Vision as Jungian Archetype," *Thought* 64 (1989): 116–129. For an analysis of some of the Freudian implications of the vision, see my "Children of Ezekiel: Biblical Prophecy, Madness, and the Cult of the Modern," *Cithara* 26 (1986): 3–22.

generation to the next. Such transformations represent the focus of the study as I undertake to explore the various forms that the visionary mode assumes from both the Judaic and the Christo-centric points of view.

In keeping with these points of view, I consider corresponding aspects of the visionary mode. These include the phenomenology of vision, the hermeneutics of vision, the esoterics of vision, the gnosis of vision, the spirituality of vision, the theosis of vision, and the poetics of vision. From a phenomenological perspective, the visionary experience is seen to manifest itself in works ranging from the pseudepigraphal books of Enoch and Abraham to the *hekhalot* literature as dimensions of the traditions surrounding the so-called *maʿaseh merkabah*, or Work of the Chariot. As a specifically hermeneutical enterprise, the *merkabah* is next explored through an analysis of its talmudic and midrashic formulations, on the one hand, and its philosophical manifestations, on the other. Within this latter context the works of Moses Maimonides receive partic-ular attention in their delineation of the *merkabah* as a metaphysical entity. Culminating the study of the Judaic renderings of the visionary mode, an investigation of the esoteric dimensions of the subject in the traditions of *kabbalah* suggests how the idea of the *merkabah* was incorporated into an entire range of works extending from such prekabbalistic texts as the *Shiʿur Komah* and *Sefer Yetsirah* to the locus classicus of kabbalistic lore, the *Sefer ha-Zohar*.

If such considerations underlie the Judaic renderings of the visionary mode, they are no less relevant to the concept as it assumes renewed significance within its Christocentric frame. Within that frame one discovers the aspects noted above, specif-ically, those designated the gnosis of vision, the spirituality of vision, the theosis of vision, and the poetics of vision. From the gnostic perspective the book focuses on the New Testament as a well-spring of the visionary outlook, especially as that outlook incorporates those elements associated with the *visio Dei* in its Judaic setting. It is argued that the *merkabah* assumes a form con-sistent with the Christocentric point of view. One is thereby em-powered to speak of a Christocentric *merkabah* that has its roots in New Testament thinking. As a gnostic phenomenon, this idea is explored not only from the perspective of the New Testament but within the context of extracanonical apocalyptic and one or two of the early church fathers concerned with the emergence of gnosticism.

Complementing the gnostic formulations of the visionary mode are those that underscore its development in the traditions of Christian spirituality. Addressing myself to representative figures within those traditions, I consider exegetes ranging from Gregory of Nyssa and Dionysius the Areopagite, on the one hand, to Jerome and Gregory the Great, on the other. An analysis of these figures demonstrates how the visionary mode assumes paramount importance in the history of Christian exegetical thought. Complementing consideration of the spirituality of vision, I proceed to an exploration of the theosis of vision. Beginning with an analysis of Johannes Scotus Eriugena, I move to a reading of figures ranging from Saint Bernard of Clairvaux to Saint Bonaventure. Doing so, I suggest how the visionary underwent a series of remarkable transformations as part of its assimilation into the history of later medieval exegesis. These transformations are seen to reinforce the investigation undertaken in the final chapter. Recalling Jung's notion that, from a literary perspective, Dante's *Commedia* represents a locus classicus of the visionary point of view, I consider that work as a primary text through which the interpretive and creative dimensions of the subject are consummated. Such, in brief, are the main lines of analysis that I adopt in this book as I address the nature of biblical prophecy, hermeneutics, and cultural change.[12]

Throughout this volume transliterations of the Hebrew are in accord with the guidelines for General Use in *The Jewish Encyclopedia*.[13] Departures are as follows: both *bet* and *vet* are transliterated with a "b"; *tsadi*, with a "ts"; and *'alef* and *'ayin*, with a ' and a ', respectively. Transliterations of the Greek are in accord with the *Chicago Manual of Style*.[14]

12. In my analysis of the Judaic and Christocentric perspectives as distinct cross-cultural entities, I adopt an approach very much in keeping with that reflected in Jeremy Cohen's important study *"Be Fertile and Increase, Fill the Earth and Master It": The Ancient and Medieval Career of a Biblical Text* (Ithaca: Cornell University Press, 1989). Like Cohen, I consider the Judaic and Christocentric perspectives in turn, "drawing attention to cross-cultural parallels and interdependence in both text and notes, when and wherever possible" (p. 68).

13. *The Jewish Encyclopedia*, ed. Cyrus Adler, 12 vols. (New York: Funk and Wagnalls, 1901–1906).

14. *The Chicago Manual of Style*, 13th ed. rev. (Chicago: University of Chicago Press, 1982).

~ *Part I*

BIBLICAL AND JUDAIC CONTEXTS

∾One

The Etiology of Vision

I

In order to establish a context through which the visionary mode can best be understood, we might well return to the Hebrew Bible.[1] There we shall discover a veritable reservoir of visionary material that will serve as the basis of an investigation of the kind of experience that puts one most compellingly in touch with the "other." From the perspective of the Hebrew Bible, that experience makes itself dramatically apparent in the panorama of biblical prophecy through which the vision of God in its various forms was made known. This fact is nowhere more graphically illustrated than in the *visio Dei* that inaugurates the book of Ezekiel. By means of that vision, one encounters the *Urerlebnis* in its most primal sense. In order to appreciate the appropriateness of such an observation, we first need to have some sense of what Ezekiel may be said to have seen. That is, we must at the outset review in brief the details that constitute the vision itself. Because of the extreme complexity of the vision, any attempt at a summary is, of course, self-defeating. As the ensuing discussion makes clear, the act of reducing the vision to its primary elements violates the basis of its conception. At most, one must be content with a crude working account that overlooks at least as much as it includes. That said,

1. Except as otherwise noted, biblical references are to the RSV *New Oxford Annotated Bible with Apocrypha*, ed. Herbert G. May and Bruce M. Metzger (New York: Oxford University Press, 1973). Hebrew references are to the Kittel *Biblia Hebraica Stuttgartensia* (Stuttgart: Deutsche Bibelstiftung, 1967–1977). In keeping with the Hebraic and Judaic contexts established in the first part of my book, I use the phrase Hebrew Bible here. In keeping with the Christocentric contexts established in the second part of my book, I employ the Old Testament–New Testament distinction there.

a summary of the main lines of the vision provides at least an initial context for interpretation.

As the vision unfolds, Ezekiel, in exile on the shores of the river Chebar in Babylon, beholds "a stormy wind" approaching from the north, "and a great cloud, with brightness round about it, and fire flashing forth continually, and in the midst of the fire, as it were gleaming bronze." "From the midst of it came the likeness of four living creatures," each with four faces (those of a man, a lion, an ox, and an eagle) and each with four wings (two of which stretched downward and two of which stretched upward). "In the midst of the living creatures there was something that looked like burning coals of fire ... and out of the fire went forth lightning." Accompanying each of the living creatures there appeared four remarkable wheels, "and the four had the same likeness, their construction being as it were a wheel within a wheel." The rims of the wheels were "full of eyes round about. And when the living creatures went, the wheels went beside them; and when the living creatures rose from the earth, the wheels rose. Wherever the spirit would go, they went, and the wheels rose along with them; for the spirit of the living creatures was in the wheels." Over the heads of the living creatures there was the likeness of a crystal firmament, and above the firmament there was the likeness of a throne, upon which was "a likeness as it were of a human form." "And upward from what had the appearance of his loins," Ezekiel says, "I saw as it were the appearance of fire, and there was brightness round about him." "Like the appearance of the bow that is in the cloud on the day of the rain, so was the appearance of the brightness round about." This, concludes Ezekiel, "was the appearance of the likeness of the glory of the Lord" (Ezek. 1:1–28). As a locus classicus of the visionary mode, this vision will serve as the core text through which we shall explore the *Urerlebnis* as archetypal phenomenon.

Any attempt to come to terms with Ezekiel's *visio Dei* must at the outset acknowledge the almost insurmountable problems attendant upon such an endeavor. Those problems are, in part, a reflection of the difficulties that have been associated with the book of Ezekiel from the earliest times. Indeed, as a prophecy, the book of Ezekiel has become legendary for all the problems it has occasioned, not the least of which was the great trepidation the inaugural vision caused among the early expositors. In the first century of the Common Era the book of Ezekiel was reputedly in danger of being withdrawn from the canon because of alleged conflicts with the Torah. According to talmudic tradition, Rabbi Hananiah ben Hezekiah had to close himself in a room with food and three hundred jars of oil for light until he was able to resolve all the discrepancies. But even then the work of Hananiah was incomplete. The difficulties that plague the book of Ezekiel, says the Talmud, will have to await the revelation of Elijah, when he returns to prepare for the onset of the Messianic age.[2] Unwilling to wait quite that long, exegetes ranging from Josephus to biblical scholars of the twentieth century have continued to raise questions and to venture solutions regarding the prophet and his book.

At the center of the contemporary critical debate resides the issue of text. As it is by now generally acknowledged, the book of Ezekiel is among the most poorly preserved texts in the Hebrew Bible.[3] Especially with regard to the inaugural vision, the text contains so many inconsistencies and apparent contradictions that an expositor is constantly faced with the dilemma of attempting to reconcile discrepancies, either through an exercise of ingenuity or through recourse to the putative authority of an earlier version. Because the ur-text is simply not to be had, expositors must finally opt for a version that most nearly approximates their sense of what the text is supposed to be. As with other books of the Bible,

2. *The Jerome Biblical Commentary*, ed. Raymond E. Brown et al. (Englewood Cliffs, N.J.: Prentice-Hall, 1968), pp. 345–346; and the *Encyclopaedia Judaica*, ed. Cecil Roth, 15 vols. (Jerusalem: Keter, 1971–1972), VI, 1094–1096.

3. According to G. A. Cooke, "in the Hebrew Bible perhaps no book, except 1 and 2 Samuel, has suffered more injury to its text than Ezekiel"; *A Critical and Exegetical Commentary on the Book of Ezekiel* (Edinburgh: T. & T. Clark, 1936), p. xi. In order to make sense of Ezekiel, one must examine the versions that were translated from an earlier form of the Hebrew text than that which we have in our Bible. First in significance is the Alexandrian Greek Version or Septuagint, dating back to the second century B.C.E., centuries before the Masoretic (hereafter referred to as the MT) assumed its present form in the fifth to eighth centuries C.E. Other translations into Greek were produced in the second century C.E. by Aquila, Symmachus, and Theodotion. The foregoing translations are known primarily through the work of Origen, who copied them into his *Hexapla*. Fragments of these Greek versions are also to be found in quotations from the fathers and in some manuscripts from the Septuagint. There are likewise other versions in Syriac, Latin, Arabic, and Ethiopic. Though made directly from the Hebrew, Saint Jerome's translation was influenced by the Septuagint. As a translation into Aramaic, the Targum is really a paraphrase, designed to edify. For a full account of the versions of the text, see Carl Heinrich Cornill, *Das Buch des Propheten Ezechiel* (Leipzig: J. C. Hinrichs'sche Buchhandlung, 1886).

so especially with Ezekiel: this dilemma has given rise to a number of exegetical approaches, among them that of the redactionists and that of the traditionalists.[4]

Most notably represented in the work of Walther Zimmerli, the redactionist approach is based on the belief that the text of Ezekiel as it has been transmitted can no longer be considered the product of a single mind during a particular period.[5] In fact, as Zimmerli points out, both the authorship and the chronology of the prophecy have been called into question by those who argue that the book of Ezekiel is a pseudepigraphon composed during a much later period than customarily assumed.[6] Although such theories no longer possess the currency they once had, the text for Zimmerli has been effectively dislodged from the secure position it enjoyed during what Zimmerli calls the "precritical phase" of biblical exegesis. For Zimmerli, that phase is indicated by Rudolf Smend, who looked upon the book of Ezekiel as "the logical development of a series of ideas in accordance with a well thought out, and in part quite schematic, plan," one in which no part might be removed "without disturbing the whole structure."[7]

Far from endorsing this view, Zimmerli conceives the book of Ezekiel as a work that stems from a "school of the prophet" that transformed the text through a complex process of redaction.[8] As a result of this process, inconsistencies, if not downright contradictions, found their way into the text. Such is especially true

4. See, in this regard, Jon D. Levenson's review of Walther Zimmerli's *Ezekiel* 2 and Moshe Greenberg's *Ezekiel 1–20*, in *Interpretation* 38 (1984): 210–217.

5. Walther Zimmerli, *Ezekiel 1 and 2*, 2 vols. (Philadelphia: Fortress Press, 1979–1983). Volume I, trans. Ronald E. Clements, ed. Frank Moore Cross and Klaus Baltzer. Vol. II, trans. James D. Martin, ed. Paul D. Hanson with Leonard Jay Greenspon.

6. Zimmerli, *Ezekiel 1 and 2*, I, 7–8. Ever since Charles Cutler Torrey (*Pseudo-Ezekiel and the Original Prophecy* [New Haven: Yale University Press, 1930]) argued that the book of Ezekiel is really a pseudepigraphon of the third century B.C.E., rather than the genuine work of an exiled prophet of the sixth century B.C.E., theories of authorship and dates of composition have proliferated. For the literature on the subject see, in addition to Torrey, Millar Burrows, *The Literary Relations of Ezekiel* (Philadelphia: Jewish Publication Society Press, 1925); and William A. Irwin, *The Problem of Ezekiel* (Chicago: University of Chicago Press, 1943). For an assertion of the traditionalist point of view, see, among others, Carl G. Howie, *The Date and Composition of Ezekiel* (Philadelphia: Society of Biblical Literature, 1950). Zimmerli's summary should be supplemented by Harold H. Rowley, "The Book of Ezekiel in Modern Study," *BJRL* 36 (1953–1954): 146–190. See also the treatment in Herbert W. Hines, "The Prophet as Mystic," *AJSL* 40 (1923): 37–71.

7. Zimmerli, I, 3, citing Smend, *Der Prophet Ezekiel* (Leipzig, 1880), p. xxi.

8. Zimmerli, *Ezekiel 1 and 2*, I, 68–74. According to Zimmerli, Ezekiel himself might have undertaken "the secondary work of learned commentary upon and further elaboration of his prophecies."

of the opening chapter, the first three verses of which contain numerous problems: "In the thirtieth year . . . as I was among the exiles by the river Chebar, the heavens were opened, and I saw visions of God. On the fifth day of the month . . . the word of the Lord came to Ezekiel the priest, the son of Buzi, in the land of the Chalde'ans by the river Chebar; and the hand of the Lord was upon him there" (1:1–3). "The thirtieth year," for example, has no definite referent: the thirtieth year of what? It has been interpreted as "the thirtieth year of the reign of Manasseh, as the thirtieth year of Ezekiel's life, as the thirtieth year since the reform of King Josiah, and as a redactor's reconciliation of the prediction of the forty-year exile in Ezek. (4:6) and the seventy-year exile in Jer. 25:12."[9] More troublesome still is the unexpected and inconsistent transition from first person ("as I was among the exiles") to the third person ("the word of the Lord came to Ezekiel the priest . . . and the hand of the Lord was upon him there"). This transition, comments Zimmerli, "betrays the fact that here a literary splicing lies before us," a situation compounded by the fact that the text tradition itself is uncertain at what point the shift back to first person occurs.[10]

These uncertainties are part of the very fabric of the text. Instances abound. We might consider, for example, the description of the four "living creatures" or *ḥayyot* (1:5–12). Zimmerli's account is apt:

> After an introductory summary of the human form of the creatures in verse 5, verse 6 describes their faces and wings, verse 7 their feet, verse 8 their hands. Verse 9 describes (after the removal of the gloss referring to the wings) the manner in which the creatures moved. Verse 10 then repeats a fuller description of their faces, verse 11 mentions the position of their wings and verse 12 finally describes once again the manner in which the creatures moved,

9. *The Interpreter's Bible*, ed. George Arthur Buttrick et al., 12 vols. (New York: Abingdon Press, 1965), VI, 81. According to Zimmerli, Ezek. 1: 1–3 provides ample evidence of "a two-or-three phase process with the secondary introduction of verse 2" (*Ezekiel 1 and 2*, I, 101).

10. Zimmerli, *Ezekiel 1 and 2*, I, 82, 100, 108. Whereas the Septuagint shifts back to the first person in 3b, the MT waits until 4a. (Cf. Ezek. 24:24 for the suggestion of another shift in person.) Furthermore, the MT has "above him" for 3b, whereas thirteen mss. have "upon me." For additional commentary, see Walther Eichrodt, *Ezekiel: A Commentary*, trans. Cosslett Quinn (Philadelphia: Westminster Press, 1970), p. 51; Julius A. Bewer, "The Text of Ezek. 1:1–3," *AJSL* 50 (1933–1934): 96–101; Irwin, *The Problem of Ezekiel*, pp. 223–226; and Cooke, *Commentary on Ezekiel*, p. 3.

with the verbal expressions of verse 9 repeated literally with reor-
dering and expansion. If we may find in vv 6–8 a tolerable order
of the listing of the bodily parts, then the account in v 9ab jumps
from one to the other, returns to what has already been mentioned
(faces, wings), and is not afraid of word by word repetitions.

"Do we," asks Zimmerli, "really have the original order of the text
before us in all this?"[11]

Not only do these inconsistencies distinguish the initial appearance of the vision in the first chapter, they are constantly arising
in later chapters. The shift in perspective between Ezekiel 1 and
10 will serve as an example. One of the most graphic instances of
this shift occurs with regard to the faces of the living creatures.
What is described as "the face of an ox [*penei-shor*]" in the first
chapter (v. 10) becomes "the face of the cherub [*penei-hakerub*]"
in the tenth chapter (v. 14). In addition, the eyes that overspread
the rims of the wheels in the first chapter (v. 18) suddenly appear
all over the bodies (including the "flesh," "backs," "hands," and
"wings") of the living creatures (v. 12) in the tenth chapter.[12]

Such alterations find precedence not only in the processes of
textual transmission dating back to the Septuagint but in the activities of those whom Zimmerli designates the school of the
prophet, contemporaneous with Ezekiel himself.[13] As a result of
the processes of textual transmission and the activities of the
school of the prophet, Zimmerli argues, the original visionary
material underwent a series of emendations that altered the *ur-*

11. Zimmerli, *Ezekiel 1 and 2*, I, 101–102.

12. There are a number of other changes as well. For example, the "wheels" in the first
chapter are referred to as *'ofannim* (v. 16). In the tenth chapter the *'ofannim* are transformed
into *galgal* (vv. 2, 6, 13, a singular noun that bears a plural sense). *Galgal* suggests the idea
of "whirling," as in "whirling wheels" (so the RSV). *The Interpreter's Bible*, p. 114, associates
the word with "whirl" and "whirlwind" (Pss. 77:19; 83:14; Isa. 17:13), as well as wagons
(Ezek. 23:24; 26:10; Isa. 5:28; Jer. 47:3). Although *'ofannim* and *galgal* may be synonymous
(and so appear in Ezek. 10:13), the use of *galgal* represents a gloss of sorts, one that
suggests the paradoxical nature of the vision.

13. Zimmerli, *Ezekiel 1 and 2*, I, 87–88, 120, 124–126, 130. Cf. Michael Fishbane, *Biblical
Interpretation in Ancient Israel* (Oxford: Clarendon Press, 1985). Distinguishing between
traditum as "the deposit of images awaiting explication" that is generated within the text
of Scripture itself and *traditio* as the process of exegesis that grows out of the text of
Scripture, he observes that "unlike other biblical visions whose explication is part of its
primary form, Ezekiel's visions are marked by clarifications and cross-references which
appear to have been added to the *traditum*—whether by prophetic tradents or by the
prophet himself" (p. 446, n. 3). See also Fishbane's *The Garments of Torah: Essays in Biblical
Hermeneutics* (Bloomington: Indiana University Press, 1989), esp. pp. 3–32.

text both within individual chapters and from one chapter to the next. The alterations were thereby at once intratextual and intertextual.[14] As a redactionist, Zimmerli responds to this situation by attempting to reclaim the *ur*-text, stripped as much as possible of all putative editorial accretions. That is, he invents his own text, one that might be called "Zimmerli's Bible." Free of any "inconsistencies" that might muddy the text or call its logic into question, Zimmerli's Bible is a version that is as direct, coherent, spare, and straightforward as one can possibly construct. A text devoid of ambiguity, it replaces poetry with exposition. For Zimmerli, this denuded version is the *ur*-text.[15]

It is against the suppositions implicit in such an approach that the traditionalists react. Moshe Greenberg is one of their most important spokesmen.[16] According to Greenberg, the attempt to reconstruct a text in order to approximate an otherwise unavailable *ur*-text (what Greenberg calls a *Vorlage*) creates more problems than it solves. At the same time, such an attempt is based upon unfounded presuppositions regarding methods of composition that may, in fact, be at variance with the actual processes of transmission during the period that the prophecy came into being as a fully realized event. The closest one can come to that event, argues Greenberg, is through recourse to the Hebrew Bible as it has been transmitted by the most reliable of received texts, in this case, the Masoretic text. Although acknowledging the difficulties attendant upon the *textus receptus* in its present form, Greenberg argues that this text, as the only Hebrew version of Ezekiel's words in existence, "must ultimately go back to him and therefore must serve as the main—often the sole—primary source for the study of his message."[17]

Whether or not one accepts Greenberg's assertion that the Masoretic text represents the most reliable index to Ezekiel's actual prophecy, Greenberg's outlook is consistent with those whose exegetical views are very much the product of a training deeply rooted in the traditions from which the Masorah emerges not just

14. They were also, of course, extratextual in that they were (and continue to be) reflected from one version to the next.

15. For Zimmerli's reconstructed text, see *Ezekiel 1 and 2*, I, 108.

16. Moshe Greenberg, *Ezekiel 1–20* (Garden City, N.Y.: Doubleday, 1983) (Volume 22 of the Anchor Bible).

17. Ibid., pp. 18–27. Even Greenberg concedes that "there is the highest probability" that changes occurred in the transmission of Ezekiel's oracles between the time of the prophet and the appearance of the MT.

as the most valid of texts but, at times, as the most sacrosanct of versions. Such an outlook prompts one to assert not only the integrity of the text but the discernible presence of a controlling aesthetic through which the text was originally conceived and executed. Far from raising questions about authorship and chronology, Greenberg reinstates the text to its privileged status as the work of a particular author during a particular period. Sharing this privileged status, the received text assumes the aura of "*the* text" through which the expositor is authorized to act as if he were in possession of "*the* book of Ezekiel."

In the hands of the expositor this book acquires an identity all its own. Once that occurs, the expositor may now see (and in fact is determined to see) in this book all the features of artistic planning and execution. In contradistinction to those who come to the text of this book with "preconceptions regarding what an ancient prophet should have said and how he should have said it," Greenberg calls for "the patient and receptive reader" to whom the text might disclose details of its "art and immanent patterning." This is what Greenberg designates his "holistic approach."[18] In response to that approach, Zimmerli would maintain that Greenberg, too, has preconceptions about what a text is and how it works that are possibly inconsistent with the book of Ezekiel in its present form. Those preconceptions incline Greenberg to underplay the disruptions in the text and to "discover" coherences that may not exist.[19] For Zimmerli, the "holistic approach" would effectively return the enterprise of biblical exegesis to its "pre-critical phase." For Greenberg, the approach restores to the prophet his artistic integrity and to the text its historical identity.

The question that confronts the literary theorist in all this is which approach is one to adopt in the treatment of the inaugural vision as a literary event? If one adopts the redactionist approach, then any attempt at a literary appraisal is compromised by a text that keeps collapsing itself into uncertainties about distinctions

18. Ibid., pp. 18, 26. For elaboration of the holistic approach, see also Greenberg's article "The Vision of Jerusalem in Ezekiel 8–11: A Holistic Interpretation," *The Divine Helmsman: Studies on God's Control of Human Events, Presented to Lou H. Silberman*, ed. J. L. Crenshaw and S. Sandmel (New York: Ktav, 1980), pp. 146–164.

19. See, for example, Greenberg's attempt to explain the transition from first person to third person in Ezekiel 1:1–3. Rather than seeing the transition as the result of an editorial insertion by another hand, Greenberg suggests that the transition represents the act of Ezekiel himself in his capacity as editor of his own text—"an extraordinary but not impossible procedure," Greenberg says (*Ezekiel*, p. 39).

between pure text and redacted text. The redactionist impulse to reduce the text to its so-called pure form undermines the literary desire to derive an aesthetic from the text that finally emerges. The instability of the text becomes a warrant for its own undoing as artistic enterprise. If the literary theorist adopts the traditionalist approach, problems of a different order surface. Any attempt at a literary appraisal is compromised not by a text that collapses itself into uncertainties but by a text that refuses to acknowledge that such uncertainties might in fact threaten its very existence. The traditionalist impulse to preserve the autonomy of the text undermines the literary desire to derive an aesthetic receptive as much to the disruptions that threaten this autonomy as to the coherences that appear to preserve it.

The result is a situation that would seem to compromise any attempt at a genuine literary appraisal. But such is not the case. If the literary theorist is willing to acknowledge that the very problems attendant upon a reading of the inaugural vision are in fact what distinguish it as a literary event, then the vision emerges as a phenomenon that embraces both the disruptions that cause the text to undermine its own integrity and the coherences that allow the text to preserve its alleged autonomy. Such a reading is neither redactionist nor traditionalist. Assimilating both approaches, the reading here proposed attempts to formulate a dialectic that reconciles the assumptions of each. If this reading acknowledges the presence of disruptions, it does so in the belief that the vision exists by means of those discrepancies that might otherwise appear to undermine it. If the reading is sensitive to the presence of coherences, it is so in the conviction that only by virtue of the coherences do the disruptions become aesthetically meaningful.

The text that results from such a reading is one that validates its existence not by appealing to *ur*-texts or by making claims that bestow upon it a privileged status it might not otherwise be able to sustain. Rather, it is one whose authenticity is determined through its ability to negotiate the demands placed upon it by the circumstances in which it finds itself at any given moment. Those circumstances are defined by the hermeneutical ground the text occupies rather than by any historical factors that might cause one "version" of a text to have more authority than another. In an environment where "the text" (as opposed to versions of an unavailable *Vorlage*) is ultimately a fiction, the definitive text is finally

that version which is so designated by informed consensus, assuming that such a consensus is within reach.[20] Such is not at issue
in the present discussion. What is at issue is the ability of the text
to liberate itself from the constraints imposed upon it by the prevailing exegetical schools, redactionist and traditionalist alike.[21] So
liberated, the text becomes self-authenticating. From the perspective of the vision that inaugurates the prophecy of Ezekiel,
the text assumes an interpretive life of its own, one fully receptive
to the visionary content it has been commissioned to transmit. It
is the vision that authorizes the text. The vision generates the text.

In fact, so crucial is this idea to the tenor of the prophecy that
Ezekiel as literary craftsman incorporates it as a dramatic device
into his narrative. Accordingly, the vision is conceived at the outset
as "the word of the Lord" (1:3) that is transmitted to Ezekiel in
the form of a vision. After Ezekiel receives the vision, he is commissioned by it not only in having its message delivered to him
orally but in being made literally to consume it as a text: "Behold,
a hand was stretched out to me, and, lo, a written scroll was in it"
(2:9). "Eat what is offered to you," Ezekiel is told; "eat this scroll,
and go, speak to the house of Israel" (3:2).[22] The consumption of
the scroll indicates how profoundly the prophecy emphasizes the

20. See in this regard, Mark C. Taylor: "In the absence of any text-in-itself, Scripture
is always a writing which is a rewriting and a rewriting which must itself be rewritten";
"Text as Victim," *Deconstruction and Theology*, ed. Thomas J. J. Altizer et al. (New York:
Crossroad, 1982), p. 72.

21. In both schools the text undergoes a reification, if not at times an ossification, that
runs counter to the concept of text as event. This reification causes the text to assume the
quality of an object: it becomes tangible. It is precisely this tangibility that the concept of
text as event seeks to transcend. In his distinction between a "work" and a "text," Roland
Barthes puts the matter succinctly. The work is "concrete, occupying a portion of book-
space." It can be seen "in bookstores, in card catalogues, and on course lists." The text,
on the other hand, "must not be thought of as a defined object": it is "a methodological
field." "While the work is held in the hand, the text is held in language: it exists only as
discourse." As such, the text is experienced as "*an activity, a production.*" That activity
involves a "movement of dislocations, overlappings, and variations." Its logic is "meto-
nymic," and its play of "associations, contiguities, and cross-references coincides with a
liberation of symbolic energy." In this respect the text is "*radically* symbolic." "*A work whose
integrally symbolic natures one conceives, perceives, and receives,*" concludes Barthes, "*is a text.*"
"From Work to Text," *Textual Strategies: Perspectives in Post-Structuralist Criticism*, ed. Josué
V. Harari (Ithaca, N.Y.: Cornell University Press, 1979), pp. 74–79.

22. The remarkable, even bizarre, nature of Ezekiel's act of consumption is reinforced
by the fact that the traditional size of a scroll during the period of Ezekiel was between
twenty and thirty feet (Cooke, *Commentary on Ezekiel*, p. 35). No wonder, God, almost as
an overbearing father, must repeat his command three times before Ezekiel finally eats
what is offered to him (2:8–3:3)!

primacy of the text in the assimilation and dissemination of God's word.[23] To understand the inaugural vision is to approach it fundamentally as a literary event, one that is not only self-generating but self-perpetuating.[24] At the very point of its conception it generates its own text, which it "hands down," as it were, for consumption and transmission by those who would spread its meaning abroad.[25]

The way in which Ezekiel conceives his mode of commissioning, however, is such as to emphasize not the literalness of the text, that is, the text as reified. Rather, the conception works paradoxically to underscore its nonliteral quality, that is, the text as event.

23. Metaphorically, the commissioning of Ezekiel assumes two forms, both having to do with the assimilation of God's word as a means of prophetic discourse. The first form is auditory, the second masticatory. For the development of these forms in corresponding biblical texts, see Exodus 3:4–12, Isaiah 6:5–9, Jeremiah 1:5–16, Revelation 10:8–10, and 2 Esdras 14:38.

24. In his "Freud and the Scene of Writing" (*Writing and Difference*, trans. Alan Bass [Chicago: University of Chicago Press, 1978], pp. 196–229), Jacques Derrida invokes precisely this reference to Ezekiel's consumption of the text as an extension of Derrida's discussion of the Freudian "writing machine."

25. The idea speaks directly to the concept of the prophet as *nabi*. Although the etymology of the term *nabi* is in dispute, the word probably finds its cognate in the Akkadian verb *nabu*, "to call." The prophet was conceived as one who calls or proclaims. So the Septuagint translates *nabi* as *prophētēs*, which signifies "one who speaks on behalf of" or "to speak for." As such, the prophet is one who calls or proclaims God's word. He is a "proclaimer." At the same time, he is also an "interpreter" of God's word. In that capacity he assumes the corresponding office of hermeneut, a concept that suggests both proclamation and interpretation. The prophet becomes, in effect, the hermeneut of what he proclaims. (See *hermēneuō* in *A Greek-English Lexicon of the New Testament and Other Early Christian Literature*, ed. W. F. Arndt and F. W. Gingrich [Chicago: University of Chicago Press, 1957], s.v.) He assumes that role because he has been chosen or called upon to perform it. His role thereby signifies not only one who calls but one who has been called upon to call.

His "calling," in turn, may be executed in one (or in both) of two ways. He may either proclaim God's word orally or disseminate God's word in writing (or both). The "pre-classical" or "popular" prophets, such as Elijah, were conceived as performing the former function; the "classical" or "literary" prophets, such as Isaiah, the latter (or a combination of the former and the latter). In either case the prophet was one called upon to assume the role of intercessor between God and His people. Because the revelation of God's presence was too awesome for the populace to endure, the prophet interceded to receive and disseminate God's word. In so doing, the prophet fulfilled his function as *nabi*. See the entry on prophets and prophecy in *The Encyclopaedia Judaica*, XIII, 1151–1158; *The Interpreter's Dictionary of the Bible*, ed. George Arthur Buttrick et al., 4 vols. (New York: Abingdon Press, 1964), III, 869–898; and Abraham J. Heschel, *The Prophets* (Philadelphia: Jewish Publication Society, 1962), pp. 347–350, as well as Michael Fishbane's excellent discussion "Biblical Prophecy as a Religious Phenomenon," *Jewish Spirituality from the Bible through the Middle Ages*, ed. Arthur Green (New York: Crossroad, 1986), pp. 62–81 (Volume 13 of the series World Spirituality: An Encyclopedic History of the Religious Quest).

Drawing upon the traditions of metaphor through which God's word is transmitted to and consumed and disseminated by his chosen, Ezekiel literalizes the process in order to demonstrate the fundamentally ungraspable nature of the divine proclamation. What results is a transposition of vehicle and tenor: word becomes flesh, flesh word. The more he emphasizes flesh, the more intangible word becomes. The consumption of the literal scroll testifies to its metaphoricalness. The text is embodied literally as a trope. Its very tangibility attests to its indefinableness. The radical presence of its nature is conceptualized in the bizarre way it is transmitted and consumed. It is in this sense that the text of the inaugural vision must be understood. The transformative quality by which vehicle becomes tenor and tenor vehicle is the quality that underscores the vision as literary event. As text, the vision constantly transforms or "reenvisions" itself in the act of making itself known. The extent to which this transformative dimension is consistent with the elements that constitute the inaugural vision will be seen upon an examination of the cultural milieu out of which the vision is thought to have arisen.

II

As scholars are well aware, the attempt to establish the nature of that milieu is at least as difficult as that involved in the establishment of text. Despite this fact, the desire to "locate" the precise cultural antecedents of the inaugural vision appear to be one of the favorite preoccupations of biblical scholarship. Drawing upon the commonplace association of the vision with chariot-like vehicles of one sort or another, scholars characteristically associate Ezekiel's *visio Dei* with the concept of the divine chariot that appears everywhere in the culture of the ancient Near East, whether among the Persians, the Egyptians, the Phoenicians, the Hittites, or the Babylonians.

Whereas some scholars point to the chariot of Mithras as a source, others find it in the chariot of Marduk. Because of Ezekiel's exilic experience, Babylonia usually emerges as a favorite candidate. According to Lorenz Dürr, practically every aspect of the inaugural vision finds its counterpart in Babylonian artifact, ritual, and myth. Although Dürr is especially fond of invoking the chariot of Marduk as antecedent, the chariots of other deities within the

Babylonian pantheon serve equally well for Dürr.[26] Scholars such as André Parrot follow Dürr in this line of thought. Like Dürr, Parrot, moreover, discerns in the fourfold creatures or *ḥayyot* that propel the chariot the influence of Assyrian artifacts, including the winged bulls that guard the entrance to the royal palace at Khorsabad. In these protective genii may be seen a composite of a man's head, eagles' wings, the breast of a lion, and the body of a bull. Such, maintains Parrot, are "precisely the elements of the prophetic vision which must have been inspired, consciously or unconsciously, by the reliefs which, in the sixth century, were still to be seen, even though the Assyrian towns, Khorsabad, Nineveh and Calah, lay in ruins."[27] Corresponding to these antecedents are many others that Hans Peter L'Orange cites, including those found on Hittite rock reliefs in Yazilikaya in Asia Minor and on Assyrian rock reliefs in Maltaya on the Tigris.[28]

As fascinating as this sort of source hunting can be, it is finally conjectural at best. If the substratum of Ezekiel's vision is discernible at all, it is to be found not in cultures alien to Ezekiel's own but most immediately within the milieu familiar to the prophet himself. That milieu, of course, is the Hebraic world centered on the figure of Yahweh enthroned upon a chariot-like vehicle that manifests his divine presence either throughout the natural and celestial worlds or localized for cultic purposes in the temple. It is specifically the renewed worship of this figure that Ezekiel as *kohen* or priest would reinstitute among his people. A glance at the Hebraic underpinnings of the inaugural vision, then, should provide significant insight into Ezekiel's *visio Dei* as a phe-

26. Lorenz Dürr, *Ezechiels Vision von der Erscheinung Gottes (Ez. c. 1 u. 10) im Licht der vorderasiatischen Altertumskunde* (Münster: Aschendorffsche Verlagsbuchhandlung, 1917), passim.

27. André Parrot, *Babylon and the Old Testament*, trans. B. E. Hooke (New York: Philosophical Library, 1958), pp. 128–136. See also P. S. Landersdorfer, *Baal Tetramorphos und die Kerube des Ezechiel* (Paderborn: Druck und Verlag von Ferdinand Schöningh, 1958); and E. Höhne, "Die Thronwagensvision Hesekiels. Eichheit und Herkunft der Vision Hes. 1: 4–28 und ihrer Züge" (diss., Erlangen, 1953–1954).

28. Hans Peter L'Orange, *Studies on the Iconography of Cosmic Kingship in the Ancient World* (Oslo: H. Aschehoug, 1953), esp. pp. 48–63. Of particular interest as well is James B. Pritchard, *The Ancient Near East in Pictures Relating to the Old Testament*, 2d ed. (Princeton: Princeton University Press, 1969), pls. 644–651. Especially significant here are the plates depicting the colossal winged lion from the doorway of the palace of Ashurnasirpal (pl. 646) and the winged bull that guarded the doorway to the palace at Nimrud (pl. 647). Moving beyond the Near Eastern world, L'Orange extends the discussion of both antecedents and analogues appreciably (*Iconography of Cosmic Kingship*, pp. 51–57).

nomenon that draws upon and transforms associations that were
the mainstay of the prophet's own outlook.

In their most primitive form the Hebraic underpinnings find
expression in the concept of a God who, coming forth "upon the
wings of the wind," "makes the clouds . . . [His] chariot" (Ps. 104:3).
"Sing to God, sing praises to his name," proclaims the Psalmist;
"lift up a song to him who rides upon the clouds; his name is the
Lord, exult before him!" (Ps. 68:4). God's presence is thereby
manifested in the very elements of the natural world, a dimension
that underlies Ezekiel's own association of the inaugural vision
with a storm-theophany (1:4). The idea is a commonplace in the
rhetoric of Hebrew prophecy: "For behold," says Isaiah, "the Lord
will come in fire, and his chariots like the stormwind to render
his anger in fury, and his rebuke with flames of fire" (Isa. 66:15).
As such, He assumes the role of a warrior who defends the faithful
and overcomes the insolence of the enemy. So Habbakuk depicts
God's appearing in His "chariot of victory" to "crush the head of
the wicked, laying him bare, from thigh to neck" (Hab. 3:8–13).
If God rides forth in His chariot as a means of destruction, He
also sends out His chariot as a means of visionary transport. So
God's "chariot of fire" appears to His faithful prophet Elijah, who
is taken into heaven by a whirlwind (2 Kings 2:11; cf. Gen. 5:24).

A crucial aspect of the outlook that conceives of God's chariot
as an expression of natural phenomena (clouds, wind, fire) is that
which associates the theophany of the divine presence with God's
enthronement in the heavenly sphere. In both respects the mysterious beings known as the cherubim serve as His throne-chariot,
either in bearing Him from one point to the next or in providing
a place for His residence. If God is celebrated as one who "rode
on a cherub, and flew" (Ps. 18:10), He is also beheld as a being who
"sits enthroned upon the cherubim" (cf. Ps. 99:1) in the heaven
of heavens, where He dwells in His celestial throne-room. Under
His feet lies a "pavement of sapphire stone, like the very heaven
for clearness" (Exod. 24:10). So Michai'ah says, "I saw the Lord
sitting on His throne, and all the host of heaven standing beside
him on his right hand and on his left" (1 Kings 22:19). Manifested
either as elemental or as celestial theophany, God resides on His
throne-chariot, where He is enthroned on (or between) His cherubim (cf. 1 Sam. 4:4). Whether portable or stationary, this vehicle
became a staple of what has often been explored as the accoutre-

ments of cosmic kingship throughout the Near Eastern world.[29] From both a celestial and an elemental perspective, the chariot that bore God's enthroned presence was fundamental to the milieu from which Ezekiel's own outlook arose.

Complementing the natural and celestial perspectives is that of the cultic. In the worship of Israel the throne-chariot is embodied in the temple as well. As the Psalmist says, God's "throne is in heaven," but God, too, "is in his holy temple" (11:4). This transposition of the throne-chariot from the heavenly domain to the earthly represents a major aspect of Hebraic cultic practice. In Exodus it is God Himself who provides Moses with detailed instructions on how this transposition is to be made: "And let them [the Israelites] make me a sanctuary, that I may dwell in their midst. According to all that I show you concerning the pattern of the tabernacle, and of all its furniture, you shall make it" (Exod. 25:8–9). It is this "pattern" that Moses follows in constructing an artifact that accommodates the conception of God's celestial chariot to the world of worship. In that world the throne-chariot assumes the form of the ark of the covenant. Constructed of acacia wood and overlaid with gold, the ark shall have a mercy seat flanked by two golden cherubim, which "shall spread out their wings above, overshadowing the mercy seat." There, says God to Moses, "I will meet with you, and from above the mercy seat, from between the two cherubim that are upon the ark of the testimony, I will speak with you of all that I will give you in commandment for the people of Israel" (Exod. 25:10–23). Enshrined within the Holy of Holies, God's presence, then, dwells enthroned upon the cherubim. From this position of enthronement God communicates with His votaries, who worship and sacrifice before the throne-chariot as cultic artifact.

It is no doubt for this reason that the Chronicler refers to the ark of the covenant as "the chariot of the cherubim [*hamerkabah hakerubim*]" (1 Chron. 28:18), an appellation that implies something not only about the cultic nature of the ark but about its physical bearing. For the ark is constructed in a way to suggest that it is actually equipped with accoutrements that resemble wheels. Surrounding it on two sides are large "rings" that aid in mobility. God says to Moses, "you shall cast four rings of

29. See L'Orange, *Iconography of Cosmic Kingship*, passim.

gold for it [the ark] and put them on its four feet, two rings on the one side of it, and two rings on the other side of it. You shall make poles of acacia wood...and put the poles into the rings on the sides of the ark, to carry the ark by them" (Exod. 25:12–14). In this way the ark, containing God's presence enthroned upon the cherubim, was transported within the Israelite encampment both during the wilderness sojourn and during the battle campaigns culminating in the conquest of Palestine. As an aspect of Israelite warfare, in fact, the ark, like a palladium, was carried into battle for the purpose of overwhelming the enemy (Josh. 6:6–7), an event celebrated in the ancient Song of the Ark, sung as Yahweh, enthroned in the ark, went forth to holy war for His people.[30] Thus, whenever the ark set out, Moses said, "Arise, O Lord, and let thy enemies be scattered; and let them that hate thee flee before thee" (Num. 10:35).

Corresponding to the military dimension reflected in the Song of the Ark is the processional dimension that underlies the installation of the ark within the Holy of Holies. Both dimensions are discernible in Psalm 68, which is at once a war song and a processional hymn. As a war song, Psalm 68 intones the verse "Let God arise, let his enemies be scattered," followed by references to God's "go[ing] forth before...[His] people" and "march[ing] through the wilderness" as a warrior (vv. 1, 7–8). As a processional hymn, Psalm 68 celebrates God's "solemn processions...into the sanctuary" (v. 24). Verse 17 is particularly to the point: "Yahweh's chariot is in the midst of the thousands of the tribes of Israel; the Lord hath come from Sinai to the sanctuary."[31] The verse clearly portrays God's sitting in His chariot, surrounded by the worshipers, as the ark that bears His presence is transported in procession to the temple.[32] This idea receives compelling treatment in the description of the installation of the ark in the Temple at Jerusalem. "And all the elders of Israel came, and the priests took up the ark. And they brought up the ark of the Lord.... And King Solomon and all the congregation of Israel, who had assembled before him, were with him before the ark.... Then the priests

30. Patrick Miller, *The Divine Warrior in Early Israel* (Cambridge: Harvard University Press, 1973), p. 104.
31. I use the rendering here of W. O. E. Oesterley, "Early Hebrew Festival Rituals," *Myth and Ritual: Essays on the Myth and Ritual of the Hebrews in Relation to the Culture Pattern of the Ancient East*, ed. S. H. Hooke et al. (London: Oxford University Press, 1933), p. 133.
32. Ibid., pp. 133–135.

brought the ark of the covenant of the Lord to its place, in the inner sanctuary of the house, in the most holy place, underneath the wings of the cherubim.... And when the priests came out of the holy place, a cloud filled the house of the Lord, so that the priests could not stand to minister because of the cloud; for the glory of the Lord filled the house of the Lord" (1 Kings 8:1–11).

If the ark of the covenant as portable vehicle represents one of the possible cultic sources of Ezekiel's vision, there are others that might be cited as well. In fact, the temple paraphernalia provides an inexhaustible reservoir of material for visionary transformation. The temple stands with their lavers are a case in point. Constructed of bronze, these "stands" were wagons, each of which had "four bronze wheels and axles of bronze." The wheels, in turn, "were made like a chariot wheel; their axles, their rims, their spokes, and their hubs, were all cast." Adorning the stands themselves were panels set with frames in which were depicted "lions, oxen, and cherubim." These stands, in turn, supported the lavers used for the purpose of purification. In fact, one such laver, unique unto itself, was a gigantic artifact known as "the molten sea." It stood upon "twelve oxen, three facing north, three facing west, three facing south, and three facing east; the sea was upon them, and all their hinder parts were inward" (1 Kings 7:23–38). The reference to bronze as the metal used for construction; the detailing of the wheels (as those of a chariot) equipped with axles, rims, spokes, and hubs; the use of lions, oxen, and cherubim as a means of adornment (cf. Ezek. 41:17–19); the description of the "molten sea" with its multidirectional oxen: these motifs and others combine with those that distinguish the ark of the covenant to suggest that any attempt to trace the sources of Ezekiel's inaugural vision (if indeed such sources are finally traceable) must concern itself with the milieu that was most familiar to Ezekiel.

On the other hand, one must be careful not to substitute these biblical underpinnings for the inaugural vision itself. As Walther Eichrodt cautions, the pursuit of "sources" for their own sake runs the risk of collapsing the visionary quality of the theophany Ezekiel describes and of thereby causing that quality to lose the overwhelming sense of awesomeness that distinguishes it.[33] The more

33. Eichrodt, *Ezekiel*, p. 56. A case in point once again is the description of the four living creatures, each with four faces. If their compositeness (zoomorphic, on the one hand, and anthropomorphic, on the other) accords fully with conceptions of ancient Near Eastern deities and mythical beings, the "multiplication of faces in the manner of Ezekiel's

one attempts to anchor the vision in a particular milieu, the more
it defies traditionalizing. The vision simply refuses to be domes-
ticated. Emerging from a rich and complex milieu of traditional
source material, the vision ultimately subverts its own lineage. It
proclaims its independence from the traditionalizing elements
that are the very source of its being. As a text it at once yields
itself willingly to a recognition of the coherences in which conventional literary analysis delights and, at the same time, undermines attempts at such analysis at the very moment of exegesis.
As a result of this tension within the text, the vision is conceptualized in such a way so as at once to suggest associations with
identifiable objects and at the same time to undermine those associations at every point.

In keeping with this situation, there is yet another factor that
must be taken into account in any attempt to assess the nature
of the vision. That factor has to do with the act of bestowing a
name upon the phenomenon Ezekiel beholds.[34] Although this
phenomenon is commonly known as that of the throne-chariot
or *merkabah*, that designation is ours, not the prophet's. Nowhere, not once, does Ezekiel refer to his vision as the *merkabah*. This name is the invention of the interpreters, who have
obviously felt the need to call it *something*. Accordingly, they
have concretized it with that name, and the name has remained. So in the Apocryphal Book of Ecclesiasticus, Joshua
ben Sira maintains that "it was Ezekiel who saw the vision of
glory which God showed him above the *chariot* [*merkabah*] of the
cherubim" (49:8; italics mine), an idea that even slipped into
the rendering of the Septuagint for Ezek. 43:3, which has "the
appearance of the *chariot* [*harmatos*] which I saw" (italics mine),
when, in fact, the word *chariot* is not present in the Hebrew.[35]

Obviously, the semantic act of concretizing the vision arose in

creatures is ... extremely rare." In fact, asserts Greenberg (*Ezekiel 1–20*, pp. 55–56), the
forms their faces assume (that of a man, a lion, an ox, and an eagle) are without precedent,
and even if such a precedent were ever found, the vision itself would contravene it because
it is finally impossible to determine (try as the expositors might) precisely in what order
the faces are arranged.

34. For the implications of naming as primal act, see Ernst Cassirer, *Language and Myth*,
trans. Susanne K. Langer (New York: Harper, 1946), passim. According to Cassirer, the
naming of something in "mythic thought" is tantamount to bringing it into being, bestowing
an identity on it, and providing it with "reality" in the objective world. This Ezekiel refuses
to do.

35. References are to *The Septuagint with Apocrypha: Greek and English* (London: Bagster,
1851; rpt. Grand Rapids: Zondervan, 1972).

response to those elements in the vision that suggest its chariot-like qualities, particularly those associated with the detailed description of the wheels that accompany the living creatures, not to mention the platform upon which the Enthroned Figure resides above the wheels. Given the nature of the vision as Ezekiel describes it, there is little wonder that the vision came to be known as the *merkabah*. It is this name, of course, that one commonly associates not only with Ezekiel's vision but, as will be discussed, with the rich traditions of Jewish mysticism that the vision inspired. All this, however, should not blind us to the fact that, as far as the prophecy itself is concerned, the vision remains *unnamed*. Not only does this fact tend to escape notice by those who have any acquaintance with the vision, but on the part of those who *are* aware of it, the fact is usually glossed over or dismissed as of relatively little importance. For the prophet and his school, I would maintain, it is of utmost importance. Any attempt to trace the sources of the vision in earlier throne-chariots (cultic or otherwise) must take into account Ezekiel's refusal to link his vision specifically with a particular object.

A number of reasons for this refusal might be cited, not the least of which is Ezekiel's responsiveness to the spirit of the Second Commandment: "You shall not make yourself a graven image, or any likeness of anything that is in heaven above, or that is in the earth beneath, or that is in the water under the earth; you shall not bow down to them or serve them" (Exod. 20:4–5). In fact, Ezekiel's entire prophecy is directed against those who violate the Second Commandment, who worship false idols. Just as Josiah "burned the chariots of the sun with fire" (2 Kings 23:11), Ezekiel castigates those who turn their backs to the temple and worship the sun (8:16). By refusing to name what he sees, Ezekiel is neither making nor worshiping "a graven image." The mystery of the name (cf. Exod. 3:14; Judg. 13:18) is too great to concretize it or perhaps mechanize it as a specific object. In this sense Ezekiel's vision has no referent—no "source"—but itself: it cannot be reduced to any *thing* that might tempt one to substitute the object for that which it is meant to represent.

Despite this circumstance, however, the vision Ezekiel portrays moves irresistibly toward concretization, if not mechanization. What Ezekiel himself admires so much about it, in fact, is its "workmanship" or "construction" (cf. 1:16: *ma'aseh*): the brilliance of the "substances" (bronze, chrysolite, crystal, sapphire) that appear to compose it, the intricacy of its "mechanical parts" (for example, the "rims" and "spokes" of the wheels), the complexity of its movements. It really is a machine to end all machines. Submerged within the mysterium of the un-named, unknowable vision is an artifact that cries out for *object-ification*, for individuation, for the bestowal of a name. If the Second Commandment prohibits the construction of graven images, God Himself, we recall, is hardly lax in providing Moses with elaborate directions for the construction of para-phernalia for the sanctuary and in particular of that one arti-fact that will accommodate most fittingly His own presence. The ark of the covenant: this very artifact comes to be "called by the name of the Lord of hosts who sits enthroned on the cherubim" (2 Sam. 6:2). Under the circumstances, the act of naming, then, becomes quite appropriate, if not inevitable. Naming the vision represents the first step in performing an exegesis upon it. The bestowal of the name *merkabah* is a her-meneutical act that releases "meanings" latent within the vision as a whole. At the precise point of denying the possibility of exegesis, the vision not only encourages but demands such an act. In response to these demands, one is inclined to become Moshe Greenberg's "patient and receptive reader" to whom the text discloses details of its "art and immanent patterning."

III

As we shall see, such details are, in fact, to be found everywhere in the coherences that underlie the vision as a subtle work of art. The arrangement of the vision is essentially bipartite: it is divisible into that which is above and that which is underneath (Ezek. 1:23, 26). Underneath are the fourfold creatures (*hayyot*), accompanied by the wheels (1:5, 16). It is this aspect that Ezekiel beholds in the first part of his vision (1:4–24). That which is above contains a throne (*kisse'*) upon which sits a manlike figure (*'adam*) (1:26). It is this aspect that Ezekiel beholds in the second part of his vision (1:25–28). Separating that which is above from that which is below is a firmament (*rakiya'*) (1:22). At once circumscribing and emanating from the vision is an overwhelming brilliance (*ḥashmal*) (1:4).[36]

This sense of balance and symmetry permeates the vision as a whole. The Enthroned Figure above the firmament is itself bipartite. Ezekiel describes him as divided by what appears "from the likeness of his loins and upward, and from the likeness of his loins and downward" (1:27). Perceptually, one is confronted with the two halves of a seated figure, upward and downward. Counterbalancing this bipartite quality above the firmament is the quadripartite nature of the visionary realm beneath the firmament. This aspect is embodied, of course, in the fourfold creatures. Each creature has four faces; the body of each creature has four wings (1:16). The four creatures are accompanied correspondingly by four wheels, each with a wheel in the middle of a wheel (1:16). The vision, then, contains its own internal coherence. Its unity (the symmetrical balance of twofold and fourfold elements) is suggested by the wings of the creatures, two of which stretch upward and two of which stretch downward (1:11), a feature that reflects the bipartite quality of the vision as a whole and of the seated figure within the vision. The cohesiveness of the vision is also suggested by those wings that extend upward (four sets of two): they are not only "stretched out straight, one toward another," but touch one another (1:11, 23). The symbolism of this two-part/four-part quality is striking. In its own way, each aspect of this cohesive union of two and four is significant for Ezekiel.

The bipartite sense of division between an upper and a lower realm that are ultimately unified, of course, reflects the symbolism of the creation account: "And God said, 'Let there be a firmament in the midst of the waters, and let it separate the waters from the waters.' And God made the firmament and separated the waters which where under the firmament from the waters which were above the firmament" (Gen. 1:6–8).[37] This act of division is equally an act of union, for the world that God creates combines the celestial and terrestrial realms into one harmonious whole: that

36. As with almost everything else regarding Ezekiel's vision, there is uncertainty over the true meaning of the word *ḥashmal*. For three informed views, see G. R. Driver, "Ezekiel's Inaugural Vision," *VT* 1 (1951): 60–63; William A. Irwin, "HASHMAL," *VT* 2 (1952): 169–170; and Zimmerli, *Ezekiel 1 and 2*, I, 122–123.

37. Cf. Greenberg, *Ezekiel 1–20*, p. 48. Ezekiel's use of *rakiyaʿ* (1:22) specifically recalls Gen. 1:6, in which the same term is used.

which is above ("the two great lights") has dominion over day and night, "the greater light to rule the day, and the lesser light to rule the night" (Gen. 1:14–18); that which is below ("the two great sexes"[38]) has dominion over "the fish of the sea, and over the birds of the air, and over the cattle, and over all the earth, and over every creeping thing that creeps upon the earth" (Gen. 1:26). The order and hierarchy reflected here are an expression of the full dominion embodied in God Himself who both creates and rules all. As a symbolic reenactment of the binary processes implicit in the creation account, the inaugural vision assumes the function of cosmic vehicle, one that coalesces the forces of heaven and earth, light and dark, God and human.

The relationship between the celestial, on the one hand, and the terrestrial, on the other, is underscored by the reference to the rainbow-like brightness that encompasses the seated figure (1:28: "Like the appearance of the bow on the day of rain, so was the appearance of the brightness round about"). The creation account in Genesis 1 finds its counterpart in the new creation account in Genesis 9. The rainbow, of course, represents a sign of the covenantal relationship between God and human as a result of the new order that is brought out of chaos (Gen. 9:8–17). After the Flood, human beings experience a renewed bond with their creator. As a promise of hope, the inaugural vision embodies a covenant theology all its own. From an aesthetic point of view the rainbow serves to enclose the vision, to frame it, to suggest its integrity as artistic enterprise, one that reconciles celestial and terrestrial within a single unified conception. Encompassing in its significance that impulse which brought the world into being, the vehicle represents Ezekiel's unique celebration of the "glory of God" (1:28).

Corresponding to the bipartite quality of the inaugural vision is the quadripartite. According to Ernst Cassirer, four is "the sacred number *par excellence*, for in it is expressed precisely the relation between every particular reality and the fundamental form of the universe."[39] Assuming archetypal status in Jungian thought, the idea is no less pertinent to Ezekiel.[40] As a reflection

---

38. The phrase "two great sexes," of course, alludes to *Paradise Lost* VIII, 151.

39. Ernst Cassirer, *The Philosophy of Symbolic Forms*, trans. Ralph Manheim, 3 vols. (New Haven: Yale University Press, 1955–1957), II, 147.

40. For the Jungian basis of the quaternary idea, see my "Ezekiel's Inaugural Vision as Jungian Archetype," *Thought* 64 (1989): passim.

of what occurs elsewhere in biblical prophecy, the quaternary in Ezekiel is associated with totality. So in Ezekiel's prophecy, the breath of Yahweh comes forth from the four points of the compass to restore the dead to life (Ezek. 37:9). In Zechariah the four chariots that come out from between two mountains go forth "to the four winds of heaven, after presenting themselves before the Lord of all the earth" (Zech. 6:1–5). Likewise, the four horns envisioned by Zechariah are "symbols of the power of earthly empires, and the four smiths who are summoned against them represent the totality of opposition appointed by Yahweh" (Zech. 1:18–21). In Daniel the four world eras represent "the whole of human history which is still to run, from Nebudchadnezzar to its end" (Daniel 2 and 7). The four creatures that bear Yahweh's throne in the vision of Ezekiel appropriately underscore "the omnipotence of Yahweh which is effective in every direction."[41] Centered in the *ḥayyot*, the quaternary nature of the vision underscores its universality as cosmic enterprise.[42] Taking that situation into account, one is impressed by the extent to which an all-pervasive symmetry underscores the artistry of the vision as a creation that invites detailed analysis.

At the same time that the vision contains its own internal coherence, it also exhibits its own internal momentum: it is self-generating and self-moving. "And when the living creatures went, the wheels went beside them; and when the living creatures rose from the earth, the wheels rose. Wherever the spirit would go, they went, and the wheels rose along with them; for the spirit of the living creatures was in the wheels" (1:19–20). The vision embodies a dynamism that is all-pervasive. Enfolding itself from within itself, the vision generates fires from out of its own midst (1:4),[43] and its creatures dart to and fro like flashes of lightning (1:14). Intensifying this self-generating dynamism, the wheels

41. Zimmerli, *Ezekiel 1 and 2*, I, 120; Greenberg, *Ezekiel 1–20*, pp. 57–58.

42. In this respect, maintains Zofia Ameisenowa, the living creatures assume a specifically zodiacal significance in keeping with the cosmic nature of the vision. "Beneath the bull, lion, human and eagle faces of the cherubs are concealed the 'zodiacal' signs of the solstices and equinoxes and perhaps the four main elements of matter. The bull represents earth, the lion fire, the eagle air, and the man water: they are the zodiacal points (separated from each other by 90 degrees on the ecliptic) of the bull, the lion, the aquarius man and of the four, the eagle, the brightest star of the constellation of Pegasus (exchanged at some unknown period for the ominous scorpion)." "Animal-Headed Gods, Evangelists, Saints and Righteous Men," *JWCI* 12 (1949): 36.

43. Although the RSV has simply "flashing forth," the AV translates the word *mitlakkaḥat* reflexively, according to the *hitpaʾ el*, as "infolding itself" (1:4).

within wheels whirl within themselves, for, after all, this is the vision of "the whirling wheels" (cf. 10:13: *hagalgal*). Paradoxically, however, neither the fourfold creatures nor the whirling wheels turn as they move (1:9, 12, 17; 10:11). The result is a tension between motion and stasis (or motion within stasis). The vision as a whole mediates between motion and stasis. When it is in motion, the creatures extend their wings (1:24); when it is at rest, the creatures let down their wings (1:24). The quality of rest is embodied in the seated figure, of motion within rest in the fourfold creatures and the wheels, both of which move without turning. Because of the dynamism, the vision itself never becomes static. Its balance and symmetry give way to an experience that is transcendent and finally overwhelming. Its effect is to cause the prophet to fall upon his face in its presence (1:28).

In his description of the vision Ezekiel achieves this sense of transcendence and awesomeness in a number of ways. Rather than clarifying what the prophet sees, a plethora of details prevents the vision from ever coming into sharp focus. The more that Ezekiel says about it, the less we know. The precise *form* of what the prophet sees finally eludes our grasp. The storm, the cloud, the fire, the creatures, the faces, the wings, the wheels, the firmament, the throne: what in fact does the prophet behold? When Ezekiel suggests comparisons between what he sees and what we know, the effect is to distance us from the "reality" of the vision rather than to bring us closer to it. For example, the fourfold creatures, the prophet says, had the likeness of a man (1:5). The description then goes on to delineate a form as unhumanlike as one can imagine: creatures with four faces (man, lion, ox, eagle), four wings, calf-like feet, all sparkling like burnished bronze. The vehicle of the comparison confounds its tenor. Nothing *is* what it appears to be: every comparison distances us more. "And when they went," Ezekiel says of the movement of the creatures, "I heard the *sound* of their wings *like* the sound of many waters, *like* the thunder of the Almighty, a sound of tumult *like* the sound of a host" (1:24; italics mine).

The *Ding an sich* is constantly occluded by the comparisons that are invoked to clarify it, a technique that is used throughout. One is constantly made to confront such phrases as "the likeness of" (*demut*) and "the appearance of" (*mar'eh*). In this regard, the final statement of the description is the most telling. What Ezekiel beholds is not the Lord, not even the glory of the Lord, not even the likeness of the glory of the Lord, but "the appearance of the likeness [*mar'eh demut*] of the glory of the Lord" (1:28). At the very point of perception, the vision reveals only to hide. If the creatures stretch two of their four wings upward in a posture of disclosure, they also cover their bodies with their other two wings in a posture of concealment (1:11). The paradox implicit in this posture establishes a metaphysics of vision: disclosure is concealment, concealment disclosure. The more we behold, the less we see. We are never permitted to penetrate the vision to its core.

This paradox is compounded, moreover, by another element that underscores the complexity. For this is a vision that is not only seen: this is a vision that likewise *sees* (cf. Ps. 11:4). Not only the wheels but the living creatures themselves are, we recall, replete with eyes (1:18, 10:12). A kind of visionary reciprocity causes subject and object to become interchangeable in the process of beholding.[44] That which is beheld also beholds. The vision mediates between seer and seen. But, of course, that which is seen ("the appearance of the likeness of the glory of the Lord") sees much more clearly than does the seer (the prophet and, in turn, the reader) who beholds. Indeed, that which is seen sees all. The seer, on the other hand, sees at three removes, in the case of the prophet, and at four removes, in the case of the reader. The situation is one that defines the act of seeing not only through its opposite (the inability to perceive) but through the disarming experience of being itself the object of perception. The vision, then, confounds both by defying full perception and by seeing back. Because that which sees back sees much more clearly than that which sees, the vision is finally not in the least reciprocal: the act of seeing becomes not the interchange of subject and object but the realization that subject and object are to be distinguished by the very experience through which they would otherwise share a common ground. The immensity that separates them is the immensity that causes the vision itself to remain forever elusive. If that which is seen through the eyes of the prophet is never concretized, that which is beheld through the eyes that see back is known only too well, for it is the prophet himself.

What begins with Ezekiel's proclamation that he saw visions of

44. In this regard, see Martin Heidegger's discussion of the "circle" of perception in *Being and Time*, trans. John Macquarrie and Edward Robinson (London: SCM Press, 1962), pp. 194–195. In that circle, says Heidegger, "is hidden a positive possibility of the most primordial kind of knowing" (p. 195).

God (*"va'er'eh mar'ot 'elohim"*) concludes with an awareness that it is not Ezekiel who beholds the vision so much as it is the vision that beholds him. Ezekiel as seer (*ro'eh*) finds himself in the paradoxical position of the one who is seen by his own vision. In a reversal of roles the vision itself becomes a seer, in fact, the seer par excellence. The phrase *mar'ot 'elohim* comes to imply not only the way in which God *appeared* but the manner in which God *saw*. What results is not just the "visions of God" (that is, God as that which is seen) but the "visions *by* God" (that is, God as that which sees). As that which is seen, the *mar'ot 'elohim* suggests the impossibility of fulfilling one's task as seer: the seer's visions are at best an approximation of what is revealed to him. As that which sees, the *mar'ot 'elohim* suggests the way in which the function of seer assumes consummate form: the seer's visions are those that are the product of absolute sight, of that which sees all and has the capacity at any moment to reveal all. As embodied in the inaugural vision and in the prophet's relationship to it, the function of *ro'eh* thereby acquires a new meaning based upon a visionary reciprocity (or, finally, the undermining of that reciprocity) that redefines the idea of the prophet as seer.[45]

Implicit in this redefinition is a new awareness of the vision as a literary event. The text of that vision remains forever impenetrable. Defying all attempts at a hermeneutics, the text distinguishes itself by virtue of its "otherness." Perpetually remote, it refuses to yield itself. It will not allow the exegete to impose his will upon it. Just the opposite is true: it imposes its will upon the exegete. It overwhelms him. It possesses him. It sees. It knows. Imbued with an awareness that far exceeds the capacity of the interpreter to understand its secrets, the text reveals more about the interpreter than the interpreter reveals about the text. Every effort at analysis becomes an exercise in self-exegesis. Seeking to provide insight into the text, the interpreter discloses himself. He becomes the text, or at least that version of the text which he reveals about himself and disseminates to others. This is the es-

45. In the traditions of prophecy to which Ezekiel was heir, a seer of visions was known as *ro'eh*, one possessed of the ability to reveal that which is concealed from ordinary mortals. This function is thought to antedate all other prophetic functions, particularly that of the *nabi*. Cf. 1 Sam. 9:9: "He who is now called a prophet [*nabi*] was formerly called a seer [*ro'eh*]." The term most often associated with the seer as visionary is *ḥozeh*, but there are corresponding terms as well. See *A Hebrew and English Lexicon of the Old Testament*, trans. Edward Robinson and ed. Francis Brown, S. R. Driver, and Charles A. Briggs (Oxford: Clarendon Press, 1907).

sence of the visionary mode. It is what underlies the vision that inaugurates the prophecy of Ezekiel.

From the perspective that such an outlook embodies, we may now attend to the traditions that constitute the history of the visionary mode as both Judaic and Christocentric phenomenon. That history is distinguished by an entire range of responses, including outright commentary, narrative reformulations, modes of mystical practice, philosophical discourse, esoteric systems of thought, apologetics, and poetic reenactments. Like the vision itself, these responses are sensitive to the transformative dynamics that are the fundamental characteristic of the visionary mode. The determinant of *"Gestaltung, Umgestaltung"* is perpetually at work in the act of reenvisioning the stuff of the *Urerlebnis*, that is, what Amos Wilder calls "the progressive culturizing of the initial vision." It is this process of acculturation with which we shall now be concerned.

~ Two

The Phenomenology of Vision

I

Having explored Ezekiel's vision as a fundamental manifestation of the *Urerlebnis*, we may now proceed to the later traditions, in which the transformative nature of the inaugural vision was given renewed impetus. Our treatment is not meant to be exhaustive. Rather, we shall focus on representative texts and significant movements that encompass a wide and diverse cultural spectrum. Doing so should suggest how the visionary impulse that originated the book of Ezekiel became a phenomenon of crucial importance not only to the religious experience but to the interpretive bearing this experience assumes as a cultural imperative. An analysis of Ezekiel's vision in these terms will demonstrate how the visionary mode is conducive to a multitude of reformulations that are themselves a reenvisioning or reenactment of a phenomenon distinguished by its capacity to reenvision itself at the very moment of perception. As such, Ezekiel's vision will be viewed as part of a network of corresponding visionary reenactments that have their sources in a multiplicity of biblical texts, prophetic and nonprophetic alike. From the perspective of this network, Ezekiel's *visio Dei* will be seen as a "model vision" that provides a focus for any treatment of the relationships between hermeneutics and cultural change.

Our point of departure will be the traditions for which the inaugural vision not only assumed a position of paramount importance but veritably provided the impetus through which those traditions were conceived and implemented. I refer, of course, to what Gershom Scholem calls "Jewish mysticism," a movement that from its earliest stages appropriated and reformulated the vision of Ezekiel to accord with its own unique outlook.[1] Scholem is unequivocal on this point. "What was the central theme of . . . [the] oldest of mystical doctrines within the framework of Judaism?" he asks rhetorically. "No doubts are possible on this point," he answers. "The earliest Jewish mysticism is throne-mysticism," the "perception of His [God's] appearance on the throne, as described by Ezekiel, and cognition of the mysteries of the celestial throne-world."[2] Conversely, we might ask in the same rhetorical vein, "What were the traditions in which the vision of Ezekiel played its most compelling role as a crucial manifestation of the visionary mode?" Like Scholem, we shall offer a response that is equally inescapable: the traditions of Jewish mysticism from their earliest stages onward. Any consideration of the visionary mode in the history of religious thought, then, must concern itself with Ezekiel's *visio Dei* as a formative experience in Jewish mysticism.

So fundamental is such an idea that, as mentioned earlier, the inaugural vision of Ezekiel received its own technical designation as Jewish mystical enterprise: *maʿaseh merkabah* or "Work of the Chariot." Composed of apocalyptic speculation, traditions of commentary, manuals of devotion, systems of numerology, magical incantations, and liturgical hymns, the *maʿaseh merkabah* reflects a wide and diverse body of thought founded not only upon the written documents that have survived but upon the transmission of oral instruction and the enactment of ritual practice among select circles of *merkabah* mystics for whom the *merkabah* and the text from which it emerged were looked upon with utmost reverence. In talmudic commentary and implicitly in the mystical literature as well, the *maʿaseh merkabah* finds its counterpart in the *maʿaseh bereʾshit*, with its source in the first chapter of Genesis, a correspondence suggesting the relationship between the visionary and the cosmogonic in Judaic thought. These relationships should become clearer in later discussion. For the present, it will be sufficient to focus upon the *maʿaseh merkabah* as an all-encompassing designation that takes into account an entire range of concerns.

In his analysis of the *merkabah* in Jewish thought, Scholem distinguishes three major stages of its development: "the anonymous

1. See Gershom Scholem, *Major Trends in Jewish Mysticism* (1941) (New York: Schocken Books, 1954), passim, as well as his *Jewish Gnosticism, Merkabah Mysticism, and Talmudic Tradition* (New York: Jewish Theological Seminary of America, 1960).

2. Scholem, *Major Trends*, pp. 33–34.

conventicles of the old apocalyptics; the Merkabah speculation of
the Mishnaic teachers who are known to us by name; and the
Merkabah mysticism of late and post-talmudic times, as reflected
in the literature which has come down to us."[3] By "anonymous
conventicles of the old apocalyptics," Scholem means primarily
the pseudepigrapha of the intertestamental period (the first two
centuries B.C.E.) and beyond; by "the Merkabah speculation of
the Mishnaic teachers," he has in mind such Tannaitic figures as
Rabbi Jochanan ben Zakkai and his pupils (the second half of the
first century C.E.); and by "the Merkabah mysticism of late and
post-talmudic times," he refers to the Amoraic period culminating
in the completion of the Talmud (the third century C.E. to the
sixth century C.E.).[4] In all three of these stages Scholem finds an
"essential continuity of thought concerning the Merkabah."[5] This
essential continuity of thought represents the working premise of
our investigation.

In our analysis of the *merkabah*, however, we shall consolidate
the first and third of Scholem's categories and expand the second
category. Specifically, we shall begin with an investigation of what
might be called apocalyptic and mystical *merkabah* and then proceed to a treatment of what might be called speculative and esoteric *merkabah*. The consolidation that results in the first category
has already been addressed by a number of scholars.[6] The ex-

3. Ibid., p. 43.

4. Tannaim ("teachers") refers to scholars active in Palestine for two and a half centuries
after the death of Hillel (ca. 60 B.C.E.–9 C.E.). They are viewed as the recognized authorities
on the Oral Law, and the Mishnah (edited 220 C.E.) is the record of their opinions.
Distinguished from the Tannaim are the Amoraim ("interpreters"), a term applied to
scholars in the Academies of Palestine and Babylonia who interpreted the Mishnah, from
the beginning of the third century of the Common Era until the completion of the Talmud
(500 C.E.). The views of the Amoraim are the basis of the *Gemara*, which represents a
commentary on the Mishnah.

5. Scholem, *Major Trends*, p. 43.

6. See in particular the works of Ithamar Gruenwald, especially *Apocalyptic and Merkavah
Mysticism* (Leiden: E. J. Brill, 1980), and more recently *From Apocalypticism to Gnosticism,
Studies in Apocalypticism, Merkavah Mysticism, and Gnosticism* (Frankfurt: P. Lang, 1988). Of
immense significance to the entire tradition is the new work of David J. Halperin, *The
Faces of the Chariot: Early Jewish Responses to Ezekiel's Vision* (Tübingen: J. C. B. Mohr, 1988).
Likewise of importance are Halperin's *The Merkabah in Rabbinic Literature* (New Haven:
American Oriental Society, 1980); F. T. Fallon, *The Enthronement of Sabaoth* (Leiden: Brill,
1977); A. F. Siegal, *Two Powers in Heaven* (Leiden: Brill, 1977); David Russell, *The Method
and Message of Jewish Apocalyptic* (Philadelphia: Westminster Press, 1964); Ioan Petru Cu-
lianu, *Psychanodia I: A Survey of the Evidence Concerning the Ascension of the Soul and Its
Relevance* (Leiden: E. J. Brill, 1983); and the studies of Ira Chernus, including *Mysticism
in Rabbinic Judaism* (Berlin: Walter de Gruyter, 1982) and "Visions of God in Merkabah

pansion that results in the second category represents what I feel
is a logical arrangement of approaches that have been treated
under various headings by scholars interested in the talmudic and
midrashic implications of the idea, on the one hand, and in the
kabbalistic implications, on the other.

Considering the complexity of the subject as a whole, it hardly
needs to be said that the *ma'aseh merkabah* defies easy categorization. The proposed categories, for example, certainly overlap: one
finds shared elements within each category. Both, moreover, are
divisible into a number of subcategories. Nor are the distinctions
between the categories that clear-cut. The categories must be
viewed as approximations of kinds rather than as generic imperatives. Like all attempts at a taxonomy, this one is provisional at
best. Nonetheless, the adoption of the foregoing categories does
have its advantages. First, it helps to impose a sense of order on
a vast amount of material, most of it as disparate as it is recondite.
At the same time these categories suggest a principle of organization by which one might be able to understand more clearly
that there is indeed an essential continuity of thought concerning
the *merkabah*. Second, the categories emphasize the fact that the
merkabah assumes a number of forms during the course of its
generation and transmission as a crucial phenomenon in the history of Judaic thought. What is known as "the *merkabah*" is neither
one dimensional nor monolithic. Multifaceted and constantly in
flux, this phenomenon is part of a vital tradition or complex of
traditions that require reassessment and redefinition at every
stage.

Rooted in the earliest concepts of *merkabah*, the apocalyptic and
mystical dimensions of the subject involve an entire literature, the
primary focus of which is third-person narrative, on the one hand,
and first-person testimony, on the other. The apocalyptic dimension is conceived primarily as narrative, the mystical dimension
as first-person testimony. As narrative, the apocalyptic dimension
portrays the encounter with the Chariot through a reformulation
of the biblical original. The purpose of this reformulation is to
transform the biblical original into a new text, one that embodies
its own myth, its own story. At times that story is part of a larger
narrative context, but underlying the story is the original text

---

Mysticism," *Journal for the Study of Judaism* 13 (1982): 123–146, as well as the important
essays in Peter Schäfer's *Hekhalot-Studien* (Tübingen: J. C. B. Mohr, 1988).

upon which the new text draws. In this atmosphere the biblical text assumes a crucial originary function: its primacy is felt throughout.

As first-person testimony, the mystical dimension portrays the encounter with the Chariot not so much through a reformulation of the biblical original as through the retelling of an individual experience.[7] The purpose of this retelling is to provide instruction in the actual implementation of a mystical (that is, ecstatic) experience. Its primary emphasis is upon praxis rather than upon story. As such, it becomes a guide, a *vade mecum* to the infinite. In this process the original biblical text loses its primacy: its function is ancillary to that of the personal testimony related. Despite this major change in focus between apocalyptic and mystical *merkabah*, both forms reflect that essential continuity of thought Gershom Scholem sees in *merkabah* literature as a whole.[8] Addressing the crucial issue of how the older apocalyptic material finds expression in the later *merkabah* accounts, Scholem is thereby prompted to observe quite categorically that "the main subjects of the later Merkabah mysticism already occupy a central position in this oldest esoteric literature."[9]

In order to assess the nature of the apocalyptic and mystical traditions that constitute the first category under consideration, we must explore in greater detail the relationships between visionary enactment in its scriptural setting and visionary enactment in its apocalyptic and mystical setting, for the transition between the two settings is of such a magnitude that the visionary mode comes to assume a new identity in its later delineations.[10] Apo-

7. In fact, this dimension, according to Peter Schäfer, is "basically independent of the Bible. To formulate it even more sharply: it appears to be autonomous." "Early Jewish Mysticism," in *Hekhalot-Studien*, p. 290.

8. It should be noted that many of Scholem's fundamental theses regarding Jewish mysticism have recently come under fire by a number of scholars. See, for example, Halperin, *Faces*, and Schäfer, *Hekhalot-Studien*, passim.

9. Scholem, *Major Trends*, p. 43.

10. The discussion of apocalypticism that follows is indebted to the excellent treatment by Ithamar Gruenwald, "Jewish Apocalypticism in the Rabbinic Period," *The Encyclopedia of Religion*, ed. Mircea Eliade, 16 vols. (New York: Macmillan, 1987), I, 336–342. This entry is part of a series of entries on the subject of apocalypse. The field of apocalypticism is immense. In addition to the items already cited, see Gruenwald, "Knowledge and Vision: Towards a Clarification of Two 'Gnostic' Concepts in the Light of Their Alleged Origins," *Israel Oriental Studies* 3 (1973): 63–107; and "The Cultural Milieu of Apocalypticism," in *From Apocalypticism to Gnosticism*, pp. 1–11.

calypticism itself is both a traditional and a radical phenomenon. As a traditional phenomenon, it self-consciously forges strong links with its scriptural forebear. It does this by bestowing upon the apocalyptic visionaries under whose names it is transmitted the identities of scriptural patriarchs, sages, and prophets, including Adam, Enoch, Abraham, Moses, Elijah, Isaiah, Baruch, and Ezra. Doing so in this pseudepigraphical fashion, it legitimates its own enterprise. It becomes thereby a new scripture, one that possesses renewed authority in the revelation of its truths. Its mode of revelation is to enlarge upon the narratives, scenes, events, and prophecies that surround the scriptural characters it appropriates as its spokesmen. In this respect, apocalyptic is a rewriting of scripture, as well as an implied exegesis upon it not by a disinterested observer but by the very individuals whose experiences are disclosed.

If apocalypticism makes a point of traditionalizing itself through the adoption of the names and events of its scriptural forebear, it departs radically from that forebear in a number of respects, the first of which has to do with the nature of the experience that is communicated and the second of which has to do with the assumptions that underlie the act of disclosure. The first comes under the heading of "vision," the second under the heading of "knowledge."[11] From the perspective of the Hebrew Bible, the visionary experience is one largely enacted by means of a revelation of deity that moves from the celestial region (the realm of God) to the terrestrial region (the human realm). Although there is at least the possibility of movement in the other direction, the sense of Prov. 30:4 still largely obtains: "Who has ascended to heaven and come down [*mi 'alah-shamayim vayyerad*]?" Departing radically from this perspective, apocalyptic reformulates the visionary experience to suggest the movement not from the realm of God to the human realm but vice versa. The all-important notion of the "ascent" makes itself known in the apocalyptic rewriting of the scriptural text. In apocalypticism the visionary mode is a phenomenon of ascent. This reversal in the nature and means of disclosure is tantamount to a "revolutioniz[ing] of the scriptural world-view." As we shall discuss, it is also a crucial feature of the

---

11. Gruenwald discusses a third issue that he terms "dualism," an idea that will not concern us at present.

visionary as a mystical category, one that suggests the ease, indeed, almost the inevitability of the transition from apocalypticism to mysticism.

Corresponding to "vision" as a distinguishing characteristic of the way apocalyptic transforms Scripture is the category of "knowledge." Once again, a reversal of sorts occurs in the movement from Scripture to apocalyptic. The attitude toward knowledge displayed in Scripture is one in which a categorical distinction is drawn between those things known to God and those things known to man. Although one may be prompted to aspire to divine knowledge, one is always made aware of one's limitations. In the world of apocalypticism, on the other hand, access to the secrets of the other world is in effect what defines the genre itself. By means of his ascent, the visionary beholds the storehouses of all the winds and the foundations of the earth; he is made aware of the workings of the universe, along with its various realms; and he comes to know the course of history from the foundation of the world to its culmination at the end of time. With this gnosis, the visionary attains to the highest plains of awareness.

The genre of apocalyptic is essentially a genre of power and the quest for power through the vehicle of ascent, on the one hand, and the vehicle of knowledge, on the other. In apocalyptic the visionary as scriptural entity is rewritten to accord with this radical point of view. Underlying that point of view is the visionary etiology centered in the prophetic milieu inspired by the event that inaugurates the book of Ezekiel and its corresponding manifestations. The force of this will be seen in an examination of some of the texts that constitute Jewish apocalyptic and mysticism.

To that end, we shall return to the pseudepigraphal accounts centered in the intertestamental period and trace the ideas embodied therein through the later mystical literature. Our point of departure will be the so-called Ethiopic Enoch or *I Enoch*.[12] A pseudepigraphon that exerted an immense influence up to the second century of the Common Era, this is a composite work composed of five shorter books conventionally referred to as "the Book of Watchers," "the Book of Parables," "the Astronomical

12. References to *I Enoch* are from *The Apocrypha and Pseudepigrapha of the Old Testament in English*, ed. R. H. Charles, 2 vols. (Oxford: Clarendon Press, 1913), hereafter referred to as Charles. I have compared this version of *I Enoch* with that in *The Old Testament Pseudepigrapha*, ed. James H. Charlesworth, 2 vols. (Garden City, N.Y.: Doubleday, 1983–1985), hereafter referred to as Charlesworth.

Book," "the Book of Dreams," and "the Epistle of Enoch." At issue is the first book (concerning the Watchers), perhaps the oldest of the five. Recalling the fallen angels of Gen. 6:1–4, the Watchers are the "sons of God" who mated with the "daughters of men" and begot giants. *I Enoch* portrays their descent, their destructive activities on earth, and their punishment. In that portrayal the angels implore Enoch to present God with their request for forgiveness. In response, Enoch ascends to the divine presence in a dream, but God rejects the angelic petition. Enoch then is given a tour of the remote and fantastic regions of the earth (chs. 6–36).[13] From the perspective that we are exploring, these events are important because they contain the oldest acknowledged *merkabah* vision from the literature outside of the canonical Scriptures.[14] That vision is contextualized ironically in an appeal of the prophet for divine mercy upon the doers of evil. The circumstances that surround the *Urerlebnis* are thereby rewritten to delineate a new narrative, one that totally reconceives the function of the prophet as visionary.

If such is true of the circumstances that surround the *Urerlebnis*, it is no less true of the visionary experience itself. Drawing upon the idea that Enoch "walked with God: and he *was* not; for God took him" (Gen. 5:22, 24), the pseudepigraphon legitimates its conception of the visionary experience as an ascent through recourse to scriptural authority, which it then transforms into its own reading of the *Urerlebnis*. This reading assumes its own decidedly architectonic focus, one reinforced by the notion of structures within structures, visions within visions, and, one might suggest, texts within texts, as the seer pursues the source of all visions, the source of all texts, the origins of knowing. The formulation of this pursuit is distinctly quadripartite. It begins with the ascent as Enoch, borne upward by winds, beholds a wall built of crystals surrounded by tongues of fire. This stage is followed by the impulse to penetrate, to move from outside to inside, from external vision, as it were, to internal vision. Penetrating the fire, Enoch draws near a large house built of crystals. It becomes clear that knowledge of the visionary is "housed" in a structure, the insides of which must be traversed in order to gain further insight.

13. This summary is derived from Halperin, *Faces*, pp. 78–79. See his account in its entirety, pp. 78–87. See also Charles, II, 168.

14. Gruenwald, *Apocalyptic*, p. 36.

The visionary text is structured throughout according to its own complex principles of organization. In Enoch's reading of this text the experience is immediately cosmicized. If the walls and floor of the house are of crystal, its ceiling is like the path of the stars and lightning, accompanied by fiery cherubim and a heaven clear as water, the crystalline sea. Surrounding the walls is a flaming fire. Within the house Enoch undergoes the extremes of one who would penetrate to the core of all knowledge. As hot as fire and as cold as ice, he is overcome with fear and trembling. Like Ezekiel before the *visio Dei*, Enoch falls upon his face.

But entrance into the visionary structure is only the first half of the experience Enoch portrays. Extending the visionary implications of the *Urerlebnis* even further, Enoch envisions yet another house, another structure that encloses additional modes of perception. This is the text within the text. Finding himself on the outside of this house in this additional stage of the visionary process, Enoch marvels that this structure is even greater than the first one. Having traversed the initial structure, however, the prophet discovers that the portal to the second one stands open before him in this myth of knowing that he formulates. Although similar in form to the first structure—in effect, a very replication of it—the second structure is nonetheless even grander and imbued with greater splendor and magnificence. Portrayed through references to lightning, stars, and celestial fires, it, too, is cosmicized. As the prophet moves to higher (that is, interior) levels of perception, then, the nature of his knowledge differs more nearly in degree than in kind. The act of penetrating the visionary text is one of reenacting the same structures of thought but in a different key.

The difference, however, is that in this higher form of knowing the seer becomes acquainted not only with the cosmic implications of his experience but with the regal implications as well. For the final stage of the quadripartite process is that of beholding the throne and its divine occupant. As Enoch makes clear in his description of the throne and its occupant, visionary seeing is concerned as much with the inability to see, that is, the failure of knowledge, as it is with the ability to see, that is, the gaining of knowledge. His description moves from the throne to the occupant himself. The appearance of the throne, declares Enoch, "was as crystal, and the wheels thereof as the shining sun, and there was the vision of the cherubim." From underneath the throne issued streams of flaming fire so that Enoch could not behold it. On the throne sat the Great Glory, whose "raiment shone more brightly than the sun and was whiter than any snow." None of the angels could enter and could behold His face because of "the magnificence and glory, and no flesh could behold Him." The flaming fire, in turn, enveloped Him, and "a great fire stood before Him, and none around could draw nigh Him." In the presence of this figure Enoch is summoned to do its bidding (14:8–25).

According to Ithamar Gruenwald, this vision represents a well-spring of later *merkabah* thought. The ascent, the passage through fire, the approach to the throne, the experience of terror, the description of the Enthroned Figure: in one form or another, all of these became the staple of visionary accounts that followed in its path. Even the concept of the vision within the vision or the house within the house is incorporated into later visionary depictions.[15] In its portrayal of Enoch's encounter with the Enthroned Figure, this account draws upon biblical antecedents and transforms them to accord with its own unique outlook. Distinguishing the portrayal is a conflation of biblical motifs that came to be associated with the *merkabah* as a distinct movement.

Foremost among these motifs, of course, are the ones that distinguish Ezekiel's vision, including the appearance of the Enthroned Figure in the context of the wheeled vehicle, the clouds, the fire, the lightning, the reference to the "terrible crystal," and the abject figure of the prophet himself. Also present, however, is the spirit of Isaiah's vision of the enthroned deity refulgent in the Holy of Holies (Isaiah 6) and Daniel's vision of the Ancient of Days with his garment white as snow and his fiery, wheeled throne (Daniel 7).[16] Coupled with these ideas is the suggestion that the building complex through which Enoch passes locates the Temple of Jerusalem in a celestial setting. Moving through this complex, Enoch enters first the walled court of the Temple, then the Temple proper, and finally the Holy of Holies.[17] From a cultic as well as a visionary point of view, one is reminded of Ezekiel's traversal of the restored Temple complex at the end of his proph-

15. Ibid., pp. 32–37.
16. For a discussion of this aspect, see, in particular, Christopher Rowland, *The Open Heaven: A Study of Apocalyptic in Judaism and Early Christianity* (New York: Crossroad, 1982), passim. Rowland dates *I Enoch* 1–36 before Daniel (p. 266).
17. Halperin, *Faces*, p. 81. Halperin associates these events with Daniel 7, for which he finds the possibility of a celestial setting.

ecy (chs. 40–48). There, he beholds the return of the inaugural vision to assume its proper place within the Temple enclosure.

I Enoch provides an apocalyptic account of such biblical occurrences. These and many more details serve as the basis of the author's conception, which he fashions into his own portrayal of the prophet's ascent to the celestial throne room to appear before the Glory of God. At the center of the prophet's experience is the *visio Dei*, awesome in its glory, overwhelming in its splendor, at once defying and inviting delineation among those committed to share with others that which is fundamentally beyond comprehension. This tension is at the heart of the apocalyptic renderings that form the basis of the *maʿaseh merkabah* from the earliest times to its later reformulation in the traditions of Jewish mysticism. Within the composite fabric that constitutes *I Enoch*, the ascent that is described in the section known as "the Book of Watchers" is only one of a number that might be cited as a foundation of *merkabah* thought.[18]

If *I Enoch* is the earliest and, in some respects, the most important document in which the visionary ascent to the *merkabah* is revealed, there are a number of other documents of significance as well. In fact, so widespread was the concept that it became part of the very culture of the Judaic world in the centuries immediately preceding and following the dawn of the Common Era. Examples abound.[19] Among the later pseudepigraphal accounts of some interest is one that develops the Enochic material still further. Probably composed by an Alexandrian Jew between 30 B.C.E. and 30 C.E., *II Enoch* or Slavonic *Enoch* (also known as *The Book of the Secrets of Enoch*) draws upon the earlier pseudepigraphon for much of its visionary

18. Such passages as *I Enoch* 18:8–9, 25:3, and parts of what is known as "the Book of Parables" in *I Enoch* (37–71), among other sections, all anticipate characteristics associated with the *maʿaseh merkabah*.

19. For other accounts, varying in times of composition, see *The Books of Adam and Eve* (25:1–28:4); *Apocalypse of Zephaniah* (33); *Syriach Baruch* (51); *4 Ezra* (8:20); and *The Testament of Job* (33 and 48). In yet another vein, see also the "Liturgy of the Angels" from the Dead Sea scrolls. Composed at various times between about 250 B.C.E. and 68 C.E., these scrolls were part of the library of the religious community at Qumran. The "Liturgy of the Angels" is represented by two extracts, the first of which is based on Ezekiel 1 and 10 and the second of which engages in a series of blessings by each of the seven archangels. See *The Dead Sea Scriptures*, trans. Theodor H. Gaster (New York: Doubleday, 1964), pp. 367–378. See also Lawrence H. Schiffman, "*Merkavah* Speculation at Qumran: The 4 Q Serekh Shirot Olat ha-Shabbat," *Mystics, Philosophers, and Politicians*, ed. Jehuda Reinharz and Daniel Swetschinski (Durham, N.C.: Duke University Press, 1982), pp. 15–47.

material.[20] At the same time, it transforms this material to accord with its own point of view.

For example, although the motif of the ascent is still very much in evidence, the means of transport are now part of the celestial rather than the natural world. In either case the implications are comparable: the visionary becomes a passive participant subject to the will of a higher order, whether manifested through natural or through supernatural forces. Thus, in *II Enoch* (1–22) the prophet relates that two huge angelic beings are revealed to him when he is asleep and bear him up on their wings to what appear to be ten celestial realms, each of which is described in varying degrees of detail.[21] A number of aspects in this description are of interest. In keeping with the angelic dimension of the account, the narrative, for example, devises an angelology that schematizes the celestial world revealed to Enoch. In that schematization one finds a distinction between the faithful and the reprobate angels, with each assigned to its own heaven. (Accordingly, the second, a portion of the third [the northern parts], and the fifth are assigned to the reprobate.) In this pseudepigraphon, then, one finds a significant emphasis on the ethical dimensions of ascent, especially as reflected in the arrangement of the angelic forces that constitute the celestial world.

The third heaven is of particular interest, because that portion assigned to the faithful angels is conceived as a paradisal realm, with "sweet-flowering trees" graced with "sweet-smelling fruits." In the midst of the trees Enoch sees the tree of life, the "place whereon the Lord rests, when he goes up into paradise." Reinforcing this paradisal description, one also finds two springs that send forth honey and milk, oil and wind. These, in turn, separate into four parts and descend into the paradise of Eden, "and thence go forth along the earth" (*II Enoch* 8–9; cf. Gen. 2:9–14). According to the schematic universe envisioned by *II Enoch*, then, the ascent to the Chariot is associated with the entrance into a paradisal realm, as distinctions are raised between those realms reserved for good behavior, on the one hand, and those reserved

20. References are to the version of *II Enoch* in Charles, which I have compared with that in Charlesworth. *II Enoch* exists in two recensions, a longer and a shorter (A and B, respectively, in Charles). The present discussion focuses on recension A.

21. There is some conjecture that the true number of heavens is really seven and that the additional numbers amount to interpolations (see Charles, II, 442, notes). Gruenwald specifies seven heavens (*Apocalyptic*, p. 49).

for bad behavior, on the other. The world of ascent is becoming humanized as well as schematized.

Such an outlook is made forcefully apparent in the higher reaches of the ascent. Thus, in the seventh heaven the *visio Dei* is reinforced by a pronounced sense of order and celestial propriety, as Enoch beholds a great light and troops of fiery archangels, as well as other forces divided into nine regiments surrounding the Lord on His throne. With a heightened sense of order and propriety, the celestial troops stand on the ten steps before the throne according to their rank. Bowing down to the Lord, they then return to their places in joy as they celebrate Him in song. The mode of celebration (as well as the description) suggests that conceived by Isaiah (6:1–3): "And the cherubim and seraphim standing about the throne, the six-winged and many-eyed ones do not depart, standing before the Lord's face doing his will, and cover his whole throne, singing with gentle voice before the Lord's face: 'Holy, holy, holy, Lord Ruler of Sabaoth, heavens and earth are full of Thy glory.'" But the emphasis upon order and propriety already establishes the idea of a celestial polity that governs the angelic behavior before the throne.

Exposed to the workings of that polity, Enoch is privileged to be guided first by Gabriel and then Michael to the highest reaches (the eighth, ninth, and tenth heavens) where he is allowed to behold God's unspeakable face. The experience, of course, is overwhelming, indeed, transformative, as Enoch is stripped of his earthly garments, anointed, and attired in the garments of God's glory. He becomes, in a sense, what he beholds, and, occupying that most privileged status, he transcends the rules governing the celestial polity to which the angelic troops must adhere and assumes a position not only of power but of authority.

Consistent with that position is the bestowal of a new vocation, that of transcriber of divine events, notably those associated with his own experience. Thus, he is given a reed with which to write and books to use for his transcriptions, as he sets about to record not only his own journeyings but such events as the creation of the universe in the form of three hundred and sixty-six books (*II Enoch* 20–23). This final dimension is apposite not only because it introduces so many of the motifs that become established *topoi* in subsequent *merkabah* literature (the ascent, the vision of the angels and the throne, and so forth) but because it provides the occasion by which Enoch is made the transcriber of those motifs

within the context of his own prophecy. As a result *II Enoch* becomes self-reflexive: it recounts the history of its own events, in
effect, the books of the secrets of Enoch within the *Book of the
Secrets of Enoch*. In the transcription of that history, it memorializes
the fact that apocalyptic is not only a vehicle of ascent but a means
of power. *II Enoch* is a text of power, one in which the visionary
assumes a paramount position in the divine world, which he not
only beholds as privileged observer but inhabits as exalted transcriber.

If the Enoch pseudepigrapha represent the kind of material
that appeared in the transitional period before and shortly after
the commencement of the Common Era, there are corresponding
documents of comparable importance to the formative stages of
the *merkabah* tradition. Reflecting the influence of the outlook embodied in the visionary ascents of Enoch is a pseudepigraphon
known as the *Apocalypse of Abraham*.[22] As a work that dates its
terminus a quo from the destruction of the Temple (70 C.E.), this
document is crucial to the development of those characteristics
that underscore the delineation of the *merkabah* in its later stages.
If the experience of Enoch in Gen. 5:22 (the "translation" of the
prophet) represents the focal point of the apocalyptic ascents considered above, the experience of Abraham in Gen. 15:3–6 (the
promise of the seed) forms the basis of the corresponding ascent
described in the present account.

Combining fictionalized autobiography and apocalyptic, the account is cast in the form of first-person narrative. This highly
personalized approach intensifies the experience and suggests a
pattern of coming to awareness that underscores the import of
what Abraham beholds on his journey to the other world. That
journey, in turn, is anticipated by the autobiographical concern
with the maturation and preparation that Abraham must undergo
before he is ready to assume the role of visionary. Within the
context of Abraham's spiritual growth, the ascent itself is seen as
a culmination of his disenchantment with idolatrous practices that
characterize his upbringing and are part of his heritage (1–8). It
is these practices that he must renounce if he is to attain the purity

22. The *Apocalypse of Abraham* is extant only in an Old Slavonic translation, which has
been transmitted in several Russian redactions. References are to the translation of R.
Rubinkiewicz in Charlesworth. This translation supersedes that of G. H. Box, *Apocalypse
of Abraham* (New York: Macmillan, 1918). Despite the shortcomings attributed to the Box
edition in modern scholarship, his introduction and comments are immensely helpful.

necessary for genuine vision. This new awareness of the propriety of cultic practice, then, reinforces the terms of the ascent and represents the means through which it is effected.

In accord with such an idea, the voice of God calls to Abraham at the appropriate time, instructs the patriarch to make a sacrifice on God's behalf, to abstain from food and wine for forty days, and to hasten to a high mountain, Horeb (9–10). As the embodiment of both divinity and cultic purity, the angel Iaoel (the counterpart of the angelic guides in the Enoch accounts) appears to Abraham in the likeness of a man (11–12). Embodying the spirit of the Tetragrammaton in his very name, Iaoel has the patriarch meditate on the *nomen ineffabile*, which becomes a source of renewed strength and wisdom.[23] Although amazed and indeed prostrate with fear, Abraham is heartened by the promise of that knowledge which is the basis of apocalyptic, as the angel promises that Abraham will be shown what is "in the heavens, on the earth and in the sea, in the abyss, and in the lower depths, in the garden of Eden and in its rivers, in the fullness of the universe." Beholding that, he will "see its circles in all" (12:10). Abiding by the injunctions of the angel and resisting the temptations of those who would dissuade him from following the true path (13–14), the patriarch is placed on the right wing of a pigeon while the angel sits on the left wing of a dove, as the two ascend to the world of God. In that ascent they attain the realm of fire, out of which emanates a sound "like a voice of many waters" (17:1; cf. Ezek. 22:24). There, Abraham, bowing low, recites a liturgy in celebration of the enthroned deity (17:8–21).

This fusion of the cultic and the liturgical distinguishes the *Apocalypse of Abraham* as a document in which these concerns assume paramount importance. In a pseudepigraphon that emphasizes worship and the trappings of worship above all other concerns, the liturgy that Abraham intones represents "the longest *Merkavah* hymn in apocalyptic literature."[24] In its celebration of God's glory the *Apocalypse of Abraham* is able to claim the liturgical

23. According to Gruenwald, Iaoel's name "is a combination of the three root-letters of the Tetragrammaton with the usual 'el' ending." Combined with this is the idea of reciting the holy name in order to bring about a mystical experience, a practice common in the later testimonies (*Apocalyptic*, pp. 52–54).

24. In form and content it resembles "a liturgical hymn or sapiental psalm" (Gruenwald, *Apocalyptic*, p. 56). In either case it is an elaborate form of the *kedushah* ("Holy, Holy, Holy"), derived from Isa. 6:3. As such, it is a staple of the *merkabah* accounts.

dimension as its singular achievement, one that involves the formulation of what might be called the cult of the *merkabah*.

In the articulation of that cult one is introduced to a rendering
of the *hayyot* that is remarkable in its implications. Surrounding
the *merkabah*, these "many-eyed ones," the "four fiery living creatures," are beheld celebrating the enthroned deity with their own
celestial liturgy. Drawing upon the protoptype of Ezekiel, the text
describes them as follows: "And the appearance of each of them
was the same, each having four faces," that of a lion, a man, an
ox, and an eagle. "Each one had four heads on its body so that
the four living creatures had sixteen faces." With this, the text
fuses the description of the seraphim in Isaiah: "Each one had
six wings: two on the shoulders, two halfway down, and two at
the loins. With the wings which were on their shoulders they
covered their faces, with the wings at their loins they clothed their
feet, and they would stretch the two middle wings out and fly, erect"
(18:1–8).

Just at the point that the description asserts its ties with the
biblical prototype, however, it departs from its sources by bestowing upon the creatures their own frightening personalities. For
"when they [the creatures] finished singing, they would look at
one another and threaten one another." In response to such behavior, Iaoel finds that he must "restrain the threats of the living
creatures of the cherubim against one another" (cf. 10:9), by turning the face of each living creature from the face opposite it so
that one face could not behold the threatening aspect of the other
face.[25] Turning their faces aside, Iaoel attempts to calm them with
"the song of peace" (18:9–12). This is a remarkable touch, one
that suggests how compellingly the author of the *Apocalypse* is
willing to exploit to its fullest the notion of the *hayyot* as genuinely
"living creatures." That which animates them has about it "something fundamentally savage and chaotic."[26] As such, these crea-

25. "This hostility of the living creatures . . . is nowhere else mentioned, at least not in
those apocalyptic texts that came down to us. Generally, the hostility of the angels is directed
only against human beings who ascend to heaven and the idea expressed here in connection
with Iaoel is thus quite extraordinary" (Gruenwald, *Apocalyptic*, p. 54).

26. The phrase is Halperin's. See his discussion entitled "*The attack of the creatures*" in
Faces, pp. 112–113. In his superb discussion Halperin has explored this dark side of the
merkabah in depth. He has found interpretations that emphasize disturbing qualities not
only with regard to the *hayyot*, especially the potentially idolatrous associations of the ox's
face and the calf's foot (cf. Ezek. 1:7, 10), but with the primordial qualities suggested by
the "terrible ice" of Ezek. 1:22. Such ideas imply that, for some interpreters, the biblical

tures are the embodiment of *das Heilige* as a phenomenon of immense danger.

At every moment the *merkabah* threatens to undo not only those who venture to approach it but its own being in the very act of celebrating its grandeur in worship and song. From this perspective the *hayyot* are a testament to the instability (indeed, the savagery) of the other world and the text through which that world is commemorated. It is this dark and potentially chaotic quality that underscores the delineation of the *merkabah* itself, as Abraham concludes his description of the vision by observing: "And while I was still standing and watching, I saw behind the living creatures a chariot with fiery wheels. Each wheel was full of eyes round about. And above the wheels was the throne which I had seen. And it was covered with fire and the fire encircled it round about, and an indescribable light surrounded the fiery crowd. And I heard the voice of their sanctification like the voice of a single man" (18:12–14). In the liturgy that the *Apocalypse of Abraham* projects, the voice of sanctification is hardly one that is fully at peace with itself.

Drawing upon conventions that are the hallmark of apocalyptic, the work concludes with an articulation of those elements that cause it to become a vehicle of gnosis. Here one finds the idea that once the visionary has attained to such heights, he has disclosed to him the drama of human history, beginning with an account of the creation of the universe, the garden of Eden, the temptation and fall, and the course of events culminating in the destruction of the Temple (19–27). Arising out of this account (and, in response to it) is the messianic promise of the seed that will be born from Abraham's line, followed by an apocalyptic judgment in the last days (28–32). Like the Enoch pseudepigrapha before it, this document establishes its own mythic framework, in this case, a mythopoeisis founded on an all-consuming concern with the destruction of the Temple as apocalyptic event. Out of that event, the pseudepigraphon forges its own soteriology and its own eschatology, both of which derive their inspiration from the promise of the seed announced to the patriarch known as the Father of Nations. At the center of this promise once again is the

---

text appeared to have "opened the window on a troubling ambiguity in the being of the Jewish God. The text's transmitters and interpreters fought a losing battle to force the window shut" (pp. 449–450, and passim).

merkabah, revealed, in this instance, not to Enoch, but to Abraham, the new voyager to the celestial realms.

The foregoing represents only a brief sampling of the apocalyptic literature that anticipates the *ma'aseh merkabah* as a fully articulated phenomenon.[27] But even on the basis of this sampling, certain motifs make themselves apparent. First, the pseudepigraphal accounts adopt as their visionary spokesmen the biblical patriarchs and ancient prophets in order to establish the integrity and legitimacy of the enterprise. Although this practice represents a defining characteristic of the pseudepigraphal form, it anticipates a corresponding practice in *merkabah* mysticism. Second, the visionary experience manifests itself in the all-important notion of the ascent, which is conceived and executed in a number of ways. Whereas in some accounts the visionary is transported suddenly and without warning, in others he is made to undergo a process of preparation. The mode of transport also varies. The visionary rises by means of clouds and winds, chariots, the wings of angels or birds, and, in later accounts, a ladder.[28]

If the mode of transport varies, so does the number of heavens that constitute the celestial realm that is the object of the ascent. The visionary may ascend to one heaven, to three heavens, to seven heavens, to ten heavens, or to an indeterminate number of heavens. In many of the accounts (both early and late) the prevailing number is seven, a concept derived largely from the traditions underlying *IV Ezra* (7:80–101). The heavens themselves are often described through a varied and elaborate topography, ranging from paradisal realms where the faithful dwell, to the realms of punishment where the unfaithful dwell. In both respects the visionary is made aware of the angelic hosts, with their formations, functions, and often their names.

The ultimate object of the quest, as we have seen, is the attainment of the heaven of heavens, there to behold and worship the enthroned deity in all His splendor. Having encountered this figure, the visionary undergoes a number of experiences. Along with

27. For additional examples see Martha Himmelfarb's discussion of the Apocalypse of Zephaniah in *Tours of Hell: An Apocalyptic Form in Jewish and Christian Literature* (Philadelphia: University of Pennsylvania Press, 1983), pp. 155–158, and passim.

28. For a study of motifs see Alexander Altmann, "The Ladder of Ascension," *Studies in Religious Philosophy and Mysticism* (Ithaca, N.Y.: Cornell University Press, 1969), pp. 41–72. In the *merkabah* literature wagons of light and carriages of fire are also used as modes of transport. In two cases the visionary is actually "dragged on his knees till he reaches the Throne of Glory" (Gruenwald, *Apocalyptic*, pp. 119–121).

the angelic hosts, he worships the Enthroned Figure through an elaborate liturgy; he is attired in a new garment or is transformed in various ways; he is the recipient of a divine gnosis that allows him to penetrate the secret ways of God, to witness the creation of the universe, to know the future of humankind, to become aware of an ultimate eschatology; and he is made a transcriber and interpreter of these events. Involving an elaborate mythology of visionary ascent, these are some of the more important aspects of the apocalyptic dimensions that anticipate the full flowering of the *merkabah* in Judaic thought.

II

Having provided a brief overview of these dimensions in our treatment of the apocalyptic *merkabah*, we may now proceed to a discussion of the mystical *merkabah* or what Gershom Scholem calls "the *Merkabah* mysticism of late and post-talmudic times."[29] Reflecting an essential continuity with the apocalyptic material considered above, the documents that constitute this stage are, nonetheless, *sui generis.* Classified under the general heading of *hekhalot* literature, they are made up of a series of texts that portray in elaborate detail the mystic's ecstatic journey of ascent through the so-called heavenly halls or *hekhalot*, there to appear before the Enthroned Figure in His celestial palace.[30] Largely edited in the fifth and sixth centuries, the texts themselves are generally divisible into what is known as the "Lesser *Hekhalot* [*Hekhalot Zutarti*]," the oldest text available, and the "Greater *Hekhalot* [*Hekhalot Rabbati*]," composed of several different strata of textual transmission.[31] Whereas the Lesser *Hekhalot* features Rabbi Akiba as its

29. According to Alexander, two views are possible in this regard: "On the one hand we could argue that the mystical tracts are post-talmudic and have grown out of attempts to understand and to explain talmudic Ma'aseh Merkabah materials. Or we could argue that the Merkabah tracts and the talmudic Merkabah texts belong to one unbroken mystical movement and that in some cases the traditions in the mystical tracts may go back to the talmudic period or may even be anterior to the talmudic Merkabah traditions." Introduction to *III Enoch*, in Charlesworth, I, 231–232. Scholars have strongly propounded both views.

30. In recent scholarship the motif of ascent has been relegated to other motifs, such as that of the adjuration and the importance of theurgy. See Schäfer, "Early Jewish Mysticism," *Hekhalot-Studien*, pp. 281–291.

31. Among the most important of these texts are (1) The Visions of Ezekiel (*Re'iyyot Yehezk'el*); (2) the Lesser *Hekhalot* (*Hekhalot Zutarti*); (3) the Greater *Hekhalot* (*Hekhalot*

principal speaker, the Greater *Hekhalot* finds its spokesman in Rabbi Ishmael. In the *hekhalot* texts these Tannaim are the primary vehicles through whom the revelation of the *merkabah* is vouch- safed and transmitted. In addition to the Lesser and Greater *hekhalot*, there are a number of other texts that constitute this special category of *maʿaseh merkabah*.[32]

In general, that category displays certain characteristics that render the texts themselves and the culture of which they are a product unique in the history of the *merkabah* as a crucial phe- nomenon. An overview of these characteristics should bring the *hekhalot* material into greater focus.[33] First, the culture out of which the texts emerge is distinguished by the presence of practicing mystics.[34] Known technically as *yordei merkabah* (literally, "descen-

---

Rabbati); (4) the *Merkabah Rabbah*; (5) the titleless *Hekhalot* (part of which appears in the form of the *Shiʿur Komah* later transmitted in the manuscripts as a separate unit); (6) the chapter on physiognomics and chiromancy; (7) the Book of the *Hekhalot* or *III Enoch*; (8) the Treatise of the *Hekhalot* (*Massekhet Hekhalot*) (Scholem, *Jewish Gnosticism*, pp. 5–7; cf. the list in Alexander's introduction to *III Enoch*, in Charlesworth, I, 250–251, and Halperin, *Faces*, pp. 363–366). Aside from the philological difficulties associated with the *hekhalot* texts, the problems that surround this material are daunting. The "texts" of this literature, observes Halperin, "float in a larger mass of unassigned *Hekhalot* material, like partly co- agulated globs floating in a thick and murky liquid." In addition to the discrepancies in manuscript sources, it is not even clear where the beginnings and endings of individual texts occur (*Faces*, p. 365). Not only are these texts completely shrouded in anonymity, their chronology is conjectural at best. Compare Joseph Dan, *Gershom Scholem and the Mystical Dimension of Jewish History* (New York: New York University Press, 1987), p. 40; and Schäfer, "Tradition and Redaction in Hekhalot Literature," *Hekhalot-Studien*, pp. 8– 16.

32. The most comprehensive and current source of *hekhalot* material to date is Peter Schäfer, *Synopse zur Hekhalot Literatur* (Tübingen: Mohr, 1981). Most of the *hekhalot* texts, as well as related material, can also be found in the three earlier anthologies of this literature: A. Jellinek, *Bet ha-Midrash*, 6 vols. (Jerusalem: Wahrmann, 1967); S. A. Werth- eimer, *Batei Midrashot*, 2 vols. (Jerusalem: Mosad ha-Rav Kook, 1950–1953); and S. Mus- sajoff, *Merkavah Shelemah* (Jerusalem: n.p., 1922). See also Ithamar Gruenwald, "New Passages from *Hekhalot* Literature," *Tarbiẓ* 38 (1968–1969): 354–372 (in Hebrew); Rachel Elior, ed., *Hekhalot Zutarti* (Jerusalem: Magnes Press, Hebrew University, 1982) (in He- brew); and the text of the tractate *Maʿaseh Merkabah* appended to Scholem's *Jewish Gnos- ticism*, pp. 101–117 (in Hebrew). An English translation of the *Maʿaseh Merkabah* has recently been made available in Naomi Janowitz's fine study, *The Poetics of Ascent: Theories of Language in a Rabbinic Ascent Text* (Albany, N.Y.: SUNY Press, 1989).

33. This discussion of the *hekhalot* material is essentially derived from Scholem's classic treatment in *Major Trends*, pp. 40–79.

34. Gruenwald raises some important distinctions between the *hekhalot* literature and apocalyptic. "Compared to the parallel experiences in the *Hekhalot* literature, the relevant experiences found in apocalyptic literature are, so-to-speak, proto-mysticism; that is, they contain all the necessary elements which could easily turn into mysticism." Unlike the *merkabah* mystics, the apocalypticists did not adopt as their *primary* goal the experience of the deity for its own sake.

ders to the *merkabah*"), they constitute actual schools of mystics exhibiting their own organization and strict rules of conduct.[35] Tracing their lineage in legendary fashion to the circle of Jochanan ben Zakkai and his disciples, they impose precise conditions of admission to their select circle.[36] These conditions are not only moral and spiritual but physical and, indeed, even physiognomic and chiromantic. Second, the texts that portray the mystical practices associated with the *yordei merkabah* are more than simply narratives of ascent: "they are essentially descriptions of a genuine religious experience."[37] As such, they are "technical guides, or manuals for mystics" that address themselves to the underlying question: "What is the mystic required to do if he wants to bring about the following mystical experience?" Embodying a complex *praxis*, the technical details involve special prayers or incantations, extended fasts and diets, the recitation of magical names, the use of magical seals, and the ritual cleansing of the body.[38]

After these elaborate preparations, the adept is ready to undergo his journey in a state of ecstasy through the heavens and through the seven palaces that constitute the highest of the heavens. The journey itself is incredibly dangerous, and, as the journey progresses, the dangers increase. The mystic is liable to be stoned or thrown into a molten lava. His flesh is transformed into fiery streams that threaten to consume him. His eyelashes become flashes of lightning, his eyeballs flaming torches. He is in danger of being

35. Although *yordei merkabah* is occasionally translated "Riders in the Chariot," this, according to Scholem (*Major Trends*, p. 47), is not the correct designation. It is not known, however, why those who "ascend" to the *merkabah* should paradoxically be referred to as those who "descend."

36. Despite the selective nature of this circle, Gruenwald disputes the idea that the testimonies of the mystics are themselves intentionally esoteric or secret. "The *Hekhalot* writings almost never require secrecy," and "no esoteric layers of Scripture are revealed in them" (*Apocalyptic*, pp. 122–123, 156–157).

37. Scholem, *Major Trends*, p. 46. Recent scholarship is increasingly questioning the distinctions between the so-called literary dimensions of the *hekhalot* material and the "practical" or "mystical" dimensions, so that one cannot simply read this material as nothing more than the first-hand descriptions of authentic mystical experiences. See Schäfer, "Tradition and Redaction," in *Hekhalot-Studien*, passim. Halperin, in turn, offers a very different picture of the *hekhalot* material and the culture of the synagogue (especially the *shabuʿot* cycle) to which it is tied (*Faces*, pp. 359–446; and in *Merkabah*, passim).

38. Gruenwald, *Apocalyptic*, p. 99. Some sense of these requirements is given already in the *Hekhalot Zutarti*: He who would endure the "the suffering of descending and ascending to the *merkabah*" must recite a fixed blessing "three times a day in the heavenly court and in the earthly court." He must also "sit fasting for forty days. He must put his head between his knees until the fast gets control of him. He must whisper towards the earth and not toward heaven, so that earth may hear and not heaven" (trans. Halperin, *Faces*, p. 374).

deluged by waves of water that represent the ethereal luminescence of the marble plates that adorn the individual palaces.

In order to ascend through the heavens to the seventh palace of the uppermost realm, the mystic must succeed in placating the angelic guards that stand watch at the entrance gates to the palaces. To do this, he fashions magic seals made of secret names, derived from his knowledge of the *merkabah* itself. Each stage of the ascension requires a new seal with which the voyager "seals himself," so that "he shall not be dragged into the fire and the flame, the vortex and the storm" that surround the throne. The seals, then, function as protective armor and as magical weapon. Initially, the magical protection of a single seal may suffice; after a while, however, the difficulties experienced by the mystic are intensified. A short and simple formula is no longer effective. Within his ecstatic trance the mystic experiences a sense of frustration that he attempts to reconcile through the adoption of longer and more elaborate magical formulae. These formulae are a reflection of the struggle that the mystic undergoes in his desire to pass the closed entrance gates that block his progress. As his energy is depleted, the attempts to marshal the theurgic powers at his disposal become progressively more strained, until finally the documents that record his ascent are filled with what appears to be "a meaningless recital of magical keywords." According to Gershom Scholem, "it is this fact which explains the abundance of magical elements in many of the *Hekhalot* texts."[39]

In this form of mysticism the quest to ascend to the realm of the Enthroned Figure is characterized not by a mystical union between the soul and God but by an emphasis upon God's *otherness* that manifests itself in an atmosphere of majesty, fear, and trembling. Finally in the presence of that Enthroned Figure, the mystic not only beholds the object of his quest in all its splendor but hears (and accompanies) the angelic hosts as they intone an elaborate *kedushah* through liturgical prayers and hymns (known as *piyyutim*) that celebrate the divine king upon His throne. Such an experience effectively represents "a Judaized form of cosmocratorial mysticism concerning the divine King (or Emperor)."[40] Undertaking the quest to behold this king represents the consummate expression of the *ma'aseh merkabah* as it is embodied in the tra-

39. Scholem, *Major Trends*, pp. 50–53.
40. Ibid., pp. 54–60.

ditions of Jewish mysticism. To understand the nature of the experience reflected in such a quest, one must review the *hekhalot* literature itself.

The point of departure will be the *Hekhalot Rabbati* or Greater *Hekhalot*, a crucial source of information on the entire tradition.[41] Essentially composite in nature, this text contains a number of different strands of *merkabah* material, aspects of which will be explored here. If we judge by the opening chapters, the purpose of the work is to instruct practicing mystics on the techniques of ascent. The spokesman for these techniques is Rabbi Ishmael, and the work itself opens with the very immediate question: "What is the meaning of the hymns [*shirot*] that one must chant when he desires to gaze into a vision of the *Merkabah*, to descend [*yarad*] in peace and to ascend [*'alah*] in peace?"[42] That is, how are the hymns formulated, what is their nature, and how does one go about chanting them in a manner to "descend" to the *merkabah* safely and to depart unharmed?[43] As technical guide, the *Hekhalot Rabbati* answers this question by offering detailed instruction in the liturgy of the *merkabah* and in the techniques of visionary transcendence. In addition to performing this function, the opening chapters describe the theurgic powers attributed to the successful mystic and include an actual dialogue between God (here given the epithet God of the Shining Light) and the mystic about the nature of the ascent. Among the powers that the *merkabah*

41. References are to the translations by Lauren Grodner in David R. Blumenthal's *Understanding Jewish Mysticism: A Source Reader: The Merkabah Tradition and the Zoharic Tradition* (New York: Ktav, 1978), pp. 56–89, and by Aryeh Kaplan in *Meditation and Kabbalah* (York Beach, Maine: Samuel Wesier, 1982), pp. 42–54. (These translations adopt the text in Wertheimer, *Batei Midrashot*, as their base text. Unless otherwise indicated, chapter references and interpolations in my text are keyed to Wertheimer. I have also made use of the renderings in Halperin, *Faces*, passim, and Gruenwald, *Apocalyptic*, passim.) For illuminating summaries and discussions of this composite work, see Morton Smith, "Observations on Hekhalot Rabbati," *Biblical and Other Studies*, ed. Alexander Altmann (Cambridge: Harvard University Press, 1963), pp. 142–160; and Gruenwald, *Apocalyptic*, pp. 150–173.

42. In Kaplan, *Meditation*, p. 42. Or "What are those songs that a person should utter if he wants to gaze at the sight of the *merkabah*, to descend safely and to ascend safely?" (Halperin, *Faces* p. 367; Schäfer, *Hekhalot-Studien*, no. 81; Wertheimer, *Batei Midrashot*, ch. 1:1.)

43. Once again, the terms *descend* and *ascend* here are not entirely clear, although they no doubt have very precise meaning. In this regard, the opening of the *hekhalot* tract entitled *Ma'aseh Merkavah* is of interest. Rabbi Ishmael asks Rabbi Akiba: "What is the prayer which one should pray when one *ascends* to the *Merkabah*?" (italics mine; in Gruenwald, *Apocalyptic*, p. 181).

mystic gains is the ability to foretell the future, to know the "secret deeds of man," to possess all kinds of sorcery, to afflict his enemies with leprosy, as well as with other diseases and punishments, and to reward his friends.[44] Like earlier apocalyptic, then, the *Hekhalot Rabbati* is a text of power, one in which the *merkabah* mystic assumes a theurgic, indeed, superhuman role as the result of his initiation into the secrets of ascent.

The precise nature of that ascent is described in detail in the latter section of the *Hekhalot Rabbati* (chs. 15–28), which will be explored here. What is so interesting about this section is the pseudo-historical nature of its setting and the dramatic context of its execution. In the background is the impending Roman persecutions of the Jews in the years 120–135 C.E.[45] Sensing the destructions to be wrought by those persecutions, the supreme mystic Rabbi Nehunya ben Hakkanah decides to reveal "the secret of the world as it appears to one who is worthy to gaze on the King and His Throne in His majesty and His beauty; [upon] the Hayot of holiness, the Cherubim of might, and the Wheels of the Shekhinah [which are] as lightning mixed with awesome electrum; [and upon] the beauty which is around the Throne" (ch. 15:1). Accompanying these revelations will be those that include the secret mysteries having to do with the creations of the heavens and the earth, the union of the two, "and the path of the heavenly ladder [*sulam*] whose one end is on earth and whose other end is in heaven at the right foot of the Throne of Glory" (ch. 16:1). His instruction, then, will include a gnosis that encompasses at once the *ma'aseh merkabah* and what has earlier been designated the *ma'aseh bere'shit*, both of which are united in the image of the ladder (cf. Gen. 28:12) through which one bridges the celestial and terrestrial realms.[46] It is these secrets that are to be revealed in the face of and in response to impending destruction, a fact that imparts to the account a certain dramatic urgency.

Reinforcing this sense of drama is its mode of execution. In order to effect his disclosures, Rabbi Nehunya directs Rabbi Ish-

44. See ibid., pp. 151–152, and the translations of chs. 1 and 2 in Kaplan, *Meditation*, pp. 42–43.

45. For a discussion of the background and the circumstances surrounding the narrative, see Joseph Dan, "The Religious Experience of the *Merkavah*," *Jewish Spirituality from the Bible through the Middle Ages*, ed. Arthur Green (New York: Crossroad, 1986), pp. 289–307.

46. See Altmann, "The Ladder of Ascension," passim, and Gruenwald, *Apocalyptic*, p. 161, n. 40.

mael to gather before him in the House of God "all the courageous members of the group and all the mighty ones of the academy." Approaching the seated mystic, this inner circle is granted the privilege of sitting before him, while others follow after to form an outer circle. As they stand beyond the inner circle, they behold "globes of fire and torches of light" that form a barrier between them and those who are seated before the master prepared to instruct them. In its own way, then, the setting recapitulates in small the drama of the celestial court with its own attendants surrounding the Enthroned Figure. This is the court, the Sanhedrin, of Rabbi Nehunya, assembled in the House of God to hear the master recount "all the matters of the Merkabah: the descent to it and the ascent, how to descend, who should descend, how to ascend, and who should ascend" (ch. 16:3). Particularly in the face of impending destruction, the dramatic context of the rendering could not be more compelling.

The instruction itself is painfully precise and involved, and, among those assembled, scribes are present to record Rabbi Nehunya's every word. When anyone wishes to "go down to the Chariot," he must first call upon Surya, the Angel of the Presence, and "make him swear [to protect him] in the name of Tootrusea-YHVH."[47] This, says Rabbi Nehunya, he must do exactly one hundred and twelve times. Any deviation from that number is dangerous. Rabbi Nehunya, in fact, suggests that the mystic count out the number with his fingers to ensure precision.[48] Having done that, the mystic may then proceed to "master the Merkabah" (ch. 16:5). Commenting upon this process in the very act of experiencing his own mystic trance, Rabbi Nehunya next describes the seven palaces in which Tootrusea-YHVH dwells, as well as the gates of each palace and the eight guardians of those gates (four to the left and four to the right). Having named each of the guardians of the first six palaces, Rabbi Nehunya then proceeds to those of the seventh palace.

These, he at first does not name. Instead, he portrays them in all their terror:

47. Tootrusea is derived from *tetra* (four), implying the Tetgragrammaton, and *ousion* (essence), implying the essence of God or the being of God in the Name YHVH (Blumenthal, *Jewish Mysticism*, p. 60). This combination of Greek and Hebrew designations is common in the *hekhalot* literature.

48. In versions of the text the prescribed number is one hundred and eleven times. See Halperin, *Faces*, pp. 378–379.

> At the gate of the seventh palace, they stand angry and war-like, strong, harsh, fearful, terrifying, taller than mountains and sharper than peaks. Their bows are strung and stand before them. Their swords are sharpened and in their hands. Bolts of lightning flow and issue forth from the balls of their eyes, and balls of fire [issue] from their nostrils, and torches of fiery coals from their mouths. They are equipped with helmets and with coats of mail, and javelins and spears are hung upon their arms. The horses upon which they ride stand beside mangers of fire, full of coals of juniper, and they eat fiery coals from the mangers, [taking] a measure of forty bushels of coals in one mouthful. (ch. 17:8–18:1)

It is these, finally, who accost the *merkabah* mystic who has successfully made his way past the guards of the first six palaces. Those of the seventh palace are another matter altogether. So fearsome are they that, unlike the guards of the first six palaces, one dare not even name them without risking disaster. As Rabbi Nehunya knows, however, the *merkabah* mystic must pronounce their names if he is to attain the ultimate vision.

Pressed by those assembled to reveal the names, Rabbi Nehunya (even while still in a trance) responds as follows: "Now that you say to me 'Specify,' come stand on your feet, every one of you. When the name of each [guard] comes forth from my mouth, bow down and fall on your faces." While the scribes continue to record every name, those assembled do precisely as their master instructs them (ch. 23:1). The "descent" to the *merkabah*, then, becomes the "descent" to the Name: it is the Name-of-All-Names, the unpronounceable Tetragrammaton itself (cf. Exod. 3:13–14) that is embodied in the angelic guards of the seventh palace.

As indicated earlier, surrounding the ascent through each one of the palaces is an entire complex of rituals that include not just the recital of names but the presentation of seals. "When you come and stand at the gate of the first palace, take two seals, one in each hand—[the seals] of Tootrusea-YHVH, Lord of Israel, to those who stand on the right, and [the seal] of Surya, the Angel of the Presence. Show the seal of Tootrusea-YHVH to those who stand on the right, and [the seal] of Surya to those on the left." Having successfully accomplished this procedure, the mystic will be sent on his way to the next palace to perform a similar set of rituals. Entrance through the gate of the sixth palace, however, is extremely dangerous, for the guards there make a practice of killing those who are unprepared (ch. 19:1).

In recounting these procedures, Rabbi Nehunya alludes rather cryptically to "those who go down to the Merkabah," on the one hand, and to "those who go and do not go down to the Merkabah," on the other (ch. 20:1). Puzzled by this distinction, the assembled members desire Rabbi Nehunya to elaborate further. In order to do so, however, he must first be awakened momentarily from his trance (that is, "brought back from the visions which he has glimpsed"). Doing so is in itself a dangerous process, one that must be undertaken with utmost care, for if the mystic is brought back too abruptly, disaster might result.

What those assembled must do is to render Rabbi Nehunya impure but not so grossly impure as to endanger his life. To that end, the members call for "a piece of very fine woolen cloth" to be applied as delicately as possible with the tip of the middle finger of the hand to the previously impure parts of a menstruating woman who has completed her period and immersed herself twice.[49] Having done so, they insert the cloth into a bough of myrtle, full of oil, that has been soaked in pure balsam, and they place it on the knees of Rabbi Nehunya. Rendered "impure" in this manner, Rabbi Nehunya is immediately dismissed before the Throne of Glory and awakens out of his trance. Fascinating in itself, this method of calling the mystic back to the present reinforces still further the immensely ritualistic nature of the entire process (ch. 20:3). The mystic of the *hekhalot* tracts is bound by ancient rituals of behavior undreamt of by the old apocalypticists. As manifested in the *hekhalot* tracts, the culture of the *maʿaseh merkabah* exhibits its own Levitical code of pure and impure.

Recalled from his trance, Rabbi Nehunya proceeds to answer

---

49. Blumenthal's explanatory note is most instructive here. "The rabbinic rule is as follows: A menstruating woman is impure. At the end of her period, she must bathe ritually. If she has doubts about her purity, she may check to see if there is still some blood present by wrapping a cloth around her finger and inserting it. If it stains, she is still impure." This procedure is brought to bear on the *Hekhalot Rabbati* in the following manner: "The woman has stopped menstruating. She has bathed ritually once but, for technical reasons, must do it again. She bathes ritually a second time and is, thus, ritually pure. This woman is then asked to 'check' herself but to do it very gently. No trace of staining is found—i.e., she is still pure. But one very, very strict rabbi might still claim she is impure because of possible irregularities in her menstrual cycle. We have, thus, a woman who is ritually pure except in the remotest sense of the word, and we have an object (the cloth) which is ritually impure in the very least degree possible. Rabbi Nehunya, upon touching it, thus becomes as minimally impure as possible." To protect Rabbi Nehunya even further, the rabbis insert the cloth into a purifying, protective case (pp. 69–70). For additional commentary on this passage, as well a translation prepared by Morton Smith, see Scholem, *Jewish Gnosticism*, pp. 9–13.

the question that is put to him: that is, what is the difference between those who go down to the *merkabah* and those who go and do not go down to the *merkabah*? The answer is a fairly straightforward one. Those who go down to the *merkabah* are the mystics themselves, and those who go down and do not go down are scribes who might be called upon to accompany the mystic and record what the mystic experiences. If these men are unfit for the task, they are attacked by the guards of the sixth palace. "Be cautious, therefore," counsels Rabbi Nehunya, "to choose men who are fit and tested *haverim*" (ch. 20:4). The response and the form in which it is cast brings to the fore, then, not just the intensely ritualistic bearing of the experience but its self-consciousness as a distinctly literary enterprise as well. This latter aspect reinforces the dramatic context in which the account is portrayed.

Having answered the question put to him by those assembled, Rabbi Nehunya returns to his trance. The remainder of the account continues to elaborate upon what the mystic beholds in his "descent" to the *merkabah* and how that "descent" is to be accomplished safely. Traversing the threshold of the sixth gate, the mystic is placed in his own "wagon of radiance," accompanied by the blowing of myriads of horns, and becomes part of something that resembles a kind of triumphal procession to the gate of the seventh palace (ch. 21:1). "As soon as the guards of the gate of the seventh palace see him, with Dumiel and Gabriel and Katspiel proceeding in front of the carriage of that man who is worthy and descends to the Merkabah, their faces, which were wrathful, are paled, they loosen their taut bows and return their sharp swords to the sheaths." Presented with appropriate seals, the guards "bring him before all types of music and song, and they make music and a parade before him until they raise him and seat him near the Cherubim, near the Wheels, and near the Holy Hayot. He sees wonders and powers, majesty and greatness, holiness and purity, terror and meekness and righteousness, at the same time" (ch. 22:2).

In that position he beholds the most awesome dimension of the vision thus far: the *hayyot* themselves. Possessing two hundred and fifty-six faces and five hundred and twelve eyes, these creatures are overwhelming in their appearance (23:5–24:1).[50] As such, they

---

50. In accord with Wertheimer, the Grodner translation has two hundred and ninety-six faces, but all the versions in Schäfer, *Hekhalot-Studien*, read two hundred and fifty-six

come to represent the very essence of the visionary as a transformative experience. This is especially true as the description intensifies the nature of the original conception through a kind of visionary *copia* at its most archaic level. The multiplication of faces is a case in point. If a relatively small number of faces is astounding, the "logic" of this *copia* implies, the effect of an even larger number will be greater yet. The *Hekhalot Rabbati* is not alone in this assumption. A similar approach is to be found not only in the *Hekhalot Zutarti* (which has two hundred and fifty-six faces) but in the Targum (which has sixty-four faces).[51]

What is true of the faces is likewise true of the eyes. Argus-like in their multiplicity, they come to assume a life of their own. So they are described in the following terms, as the seer beholds them on the threshold of the gate of the seventh palace: "The holy *ḥayyot* then look at him with their five hundred and twelve eyes. Each one of the eyes of the *ḥayyot* is split open [*peku'ah*], the size of a large winnowers' [?] sieve; and their eyes look as if they *race like lightnings*. . . . Besides them, there are the eyes of the mighty cherubim and of the *'ofannim* of the Shekhinah, which look like torches and flaming coals."[52]

As David Halperin has demonstrated, the uncanny quality of this description assumes unique significance by virtue of the reference to the sieve that is split open. In the *Hekhalot Rabbati* the idea of an open sieve is overtly sexual. It is earlier used in connection with the blatantly erotic language that describes the passionate embraces the *ḥayyot* bestow upon the Enthroned Figure as they hug and kiss him with uncovered faces during their act of worship. In response to such behavior, the heavenly realm "splits open like a sieve." The sexuality of the event is inescapable. The desire (*ḥemdah*) and passion (*ta'avah*), as Halperin makes clear, are tantamount to "sexual lust," and the root (*peh, resh, 'ayin*) employed here for the uncovering of the faces of the *ḥayyot* is also used in conjunction with the idea of circumcision to indicate "the

faces (no. 245), which, given the five hundred and twelve eyes, appears to be the logical number. See Halperin, *Faces*, pp. 393 and 543n.

51. For the *Hekhalot Zutarti*, see Schäfer, *Hekhalot-Studien* (nos. 353–355) and Halperin's translation, *Faces*, p. 388. For the Targum, see Ezek. 1:6 in *The Targum of Ezekiel*, trans. Samson H. Levey (Wilmington: Michael Glazier, 1987).

52. The translation here is that of Halperin, based on Schäfer, *Hekhalot-Studien*, no. 247. Compare Grodner's rendering, based on Wertheimer, *Batei Midrashot*, ch. 24:2: "Five-hundred-and-twelve eyes, and each and every eye of the eyes of the Holy Hayot is hollow like the holes in a sieve woven of branches."

uncovering of the corona." When the celestial realm, then, "splits open like a sieve" before the splendor and passion of the denuded faces of the *hayyot*, this act commemorates in sexual terms the eroticism of the event through which the Enthroned Figure is worshiped. The later reference to the eyes of the *hayyot* split open in the fashion of a large winnowers' sieve comes to assume the sexuality that only such a context might provide. When one journeys to the *merkabah*, one is confronted not only with a multitude of faces and eyes but with an experience that is as erotic as it is terrifying.[53] In response to such an experience, the visionary, like the prophet before him, is overcome by the vision. The *hayyot*, however, lift him up and give him strength, as he hears the elaborate celestial liturgy sung before the Throne (chs. 24–25).

In brief, this represents the basis of Rabbi Nehunya ben Hakkanah's experience as portrayed in the *Hekhalot Rabbati*, a remarkable work that brings to the fore many of the fundamental motifs that characterize the *ma'aseh merkabah* as a vital enterprise among practicing mystics. In the world of those mystics the essence of the visionary experience is to "penetrate" to the world that is itself "vision" incarnate. Truly a world in which the means of seeing becomes the object of sight, the experience of the *merkabah* is conceived through a multitude of complex associations that transform and reenvision the *Urerlebnis* in an entirely unique and fascinating way. One is reminded once again of Jung's allusion to Goethe: *"Gestaltung, Umgestaltung, / Des ewigen Sinnes ewige Unterhaltung."* Such is certainly true of the *Hekhalot Rabbati*, a work of paramount importance to the development of the visionary mode.

III

As interesting as the *Hekhalot Rabbati* might be, the *Sefer Hekhalot* is equally fascinating. Commonly known as *III Enoch* (fifth to sixth century C.E.), this is the longest and most complex work in the *hekhalot* traditions.[54] What makes *III Enoch* so significant is its en-

53. Halperin, *Faces*, pp. 394–395.

54. References by chapter and verse to *III Enoch* in my text are to the translation in Charlesworth, I, 255–315. In addition to the excellent translation, Alexander provides an informative introduction not only to the text but to the traditions of the *merkabah*. Still useful but now superseded by Charlesworth is Hugo Odeberg's edition and translation of *III Enoch or The Hebrew Book of Enoch* (1928), with a prolegomenon by Jonas C. Greenfield (New York: Ktav, 1973).

tirely uncharacteristic nature. At once a consummate expression
of the *hekhalot* spirit, *III Enoch* contains none of the "utilitarian"
features normally associated with the *hekhalot* tracts. It is not a
"how to" work: "Nothing is said in it about the special technique
of the ascent; it lacks any reference to the theurgical means which
protect the mystic on his journey in heaven; and it contains no
Hekhalot hymns."[55] In fact, it is not a tract or a manual at all.
Rather, it is a genuine literary production (albeit, no doubt a
composite one) that draws upon and transforms earlier traditions
of the *hekhalot*. As such, it is a self-conscious literary artifact with
its own sense of integrity, as well as a veritable "treasure-house of
information about the esoteric traditions."[56]

Addressing the genre of this work, Ithamar Gruenwald observes
that "by the manner in which it fuses together a number of esoteric
traditions it can be viewed as a romance or grand summary of the
Jewish apocalyptic and mystical traditions."[57] The term *romance*
here is apposite, for it brings to mind the kinds of distinctions
that Northrop Frye invokes in his taxonomy of genres. "The complete form of the romance," Frye maintains, "is clearly the successful quest, and such a completed form has three main stages:
the stage of the perilous journey and the preliminary minor adventures; the crucial struggle, usually some kind of battle in which
either the hero or his foe, or both, must die; and the exaltation
of the hero."[58] Whether or not Gruenwald would agree that *III
Enoch* subscribes to such a delineation remains to be seen. The
point is, however, that the work embodies what Frye calls the
"mythos" of romance as a self-conscious archetypal mode that
assimilates earlier, legendary material and recasts that material in
a form at once highly conventional and highly unique. As a work
that is *sui generis* within a body of works by their very nature *sui
generis*, *III Enoch* "belatedly" recalls the traditions of the old apocalyptic texts (which already contain elements of "romance" in the
sense that Frye intends) and incorporates those traditions into the
"newer" sensibility (but not the utilitarian outlook) of the *hekhalot*
material.

Responding to the structure of *III Enoch*, P. Alexander sees four

55. Gruenwald, *Apocalyptic*, p. 191.
56. The phrase is Gruenwald's, ibid., pp. 191–192.
57. Ibid., p. 191.
58. Northrop Frye, *The Anatomy of Criticism* (Princeton: Princeton University Press,
1975), p. 187.

main divisions in the work: (1) chapters 1–2, "The Ascension of Ishmael"; (2) chapters 3–16, "The Exaltation of Enoch"; (3) chapters 17–40, "The Heavenly Household"; (4) chapters 41–48, "The Sights of Heaven."[59] As suggested by this division, the action of *III Enoch* assumes the form of a frame narrative organized around the ascent of Rabbi Ishmael, who is in turn introduced to the celestial mysteries by Enoch. The outlook is much like that of the earlier Enoch material upon which it draws: one encounters such *topoi* as the ascent, the guide, the transformation, the vision of the Enthroned Figure, and instruction in matters both cosmogonical and eschatological. As self-conscious literary enterprise, moreover, *III Enoch* draws upon the self-reflexive quality of such works as *II Enoch* and intensifies that quality even further. As a result, *III Enoch* becomes a multidimensional work as sensitive to the traditions from which it emerges as any previously considered.

Initiating the action, the first two chapters provide a first-person account of Rabbi Ishmael's ascent to the seventh palace to behold "the vision of the chariot." From a literary point of view, the account is interesting because it adopts the persona of the famous Palestinian scholar and mystic encountered in the earlier *hekhalot* treatises in order to establish a setting for the narrative that follows. *III Enoch*, in short, sees itself as part of a tradition already well known to an audience familiar with the genre that it embodies. As such, the work abides by the conventions of that genre. Having ascended to the seventh palace, the visionary prays to God for protection from the angelic gatekeepers who might seek to cast him out of the celestial realm. In response to that prayer the angel Metatron, Prince of the Divine Presence, flies out to meet Rabbi Ishmael. Grasping the visionary with his hand, Metatron encourages him, "Come in peace into the presence of the high and exalted King to behold the likeness of the chariot" (1:1–7). Stunned by the fearsome gaze of the seraphim, Rabbi Ishmael is revived by Metatron and is finally able to accompany the hosts in an angelic *kedushah* in praise of God (1:8–12), after which Metatron is called upon by the angelic hosts to establish Rabbi Ishmael's worthiness as "one born of woman to come in and behold the chariot" (2:1–4). Such is the frame that introduces the main narrative, involving the exaltation and transformation of Enoch, the portrayal of the heavenly household, and the revelation of the celestial mysteries.

59. Charlesworth, p. 223.

The frame is significant first as a means of preparing for the narrative that is to follow and second as a way of providing an "historical" (albeit, pseudonymous) context for the mythical elements implicit in the narrative itself. It is in the main body of the narrative that what has been defined as the dimensions of the romance (the journey, the struggle, and the exaltation of the hero) emerges.

All three dimensions are implicit in the revelation of the identity of Metatron. Asked by Rabbi Ishmael to reveal his name, Metatron responds: "I have seventy names, corresponding to the seventy nations of the world, and all of them are based on the name of the King of the kings of kings" (3:2). Embodied in Metatron is not only the cosmocratorial sense of rulership but the divine sense of deriving one's authority and power from the Most High, whose names also total seventy and in whose tetragram YHVH resides the meanings of all the names.[60] As Metatron makes clear, however, the name by which he is most commonly known is that of "Youth" (na'ar).[61] He is called this name because he is young in the company of the angelic hosts "and a mere youth among them in days and months and years" (4:10). Having established his identity through a delineation of his names, Metatron then traces his lineage. As the youngest among the company of the angelic hosts, he was originally created not as an angel but as a man. In short, his lineage is that of one of low degree, translated through the auspices of the Most High to take his place among the angels. The person in question is none other than Enoch, the son of Jared, who lived among the "generation of the Flood" that "sinned and turned to evil deeds." As one faithful to the Most High, Enoch testifies to Rabbi Ishmael that God "brought me up in their lifetime, before their very eyes, to the heavenly height," to bear witness to God's greatness among not only his own generation but all those who should come into the world in future generations (cf. Gen. 5:18–24). So translated, Enoch is then exalted by being made "a prince and a ruler among the ministering angels." In Enoch, then, one finds the perfect type of the romance hero: born

---

60. For the seventy names of Metatron, see Appendix to *III Enoch* (48D:1–5), in Charlesworth. The precise meaning of the name Metatron has been long disputed. See, in particular, the appendix by Saul Lieberman in Gruenwald, *Apocalyptic*, pp. 235–240, as well as the discussion in Odeberg, *III Enoch*, pp. 79–90.

61. Originally, this term meant "servant" (cf. Exod. 24:5) and may suggest Metatron's service in the heavenly sanctuary. See Charlesworth, I, 259n.

of low degree, he is elevated (by means of a journey of ascent) to the highest stature and given supremacy as one exalted over those traditionally placed above him (4:2–5).

The ascent and exaltation, in turn, are not realized without a struggle: there are those among the ministering angels who attempt to lay charges against Enoch and to dispossess him of his exalted station, but the Holy One himself intervenes to vindicate Enoch from those who would undermine him (4:6–9).[62] The idea recalls the experience that initiates the frame narrative: following his ascent, Rabbi Ishmael's worthiness, too, is called into question and must be vindicated through the efforts of Metatron (2:1–4). The preparatory narrative is thereby proleptic: it anticipates and encapsulates as "historical" event the romance *mythos* of ascent, exaltation, and struggle that the main narrative expounds in detail. Doing so, it draws upon and reenvisions the apocalyptic elements already established in the earlier Enoch pseudepigrapha. In this way *III Enoch* becomes both a self-conscious and self-reflexive literary artifact, fusing the *topoi* of apocalyptic, on the one hand, with the conventions of the *hekhalot* tracts, on the other. The result is a new myth of ascent, one that finds detailed elaboration in the narrative that follows.

Accordingly, chapters 6–16 recapitulate and elaborate the motifs initiated in the opening chapters of the second division. The journey to the celestial realms is conceived first as an ascent in "a fiery chariot, with fiery horses and glorious attendants," an event that associates the translation of Enoch with that of Elijah (2 Kings 2:11), and second as an ascent "on the stormy wings of the Shekhinah," an event that talmudic commentary looked upon as the supreme assertion of faith in the Judaic traditions (6:1, 7:1; cf. Ruth 2: 12).[63] Having achieved the celestial realms, Enoch undergoes a transformation unrivaled in either the apocalyptic or the mystical traditions.[64] The experience is initially a terrifying one.

62. Cf. 6:2: "As soon as I reached the heavenly heights, the holy creatures, the ophanim, the seraphim, the cherubim, the wheels of the chariot and the ministers of consuming fire, smelled my odor 365,000 myriads of parasangs off; they said, 'What is this smell of one born of a woman?' " (cf. Job 14:1 and 15:14). The reference is contemptuous.

63. See Charlesworth, I, 262n. The proper context for the expression "wings of the Shekhinah" is conversion to Judaism, as indicated in the Talmud.

64. In fact, nowhere else in either the apocalyptic or mystical traditions does one encounter so profound or elaborate a transformation, and "it should be noted that although Metatron is mentioned in other *Hekhalot* writings, he is nowhere else identified with the transfigured Enoch." Gruenwald, *Apocalyptic*, p. 195.

As Enoch relates, "When the Holy One, blessed be he, took me to serve the throne of glory, the wheels of the chariot and all the needs of the Shekhinah, at once my flesh turned to flame, my sinews to blazing fire, my bones to juniper coals, my eyelashes to lightning flashes, my eyeballs to fiery torches, the hairs of my head to hot flames, all my limbs to wings of burning fire, and the substance of my body to blazing fire" (15:1–2).

Undergoing such a transformation, Enoch veritably assumes the form of a god. All the gates of the heavenly treasuries are opened to him: he is imbued with great wisdom, understanding, prudence, life, grace and favor, love, Torah, humility, sustenance, mercy, reverence (8:1–2). As the recipient of all wisdom and all knowledge, he has access to "all the mysteries of the world and all the orders of nature." "Before a man thinks in secret," says Enoch, "I see his thought; before he acts, I see his act. There is nothing in heaven above or deep within the earth concealed from me" (11:1–3). Such gnosis is the characteristic hallmark not just of the earlier Enoch pseudepigrapha (particularly *II Enoch*) but of the *hekhalot* tracts (particularly the *Hekhalot Rabbati*). Combining both traditions, *III Enoch* causes them to assume consummate form in the bestowal of gnosis upon Enoch in his transformation into Metatron. As indicated, that transformation is not only intellectual; it is also physical. Thus, in keeping with his new mental stature, Enoch as Metatron is physically enlarged until he matches the world in length and breadth. Seventy-two wings are made to grow on him (thirty-six on each side), and each wing covers the entire world. He is given three hundred and sixty-five thousand eyes, each of which is like a great light. "There was," says Enoch, "no sort of splendor, brilliance, brightness, or beauty in the luminaries of the world that he [the Holy One] failed to fix in me" (9:1–5).

After these transformations Enoch is placed on a throne before the gate of the seventh palace. His throne is like that of the throne of glory itself, and over the throne is spread a coverlet of splendor, once again, like that overspreading the throne of glory. Suggesting the cosmic nature of Enoch's enthronement, the coverlet is inscribed with "all the varied splendor of the luminaries that are in the world" (10:1–2). In addition to the enthronement of Enoch and the spreading of a cosmic coverlet upon the throne, the transformation into Metatron is accompanied by an attiring and a coronation of this Prince of the Divine Presence. Accordingly, the

Holy One fashions for Enoch a majestic robe, which, like the coverlet for the throne, is set with all kinds of luminaries. In addition to the robe, Enoch is attired in a glorious cloak and a kingly crown, in which are placed forty-nine refulgent stones, each like the orb of the sun. The brilliance of this crown shines "into the four quarters of the heaven of ʿArabot, into the seven heavens, and into the four quarters of the world" (12:1–4). On the crown the Holy One inscribes "with his finger, as with a pen of flame" the divine letters by which all the terrestrial and celestial realms and orders were created. Representing the twenty-two letters of the Hebrew alphabet, these letters "flashed time after time like lightnings, time after time like torches, time after time like flames, time after time like the rising of the sun, moon, and stars" (13:1–2). In them is all cosmology, all cosmogony, and all theurgy: Enoch is master of them all. Ruler of the letters, he is ruler of the words that the letters form. As cosmocrator par excellence, he is not only high priest of the celestial sanctuary and lord of all the celestial realms but the king of the creative forces.

It is only appropriate, then, that he is known as "The Lesser Yahweh" (*Yaweh ha-Katan*), one in whom God's very name is fully embodied (12:5; cf. Exod. 23:21).[65] So he is proclaimed by a herald to every heaven:

> "I [the Holy One] have appointed Metatron my servant [ʿ*ebed*] as a prince and a ruler over all the denizens of the heights. . . . Any angel and any prince who has anything to say in my presence should go before him and speak to him. Whatever he says to you in my name you must observe and do, because I have committed to him the Prince of Wisdom and the Prince of Understanding, to teach him the wisdom of those above and of those below, the wisdom of this world and of the world to come. Moreover I have put him in charge of all the stores of the palaces of ʿArabot, and all the treasuries that are in the heavenly heights." (10:3–6)

Hearing this proclamation and witnessing the coronation, the angelic hosts tremble and shrink from before the presence of Enoch-Metatron. More than that, they fall prostrate and cannot bear to behold him because of the majesty and radiance that emanate from his glorious crown (14:1–5). Enoch-Metatron's ascendancy

---

65. For a discussion of "Lesser Yahweh," see Scholem, *Jewish Gnosticism*, p. 43; and Gruenwald, *Apocalyptic*, pp. 196–197.

does not go entirely unchallenged, to be sure. Once again, there are those who would undermine it (16:1–5). Nonetheless, the powers of the transformed Enoch remain ultimately intact.

What is significant about the account of the ascent and exaltation as it appears in *III Enoch*, finally, is the way this document draws upon earlier traditions to forge its own unique myth both of the *hekhalot* and of the *yordei merkabah*. If the earlier traditions conceive of the ascent (or "descent," as the case may be) to the *merkabah* as primarily a means of achieving the ultimate realm in order to celebrate deity in all its glory, *III Enoch* conceives of this experience as a means of sharing as much as possible in the attributes of deity. The impulse here is, in a very real sense, dynastic as much as it is "mystic." Not to put too fine a point on it, one might observe that what the earlier traditions conceive as an ascent of the visionary to *see* God becomes in *III Enoch* an ascent of the visionary to *be* God, or at least something as close to that concept as one can possibly get without being guilty of outright heresy.[66] But elements of this idea, as we have discussed, were already present in the oldest apocalyptic texts, which are as much narratives of power as narratives of transcendence. From the very outset in which the visionary is conceived through the notion of ascent, the two ideas go hand in hand both as apocalyptic and as mystical enterprise. In *III Enoch* it receives its most graphic dramatization.

Having examined the first two divisions of this work, we may now conclude with some observations concerning the final two divisions: "The Heavenly Household" (chs. 17–40) and "The Sights of Heaven" (chs. 41–48). The third division falls roughly into three sections: the first dealing with the angelic hierarchies, the second describing the sessions of the celestial law court, the third elaborating on the singing of the heavenly *kedushah*. The fourth division, in turn, falls roughly into two sections: the first propounding matters cosmogonical in the form of a *maʿaseh be-reʾshit*, the second exploring matters eschatological in the form of an apocalypse. Exceedingly detailed and complex, the chapters that constitute these divisions recapitulate and elaborate concepts raised in the first two divisions as well as introduce and refashion ideas implicit in both the apocalyptic and the mystical traditions.

---

66. Gruenwald makes the interesting point that in the third century certain Palestinian sages expressed negative views regarding Enoch. Assuming the form of polemics against the *minim* ("heretics"), these views reflect an anti-Christian outlook. *Apocalyptic*, pp. 200–201.

The primary focus of the last two divisions is encyclopedic: they are repositories of lore concerning the most secret of matters. As such, the divisions are heuristic in nature. Their purpose is to instruct the adept in the ways of the celestial realm. In the third division, for example, one discovers the names and functions of the seven princes that oversee the seven heavens (ch. 17), the classes of angels that occupy the celestial hierarchy (ch. 18), and the placement of the angels that preside over various parts of the Chariot (the *ḥayyot*, the *kerubim*, the *'ofannim*, and the *serafim*) (chs. 19–26). Crucial to this delineation of angelic names and functions is the image of the *merkabah*. So crucial is it, in fact, that the author becomes veritably rhapsodic in his envisioning of the Chariot in all realms of the universe. So Metatron asks "How many chariots has the Holy One, blessed be he?" and then answers his own question with an elaborate poetical list that draws together references from a multitude of biblical sources: He has the chariots of the cherubim, the chariots of wind, the chariots of swift cloud, the chariots of the altar, the chariots of the tent, the chariots of the mercy seat, the chariots of sapphire stone, the chariots of eagles, the chariots of acclamation, the chariots of *'arabot*, the chariots of the creatures, the chariots of wheels, the chariots of the swift cherub, the chariots of the *'ofannim*, and the chariots of the holy throne, subdivided into the throne of Yah, the throne of Judgment, and the throne of glory (24:1–23).[67] Beginning principally with the natural realm, the list progresses to the sphere of the Temple and culminates in the divine, which recapitulates a brief angelogical system (wheels, *kerubim*, *'ofannim*, and thrones). Each sphere, in turn, seems to be reflected in the next, as the list encircles itself concentrically to create both a sense of movement and recapitulation. What results is a poem of the *merkabah* within a self-reflexive text that represents its own unique version of the *ma'aseh merkabah*.

Constructing an elaborate mythos to portray that experience, the account reconceives it in apocalyptic terms, as it next fashions a compelling drama that occurs in the highest realm. There, the angel in charge of the celestial archives presents the book of records to the Holy One to pronounce judgment in the Great Law

---

67. This chapter appears in the appendix to *III Enoch* in Charlesworth (I, 308–309). For the biblical texts alluded to in the chapter, see the marginal glosses provided by Alexander. The idea finds further elaboration later in the text (37:1–2).

Court (*bet din haggadol*) (ch. 27). In its account of this event, the description draws upon the language of Daniel 7, so important to the earlier Enoch pseudepigrapha, as well as to apocalyptic in general. Presented with the scrolls from the scroll box, the Holy One is beheld sitting in judgment on the throne of judgment, his garment white as snow, the hair of his head like pure wool, his robe emanating light, and he himself covered with righteousness as with a coat of mail (28:7). He, in turn, is surrounded by the celestial hosts that debate each matter "like court officers before the judge" (28:8). "Justice stands on his right hand, Mercy on his left, and Truth stands directly facing him" (31:1; cf. Ps. 89:14). Scribes record His every word, and angels of destruction execute His judgment against the wicked with the terrible unsheathed sword of God (32:1–33:2). In this manner, the vision of the *mer-kabah* that occupies the delineation of the celestial household culminates in the divine moment of apocalyptic judgment, an anticipation of the eschatological dimension portrayed in the final chapters of the document. At the same time, the reference both to the archives that contain the books of accounts and to the transcriptions that record God's judgments suggests once again the self-conscious and self-reflexive nature of *III Enoch* as a work fully aware of its own "archival" and "transcriptional" status (cf. *II Enoch* 20–23).[68] Itself the official record of the doings of both man and God, *III Enoch* emerges as sacred writing (*ketab*), one in which the transcriber and the word transcribed assume consummate importance.

Having portrayed the heavenly hierarchies and the celestial law court, the third division proceeds to the *kedushah* (cf. Isa. 6:3), a staple of both apocalyptic and mystical texts. Once more, at the center of the angelic liturgy resides the *merkabah*, again depicted through the image of concentric circles (but much more graphically so), as the hooves of the *hayyot* bearing the *merkabah* are encircled by seven clouds of burning coal, the clouds of burning coal by seven walls of flame, the walls of flame by seven walls of firebrands, the walls of firebrands by seven walls of hailstones, the walls of hailstones by hurricane and fire and water, and these by those who say "Holy" (34:1–2). Particularly characteristic of later midrashic commentary, this delineation draws upon the atmo-

---

68. Enoch himself is traditionally depicted as a scribe. Compare the Book of Jubilees 4:23.

spheric and elemental dimensions of Ezekiel's vision (whirlwind, fire, water, and so on) to portray its own concentric universe. That universe, in turn, is distinguished by the myriads of camps or armies of angels, once again common to midrashic commentary as well as to other depictions of the *kedushah*.[69] In *III Enoch*, they assume a traditional order: "They all stand before the throne of glory in four rows and mighty princes stand at the head of each row. Some of them say 'Holy' and some of them say 'Blessed'; some run on missions and some stand and serve" (35:1–2). When they intone their celestial liturgy, the entire universe resounds, and all the sacred names "engraved with a pen of flame on the throne of glory fly off like eagles" and encompass the Holy One. Those who recite the *kedushah* properly are rewarded with crowns; those who do not recite the *kedushah* properly are devoured by flames (chs. 38–40). As in the depiction of the great court, so in the rendering of the *kedushah*, the element of terror is ever present. Even in the act of celebration, there is the possibility of annihilation, a dimension that is an enduring part of the *ma'aseh merkabah* in all its forms.

From the perspective offered by this overview of the third division of *III Enoch*, we shall conclude with a brief analysis of the fourth. As indicated, the fourth division ("The Sights of Heaven" [chs. 41–48]) falls roughly into two sections. The first is cast in the form of a *ma'aseh bere'shit* that propounds matters cosmogonical; the second is cast in the form of an apocalypse that dramatizes matters eschatological. Recalling the divine letters inscribed on the crown of Enoch-Metatron (13:1–2), the opening chapters of this division rearticulate the concept of sacred letters and sacred names by revealing to the visionary a gnosis of the sources of power through which all aspects of the universe come into being. As in earlier chapters, this encyclopedic dimension is portrayed through a hierarchical ordering that moves from the terrestrial through the celestial. Beginning with the terrestrial universe (seas and rivers, mountains and hills, trees and grasses) the account progresses to the planetary realm (stars and constellations, sun and moon), and then to the celestial sphere (the angels, the *serafim*, and the *ḥayyot*). Characteristically, the account concludes with a reference to the *merkabah*, that is, "the throne of glory and the wheels of the chariot" (41:1–2). In its revelation of secret knowl-

69. See Odeberg, *III Enoch*, pp. 116–118.

edge, then, what begins as *ma'aseh bere'shit* ends as *ma'aseh mer-kabah*: the sense of order is all-pervasive. Underlying the conception as a whole is the emphasis upon the cosmic letters through which both the divine cosmogony and the ascent from *bere'shit* to *merkabah* occur. In an attestation to this idea, Rabbi Ishmael, as the recipient of gnosis, says of Metatron, "I went with him and he took me by his hand, bore me up on his wings, and showed me those letters, engraved with a pen of flame upon the throne of glory, and sparks of lightnings shoot from them and cover all the chambers of 'Arabot" (41:3).

Corresponding to this account of the letters is that which occupies the following chapter on the cosmic power of divine names. Once again, the visionary is borne on the wings of Metatron to the realms that reveal the inner workings of all that the Tetragrammaton in its various forms implies. Particularly in its manifestation of ultimate Being, the Tetragrammaton as "I am that I am" (Exod. 3:14) suggests, among other ideas, that the Holy One is a consuming fire (cf. Deut. 4:24), that He is an everlasting rock (cf. Isa. 26:4), and, of course, that He is God Almighty (42:1–7; cf. Gen. 17:1). Whereas the previous chapter focuses upon the cosmogonic aspects of the letters, this chapter formulates a variety of perspectives concerning what might be called the ontological functions of the names that occur when the letters are combined to form the Name of Names.[70]

Moving from the cosmogonical section to the eschatological section, one discerns a number of motifs implicit not only in earlier sections of *III Enoch* but in the apocalyptic and mystical writings as a whole. As in the earlier apocalypses, the visionary is shown the realms of both the righteous and the reprobate (ch. 43–44). Even more to the point, however, is the elaborate description of the "curtain [*pargod*] of the Omnipresent One" (ch. 45). With its correspondence in the veil (*paroket*) that separates the Holy Place from the Holy of Holies in the earthly sanctuary (cf. Exod. 26:31; 2 Chron. 3:14), the curtain of the Omnipresent One traditionally separates the immediate presence of God from the rest of heaven. Concealing the ultimate mysteries of deity, it permits access only

70. Compare the emphasis upon names here with the corresponding emphasis in other chapters, as well as in *merkabah* literature in general. In *III Enoch*, for example, see especially chapters 48B ("The [Seventy] Names of God") and 48D ("The Seventy Names of Metatron"; Appendix to *III Enoch*, Charlesworth, I, 310–311, 313–315).

to the Prince of the Divine Presence.[71] In the present context, the *pargod* is of such interest because on it are inscribed "all the generations of the world, and all their deeds, whether done or to be done, till the last generation." It is these that the visionary beholds, as he is instructed in the course of history by Metatron. The event is likened to a father teaching his son by pointing to the letters of the Torah with his fingers: the recitation of the letters is the recitation of sacred history. Beginning with Adam and his generation, Metatron reveals to Rabbi Ishmael the story of Noah, Nimrod, Abraham, Isaac, Ishmael, Jacob, Amram, Moses, Aaron, Joshua, the judges, kings, and prophets. The account culminates in a vision of apocalyptic battle and the coming of the Messiah both during the period of recorded history and in "the time to come" (45:2–6; cf. 48A).[72] The sense of messianic fervor that underscores the earlier apocalypses, then, is equally present in *III Enoch*, which transforms sacred history into providential history, inscribed (that is, "interwoven") here as a text in the very fabric of the *pargod*. To know the *merkabah* is to read it and recite it as a text, an idea that receives consummate expression in that most self-conscious and self-reflexive of texts *III Enoch*.

With the discussion of *III Enoch* we have reached the end of our treatment of the apocalyptic and mystical material that underlies the transformations of the visionary mode in the traditions of Judaica. As I have attempted to suggest, the originary content of the visionary mode is never stable. Constantly in the process of flux, constantly undergoing a series of metamorphoses at the very point of inception, the visionary mode, as a manifestation of ultimacy, of "seeing God," gives rise to a whole complex of associations that reveal more about the perceiver than the perceived, the seer than the seen. In the process of attempting to reveal the mystery of what he seeks to behold, the visionary discloses himself.

In the traditions of Jewish apocalyptic and mystical *praxis*, this disclosure has its source in the vision that first revealed itself on the shores of the Chebar but now resides worlds apart in realms beyond perception. Having appeared initially in thunder and lightning to the exiled prophet, the divine presence must now be

71. Charlesworth, I, 296n.
72. Implied are two Messiahs, a Messiah ben Joseph and a Messiah ben David. For a full discussion, see Odeberg, *III Enoch*, pp. 145–147.

sought through elaborate procedures of ascent into the celestial spheres. As a result of that reorientation, an entire literature of transcendence emerges, accompanied by its own *topoi* and its own *mythos*. Ultimately self-reflexive, this literature textualizes itself, comments upon itself, transcribes itself, renders its own hermeneutics. At the center of this hermeneutics resides the *merkabah*, awesome in its splendor, terrifying in its presence, at once inviting and defying disclosure. If this is the essence of the visionary mode as apocalyptic and mystical enterprise, that dimension finds its correspondence among the generations of exegetes for whom the experience of the *merkabah* was as much an interpretive activity as it was a mystical endeavor. It is to this particular form of acculturation that we shall now attend.

~ *Three*

The Hermeneutics of Vision

I

No treatment of the visionary mode would be complete without a discussion of its exegetical bearing as a distinct subject of
discourse among the rabbinical authorities dating back to the earliest periods of Judaic thought and extending into the later Middle
Ages. Taking into account Gershom Scholem's second category
(the speculation of the mishnaic teachers) in his taxonomy of the
merkabah, we shall considerably expand this aspect to include not
only talmudic and midrashic commentary but related endeavors
as dimensions of what I call speculative and esoteric *merkabah*. As
we shall see, this enterprise at once complements and distinguishes
itself from the apocalyptic and mystical *merkabah* discussed in the
previous chapter. Speculative and esoteric *merkabah* provides its
own unique rendering of the visionary mode, one in which the
inaugural vision of Ezekiel undergoes a series of metamorphoses
as fascinating as those associated with the *merkabah* as apocalyptic
and mystical enterprise. In its various forms speculative *merkabah*
is the subject of this chapter, esoteric *merkabah* the subject of the
next. Once again, categories are seen to overlap and intersect
throughout.

From the early rabbinical perspective, the most direct acknowledgment of the *merkabah* as a topic of speculation appears in the
Mishnah, which forms the halakhic core of both the Palestinian
and Babylonian Talmuds. Although the putative editor of the
Mishnah, the patriarch Rabbi Judah "the Saint," is supposed to
have attempted to exclude references to the *merkabah*, the phenomenon is nonetheless addressed in such tractates of the Mishnah as the *Ḥagigah* ("Festal Offering") of the Second Division

(*Mo'ed*).¹ Particularly as these references appear in the Babylonian Talmud, the locus classicus is that which is expounded, with its accompanying commentary or *Gemara*, in the *Hagigah* (2:1).² Designating in ascending order what it considers to be the subjects that are absolutely sacrosanct in any encounter with the biblical text, the *Hagigah* (2:1) makes the following pronouncement: "THE [SUBJECT OF] FORBIDDEN RELATIONS MAY NOT BE EXPOUNDED IN THE PRESENCE OF THREE, NOR THE WORK OF CREATION IN THE PRESENCE OF TWO, NOR [THE WORK OF] THE CHARIOT IN THE PRESENCE OF ONE, UNLESS HE IS A SAGE AND UNDERSTANDS OF HIS OWN KNOWLEDGE."³

The pronouncement is important for a number of reasons, first because it provides a nomenclature for specific subjects of discourse prominent in rabbinical circles; second, because it suggests the prevailing attitude among the rabbinical schools toward those subjects; third, because it implies an ordering in which those subjects are to be considered; and fourth, because it indicates the appropriate audience and occasion for embarking upon such a consideration.⁴ The *Hagigah*, in short, provides a veritable rhetoric

---

1. According to Gershom Scholem, "it is a well-known fact that the editor of the Mishnah, the patriarch Jehudah 'the Saint' [i.e., Judah the 'Rabbi'], a pronounced rationalist, did all he could to exclude references to the Merkabah." *Major Trends in Jewish Mysticism* (New York: Schocken Books, 1954), pp. 42–43. This attitude prevails in the midrashic compendium, the Mekhilta: "R. Eliezer says: Why can you say that a maid-servant at the Sea saw what Isaiah and Ezekiel never saw? For it is said, 'And through the prophets I gave parables' [Hos. 12:11], and it is written, 'And the heavens were opened and I saw the visions of God' [Ezek. 1:1]." Such a view is elaborated upon in the later midrashim (Ira Chernus, *Mysticism in Rabbinic Judaism* [Berlin: Walter de Gruyter, 1982], p. 21). In *Megillah* 4.10, however, one finds, along with a list of proscribed texts, the following statement: "They may not use the chapter of the Chariot as a reading from the Prophets; but R. Judah permits it," an assertion that at least suggests the possibility of conflicting traditions. (Compare *Megillah* 2.6 and *Hullin* 5.5, regarding the corresponding chapter on Creation.) References are to *The Mishnah*, trans. Herbert Danby (London: Oxford University Press, 1933), pp. 205, 207, 212, 522.

2. Although corresponding accounts are present in the Palestinian Talmud, the Babylonian Talmud, as that which is generally looked upon as the more authoritative and comprehensive of the two, serves as the primary focal point of the present discussion.

3. For additional talmudic references that either allude directly to the concept of the *merkabah* or interpret various aspects of it, see the commentary in *Megillah* (24b), *Pesahim* (119a), *Menahot* (43b), and *Berakot* (21b).

4. Despite the mishnaic injunctions against speculating on the *ma'aseh merkabah*, the inaugural vision of Ezekiel was widely interpreted in rabbinical circles. So widely disseminated were the exegeses of Ezekiel's vision, in fact, that they were incorporated into the synagogue service for *shabu'ot*, the festival on which the revelation at Sinai is celebrated (cf. Exod. 19:16–20). David J. Halperin, *The Merkabah in Rabbinic Literature* (New Haven: American Oriental Society, 1980), pp. 182–183.

of discourse for the investigation of acknowledged (yet ostensibly interdicted) topics dating back to the period of the Tannaim.

For our purposes the topics of primary importance, of course, are the *ma'aseh bere'shit* and the *ma'aseh merkabah*, the first with its source in the first chapter of Genesis, the second with its source in the first chapter of Ezekiel.[5] As an attestation to the halakhic weight that was placed upon these subjects in rabbinical circles from the earliest period, the pronouncement in the *Ḥagigah* (2:1) could not be stronger. In the traditions of rabbinical commentary, the *ma'aseh bere'shit* and the *ma'aseh merkabah* became the focus of cosmogonic and cosmological speculation on the manifestation of godhead in all realms of the universe. In keeping with that focus the *Ḥagigah* declares: "WHOSOEVER SPECULATES UPON FOUR THINGS, A PITY FOR HIM! HE IS AS THOUGH HE HAD NOT COME INTO THE WORLD, [TO WIT], WHAT IS ABOVE, WHAT IS BENEATH, WHAT BEFORE, WHAT AFTER. AND WHOSOEVER TAKES NO THOUGHT FOR THE HONOUR OF HIS MAKER, IT WERE A MERCY IF HE HAD NOT COME INTO THE WORLD" (2:1). Although the precise meaning of the "four things" is open to debate, the consensus is that "what is above" refers to the firmament stretching over the heads of the living creatures of the Chariot; "what is beneath" refers to the realm beneath the living creatures; and "what before" and "what after" refer both spatially to what lies before and beyond the Chariot and temporally to what happened before and after the creation.

The conjunction of these temporal and spatial coordinates suggests how intimately the *ma'aseh bere'shit* and the *ma'aseh merkabah* were related in rabbinical thought. An examination of the *Gemara* and its related *'aggadot* or narrative formulations within the *Ḥagigah* should confirm not only this fact but the nature of the interdictions imposed upon the subjects in question. In its word-by-word dissection of the mishnaic text, the *Ḥagigah* generally divides its treatment into an elaborate discourse on the *ma'aseh bere'shit*, on the one hand, and the *ma'aseh merkabah*, on the other. Proceeding topically, it incorporates a vast amount of material, bolstered through recourse to rabbinical authority. From the perspective of the *ma'aseh bere'shit*, for example, it returns to the

5. The subject of Forbidden Relations (*'arayot*) alludes to the kinds of sexual relations interdicted in Leviticus (see Lev. 18:6–30). Its presence in the list bestows upon the other two topics, one supposes, a kind of ceremonial sanctity as expressed in distinctions between sacred and profane. See the *Ḥagigah* (11b).

secrets of the precosmogonic period (that which is "before") and moves through an account of the creation to the events following the period of the six days and beyond (that which is "after"). Emphasizing the severe restrictions placed upon the study of these matters, the *Ḥagigah* ironically proceeds to violate its own caveat by making them the subject of its discourse. It does so by generating a complex mythology that takes into account both the process of creation and the nature of that which is created.

Of the process of creation, the *Ḥagigah* (12a) comments: "By ten things was the world created: By wisdom and by understanding, and by reason, and by strength, and by rebuke, and by might, by righteousnes and by judgment, by lovingkindness and by compassion." For each of these attributes or potencies, the *Ḥagigah* has an explanation that elaborates the process even further. In that elaboration one finds a discussion of the first man and his immense proportions, as well as a discourse on the various parts of the created universe. In its discussion of heaven and earth, for example, it attempts to determine which was created first and compares their creation to the construction of a house, with its upper stories and its lower portions. Offering contrasting opinions concerning such matters, it refuses to resolve the issue but, rather, delights in apparent contradictions.[6] Accompanying this discourse is the kind of etymological wordplay that underscores talmudic discussion of abstruse subjects. "What does 'heaven' [*shamayim*] mean?" the *Ḥagigah* (12a) asks. Citing rabbinical authority, it observes that the word implies both "There is water" (combining *sham* and *maim*) and "fire and water" (combining *'esh* and *maim*). This ludic quality is not gratuitous: it underscores the sense of mystery surrounding both the *maʿaseh bereʾshit* and the *maʿaseh merkabah* as speculative enterprises.

Continuing its speculation on the *maʿaseh bereʾshit*, the *Ḥagigah* (12b–13a) focuses its attention in greater detail on the celestial spheres. It begins by invoking rabbinical authority on the number and names of the firmaments. Whereas Rabbi Judah maintains there are two firmaments, Resh Lakish holds out for seven, which he names as follows: *Wilon* or curtain, *Rakiyaʿ* or expanse, *Shehakim* or clouds, *Zebul* or lofty abode, *Maʿon* or dwelling, *Makon* or place, and *ʿArabot* or darkness (12b). Recalling the seven heavens of

---

6. The scriptural verses upon which such arguments are based, the *Ḥagigah* (12a) declares, "contradict one another!"

apocalyptic and mystical *merkabah*, these designations represent an act of structuring the celestial worlds to accord with the speculative outlook of talmudic commentary. Each heaven, in turn, reveals its own characteristics. *Wilon* "enters in the morning and goes forth in the evening," a diurnal pattern of movement that suggests the sense of renewal associated with "the work of creation" (cf. Isa. 40:22). *Rakiya*, in turn, is that in which the "sun and moon, the stars and constellations are set" (cf. Gen. 1:17). Probably because of its etymological association with the idea of pulverizing or grinding, *Shehakim* is the heaven in which "millstones stand and grind manna for the righteous" (cf. Ps. 78:23–24).

In *Zebul* resides the celestial Jerusalem with its temple and altar, where "Michael the great Prince stands and offers up thereon an offering" (cf. 1 Kings 8:13). *Ma'on* is important, because in that heaven the ministering angels utter divine song by night and are silent by day in order that Israel may celebrate God during that period (cf. Ps. 42:9). In *Makon* there are "the stores of snow and stores of hail, and the loft of harmful dews and the loft of raindrops, the chamber of the whirlwind and storm, and the cave of vapour, and their doors are of fire" (cf. Deut. 28:12; Ps. 118: 7, 8). Because the stores within this heaven are used both for rewards and for punishments, David, according to one tradition, caused them to come down to earth. *'Arabot* , finally, is "that in which there are Right and Judgment and Righteousness [or *Tsedakah*], the treasures of life and the treasures of peace and the treasures of blessing, the souls of the righteous and the spirits and the souls which are yet to be born, and the dew wherewith the Holy One, blessed be He, will hereafter revive the dead" (12b; cf. Ps. 36:10, 89:15; Isa. 59:17, among others).

As the foregoing suggests, the act of naming and delineating the celestial spheres that constitute the *ma'aseh bere'shit* involves the creation of an elaborate mythology through which we are able to gain insight into the workings of the divine. With the *Hagigah* as guide, moreover, we ascend as speculative participants into the heavens. In the highest of heavens we encounter the Enthroned Figure surrounded by His attendants: "There ... are the Ofanim and the Seraphim, and the Holy Living Creatures, and the Ministering Angels, and the Throne of God; and the King, the Living God, high and exalted, dwells over them in *'Arabot*, for its is said: *Extol Him that rideth upon 'Arabot whose name is the Lord* [cf. Ps.

68:4]." Implied in the reference to ʿArabot, of course, is the concept of the chariot that underscores the Psalm 68. "And whence do we derive that it [ʿArabot] is called heaven?" the Ḥagigah asks. The answer, as the Ḥagigah is aware, resides in the "mighty chariotry" (Ps. 68:17) that distinguishes "*Him that rideth upon ʿArabot*" (cf. Deut. 33:26). Surrounded by cloud and thick darkness, the Enthroned Figure is He who "dwells above the heads of the living creatures." Although we have moved from outer chamber to inner chamber in our quest for this Figure, the Ḥagigah (12b–13a) observes, we may speak no further of Him, an injunction that is reinforced by the Book of Ben Sira: "*Seek not things that are too hard for thee, and search not out things that are hidden from thee. The things that have been permitted thee, think thereupon; thou hast no business with the things that are secret*" (Ecclus. 3:21–22).

Defying this injunction will be tantamount to following in the footsteps of that wicked one portrayed by the prophet Isaiah. Seeking to "*ascend above the heights of the clouds*," the wicked one stirred the entire world to rebellion against God by desiring to "*be like the Most High*" (Isa. 14:14). In response to this act of defiance, the Ḥagigah (13a) relates that a divine voice (*bat kol*) went forth and said to the wicked one: "How many are the years of man? Seventy." However, "the distance from the earth to the firmament is a journey of five hundred years, and the thickness of the firmament is a journey of five hundred years, and likewise [the distance] between one firmament and the other." Above these seven firmaments are the holy living creatures:

> The feet of the living creatures are equal to all of them [together]; the ankles of the living creatures are equal to all of them; the legs of the living creatures are equal to all of them; the knees of the living creatures are equal to all of them; the thighs of the living creatures are equal to all of them; the bodies of the living creatures are equal to all of them; the necks of the living creatures are equal to all of them; the horns of the living creatures are equal to all of them. Above them is the throne of glory; the feet of the throne of glory are equal to all of them; the throne of glory is equal to all of them. The King, the Living and Eternal God, High and Exalted, dwelleth above them.

Because of the audacity and presumption of the wicked one in desiring to attain to these reaches, the *bat kol* proclaims, "*thou shalt be brought down to the nether-world, to the uttermost parts of the pit"* (13a; cf. Isa. 14:15).

The narrative and the form in which it is cast are interesting for a number of reasons. The *Ḥagigah* resorts to Isaiah 14 in order to portray its own myth of ascent (which also involves the myth of a fall): the wicked one who attempts to ascend to the heights of the clouds in order to be like the Most High is cast into the depths below. The point of the myth is to drive home the immense dangers, as well as the potential evils, associated with the idea of presuming to journey to the throne of God. Framed by Isaiah's account, the portrayal of the journey itself is rendered in a form that provides a detailed description of what such an enterprise entails. In keeping with the spirit of the Mishnah, that description conflates temporal and spatial coordinates (years of the journey conceived through the measurement of sizes and distances) as a means of demonstrating the difficulties attendant upon an undertaking of this sort.

Recalling the elaborate depictions characteristic of apocalyptic and mystical *merkabah*, the account begins with the firmaments and then proceeds to the details associated with the inaugural vision of Ezekiel. In its recapitulation of that vision it moves in ascending order from the *ḥayyot* to the King upon His throne. Beginning with the feet of the *ḥayyot*, it ascends to their ankles, next to their legs, then to their knees, and thereafter to their thighs, their upper bodies, their necks, their heads, and finally to their horns (a reference to the oxen as a symbol of the whole). From that point the description proceeds upward to the throne of glory (beginning once again at the feet of the throne and from there to the throne proper) and ends with a reference to the Enthroned Figure, who dwells in the height of heights. In this process of ascent by means of enumeration, the description engages in a rhetoric of formulaic and reiterated measurement ("are equal to all of them") that underscores the impossibility of perceiving or knowing the whole in its entirety. Such is the form that the visionary mode assumes at this point in the *Ḥagigah*.

Warning all those who would engage in an ascent of this kind, the *Ḥagigah* ironically does precisely what it warns against as it undertakes its own rhetorical ascent from firmament to firmament and from the feet of the *ḥayyot* to the heights of the Enthroned Figure. In the process the *Ḥagigah* reformulates the inaugural vision of Ezekiel in its own terms. Relocating the vision above the

firmaments, it participates interpretively in the experience of the
yordei merkabah. From a hermeneutical perspective the account
represents a kind of visionary matrix for the *Ḥagigah* as well. In
this transitional moment the tractate adopts the occasion to turn
its attention from its speculations on the *maʿaseh bereʾshit* as a stated
subject of discourse and to address the complex nature of the
maʿaseh merkabah as a "new" topic of discourse. The effect is to
demonstrate in rhetorical terms the fundamental premise of rabbinical Judaism that *maʿaseh bereʾshit* and *maʿaseh merkabah* are intimately related (indeed, at times, overlapping) phenomena.

As with the *maʿaseh bereʾshit*, the *Ḥagigah* (13a) begins its discussion of the *maʿaseh merkabah* with a consideration of the injunction concerning who may or may not expound the *maʿaseh
merkabah* ("Nor [the work of the chariot] in the presence of one,
unless he is a sage") and what the consequences of disobedience
are ("it were a mercy if he had not come into the world"). Likewise
in keeping with the *maʿaseh bereʾshit*, there is considerable debate
over these points. According to one rabbinical tradition, the "chapter headings" or the initial words of each section of the description
may be transmitted to an individual, but that is all. According to
another tradition, those chapter headings may be transmitted ex-
clusively to the head of a rabbinical court (*ʾab bet din*) and only to
such a head who is entirely reverential. A further tradition avers
that such matters may be shared only with one who possesses five
attributes, namely, *"the captain of fifty, and the man of rank, and the
counsellor, and the cunning charmer, and the skilful enchanter"* (13a).
"What are these?" we are prompted to ask. The answer, we might
suggest, lies in the very need to ask the question. Deliberately
obscure in themselves, these enigmatic phrases are part of what
the *maʿaseh merkabah* is meant to imply. As such, they suggest the
occlusive bearing of the subject as a whole.

What the phrases probably mean is expounded only later (and
without warning) in the *Ḥagigah* (14a). There, the phrases reap-
pear as part of a discussion of another subject. We infer from this
discussion possible interpretations of the phrases that appear earlier. But the interpretations themselves are open-ended. We find,
for example, that "the captain of fifty" (cf. Isa. 3:3) has two definitions. Interpreting "fifty" (*ḥamishim*) as "fifths" (*ḥumashim*), one
rabbinical tradition explains the phrase as "the captain of the
Pentateuch," that is, one who is presumably able to expound the
five books of the Torah. Interpreting "fifty" as fifty years of age,

however, another rabbinical tradition maintains that a *Methurge-man* or interpreter may not be appointed over a congregation who is not sufficiently ripened in years. This definition, in turn, is followed by another that "elucidates" the next phrase, "the man of rank." That phrase supposedly implies "one for whose sake favour is shown to his [entire] generation" both "on high" and "below." What "on high" and "below" mean is not defined. Presumably, they suggest something like "in heaven" and "on earth." What about "the counsellor"? He is one who is well acquainted with "the intercalation of years and the fixation of months." That definition probably suggests a person who knows what festivals are appropriate for a given season in the Jewish calendar. "The cunning charmer" is explained as the wise man, a disciple who is able to instruct his own teachers and to make them wise. At the very moment that he begins to expound the Torah, he charms them with his wisdom, it is supposed, and they become silent. Finally, "the skilful enchanter," like the cunning charmer, is able to discern one fine point from another. Having had the secrets of the Torah bestowed upon him in a "whisper," he is, we assume, able to expound the highest mysteries and enchant others with his profound knowledge (14a).

These definitions and the manner in which they are communicated reveal a great deal about the talmudic view of the *ma'aseh merkabah*. Of immediate importance are the qualifications that distinguish the hermeneut or *Methurgeman* himself. From what the definitions do suggest, we can gather the following. Ripened in years and gifted with immense wisdom, he is an individual who is able to teach his own teachers. So accomplished is he that he holds high rank and authority in the rabbinical academies and among his congregation. Attentive to the ceremonies of his calling, he is at once an *'ab bet din* or head of a rabbinical court and a person whose lineage and conduct are above reproach. More than that, however, he is endowed with certain theurgical, even oracular, abilities: he is able to charm and enchant with the secret knowledge that he possesses. As paragon of paragons, then, he is a charismatic person in whom there dwells great power.

Such are the ostensible qualifications necessary for anyone who would presume to expound the *ma'aseh merkabah*. But these qualifications are not meant to preclude others, or at least other interpretations of the definitions from which they emerge. Couched in a language of indeterminacy, they are delineated in a manner that invites further elaboration, additional debate. Although implicitly illuminating certain enigmatic phrases that have appeared earlier in the text, the definitions that address these qualifications present their own problems, embody their own uncertainties. That is precisely as it should be: the delineation of the *ma'aseh merkabah* as talmudic enterprise gives rise to a heuristic process that resists direct disclosure and that revels in the complexities of the very subject it presumes to elucidate. If such is true of the foregoing, it is no less so of other aspects of the *ma'aseh merkabah* that the *Ḥagigah* undertakes to consider.

Among these aspects is the form that the *ma'aseh merkabah* assumes as a distinct subject of discourse. The *Ḥagigah* (13a) addresses this issue through an *'aggadah* that again reinforces the intimate relationship between the *ma'aseh bere'shit* and the *ma'aseh merkabah*. So it is related that Rabbi Joseph was studying the "Work of the Chariot" and the elders of Pumbeditha were studying the "Work of Creation." When asked by the elders to instruct them in the "Work of the Chariot," Rabbi Joseph responds by requesting them to recite the "Work of Creation" first. Having done so, they are now ready to hear about the corresponding subject, the "Work of the Chariot." If both subjects appear to exist in an atmosphere of reciprocity, however, that reciprocity is limited by the extent to which one is able to understand secrets of the most occlusive sort.

It is, in fact, the very nature of the "Work of the Chariot" not to be fully understood, for the purpose of which Rabbi Joseph draws upon an analogy from the Song of Songs: "Honey and milk are under thy tongue" (5:11). The analogy, of course, recalls the act of consumption so important to the originary content of the vision: "And he said to me, 'Son of man, eat this scroll that I give you and fill your stomach with it.' Then I ate it; and it was in my mouth as sweet as honey" (Ezek. 3:3). If to know the *merkabah* is once again to consume it as a text, this new act of consumption is particularly apposite, for it suggests the transformative bearing of the *merkabah* in the movement from its original biblical milieu, grounded in the commissioning of the prophet, to its new talmudic environment, grounded in the discourse of rabbinical authorities. As a unique and indeed ostensibly prohibited subject of discourse, the *merkabah* assumes a form consonant with the outlook of those who consume it. In this form, it is consumed not so much for the purpose of prophetic commissioning and transmission as to sug-

gest the peculiarly occlusive nature it has now assumed under the
tutelage of the rabbis. So Rabbi Joseph glosses the passage from
the Song of Songs ("Honey and milk are under thy tongue") by
observing that "the things that are sweeter than honey and milk
should be *under* thy tongue"; that is, they should remain hidden,
for they are a mystery (13a).

Reinforcing this sense of mystery are the textual uncertainties
that surround the *merkabah* as a subject of discourse (*Ḥagigah* 13a).
Here, the fundamental consideration has to do with the very act
of "locating" the *merkabah* in the text to be interpreted. In an
encounter with the first chapter of Ezekiel, the rabbis ask, wherein
precisely does the *merkabah* lie? What are the parameters of its
delineation? How far may one read through the text before one
begins running into dangerous territory? These questions are of
crucial concern to those who want to be able to recognize the
merkabah when they see it in the text. The way these questions are
raised and negotiated is as interesting as the questions themselves,
for there is no one answer, only debate. After Rabbi Joseph, in
the presence of the elders of Pumbeditha, maintains that the *maʿaseh merkabah* extends as far as the words "*And he said unto me; 'Son
of man'*" (cf. Ezek. 2:1), an objection is raised that, according to
authoritative tradition, it extends only as far as "the second *I saw*"
(cf. Ezek. 1:27). The elders are not satisfied. Rabbi Isaac maintains
that it extends as far as *ḥashmal* (Ezek. 1:28), after which only the
chapter headings may be taught. Others voice their own opinions.
The subject itself and the text in which it appears are part of a
continuing interchange of views that alter and transform the *merkabah* in the very act of considering it. What the *merkabah* is and
where it appears in the text are both open to interpretation and
dialogic interchange (13a).

Correspondingly open to interpretation is what the *merkabah*
means, the nature of the significations it engenders as a visionary
event. An entire constellation of meanings, indeed, an entire mythology of associations, accrues to its various components (*Ḥagigah*
13a–13b). The electrum or *ḥashmal* that surrounds the Enthroned
Figure is a case in point. Even as it is encountered in the text, the
ḥashmal is a dangerous phenomenon. To understand its meanings
in the act of reading can lead to disaster. One always runs the risk
of being overwhelmed by the power of the text. So the rabbis
taught that "there was once a child who was reading at his teacher's
house the Book of Ezekiel, and he apprehended what *ḥashmal* was,

whereupon a fire went forth from *ḥashmal* and consumed him."
For this reason, we are told, the rabbis sought to suppress the
book of Ezekiel. As with other aspects of the *merkabah*, the language that delineates it is open to a variety of interpretations.
Once again, *ḥashmal* serves as an example. For some, this word
means "living creatures speaking fire": at times the *ḥayyot* are silent, at times they speak. "When the utterance goes forth from
the mouth of the Holy One, blessed be He, they are silent, and
when the utterance goes not forth from the mouth of the Holy
One, blessed be He, they speak" (13a–13b). As a purveyor of
discourse, the *merkabah* manifests itself in its ability to communicate, either in its silences or in its utterances.

Other meanings accrue to its many aspects as well. That it is
initially beheld as a stormy wind coming out of the north is meaningful. In that movement one may see how the destructions
wrought by the wicked Nebuchadnezzar serve as an example of
the punishment that evil-doers and idol-worshipers bring upon
themselves. In this respect the *merkabah* becomes a symbol of divine anger. As such, the phenomenon is associated with war chariots, and the numberless "troops" of the *merkabah* surround the
Divine Warrior as He goes forth to battle. According to another
tradition, an angel by the name of Sandalfon accompanies the
Chariot. Of gigantic proportions, Sandalfon stands behind the
Chariot and at once "wreathes crowns for his Maker" and "pro-
nounces the Divine Name over the crowns." The *ḥayyot* themselves
are emblematized to suggest the regal nature of the Enthroned
Figure that presides over the vision as a whole: the lion is seen as
king of the wild animals, the ox as king of the cattle, the eagle as
king of the birds, and man as exalted over them (13a–13b).

Finally, the vision is contextualized so that it is understood in
terms of comparable biblical events, notably Isaiah 6 and Daniel
7 (*Ḥagigah* 13a–14b). From the perspective of Isaiah 6, the question is raised concerning the number of wings the *ḥayyot* have.
Whereas the *serafim* of Isaiah have six, the *ḥayyot* of Ezekiel are
described as having four. One answer to the question resides in
the environment of each vision. Isaiah's is a pre-exilic environment: the Temple still stands. Ezekiel's is post-exilic: the Temple
is destroyed. For this reason the wings of the *ḥayyot* are diminished,
with the implied expectation that they will grow back once the
Temple has been restored and the Divine Presence returns to its
residence. Compounding such considerations, moreover, is a de-

bate about which of the two wings is missing. Nothing is entirely settled. In fact, controversy is the order of the day. Comparing what Isaiah saw with what Ezekiel saw, the rabbis maintain that they beheld essentially the same thing; only the circumstances have changed according once again to their respective environments, pre-exilic, one the one hand, and post-exilic, on the other. Accordingly, Isaiah resembles "a townsman who saw the king": the royal court with its entourage is much more accessible to one situated within immediate proximity of the king upon his throne. Ezekiel, on the other hand, resembles "a villager who saw the king": the royal court with its entourage is rarely or ever seen beyond the city confines. For that reason it is much more daunting to one for whom a royal visitation is an occasion that rarely, if ever, occurs (13a–13b).

If this process of contextualization is true of Isaiah 6, it is no less so of Daniel 7. Here, the focus is primarily upon the Enthroned Figure described by Ezekiel (1:26–28). This figure is likened to the Ancient of Days described by Daniel (7:9–10). As conceived by Daniel, the Ancient of Days, in turn, finds its counterpart in the divine groom depicted in the Song of Songs (5:11). From these corresponding perspectives, the Enthroned Figure is implicitly both old and young. As he is old, his raiment is as "white as snow," and "the hair of his head is like pure wool." He is beheld as an ancient judge who holds court in session. But he is also young, a characteristic that causes him in the Song of Songs to be described as a figure whose "locks are curled and black as a raven." He is accordingly beheld as a young warrior ready to do battle. Other correspondences follow suit. If the Enthroned Figure is surrounded by *hashmal*, the Ancient of Days, we recall, resides upon a throne from which issues "a stream of fire." "What is the source of the stream of fire?" This stream comes, we are told, "from the sweat of the 'living creatures,'" which pours forth "upon the head of the wicked in Gehinnom" (13b–14a).

Fundamental to the conception of the *ma'aseh merkabah* as a talmudic enterprise is the kind of intercalation and contextualization that distinguish the hermeneutical practices of the rabbinical authorities. In the hands of these authorities the *merkabah* is a constantly changing phenomenon, one that gives rise to an entire constellation of meanings. These meanings are never fixed, never static. They exist in an environment of dialogue, debate, even controversy that renders the *merkabah* forever dynamic, forever indeterminate, like the vision itself from which it emerges as a subject of interpretation and investigation.

In its delineation of the *maʿaseh merkabah* the *Ḥagigah* relates a number of *ʾaggadot* that are essential to an understanding of the rabbinical attitude toward the subject and what it implies. Among these *ʾaggadot* there are two in particular that are important for our purposes. The first concerns a dialogue between Rabbi Jochanan ben Zakkai and his pupil Rabbi Eleazar ben Arak (14a–14b), the second, an experience that features Rabbi Akiba and three other Tannaim (14b–15a). Both *ʾaggadot* are of interest to the formulation of the *merkabah* as a rabbinical enterprise founded upon the concept of narrative as a mode of exposition.

According to the first narrative, the teacher Rabbi Jochanan ben Zakkai and his pupil Rabbi Eleazar ben Arak are embarked upon a journey.[7] The teacher is riding upon an ass in front, and the student is appropriately driving the ass from behind. "Teach me a chapter of the 'Work of the Chariot,' " Rabbi Eleazar requests of his master, who responds with the mishnaic admonition, " 'Nor [the work of] the chariot in the presence of one, unless he is a Sage and understands of his own knowledge.' " Undeterred by his teacher's refusal, the persistent student exercises his ingenuity in order to accommodate the spirit of the admonition and still make use of the opportunity to discuss the *merkabah*. "Master," Rabbi Eleazar says, "permit me to say before thee something which thou hast taught me." In other words, "if you will not teach me, then, allow me to instruct you by sharing with you what I have learned from your earlier instruction." So the student instructs the teacher.

Encouraged by Rabbi Eleazar's persistence, Rabbi Jochanan answers, "Say on!" after which he dismounts from his ass, wraps himself in his *tallit* or prayer shawl, and sits upon a stone

7. There are four versions of this narrative that invite comparison: (1) the Babylonian Talmud (the subject of the present investigation); (2) the Palestinian Talmud; (3) the Mekhilta of Rabbi Simeon ben Yochai; and (4) the Tosefta. Aspects of the narrative in each differ. Among the various studies devoted to the narrative, as well as to Rabbi Jochanan ben Zakkai, see Christopher Rowland, *The Open Heaven: A Study of Apocalyptic in Judaism and Early Christianity* (New York: Crossroad, 1982), pp. 269–348; Jacob Neusner, *A Life of Rabban Yoḥanan b. Zakkai* (Leiden: Brill, 1962), and *The Development of a Legend: Studies on the Traditions concerning Yoḥanan ben Zakkai* (Leiden: Brill, 1970); E. E. Urbach, "The Traditions about the Religion of Esoteric Groups in the Tannaitic Period" (in Hebrew) in *Studies in Mysticism and Religion for G. Scholem* (Jerusalem: Ktav, 1967); and Halperin, *Merkabah*, passim.

beneath an olive tree.[8] All his actions represent a recognition of the importance and sanctity of the occasion.[9] Accordingly, when his pupil asks, "Master, wherefore didst thou dismount from the ass?" Rabbi Jochanan responds with a rhetorical question that, in its implied humor, paradoxically reinforces the momentous nature of what is to be communicated: "Is it proper," he asks, "that whilst thou art expounding the 'Work of the Chariot,' and the Divine Presence is with us, and the ministering angels accompany us, I should ride on the ass!" Chastened, the pupil begins his exposition.

Unlike the child who is consumed by the fires from the *hashmal*, Rabbi Eleazar is successful: fire comes down from heaven and encompasses all the trees in the field, which, in turn, begin to utter a divine song of celebration, derived from Psalm 148: *"Praise the Lord from the earth, ye sea-monsters, and all deeps . . . fruitful trees and all cedars . . . Hallelujah."*[10] In a kind of responsum, an angel then proclaims from the fire, "This is the very 'Work of the Chariot,' " after which the master rises, kisses his pupil on his head, and blesses him: "Blessed be the Lord God of Israel, Who hath given a son to Abraham our father, who knoweth to speculate upon, and to investigate, and to expound the 'Work of the Chariot.' There are some who preach well but do not act well, others act well but do not preach well, but thou doest preach well and act well. Happy art thou, O Abraham our father, that R. Eleazar b. Arak hath come forth from thy loins" (14a–14b).

Both the narrative and its mode of execution suggest a great deal about the *maʿaseh merkabah* as a rabbinical enterprise. The use of narrative provides a fictive occasion for the exposition as a whole, a means of suggesting that a knowledge of divine things

8. The Babylonian Talmud offers the fullest account at this point, one that does not find its correspondence in the Mekhilta, the Tosefta, and the Palestinian Talmud. See Rowland for a comparison of the accounts, *Open Heaven*, pp. 284–288.

9. Wrapping oneself in a prayer shawl obviously suggests the sanctity of the enterprise. The act of sitting on a stone perhaps implies expectation and attentiveness. Finally, the olive tree has many associations, among them, those having to do with the creation of the holy of holies (such as the cherubim of olivewood), man's faith in God, and a renewal of divine favor (cf. 1 Kings 6:23, 31–33; Ps. 52:8; Hos. 14:6; and Hag. 2:9).

10. In the Palestinian Talmud the account is expanded at this point: "Fire came down from heaven and surrounded them and the ministering angels were dancing before them like wedding-guests in the presence of the bridegroom. An angel replied from the middle of the fire and said, 'According to your words Eleazar b. Arak is the story of the chariot.' Immediately all the trees opened their mouths and sang a song. Then all the trees of the forest began to rejoice." (Cited in Rowland, *Open Heaven*, pp. 286–287.)

is best communicated through story. By means of story one is able to arrive at a higher truth than through the vehicle of direct exposition. Story allows for setting, dialogue, character, humor, dramatic interchange, conflict, and resolution. These create the most appropriate environment for the *ma'aseh merkabah*, which is best apprehended through the interpretation of the various elements that constitute story. In the transmission of story the mode of execution is also important. It is a mode that invokes the mishnaic injunction ("nor [the work of] the chariot in the presence of one"), only to discover a means of expounding the *ma'aseh merkabah* despite the injunction. That means is through the act of having the student instruct the teacher, that is, of having the student interpret for the teacher what the student has been taught. In this social context of dialogue and mutual interchange, not only is a hermeneutic circle established but the student himself is tested, and, as a result of that test, proves himself equal to the task.

Significantly, the student's discourse itself is not included in the narrative. We don't know precisely what he says, what his exposition is. In the context of the narrative itself, it appears that what is important is not so much the substance of the student's actual discourse as his success in executing it. Perhaps the suggestion is that, as students of the *merkabah*, we are left to devise our own expositions, our own interpretations, in the expectation that we, too, will be successful, assuming that we are wise enough. Interpretation is an open-ended endeavor: we are permitted to share the story of its execution but not the substance of its content. What results is a narrative that encourages us, too, to be tested, to recite the "Work of the Chariot" before our teachers, to engage in our own interpretations, and to do so in the very teeth of the mishnaic admonition to refrain, unless we wish to risk ultimate disaster like that child for whom reading proved to be a dangerous enterprise indeed. Not to be put off by the fate of the child, however, we are prompted to keep in mind the good fortune of Rabbi Eleazar, who was able to sustain the test and, having taught his own teacher, was celebrated by the heavens and received the blessings of his master. At the very point of interdicting the *ma'aseh merkabah* as a subject of interpretation, then, the *Ḥagigah* provides the occasion for its elucidation. This paradox is fundamental to the "Work of the Chariot" as an enterprise of greatest moment among the Tannaim and their followers. As dangerous as reading can be, it has its immense rewards too.

The foregoing *'aggadah* is only one of a number that develop similar ideas. Complementing this *'aggadah* is that which concerns the experience of Rabbi Akiba and his cohorts in the mysterious realm known as *pardes*.[11] Because of its enigmatic quality, it is a narrative that has occasioned much discussion and controversy concerning its meaning, its significance, and its relation to the traditions of the *ma'aseh merkabah*.[12] According to the narrative, "Four men entered the 'Garden' [*pardes*], namely, Ben Azzai and Ben Zoma, Acher, and Rabbi Akiba. Rabbi Akiba said to them: When ye arrive at the stones of pure marble, say not, Water, water! For it is said: *He that speaketh falsehood shall not be established before mine eyes* [Ps. 101:7]. Ben Azzai cast a look and died. Of him Scripture says: *Precious in the sight of the Lord is the death of His saints* [Ps. 116:15]. Ben Zoma looked and became demented [lit. stricken]. Of him Scripture says: *Hast thou found honey? Eat so much as is sufficient for thee, lest thou be filled therewith, and vomit it* [Prov. 25:16]. Acher mutilated the shoots. Rabbi Akiba departed unhurt" (14b).[13]

Whatever the precise meaning of this *'aggadah*, the later responsa interpreted it as an expression of the kinds of experiences recorded in the various *hekhalot* documents examined in the previous chapter. To confirm this notion, one need only glance at the accounts of the later *geonim* who resorted to the *pardes* narrative in order to describe the practices and experiences of the *yordei merkabah*.[14] One such account is that of Hai ben Sherira (939–1038), *gaon* of Pumbeditha. The most prominent figure of his time, Hai Gaon was himself a mystic and heir to the traditions of the *hekhalot*. Although he vigorously opposed those who held that

11. Like the previous *'aggadah* this one also exists in a number of forms, including those featured in the Babylonian Talmud (the subject of the present discussion), the Palestinian Talmud, the Tosefta, and the Song of Songs Rabbah. See in particular *The Tosefta [Second Division: Mo'ed]*, trans. Jacob Nuesner (New York: Ktav, 1981), pp. 312–318.

12. Both in his commentary and in his notes Rowland provides a review of the scholarship (see *Open Heaven*, esp. pp. 491–497).

13. Acher (lit. "another") is presumably Elisha ben Abuyah, the apostate.

14. Accounts appear in Aryeh Kaplan, *Meditation and Kabbalah* (York Beach, Maine: Samuel Weiser, 1982), pp. 24–27. For the full responsa to *Hagigah* (14b), see *Otzar ha-Geonim: Thesaurus of the Gaonic Responsa and Commentaries*, comp. Benjamin M. Lewin, 13 vols. (Haifa and Jerusalem: n.p., 1928–1943), vol. IV/2 (*Hagigah*), part 1 (*Teshubot*).

the divine names and charms could effect miraculous occurrences, he believed that whoever studied the *hekhalot* could ascend to the celestial realms and to the world of the *merkabah*.[15] In this regard, his testimony is of great value in assessing the practices of the *yordei merkabah*.

In a responsum that has assumed the status of a classic on the subject, he observes that one in possession of all the necessary qualifications has methods through which he can gaze at the *merkabah* and look into the celestial chambers. One must first fast for a certain number of days. He then "places his head between his knees, and whispers into the ground many songs and praises known from tradition. From his innermost being and its chambers he will then perceive the Seven Chambers." In that vision it will be as if he were entering one chamber after another, beholding what is in each one. Having alluded to such practices and the experience they bring about, Hai Gaon invokes the talmudic 'aggadah* in question. It is with respect to this experience, he observes, that the Talmud teaches, "Four entered the Orchard." The chambers, he says are compared to an orchard and are given this name. The four who entered the *merkabah* and passed through the chambers are similar to people entering an orchard.

Ben Azzai gazed and died, because it was his time to leave the world. Ben Zoma gazed and was stricken, a reference implying that "he became insane because of the confounding visions that his mind could not tolerate." Acher "cut his plantings" in the sense that he did irreparable damage by not comprehending the full significance of the vision. Rabbi Akiba, on the other hand, was the most perfect of them all. Not exceeding his limitations, he gazed properly, as the result of which his mind was able to encompass these remarkable visions. As long as he gazed, he kept proper thoughts and maintained a proper mental state. God gave him power to endure. This, Hai Gaon says, was acknowledged by all the early sages and none denied it. They believed that God would work wonders and fearsome things through His saints, just as He did through His prophets.[16]

As the *geonim* would heartily concur, then, the talmudic 'aggadah* in question fully confirms the experience depicted in the *hekhalot*

---

15. *Encyclopaedia Judaica*, ed. Cecil Roth et al., 16 vols. (Jerusalem: Keter, 1971–1972), VII, 1130–1131.

16. In Kaplan, *Meditation*, pp. 26–27.

tracts. This experience, as we have seen, carries with it an awesome responsibility, one tantamount to risking, at the very least, something like the total annihilation of the personality in the quest to behold the Enthroned Figure in the chambers of His glory. Fulfilling that quest is the essential goal of the *ma'aseh merkabah* as it is embodied in the traditions of Jewish mysticism. With the talmudic *'aggadah* concerning *pardes* as a locus classicus of the *merkabah* experience, Scholem observed that "the later *Merkabah* mystics showed a perfectly correct understanding of this passage, and their interpretation offers striking proof that the traditions of Tannaitic mysticism and theosophy was really alive among them."[17] Be that as it may, our discussion of the *pardes* narrative has demonstrated what is true of the talmudic dimensions of speculative *merkabah* as a whole. In the traditions of rabbinic Judaism the visionary mode, grounded in Ezekiel's *visio Dei*, finds consummate expression as a hermeneutic enterprise of the first order.

II

If such is true of talmudic commentary, it is no less true of the midrashim, in which the vision that inaugurates the prophecy of Ezekiel assumes major import. Implying in its very root the idea of "searching out" or "seeking," midrash embodies that heuristic activity so crucial to the originary foundations of the visionary experience.[18] As a mode of discourse that spans centuries from the period of the Tannaim through the later Middle Ages, midrashic interpretation assumes many forms, both halakhic and aggadic. In the collections of midrashim through which this exegetical impulse manifested itself, one finds an entire panoply of texts and approaches, ranging from biblical commentary and homiletic discourse to narrative creation. Our concern will be with representative collections that provide their own rendering of the *merkabah* as visionary enterprise.

17. Scholem, *Major Trends*, pp. 52–53. David J. Halperin, however, calls Scholem's observations into question in a number of respects. See *The Faces of the Chariot: Early Jewish Responses to Ezekiel's Vision* (Tübingen: J. C. B. Mohr, 1988), pp. 6–7, and passim.

18. For a fine collection of essays on midrash as an interpretive activity, see *Midrash and Literature*, ed. Geoffrey Hartman and Sanford Budick (New Haven: Yale University Press, 1986). Barry W. Holtz offers an excellent introduction to midrash in *Back to the Sources: Reading the Classic Jewish Texts*, ed. Barry W. Holtz (New York: Summit Books, 1984), pp. 177–211.

The *Midrash Tehilim* (comp. 900–1000 C.E.) will serve as an appropriate point of departure.[19] Engaging in an interpretation of Psalm 90:12 that combines *ma'aseh bere'shit* and *ma'aseh merkabah*, the expositors observe that "seven things, by two thousand years, preceded the creation of the world: the Torah, the throne of glory, the Garden of Eden, Gehenna, repentance, the sanctuary in heaven, and the name of the Messiah." "How," the expositors ask, "was the Torah written?" It was written, they respond, "with black fire upon white fire as it rested on the knee of the Holy One," while He was seated on the throne of glory "set upright on the firmament which is above the heads of the celestial creatures," even before the *hayyot* were created. On His right was the Garden of Eden, on His left Gehenna, in front of Him the sanctuary, "and the name of the Messiah was engraved in a precious stone upon the altar," while His voice proclaimed repentance. "All the seven were borne up by the power of the Holy One, blessed be He" (II, 94). At the very center of this precosmogonic formulation is the *merkabah*. With the creation, these seven things are actualized: only after the Holy One created the world and the *hayyot* did He establish the firmament with all the seven upon the creatures themselves.

Commenting further on the significance of the *hayyot*, the *Midrash Tehilim* suggests in its analysis of Ps. 103:16 that "there are four rulers in the world who are proud because they are exalted over all others, but the Holy One, blessed be He, is exalted even over these four." The expositors elucidate as follows: "The bullock is proud in his rule of cattle, the lion in his rule of wild beasts, the eagle in his rule of creatures that fly. But who in his rule is prouder than all of these? Man." Setting these four into the throne of glory, the Holy One declared: "They, to be sure, are exalted, but I am exalted over them" (II, 163). In the *Midrash Tehilim*, then, the precosmogonic vision of the *merkabah* finds its counterpart in an assertion of that ethical and spiritual hierarchy that informs the rabbinical outlook toward all the events of sacred history, human and divine.

This outlook, in turn, assumes a distinctly eschatological and, indeed, Jerusalemic, bearing in the *Midrash Tanhuma* (comp. 650–900): "And thus you find in the world to come, that the Holy One

---

19. References by volume and page are to *The Midrash on Psalms*, trans. William G. Braude, 2 vols. (New Haven: Yale University Press, 1959).

blessed be He will enlarge Jerusalem, as it is said, 'And it was enlarged as it was surrounded and it rose story by story' (Ezek. 41:7), until it rises to the heavens." From there, God raises it "to the firmament, from the second firmament to the third, from the third to the fourth, from the fourth to the fifth, from the fifth to the sixth, from the sixth to the seventh. R. Eliezer b. Jacob said: Until it reaches the throne of glory." In their ascent to the highest firmament the righteous are charioted in clouds, each chariot with its own canopy (cf. Isa. 4:5, 60:8). When they reach the throne of glory, God says to them, "You and I will walk together through the universe." On His throne of glory God sits in the middle and is worshiped by the righteous.[20] This eschatological reformulation of the *merkabah* suggests once again not only the centrality of the concept to midrashic thought but how extensively the concept was able to accommodate itself to an entire range of interpretive response among those adept at a hermeneutics of the *merkabah*. In the exoteric sphere one did not need to cultivate a secret form of mystical *praxis* in order to participate in the *maʿaseh merkabah*. An acquaintance with the specifically exegetical implications of the *merkabah* was as valuable, in its own way, as an awareness of the phenomenon specifically as a means of ecstatic ascent.

Already implicit in talmudic formulations, this idea finds graphic expression in the compendious *Midrash Rabbah* (comp. 400–1200 C.E.).[21] There, ben Azzai of *pardes* fame reappears in another (but related) context. He is found sitting and expounding the Tanakh while fire plays around him. Those who discover ben Azzai so enveloped in flame go and inform Rabbi Akiba, saying, "Sir, as ben Azzai sits and expounds, the fire is flashing round him." Rabbi Akiba then goes to him and says: "I hear that as you were expounding the fire flashed round you." Ben Azzai responds, "That is so." Rabbi Akiba accordingly asks, "Were you perhaps treating of the secrets of the divine Chariot?" "No," ben Azzai says, "I was only linking up the words of the Torah with one another and then with the words of the Prophets, and the Prophets with the

20. Cited in Chernus, *Mysticism*, p. 95. According to Chernus, this passage is significant because it implies that the eschatological reward of the righteous is "closely akin to the experience of the *Merkabah* mystics." Chernus proceeds to argue, however, that such a text is unusual in the corpus, and that "among the motifs which are of central importance in the *Merkabah* texts, those which also appear in exoteric rabbinic eschatology often play a relatively minor role there" (p. 99).

21. References to the *Midrash Rabbah* by volume and page are to the edition of H. Friedman and Maurice Simon, 10 vols. (London: Soncino Press, 1939).

Writings." If ben Azzai was not treating of the secrets of the divine
Chariot as the esoteric product of a *ma'aseh merkabah*, he was,
nevertheless, engaged in a corresponding (and equally enlightening) activity. He was linking up the Torah with the rest of the
Tanakh, an act, this little story implies, tantamount to engaging
in a *ma'aseh merkabah* as profound as any those who entered *pardes*
might have performed.

The hermeneutical enterprise represents an engagement with
the secrets of the divine Chariot all its own. That engagement can
best be appreciated through the wider context that only the Tanakh as a whole provides. So the *haggadah* in question concludes:
"Some are able to link together but not to penetrate, and some
are able to penetrate but not to link together" (IX, 74). As hermeneutical phenomenon, the true *ma'aseh merkabah* involves both.
True success results in the experience of being surrounded by
fire in the fashion of the successful practitioner of the *ma'aseh
merkabah*. It is from this perspective that the *Midrash Rabbah*,
among the other midrashic compendia, assimilates the *merkabah*
into its commentary. In the *Midrash Rabbah* the presence of the
merkabah is accordingly all pervasive.

The midrashim to Genesis are a case in point. In its explication
of Gen. 1: 17 ("And God set them [the sun, moon, and stars] in
the firmament of heaven"), for example, the *Midrash Rabbah* interprets "firmament" (*rakiya'*) within the context of the *merkabah*
firmament as depicted in the *Ḥagigah*: "Thus where are all their
hosts set? In the second *rakiya'*, which is above the heaven. From
the earth to the *rakiya'* is a five hundred years' journey, and the
thickness of the *rakiya'* is a five hundred years' journey, and from
the first *rakiya'* to the next *rakiya'* is a five hundred years' journey:
see then how high it is!" (I, 45–46). The formulaic nature of the
midrash suggests once again how commonplace the association of
bere'shit with *merkabah* was in rabbinical circles. A similar outlook
is discernible in the midrashim to Exodus. Alluding to the throne
of Solomon in the context of its interpretation of Exod. 12:2, the
midrash first invokes the *ḥayyot* of Ezekiel and then observes: "God
made six heavens and resides in the seventh, and of the throne
of Solomon we read: *There were six steps to the throne*" (III, 197; cf.
1 Kings 10:19).

In its interpretation of Numbers the *Midrash Rabbah* likewise
causes the *merkabah* to assume a central importance. Focusing
upon the ordering of the Israelite camps in Num. 2:3, the midrash

observes that the Holy One "created four cardinal directions in the world—East, West, North, and South." The east is represented by the standard of Judah, Issachar, and Zabulon; the west, by the standard of Ephraim, Manasseh, and Benjamin; the north, by the standard of Dan, Asher, and Naphtali; and the south, by the standard of Reuben, Simeon, and Gad. In the same manner that He created these four cardinal directions with their corresponding standards, the Holy One similarly set about His throne the four *hayyot* and above them the Throne of Glory. Extending this idea even further, the midrash maintains that the four directions and four standards embodied in the *hayyot* find their counterparts in the four angels that the Holy One set about His throne: Michael at His right, corresponding to Reuben; Uriel at His left, corresponding to Dan; Gabriel in front, corresponding to Judah; and Raphael behind, corresponding to Ephraim (V, 34–39). Underscoring the arrangement as a whole is the concept of the *merkabah* represented spatially through an elaborate metaphor of placement and direction. It is a sublime and complex architectonics of the *merkabah* that distinguishes the midrash in question.

In keeping with the foregoing midrashim, a crucial text in the delineation of the *merkabah* is the Song of Solomon 6:10 ("terrible as an army with banners"). Responding to this text, the *Midrash Rabbah* comments: "Shall I say that just as the sun and moon do not inspire fear, so Israel? Not so, since it says, TERRIBLE AS AN ARMY WITH BANNERS: like the bannered hosts of heaven, such as Michael and his host and Gabriel and his host. How do we know that they inspire fear? Because it says, *As for their rings, they were high and they were dreadful*" (IX, 268–269; cf. Ezek. 1:18). Riding forth in His war chariot, God parts the Red Sea to overwhelm Pharaoh (IX, 68–70). He also descends in His celestial chariot to give His laws on Sinai, and, having bestowed His laws, He returns to heaven in His chariot. For the *Midrash Rabbah* this is nothing less than God's "state-carriage" in which He rides and which is drawn by the *hayyot* that propel it forward (III, 60–61, 487, 504).[22]

22. As Halperin, *Faces*, pp. 289–322, has amply demonstrated, the *merkabah* has close affinities in the interpretive traditions with the Sinai theophany and the festivals surrounding it. See *Piska* 20 in the *Pesikta Rabbati: Discourses for Feasts, Fasts, and Special Sabbaths*, trans. William G. Braude, 2 vols. (New Haven: Yale University Press, 1968), I, 396–411. Compare also the Ascension of Moses in the *Gedullat Mosheh*. The document is summarized by Louis Ginzburg in *The Legends of the Jews*, trans. Henrietta Szold, 7 vols. (Philadelphia: Jewish Publication Society of America, 1913), II, 304–316, V, 416–419.

So difficult is it to bear God's throne and to draw His chariot that the *ḥayyot* perspire under the burden, a perspiration that, as indicated earlier in the discussion of the *Ḥagigah*, is a fiery river (cf. Dan. 7:10). Nonetheless, the *ḥayyot* that bear the throne are nourished by the splendor of the Shekhinah (VII, 201–202; III, 541).

The outlook made evident here suggests that midrashic commentary, like talmudic commentary, engendered a complex mythology of the *merkabah*. By means of that mythology the commentators not only bestowed meaning and significance upon the events of biblical history but structured those events to accord with a theophany that proved to be of fundamental import in the portrayal of the individual's encounter with the divine. Such was the *maʿaseh merkabah* in the hands of those interpreters whose collective insights constitute the midrashim.

Complementing and augmenting the midrashic commentaries considered above are a number of related texts that bring the *merkabah* into even greater focus as an exegetical enterprise. These texts suggest how widely the stock of mythological ideas surrounding the *merkabah* was disseminated in the traditions of Judaica throughout the Middle Ages. One text is particularly significant as a means of extending our understanding of the transformations that the *merkabah* underwent among the medieval exegetes. This is the *Re'iyyot Yeḥezk'el* (*Visions of Ezekiel*), one of the documents found in the Cairo *Genizah*. Probably dating from the fourth or fifth century c.e., the text has been designated among the earliest examples of *merkabah* literature as a separate, identifiable category of Jewish mysticism.[23] As such, it is a "mystical midrash," one that draws upon the exegetical assumptions of midrashic activity and reflects that sense of divine transcendence normally associated with the mystical texts.[24] As a commentary on the *merkabah*, it projects its own universe, distinguished both by complex structures and an elaborate terminology.

Approaching the *merkabah* as cosmic entity, it conceives a world

23. References are to the translation in *Jewish Mystical Testimonies*, ed. Louis Jacobs (New York: Schocken Books, 1976), pp. 26–34, which has been compared with that in Halperin, *Faces*, pp. 264–268. The Hebrew text with notes by Ithamar Gruenwald is in *Temerin* 1 (1972): 101–139. See also A. Marmorstein, "A Fragment of the Visions of Ezekiel," *JQR* 8 (1917–1918): 367–378. Halperin questions the customary dating of the text, *Faces*, pp. 268–277.

24. Ithamar Gruenwald, *Apocalyptic and Merkavah Mysticism* (Leiden: E. J. Brill, 1980), p. 134.

in which what is above is mirrored in what is below.[25] Accordingly, it suggests that the visionary experience is a seeing that encompasses the subterranean realm as well as the celestial realm. In fact, it is the subterranean realm that is revealed to Ezekiel first in his encounter with the *merkabah*. Thus, in the revelation of the *merkabah* the Holy One "opened seven compartments down below" for Ezekiel to "gaze into." These compartments include the following: *'Adamah* (Ground); *'Erets* (Earth), *Ḥeled* (World), *Neshiyyah* (Forgetfulness), *Dumah* (Silence), *She'ol* (Pit), and *Tit ha-Yaven* (Miry Clay). In the biblical references that the text invokes, each of these designations is significant and suggestive. *'Adamah*, *'Erets*, and *She'ol* recall the destruction of Korah and his followers because they have despised the Lord: the earth opens its mouth and swallows them up as they go down alive into the pit (Num. 16:30–35).

Drawn from Psalms, all the other references are in accord with this idea. *Ḥeled* alludes to what will become of those who do not heed the fate of the ungodly (Ps. 49:2); *Neshiyyah* to the desire to be reclaimed from the realm of the underworld (Ps. 88:13); *Dumah* to the suffering associated with being exiled to the realm of silence (Ps. 115:17); and *Tit ha-Yaven* to the experience of one who has been reclaimed from that realm (Ps. 40:3). The seer is made to behold this subterranean world so that, remembering both his mortality and his allegiance to One who brought him out of the pit, he might "see all that is on high." In a remarkable gesture that approaches the celestial realm by means of its opposite, the text provides its own theodicy as an underlying factor in its vision of the *merkabah*.[26]

Having established this preparatory dimension, the document then declares that the Holy One opened to Ezekiel the seven heavens and revealed the Power (*geburah*). Even these he does not

25. "While the actual divisions [of the netherworld] are found in other texts, the idea that Ezekiel saw his vision of the world on high through the seven compartments of the netherworld is peculiar to our text." Jacobs, *Jewish Mystical Testimonies*, citing Gruenwald, p. 33.

26. Reinforcing the underworld dimension of its outlook, the text comments that Ezekiel is shown "the primordial waters" and "the mountain beneath the sea from when the sacred vessels of the Temple will be restored in the future." Whatever the meanings implicit in these enigmatic images, they do bring into focus ideas latent in Ezekiel's own vision, ideas that invite us to conceive the prophet as one intimately concerned with the cosmogonic act of taming the primeval waters in the creation of the universe, on the one hand, and with the eschatological act of envisioning the restoration of the Temple, on the other. See Halperin's detailed explanation in Appendix IV to *Faces*, pp. 494–498.

behold directly, however. In what amounts to a kind of Neoplatonic formulation of the visionary process, the document offers a parable to suggest what Ezekiel beheld and how he saw:

> A parable was told. To what can this [the vision of the *merkabah*] be compared? To a man who visited his barber. After the barber had cut his hair he gave him a mirror [*mar'ah*] in which to look. As he was looking into the mirror the king passed by and he saw the king and his armies passing by the door (reflected in the mirror). The barber said to him: Look behind you and you will see the king. The man replied: I have already seen. Thus Ezekiel stood beside the river Chebar gazing into the water and the seven heavens were opened to him so that he saw the Glory of the Holy One, blessed be He, the *ḥayyot*, the ministering angels, the angelic hosts, the seraphim, those of sparkling wings, all attached to the *merkabah*. They passed by in heaven while Ezekiel saw them (reflected) in the water. Hence the verse says: "by the river Chebar." (Ezek. 1:1)

The parable is interesting because, in true aggadic fashion, it reformulates the visionary experience as story. Doing so, it paradoxically reinforces the profundity of the experience by domesticating it with humor. The humor is one that ironically draws upon the act of self-admiration as a means of beholding that which is "other," that is, God and His retinue. This vision can be seen only in a reflected form, that is, only as in a mirror (*mar'ah*), here, invoked as a metaphor for Ezekiel's looking into the river Chebar.[27] Reinterpreting the original event and recontextualizing it as parable, the text drives home the point that what the prophet sees is only a reflection of what is: God and His retinue are never beheld directly. More than that, they are seen only in the context of the subterranean world that anticipates and mirrors their revelation.

Corresponding to the seven compartments of the subterranean world, the seven compartments or heavens that Ezekiel beholds in reflected form are named (*Shamayyim, Shemei ha-Shamayyim, Zevul, Arafel, Sheḥakim, 'Arabot,* and *Kisse' ha-Kabod*), and each has its

27. According to Gruenwald, the reference to the mirror likewise suggests the additional idea that the *merkabah* mystics employed the technique of gazing into a mirror or into water before embarking on their ascents. Jacobs, *Jewish Mystical Testimonies,* however, questions this interpretation (p. 33).

functions and associations.[28] *Shamayyim* is associated with the watery firmament as the place of the sun, moon, and stars; *Shemei ha-Shamayyim* is the heaven of heavens, where the angels perform the *kedushah*; *Zevul* is associated with the theurgical use of divine names (such as *Metatron*); *'Arafel* is associated with the canopy of the Torah; *Sheḥakim* is the place of "the rebuilt Jerusalem, the Temple and the Sanctuary, the Testimony, the Ark, the *Menorah*, the Table, the sacred vessels and all the adornments of the Temple together with the Manna that was eaten by the Israelites"; *'Arabot* contains the treasurehouses of blessing, peace, the souls of the righteous and the unborn, as well as both the punishments reserved for the wicked and the rewards for the righteous; finally, the *Kisse' ha-Kabod* is associated with the Throne of Glory, which contains the *ḥayyot* and the "great chariot upon which the Holy One, blessed be He, will descend in the future to judge all the nations, concerning which Isaiah said: 'For, behold, the Lord will come in fire, And His chariots shall be like the whirlwind' [Isa. 66:15]." In accord with the function that is assigned to it, this chariot appropriately has a name: it is called *Markabot 'Esh va-Sa'arah* (Chariots of Fire and Whirlwind). The account of the seven heavens, then, culminates in the apocalyptic and the eschatological.

From the perspective of the chariot that one finds in the seventh heaven, moreover, what is particularly unique about the *Re'iyyot Yeḥezk'el* is the idea that not just the seventh heaven contains a chariot. If the chariot of chariots is to be found in the highest of heavens, each of the other heavens likewise contains its own *merkabah*, and each *merkabah* has not only its own name but its own biblical associations, culminating in those that distinguish the chariot of chariots in the seventh heaven.[29] Such is the bearing that the *ma'aseh merkabah* assumes in the *Re'iyyot Yeḥezk'el*. As a mystical midrash that reflects its own unique understanding of Ezekiel's inaugural vision, this document provides additional insight into

28. Suggesting the talmudic account, the journey from one heaven to the next is five hundred years. Marmorstein ("A Fragment," p. 372) appropriately observes that "the measure given between the heavens is also to be found in Greek philosophy," as well as in the pseudepigrapha and in the rabbinical sources. "The teaching that to travel from earth to heaven takes five hundred years is . . . identical with Plato's reckoning of the world year." Cf. *III Baruch* 2:5.

29. The chariot of the first heaven is called "steed"; that of the second "horses"; that of the third "escort"; that of the fourth "chariot of kings"; that of the fifth "cherubim"; and that of the sixth "cloud." See Halperin's discussion, *Faces*, pp. 284–288, 503–504.

the range and complexity of interpretations that this vision inspired in the Middle Ages.

In the enactment of those interpretations, one fact remains
clear. The impulse to create new hermeneutical contexts as a
means of suggesting a multiplicity of dimensions and approaches
to the originary event proved to be overwhelming from the outset.
What did Ezekiel see? What did his vision mean? How does one
deal with the text of the vision, where it begins and where it ends,
how it is to be read, the dangers, as well as the rewards, of reading
it, who is entitled to read it and who not? How does it help us to
come to terms with the nature of the universe, the course of
history, matters of theology, theodicy, individual experience, our
own dreams, our need to transcend human limits, the desire for
power? These and other considerations underlie the transformations that the visionary experience is made to undergo in the
infinite variety of its formulations. Just as the apocalyptic and
mystical accounts address some of these issues in their recreation
of the vision, the talmudic and midrashic accounts address others.
The concerns and methodologies of these accounts overlap. But
they all involve that fundamental act of acculturation that Amos
Wilder speaks of in his reference to "the progressive culturizing
of the initial vision." In our account of this acculturation in the
Middle Ages, a number of other documents might be cited and
explored.[30] The foregoing, however, should be sufficient to suggest the manner in which those texts that fall under the heading
of midrashic commentary became the source of a renewed appreciation of the meaning and significance of the *merkabah*.

III

Moving from the anonymity and pseudonymity of talmudic and
midrashic commentary to the cross-cultural milieus of individual

30. One such document is the *Pirke de Rabbi Eliezer*, a ninth-century pseudepigraphon
attributed to the Tanna Rabbi Eliezer ben Hyrkanos, a pupil of Rabbi Jochanan ben Zakkai.
See the 1919 translation of Gerald Friedlander, *Pirke de Rabbi Eliezer (The Chapters of Rabbi
Eliezer the Great) According to the Text of the Manuscript Belonging to Abraham Epstein of Vienna*
(New York: Hermon Press, 1965). For a later restatement of the *merkabah* material covered
in the *Pirke*, see Eleazar ben Asher ha-Levi (fourteenth century), *The Chronicles of Jerahmeel;
or, The Hebrew Bible Historiale*, trans. M. Gaster (New York: Ktav, 1971).

authorship in the later Middle Ages, we shall now concern ourselves with two major figures, roughly contemporaneous: Eleazar
ben Jehuda of Worms (ca. 1160–1238 C.E.) and Moses ben Maimon or Maimonides (1135–1204 C.E.). The products of radically
different cultural milieus, these two figures will provide additional
insight into the processes of transformation undergone by the
merkabah as a distinct subject of speculation in medieval thought.
Whereas the deliberations of Eleazar spring from the *hasidic* environment of Germanic Jewry, those of Maimonides are the product of the philosophical predilections grounded in the culture of
Islamic Spain. Approaching the *merkabah* from their own unique
points of view, Eleazar, on the one hand, and Maimonides, on the
other, will suggest how the visionary assumed renewed life in
diverse interpretive environments.

A major representative of the *hasidei ashkanaz* (devout of Germany) that flourished between 1150 and 1250, Eleazar produced
a number of important works, both halakhic and mystical.[31] Because of their ties with the *hasidic* ideals manifested in this early
movement among German Jewry, these works reflect an intense
concern with the pietistic dimensions (*hasidut*) of religious observ-
ance. According to this pietistic point of view, the seeker after
visions is at once the keeper of the holy mysteries but, at the same
time, a figure for whom the virtues of humility, restraint, and self-
denial assume greater import than the pride that infuses the *merkabah* visionary in the mystical presence of God. In place of the
ecstatic seer, whose mystical élan transports him beyond all bar-
riers and obstacles to the steps of the celestial throne, one discovers
the meditative devotee, immersed in humble contemplation of the
Omnipresent Infinite.[32]

Equally important to the outlook expressed by the *hasidei ashkanaz* in general and the works of Eleazar in particular is an emphasis upon the act of speculation. Indeed, "the scope and variety
of *hasidic* speculation is far greater than that of the old *merkabah*
mysticism." Whereas earlier *merkabah* visions left little room for
exegetical speculation, the enactment of textual hermeneutics oc-

31. For an enlightening treatment of both the *hasidei ashkanaz* and Eleazor of Worms,
see Scholem's chapter "Hasidism in Mediaeval Germany" in *Major Trends*, pp. 80–118. For
a full study of the *hasidei ashkanaz*, see Joseph Dan, *The Esoteric Theology of Ashkenazi Hasidim*
[in Hebrew] (Jerusalem: Mosad Bialik, 1968).
32. Scholem, *Major Trends*, p. 98.

cupies a central place among the *ḥasidim*. Textuality is at the very heart of this point of view.[33] As one in whom this point of view finds profound expression, Eleazar of Worms affords remarkable insight into the workings of the *merkabah* as a speculative enterprise. One need only glance at Eleazar's commentaries on the *merkabah* to confirm this observation. In Eleazar of Worms both the *merkabah* and the way it is conceived assume a unique and fascinating form.

For Eleazar an understanding of the *merkabah* involves a knowledge of what he playfully calls the "science of the nut [*ḥochmat ha-'egoz*]."[34] "Anyone who does not know the mystical meaning of the nut," declares Eleazar, "does not know the *maʿaseh merkabah*" (p. 164). As a means of disclosing the science of the nut, Eleazar approaches the *merkabah* through an examination of a passage from the Song of Songs: "I went down into the garden of nuts" (6:11). Suggesting both the idea of the *yordei merkabah* ("I went down [*yaradeti*]") and the concept of *pardes* (garden), this passage is most appropriate. As Alexander Altmann with corresponding playfulness observes, the passage affords Eleazar a wonderful opportunity to disclose the secrets of the *merkabah*, as it were, "in a nutshell."[35]

The effect is to localize the *merkabah*, to contain it, and finally to textualize it, so that, by means of an elaborate process of exegesis, its meanings can be analyzed. Despite this act of localization, containment, and textualization, however, the analysis itself is profoundly obscure and abstruse. Like the vision that it purports to illuminate, the analysis effectively occludes attempts at comprehension at the very point of offering to facilitate understanding. The result is a process that ostensibly engages in a step-by-step laying bare of meaning, while it paradoxically (indeed, methodically) confounds meaning in the implementation of that process. The nut itself is the objective correlative through which this process is implemented.

Conceiving the nut as an object with four segments and a ridge

33. Ibid., pp. 90, 101.

34. This "science" is treated in Altmann's illuminating essay "Eleazar of Worms' Symbol of the Merkabah," *Studies in Religious Philosophy and Mysticism* (Ithaca, N. Y.: Cornell University Press, 1969), pp. 160–171. This study contains the translations used in the present analysis, including passages from *Ḥokhmat ha-Nefesh, Shaʾar Sod ha-Merkabah*, and *Hilḥot ha-Kisseʾ*, as well as manuscript material. Page references in my text are to these translations.

35. Altmann, "Eleazar of Worms' Symbol," p. 168.

in its center, Eleazar engages in a fourfold analysis that addresses each of the segments and what they signify. In preparation for this fourfold analysis, he begins by examining the outer shell of the nut. This, he observes, is like the Scroll of the Torah, which covers the secrets within. The outer shell likewise corresponds to "the heaven which encompasses everything." In short, the nut as a whole represents the book of the universe in which are to be read the most profound of mysteries. At the same time the outer shell of the nut is green and bitter to the taste like the salty ocean. This bitterness suggests the admonitions and punishments that await those who disregard the sacred laws of the Torah. Thus, "even as the shell of the nut, because it is bitter, protects the kernel against worms, seeing that worms are found only in sweet things, so do the admonitions and punishments protect the commandments."

As for the four segments within, Eleazar says that they are in the center of the kernel and are divided in four directions like the camps of Israel. "The kernel is shaped like four double-columns corresponding to the four camps." These camps, in turn, find their counterparts in the four *ḥayyot*, and the ridge or stalk in the center is raised to suggest the throne. The edible fruit within the nut, finally, is white "even as *His throne was flames of fire* [Dan. 7:9]" (pp. 163–164). The concept of eating the fruit of the nut returns us, of course, to the biblical and talmudic notion of the *merkabah* as a text to be consumed by the interpreter who is empowered to transform it in the process of consumption.

In corresponding analyses Eleazar elaborates still further his interpretation of the nut. Like the outer shell that surrounds the nut, the glory of God in Ezekiel's vision is protected by the brightness of fire. Beneath the outer shell there are two other shells that are separate but stick together when the nut is dry. In this respect the outer shell is like the whirlwind that Ezekiel beholds, and the two inner shells are like the great cloud contained within the whirlwind. The fruit of the nut is placed within these two shells, as the internal theophany of enthronement with its fourfold *ḥayyot* is situated within the whirlwind with its great cloud. The four faces of the *ḥayyot* are represented by the four heads of the kernel. The wings of the *ḥayyot*, embodied in the four segments of the nut, are beneath these four faces. Represented by the stalk, which is cut, the throne at the center corresponds to the throne of justice and the throne of mercy. The nut itself is round, a fact that suggests the wheels of the *merkabah*, and the soft shell attached to the fruit suggests the wheel within the wheel. "The side of the kernel facing towards the outer shell is red, green and yellow like the [*rain*]*bow*."

Eleazar attributes gender designations to the nut as well. The four segments or compartments of the nut are female; in the center of them rises the stalk as a throne. This is the *membrum virile*. The fruit of the compartments sucks some bitterness from the shell, so that no worms are found in the nut. "In case, however, one removes the bitter shell before the kernel has ripened and whilst it is still on the tree, worms will be found to develop in the kernel." The virginity of the nut will then have been violated. In order to keep the nut inviolate, "a black shell divides the kernel from the head of the *membrum virile*." As an expression of *ḥasidic* piety, Eleazar likens this black shell to "the strap of the *tefillin* upon the head of the *kabod*." In keeping with this sense of piety, he maintains that, just as beneath the kernel there is a space, so "beneath the throne of glory is a space like an ark, and in it are the souls of the righteous." "He who knoweth the science of the nut," Eleazar concludes, "will know the depth of the *Merkabah*" (pp. 165–167).

In its account of Eleazar's *merkabah* speculations, the foregoing falls short of suggesting the complexities involved in the kinds of correspondences that Eleazar conceives. If Eleazar's purpose is to introduce one to the mysteries of the *merkabah*, the "window" (to use his term) that he opens into the fruit of the nut still reflects like a glass darkly rather than allowing us to encounter the inner glory face to face. But this is part of Eleazar's implied purpose. The very act of implementing his methodology of step-by-step correspondences undermines the appearance of logical analysis that his methodology suggests. The fourfold nature of the analysis as a whole gives every appearance of deploying the kind of four-fold methodology familiar to medieval rabbinical interpretation. In fact, that mode of interpretive response drew upon the concepts underlying the *merkabah* itself in order to implement its methodological scheme.[36] Whether or not Eleazar had such an approach in mind as he set about to lay bare the mysteries of the nut, his hermeneutics remains true to the spirit of the original vision, which is as inscrutable in his hands as in the hands of the

36. This idea will be discussed in greater detail in the next chapter.

prophet through whom the originary content of the vision is finally and indeed triumphantly impenetrable.

If Eleazar of Worms suggests one form that the *merkabah* as speculative enterprise assumed toward the end of the twelfth century, Moses Maimonides represents still another form. Emerging from the culture of Islamic Spain and influenced by the crosscurrents of thought and custom that followed him into Morocco and Egypt, Maimonides is not only one of the foremost intellectual figures of medieval Judaism but a scholar who exerted a profound influence on the philosophers and exegetes who followed in his path. As a result of a vast erudition indebted to Arabic renderings of Greek philosophical thought, Maimonides infused into the *merkabah* his own sense of what constitutes the visionary mode as a speculative enterprise. Avowing throughout his works a compelling interest in the *merkabah*, he approached that phenomenon in a manner that might accord with his own philosophical predilections.

His major philosophical work, the *Moreh Nebukhim* or *The Guide of the Perplexed* (composed between ca. 1176 and 1190), represents his most penetrating analysis of the subject.[37] According to the expressed intention of the introduction to the third (and final) part of the *Guide*, "the chief aim of this Treatise is to explain what can be explained of the *Account of the Beginning* and the *Account of the Chariot*" (Introduction to Part III). Undertaking such an explanation, Maimonides is fully aware of the awesome responsibility he has assumed. Alluding to the *Mishneh Torah*, his earlier codification of Jewish law, he says: "We have already made it clear that these matters belong to *the mysteries of the Torah*," the disclosure of which renders the commentator potentially culpable of violating a divine secret to those who are not worthy or prepared to receive it.[38]

Accordingly, the Sages have already revealed how secret the *Account of the Chariot* was and how alien to the mind of the multitude. Furthermore, one must acknowledge that even that portion

37. References in my text are to *The Guide of the Perplexed*, trans. Shlomo Pines (Chicago: University of Chicago Press, 1963). Originally composed in Arabic, the *Guide* was shortly thereafter translated into Hebrew as *Moreh Nebukhim*.

38. Maimonides engaged in extensive discussions of the *maʿaseh merkabah* and *maʿaseh bereʾshit* in the *Sefer Hanada* (*Book of Knowledge*) prefaced to his *Mishneh Torah* (composed between 1168 and 1178). See *The Mishneh Torah*, ed. Moses Hyamson, 2 vols. (New York: Bloch, 1947–1949).

of it that is discernible to him who is capable of understanding it is subject to "a legal prohibition against its being taught and explained except orally to one man having certain stated qualities, and even to that one only the *chapter headings* may be mentioned." It is as the result of such injunctions, observes Maimonides, that "the knowledge of this matter has ceased to exist in the entire religious community, so that nothing great or small remains of it." Such an outcome was inevitable, because "this knowledge was only transmitted from one chief to another and has never been set down in writing" (Introduction to Part III). Whether or not Maimonides is being deliberately hyperbolical in emphasizing the alleged disappearance of the *maʿaseh merkabah* from the religious community and in providing an explanation for that disappearance based upon the talmudic notion of oral transmission among a very select circle, his approach serves to underscore his purpose of being the repository of a secret knowledge that he now plans to share with an audience fit to receive it.[39]

In short, Maimonides is assuming the exalted and privileged role of the ancient purveyors of the *merkabah*. He justifies such an act by saying that "if I had omitted setting down something of that which has appeared to me as clear, so that the knowledge would perish when I perish, as is inevitable, I should have considered that conduct as extremely cowardly." It is for this reason that he has elected to share his knowledge and to enlighten all those who are perplexed about the true meaning of the *maʿaseh merkabah*. As the new authority in such matters, he makes it clear that his knowledge is derived neither from "divine revelation" nor from the secret oral instruction of a specific teacher. Rather, he acknowledges that "the texts of the prophetic books and the dicta of the *Sages*, together with the speculative premises that I possess, showed me that things are indubitably so and so."

Adopting an entirely rationalistic approach in keeping with his philosophical outlook, he proposes to adhere strictly to the meanings implicit in the biblical text. "I shall," he says, "interpret to

---

39. Compare Maimonides's earlier statement: "Know that the many sciences devoted to establishing the truth regarding these matters [i.e., *The Account of the Beginning* and *The Account of the Chariot*] that have existed in our religious community have perished because of the length of the time that has passed, because of our being dominated by the pagan nations, and because . . . it is not permitted to divulge these matters to all people" (I.71). See Halperin, *Merkabah*, passim, for the "myth" of the *maʿaseh merkabah* as entirely a closed system of oral discourse.

you that which was said by *Ezekiel the prophet* ... in such a way that anyone who heard that interpretation would think that I do not say anything over and beyond what is indicated by the text, but that it is as if I translated words from one language to another or summarized the meaning of the external sense of the speech." Such an approach will emphasize the "utility" embodied in the truly informed interpretation of the *Account of the Chariot* (Introduction to Part III). This is the new *ma῾aseh merkabah*, one that restores to the text its original integrity and to the interpeter of the text the ability to understand the meanings it embodies.

Implicit in the outlook that Maimonides endorses is a science of interpretation that renders the most secret of doctrines accessible to those capable of receiving it, while ostensibly maintaining the sacrosanct nature of the traditions indebted to that doctrine. It is on this basis that Maimonides proceeds to discourse on the *Account of the Chariot*, along with its corresponding subject *The Account of the Beginning*. He does this first by making what he considers an all-important distinction between the two subjects: whereas *The Account of the Beginning* is identical with "natural science," *The Account of the Chariot* is identical with "divine science" (Introduction to Part I). The first encompasses the laws of the natural universe; the second embraces the laws of the divine world. What these two enterprises entail in the *Guide* is implicit in the nature of the discussions that focus upon them.

In his discussion of natural science, for example, Maimonides invokes such authorities as Plato and Aristotle to discuss first principles, the nature of matter and form, the elements, light and dark, generation and corruption, concepts of motion, astronomy of the spheres, and matters related to cosmogony in general.[40] Although mysterious in nature and often related in parables, these matters, Maimonides makes clear, have been the concern of philosophers from the very beginning. In the *Guide* Maimonides is now bringing to bear upon these matters his own enlightened point of view, one that benefits not only from the pagan traditions of the past but from the secret knowledge possessed only by that sage versed in the ways of *ma῾aseh bere᾽shit*.

If *The Account of the Beginning* embodies a physics of the natural

40. Maimonides's discussion of the principles underlying *The Account of the Beginning* appears in various forms throughout the *Guide*. See in particular the treatment of the concepts called "the first" and "the principle" in II.30. This chapter is interesting because it takes to task the *ma῾aseh bere᾽shit* of Rabbi Eliezer (cf. II.26).

universe, *The Account of the Chariot* embodies a metaphysics of the divine universe. The nature of this enterprise involves "the study concerning the totality of existence, the existence of the Creator, His knowledge, His attributes, the things that derive from Him, the angels, the soul, and the mind which is joined to man. Also that which comes after death."[41] In the *Guide* these matters are discussed throughout as aspects of divine science.[42] Once again, Maimonides draws upon the philosophical traditions of the past in order to delineate his sense of such topics, but because of the profound mysteries that these topics entail, he brings to bear that special knowledge bestowed only on that sage versed in the ways of *merkabah*. In his treatment of the divine science Maimonides makes it perfectly clear that what he proposes to discuss is potentially quite harmful.[43] One needs to be prepared to receive such matter; otherwise, he will be misled. Accordingly, Maimonides maintains that "he who is seen to be perfect in mind and to be formed for that high rank—that is to say, demonstrative speculation and true intellectual inferences—should be elevated step by step, either by someone who directs his attention or by himself, until he achieves his perfection" (I.33).

This step-by-step process of elevation to the higher reaches encompassed by the divine science involves not simply a moral and spiritual perfecting of the self: it is also curricular. One may not undertake to master the divine science without a thorough preparation in what precedes it. "Divine science," maintains Maimonides, "cannot become actual except after a study of natural science. This is so since natural science borders on divine science,

41. The statement comes from Maimonides's early *Commentary on the Mishnah* (1168), as cited in *Ezekiel/ A New Translation with a Commentary Anthologized from Talmudic, Midrashic and Rabbinic Sources*, ed. Rabbis Nosson Scherman and Meir Zlototwitz, Art Scroll Tanach Series (New York: Mesorah Publications, 1977), p. 69. See also the summary in the *Mishnah*, ed. Rabbis Nosson Scherman and Meir Zlotowitz, Art Scroll Mishnah Series (New York: Mesorah Publications, 1979), p. 24.

42. Among many examples, see the discussion of the concept of "riding" (a God who rides) in I.70 of the *Guide*. Beginning with an analysis of riding in its various forms, the discussion moves to the nature of *'arabot*, the highest of the seven heavens encompassing the universe. From the perspective of the *Ḥagigah*, God is said to be a rider on *'arabot*, one explanation of the *ma'aseh merkabah*. Maimonides discusses this idea in detail (particularly within the context of divine motion). Such detailed treatments of various aspects of the divine science (particularly as that science is manifested in individual words) permeate the *Guide*. Taken together, these treatments (embodying what Maimonides would call flashes of insight concerning the divine) form a unified whole.

43. "Know that to begin with this science is very harmful, I mean the divine science" (*Guide*, I.33).

and its study precedes that of divine science in time" (Introduction to Part I). In fact, Maimonides advocates an entire course of study in preparation for encountering the divine science. Thus, "it is certainly necessary," he says, "for whoever wishes to achieve human perfection to train himself at first in the art of logic, then in the mathematical sciences according to the proper order, then in the natural sciences, and after that in the divine science" (I.34). This is Maimonides's *quadrivium*: moving from logic through mathematics to physics and finally metaphysics, one arrives at an understanding of those sciences that encompass the *ma'aseh be-re'shit*, on the one hand, and the *ma'aseh merkabah*, on the other. Beyond such heights no one can possibly go.

Toward the end of his treatise Maimonides conceives of this idea by way of an elaborate but fascinating parable:

> I say then: The ruler is in his palace, and all his subjects are partly within the city and partly outside the city. Of those who are within the city, some have turned their backs upon the ruler's habitation, their faces being turned another way. Others seek to reach the ruler's habitation, turn toward it, and desire to enter it and to stand before him, but up to now they have not yet seen the wall of the habitation. Some of those who seek to reach it have come up to the habitation and walk around it searching for its gate. Some of them have entered the gate and walk about in the antechambers. Some of them have entered the inner court of the habitation and have come to be with the king, in one and the same place with him, namely, in the ruler's habitation. But their having come into the inner part of the habitation does not mean that they see the ruler or speak to him. For after their coming into the inner part of the habitation, it is indispensable that they should make another effort; then they will be in the presence of the ruler, see him from afar or from nearby, or hear the ruler's speech or speak to him. (III.51)

Recalling both in spirit and in circumstance the allegory of the cave in Plato's *Republic* (7.514–518), the parable of Maimonides is to be interpreted according to the *quadrivium* embodied in the true study of the *merkabah*. "As long as you are engaged in studying the mathematical sciences and the art of logic, you are one of those who walk around the house searching for its gate," observes Maimonides. "If, however, you have understood the natural things, you have entered the habitation and are walking in the antechambers. If, however, you have achieved perfection in the natural things and have understood divine science, you have entered into the ruler's place *into the inner court* and are with him in one habitation. This is the rank of the men of science; they, however, are of different grades of perfection." Those who have attained the highest grade are themselves prophets: having achieved perfection in the divine science, they "turn wholly toward God" and "renounce what is other than He" (III.51).

As Maimonides makes clear, that which underlies both the parable and his interpretation of it is the talmudic account of the four who "entered the 'Garden'," that is, penetrated into the presence chambers of the Enthroned Figure who is the focus of the *maʿaseh merkabah*.[44] Undergoing the *quadrivium* that the full understanding of the *merkabah* entails, one is able to stand in the presence of the ruler, to behold him, and finally to enter into discourse with him. For Maimonides, the divine science represents the very pinnacle by which this process is realized, the consummation of all that a knowledge of God's ways has to offer. Having achieved that pinnacle, one knows all and experiences all: one's education is complete. It is the achievement of this pinnacle that *The Guide of the Perplexed* sets out to make possible in its disclosure of the secret knowledge to those capable of receiving it.

The supreme moment of that disclosure occurs in the third part of the treatise. Having reiterated his interpretive outlook toward the *merkabah* in the introduction to the third part, Maimonides next proceeds to a detailed explication of the text upon which *The Account of the Chariot* is based. He begins first with an account of the *ḥayyot*, which, according to the biblical text, are consummated in *"the face of a man."* The purpose here is to suggest that, despite the apparent strangeness of the vision, it resolves itself finally in a human form. With Maimonides one encounters a humanizing of vision (III.1–2). Along with this humanizing, there occurs in Maimonides an emphasis upon the utility of what the prophet beholds. Focusing upon the hands of the living creatures, Maimonides observes that "a man's hands are indubitably formed as they are in order to be engaged in the arts of craftsmanship" (III.2). Complementing this humanistic and utilitarian approach is a concern with what might be called kinetics, a concern that, in

---

44. Explaining the plight of those who "walk around the house searching for its gate," Maimonides invokes the talmudic statement: *"Ben Zoma is still outside,"* a reference to one of the four who was unable to realize what the "Garden" had to offer (III.51). (See *Ḥagigah* 14b–15a, particularly with regard to Ben Zoma's placement outside the Temple Mount.)

fact, is all-pervasive in the *Guide* as it undertakes to explore the philosophical antecedents of the concept of motion.

According to Maimonides, the motion of the living creatures (that of running and retracing their path) is undertaken according to a "divine purpose." Motion accords with the will of God. Thus, says Maimonides, the direction in which God wishes the living creatures to go has been "determined"; the living creatures take the direction that God wishes them to take; and the divine will is "constant" regarding this direction. The concept of motion implicit in the living creatures is, for Maimonides, correspondingly operative in the wheels, but, unlike the living creatures, the wheels are propelled not from any spirit latent within them but as the result of the creatures themselves. If the wheels reflect God's will, they do so through the agency of the creatures. Accordingly, "the relation of a *wheel* to a *living creature* could be likened," suggests Maimonides, "to what happens when one ties an inanimate body to the hands and the feet of a living being: every time the living being moves, the piece of timber or the stone tied to a limb of that living being moves likewise" (III.2). The point of all this is to suggest the way the divine science operates according to its own laws: embodied in that science is what might be called a technology of vision, one that manifests itself in distinctions of form, utility, motion, and agency. In short, Maimonides approaches the *maʿaseh merkabah* the way a philosopher would approach a problem in metaphysics, but for the Rambam this is a metaphysics of the highest order.

Moving from these metaphysical concerns to the way in which the *merkabah* is perceived by the prophet, Maimonides next addresses himself to the nature of the visionary experience, a topic that, in fact, concerns him throughout the *Guide*.[45] Among those aspects to which one's attention should be directed, observes Maimonides, is Ezekiel's expression "*visions of God*" (1:1). Ezekiel "does not say *vision*, in the singular, but *visions*, because there were many apprehensions differing in species; I mean to say three apprehensions, that of the *wheels*, that of the *living creatures*, and that of the *man*, who is above the *living creatures*" (III.5). Each of these visions is preceded by the phrase "*and I saw*," which signifies the announcement of a new visionary event. According to Maimonides, this phrase, as it is repeated from one verse to the next,

45. See, e.g., II.41–46.

represents the so-called chapter headings referred to in the Mishnah. Although there is apparently some disagreement among the ancient rabbinical compilers of the Mishnah which occurrence of the phrase (the first, the second, or the third) signals the actual commencement of *The Account of the Chariot,* Maimonides feels that the *merkabah* encompasses all three visionary events announced by the repeated phrase.

In any case, Maimonides sees in the progression from "wheels" to "creatures" to "man" a tripartite movement from lower to higher, a heuristic scale, as it were, toward the moment of ultimate perception. It is accordingly clear, he says,

> that there were various apprehensions to which attention is drawn by the expression: *And I saw, And I saw, And I saw*: that these signified different degrees; and that the last apprehension, that referred to in the words: *And I saw as the color of ḥashmal* [Ezek. 1:27]—I mean the apprehension of the form of the divided man of which it is said: *From the appearance of his loins and upward, and from the appearance of his loins and downward*—is the ultimate perception and the highest of all. (III.5)

For Maimonides, then, the *maʿaseh merkabah* is consummated through a tripartite progression of discovery, in the Enthroned Figure enveloped in the *ḥashmal.* To arrive at that moment in the ascent from visionary event to visionary event is to undergo the most profound of hermeneutical experiences, one reserved only for the sagest of the sage. It is toward the consummation of this experience that *The Guide of the Perplexed* moves in its exposition of the "sciences" that constitute *The Account of the Beginning,* on the one hand, and *The Account of the Chariot,* on the other.

In this respect the *Guide* becomes a key enabling one to enter areas the gates to which were sealed. When these gates are opened and these areas entered, "the souls will find rest therin, the eyes will be delighted, and the bodies will be eased of their toil and of their labor" (Introduction to Part I). Accordingly, Maimonides concludes his discussion of the *merkabah* by observing: "We have thus given you ... such *chapter headings* that if you combine the *headings* there will emerge from them a whole that is useful with regard to this theme." Combining or completing the chapter headings (that is, the visionary events contained within them) will yield an understanding of the vision in its entirety. If one considers everything that has been said in the treatise up to the present chapter, Maimonides observes, "the subject in its entirety will become clear." With that assertion Maimonides closes his discourse on *The Account of the Chariot* by issuing the following disclaimer: "Do not hope that, after this chapter, you will hear from me even a single word about this subject, be it as an explicit statement or in a flashlike allusion. For everything that it is possible to say about this has been said; I have even plunged deep into this with temerity" (III. 7). The pronouncement is that of both the hermeneut and the oracle: the prophet has concluded with a final flourish that precludes further comment. If the disciple is still perplexed, his perplexity is the result not of the master's inability to explain but of his own interpretive shortcomings.

Such categorical pronouncements are the hallmark of one for whom the act of interpretation is tantamount to the reenactment of the event that is being interpreted. The hermeneut becomes the prophet, and *The Account of the Chariot* is now the property of one who reconceives it (that is, reenvisions it) in his own terms. That reconception is an appropriation: the *merkabah* is no longer Ezekiel's nor even that of the Tannaim who first codified it as such. It now belongs to the Rambam, who has plumbed its depths and has made it his own.

In Maimonides the *merkabah* assumes a metaphysical identity unlike any identity it has heretofore possessed. Previously, it existed as story. As such, its presence was aggadic. Such is the way the talmudists and midrashists reformulated the halakhic character of its codification in the Mishnah. Now, it exists as "demonstrative speculation" and "intellectual inference" (to use Maimonides's own terms). Moving from the text of the prophecy to the dicta of the sages, Maimonides arrives at his own speculative outlook that is founded upon an act of "translating" (an idea already implicit in the concept of *hermēneuō*) as from one language to another. To understand Maimonides's interpretation is to understand his new language. It is a language understood only after a course of study that encompasses a *quadrivium* that proceeds from logic to mathematics and from there to physics and metaphysics. Only after having undergone such a course of study will one be able to appreciate the concepts of form, utility, motion, agency, and perception that the vision embodies.

Approaching the vision from these perspectives, one will be able to appreciate the *merkabah* in a way that it has not been appreciated before. For what Maimonides provides is a new *halakhah*, with its own *merkabah* and its own mode of perception. Espousing that *halakhah*, Maimonides becomes a sage who fosters an interpretive community that is uniquely of his calling. Whether it is the individual known as Rabbi Joseph ben Judah to whom the *Guide* is addressed or an entire line of interpreters with a professed allegiance to the ways of their master, this is an interpretive community consistent in its outlook with the speculative traditions that Maimonides embodies.[46]

Concern with the category of speculative *merkabah* has demonstrated the degree to which the visionary mode is adaptable to an entire range of interpretive strategies. As we trace the course of those strategies throughout the centuries, we behold the talmudic and midrashic masters, on the one hand, and the philosophers, on the other, bestowing on the visionary a renewed sense of its own significance as speculative enterprise. We are made to think once again of the wonderful story concerning ben Azzai who is sitting and meditating on the Tanakh, while fire plays around him. Like ben Azzai, those who speculate on the originary text are exploring the secrets of the divine Chariot. Like ben Azzai, they, too, are linking up the words of the Torah with those of the Prophets and those of the Prophets with those of the Writings, an act that causes the originary text to become the well-spring of speculative thought. In their own way, the interpreters of the originary text assume a numinous quality as well: they, too, have fire playing about them. They assume the originary role of one who invents the text. Doing so, they promote a new order of knowing, one in which the interpreter becomes the originator and the interpretation supersedes all other acts. If such is true of speculative *merkabah*, it is, as we shall see, no less true of esoteric *merkabah*. From both points of view, the visionary mode is seen to flourish.

46. For an account of Rabbi Joseph ben Judah, see the Epistle Dedicatory to the *Guide*. Among the many disciples of Maimonides, one thinks of such thirteenth-century figures as Moses ben Nachman or Nachmanides (the Ramban), Isaac ibn Latif, Abraham Abulafia, and Moses ben Shem Tob de Leon. Extending the many insights of their master, these figures transformed the Rambam into a kabbalist. For a discussion of the philosophical-mystical dimensions of Maimonides's own thought as well as his influence on the mystical traditions, see David Blumenthal, "Maimonides' Intellectual Mysticism and the Superiority of the Prophecy of Moses," *Studies in Medieval Culture* 10 (1977): 51–67; and the discussions and readings in volume II of Blumenthal's *Understanding Jewish Mysticism* (New York: Ktav, 1982), passim.

～ Four

The Esoterics of Vision

I

Having explored the phenomenological and hermeneutical dimensions of the visionary mode, we may now consider that aspect of the *merkabah* reflected in the esoteric traditions customarily designated *kabbalah*. Although this designation has been loosely applied to the traditions of Jewish mysticism as a whole, I am reserving it as a term that is to be associated with the category of speculative and esoteric *merkabah*. But even here significant qualifications must be made, for *kabbalah* in some forms is as much concerned with the phenomenological or mystical dimensions of *merkabah* as it is with the speculative and esoteric dimensions. As we discussed much earlier, categories overlap, and it is inadvisable and even foolhardy to make rigid distinctions. In order to have some sense of what amounts to a unique formulation of the *merkabah* among certain generations of writers who looked upon themselves as engaging in a common enterprise, the designation of *kabbalah* seems most appropriate to apply to this dimension of the visionary mode, particularly as it was manifested in the later Middle Ages. Because the history and doctrines of *kabbalah* have already been amply explored by a host of scholars, there is little need to rehearse their findings here.[1] On the other hand, some

1. Among the numerous studies devoted to the subject, see in particular the works of Gershom Scholem, especially his *Kabbalah* (Jerusalem: Keter, 1974). My references are to the New American Library edition (New York, 1978). In addition to his *Major Trends in Jewish Mysticism* (New York: Schocken Books, 1954), see his *Ursprung und Anfänge der Kabbala* (Berlin: W. de Gruyter, 1962), newly translated by Allan Arkush and edited by R. J. Zwi Werblowsky as *Origins of the Kabbalah* (Princeton: Princeton University Press, 1987); and *On the Kabbalah and Its Symbolism*, trans. Ralph Manheim (New York: Schocken, 1965). Of major importance are G. Vajda's *Recherches sur la philosophie et la Kabbale dans la pensée juive du moyen-âge* (The Hague: Mouton, 1962) and the essays in Alexander Altmann,

sense of what is meant by this designation is in order before we proceed to a discussion of specific writers and texts in which the inaugural vision of Ezekiel assumes a renewed significance.

As that which implies "something handed down by tradition," *kabbalah* (from *kibbel*, "receive") is one of a number of terms that characterize the transformation of the *merkabah* into a unique subject of esoteric and theosophic speculation in the later Middle Ages. Emerging as a distinct entity in Provence, in southern France, during the latter part of the twelfth century, it reemerged in the thirteenth century as a fully conceived movement in northeastern Spain, especially in the kabbalist center in Gerona. During this period its primary exponents in France were such figures as the author of the *Sefer ha-Bahir* and Isaac the Blind, and in Spain such figures as Isaac ibn Latif, Azriel ben Menachem, Moses ben Nachman, Abraham Abulafia, Joseph Gikatilla, and Moses ben Shem Tob de Leon. In fourteenth-century Spain it found expression in the writings of Solomon ben Abraham Adret and Isaac ben Todros; at the same time, it spread into Italy, where it was reformulated in the works of such writers as Menachem Recanati. After the expulsion from Spain in 1492, it assumed compelling form in the sixteenth century in what became a major kabbalistic center, the Galilean city of Safed, where such major kabbalists as Moses ben Jacob Cordovero and, of course, Isaac Luria and his school flourished. Each of these figures has his own conception of *kabbalah*, a movement that was formulated and reformulated over the centuries. Although it is dangerous to generalize, we are still able to have a sense of the basic concepts normally associated with this movement. Because a knowledge of those concepts, as well

---

Studies in Religious Philosophy and Mysticism (Ithaca, N.Y.: Cornell University Press, 1969). More recently, see the important studies of Moshe Idel, particularly his major work *Kabbalah: New Perspectives* (New Haven: Yale University Press, 1988), which provides renewed emphasis upon the mystical and ecstatic dimensions of the subject while reassessing both the approach and some of the basic assumptions of Scholem's work. Earlier studies of interest include Adolph Franck, *The Kabbalah* (1843), trans. I. Sossnitz (New York: Kabbalah Publishing, 1926) and Adolph Jellinek, *Beiträge zur Geschichte der Kabbala* (Leipzig: C. L. Fritzsche, 1852). Excellent introductory and historical essays can be found by Lawrence Fine in *Back to the Sources: Reading the Classic Jewish Texts*, ed. Barry W. Holtz (New York: Summit Books, 1984), pp. 305–359; and Joseph Dan, ed., *The Early Kabbalah* (New York: Paulist Press, 1986), pp. 1–41. From the perspective of literary analysis, the works of Harold Bloom are of crucial importance. See, among other studies, *Kabbalah and Criticism* (New York: Seabury Press, 1975). For an extremely helpful bibliographical guide, see Sheila A. Spector, *Jewish Mysticism: An Annotated Bibliography on the Kabbalah in English* (New York: Garland, 1984).

as the terminology in which they are couched, is fundamaental both to the movement as a whole and to the function of the *merkabah* within that movement, a brief overview of the conceptual framework of *kabbalah* would appear to be in order here.[2]

Particularly as a speculative phenomenon, *kabbalah* represented a way of coming to terms with the nature of deity. For the kabbalists, deity itself is fundamentally unknowable. This unknowableness in kabbalistic lore is designated *ein-sof*, "infinite," "without limit", and God Himself is often referred to as *ha-Ein-Sof*, "the infinite." Such an approach is characteristic of a theology founded upon a *via negative*, in which God is conceived as a *deus absconditus*. Even within His hiddenness and unknowableness, however, *ha-Ein-Sof* is distinguished by the impulse to emerge from His own depths into what might be called the realm of creation. The process of emergence by which God manifests His various attributes is called the *sefirot* (from *safar*, "count"). Although originally used to suggest the idea of numeration, the term *sefirot* came to be associated with the concept of emanation, an idea that finds extensive correspondences in the traditions of Neoplatonism that became a crucial dimension of kabbalistic thought from the very outset. As a specifically kabbalistic phenomenon, the concept of *sefirot* represents the emanation of deity in its emergence from the hidden and unknowable realms of its own divinity. The kabbalists looked upon the *sefirot* as an activity that occurs within the very nature of the divine, as that which occurs within God Himself. So Gershom Scholem observes, "the hidden God in the aspect of *Ein-Sof* and the God manifested in the emanation of *Sefirot* are one and the same, viewed from two different angles."[3]

According to kabbalistic tradition, there are ten *sefirot* that emanate from *ein-sof* in hierarchical succession from above to below. In the process of emanation each *sefirah* of the *sefirot*, moreover, has a name that signifies the attributes of deity. These are: (1) *keter ʿelyon* (supreme crown) or simply *keter*, (2) *hokhmah* (wisdom), (3) *binah* (intelligence), (4) *gedullah* (greatness) or *hesed* (love), (5) *geburah* (power) or *din* (judgment), (6) *tiferet* (beauty) or *rahamim* (compassion), (7) *netsah* (lasting endurance), (8) *hod* (majesty), (9) *tsaddik* (righteous one) or *yesod ʿolam* (foundation of the world),

2. The following discussion makes extensive use of Scholem's *Kabbalah*, esp. pp. 42–79, 87–175.
3. Ibid., p. 98.

and (10) *malkhut* (kingdom) or ʿ*atarah* (diadem).[4] These constitute the forms that *ein-sof* assumes in its emanative capacity. So conceived, the *sefirot* suggest the richly symbolic and mythic world of *kabbalah*.

Within that world of symbol and myth the *sefirot*, moreover, came to be associated with an entire constellation of images and meanings that helped to define the process of emanation even further.[5] As a manifestation of the unknowable, the *sefirot* were thought to exhibit a formalized structure that suggests a kind of diagram of the divine. In the depiction of this diagram the kabbalists conceived of the *sefirot* in a number of ways. For example, they viewed the *sefirot* in organic terms as assuming the character of a cosmic tree, on the one hand, and a human form, on the other. As the mystical tree, the *sefirot* are seen to grow downward from the root (the first *sefirah*) and spread out through their corresponding emanations or branches. From an anthropomorphic perspective these branches, in turn, suggest the skeleton of the universe that constitutes the primordial man (ʾ*adam kadmon*) or cosmic man (ʾ*adam ha-gadol*). Whereas the tree grows from the top down, the human form is properly conceived with its head on top, followed by a torso containing arms, legs, and the sexual organ. Given the implied sexual basis of such an image, one should not be surprised to discover that kabbalists made a great deal of both the gender-related and generative dimensions of the *sefirot*. Both phallic and vaginal references underscore the kabbalistic outlook.

These are not the only images through which the *sefirot* in their entirety are depicted, however. As cosmic manifestations of the universe of the divine, the *sefirot* assume the form either as "adjoining arcs of a single circle surrounding a central Emanator, or as ten concentric spheres (called 'circles') with the power of emanation diminishing as it moves away from the center." From the perspective of the ten concentric spheres, one is immediately reminded of depictions of the ten-sphered universe commonplace

4. The terminology derives largely from 1 Chron. 29:11: "Thine, O Lord is the greatness, and the power, and the glory, and the victory, and the majesty; for all that is in the heavens and in the earth is thine; thine is the kingdom, O Lord, and thou art exalted as head above all." See ibid., p. 106.

5. "The *sefirot* are also called *maʾamarot* and *dibburim* ('sayings'), *shemot* ('names'), ʾ*orot* ('lights'), *koḥot* ('powers'), *ketarim* ('crowns'), *middot* in the sense of qualities, *madregot* ('stages'), *lebushim* ('garments'), *marʾot* ('mirrors'), *netiʾot* ('shoots'), *mekorot* ('sources'), *yamim elyonim* or *yemei kedem* ('supernal or primordial days'), *sitrin* ('aspects'), *ha-panim ha-penimiyyot* ('the inner faces of God')." Ibid., p. 100.

in medieval cosmology.[6] In later formulations of the cosmic dimensions of the *sefirot* there appeared the concept that from the emanations arose four worlds extending from above to below and "forming one basic vector along which creation passes from its primeval point to its finalization in the material world." Referred to as divine emanation (*ʿolam ha-ʾatsilut*), creation (*ʿolam ha-beriah*), formation (*ʿolam ha-yetsirah*), and activation (*ʿolam ha-ʿasiyyah*), these worlds represent the different stages through which the creative power of God is actualized.[7]

Along with such formulations, there are many others. Underlying the emanative quality of the *sefirot*, for example, is the concept of light, an idea implicit in the kabbalistic association of *sefirot* with the Hebrew *sappir* (sapphire), that which radiates from the divine throne (cf. Ezek. 1:26).[8] In this sense the *sefirot* are conceived specifically as radiations of divine light from a cental emanative source. (The lights themselves are often multicolored.) In the process of radiation, moreover, one *sefirah* reflects back upon the other in a mutual reciprocity of shared splendor. The idea of reflected light, in turn, finds its counterpart in such images as the varying aspects of the divine reflected from one *sefirah* to the next, as they are emanated from the "inner, intrinsic or mystical Face of God."[9]

As they are delineated, the *sefirot* find their correspondence in the names most common to God (*ʾEhyeh, Yah, ʾEl, ʾElohim, ʾElohim Tsebaʾot, YHVH, YHVH Tsebaʾot, ʾEl Ḥai,* or *Shaddai, ʾAdonai*), and taken as a whole they constitute His one great Name.[10] This linguistic dimension of the *sefirot* gives rise to another crucial aspect, that of divine speech. From the very outset of *kabbalah*, ideas concerning emanation were intimately related to a concern with the nature of language. If the manifestation of God's attributes in the *sefirot* was looked upon as a revelation of His various names, this process was likewise seen as a disclosure of His voice in the form of speech. "The process by which the power of emanation manifests itself from concealment into revelation is paralleled by the manifestation of divine speech from its inner essence in thought, through sound that as yet cannot be heard, into the

6. Ibid., p. 109.

7. Ibid., pp. 118–119; and *On the Kabbalah and Its Symbolism*, pp. 72–73.

8. Although the term *sefirah* has nothing etymologically to do with the Greek *sphaira*, the association was common in kabbalistic practice. Scholem, *Kabbalah*, p. 99; *Major Trends*, p. 206.

9. Scholem, *Major Trends*, pp. 213–214.

10. See Scholem, *Kabbalah*, pp. 107–108, and *Major Trends*, p. 213.

articulation of speech."¹¹ As that document in which divine speech (the *word* of God) is most anciently, fully, and authoritatively revealed, the Torah represents for the kabbalists the consummate source of deific articulation, the letters of which are nothing less than the configurations of the divine light of the *sefirot*. To know the meanings of the *sefirot* as manifestations of the word of God is to know the hidden meanings of the Torah. Kabbalistic commentary provides access to those hidden meanings, to the true word of God in its absolute essence. Although that essence will not be entirely disclosed until the time of the Messiah, some sense of its meaning can be understood through an encounter with the *sefirot*. Various dimensions of the *sefirot* will be discussed in the analysis that follows.

In his discussion of the *sefirot* Harold Bloom observes that, "more audaciously than any developments in recent French criticism," *kabbalah* is "a theory of writing," one that speaks not only of "a writing before writing" but of "a speech before speech, a Primal Instruction preceding all traces of speech."¹² With this idea in mind, the kabbalists drew upon the midrashic idea, discussed earlier, that before the creation of the world the Torah was written in black fire on white fire. For the kabbalists the white fire constituted the true text of the Torah, whereas the text that appeared in black fire was the oral law. Now that the true written law has become invisible to human perception, what remains "is nothing more than a commentary on this vanished text."¹³ Scholem elaborates as follows:

> Strictly speaking, there is no written Torah here on earth.... What we call the written Torah has itself passed through the medium of the oral Torah, it is no longer a form concealed in white light; rather, it has emerged from the black light.... Everything that we perceive in the fixed forms of the Torah, written in ink on parchment, consists, in the last analysis, of interpretations and definitions of what is hidden. *There is only an oral Torah*: that is the esoteric meaning of these words, and the written Torah is a purely mystical

11. Scholem, *Kabbalah*, p. 99.

12. Bloom, *Kabbalah and Criticism*, pp. 52–53. As Bloom makes clear, he has in mind, of course, the Derridean concept of the "trace." According to Bloom, the *sefirot* themselves are to be interpreted rhetorically as ranging over "the entire realm of the classical trope, including metaphor, metonymy, synecdoche, and hyperbole." In this sense *kabbalah* is not only a theory of writing but a theory of rhetoric, and the *sefirot* are poetic documents (p. 26).

13. Scholem, *Kabbalah*, pp. 168–174.

concept. It is embodied in a sphere that is accessible to prophets
alone. It was, to be sure, revealed to Moses, but what he gave to
the world as the written Torah has acquired its present form by
passing through the medium of the oral Torah.[14]

What is true of the inaugural vision as a biblical phenomenon is
true of the kabbalistic attitude toward the Torah itself: the true
text does not exist. Written on white fire, it cannot be seen. All
that remains is that which is the residue of black fire, that is,
interpretation itself. This is the oral Torah as it is disseminated
from one generation to the next in the dynamics of transformation
that lie at the heart of the visionary mode. In its attempts to
confront a text that no longer exists, *kabbalah* offers its own
method of retrieving the nonexistent text, of reclaiming the white
fire that has disappeared. Formulating a new Torah of its own,
it seeks to penetrate to the source of all utterance, to the unknowable word through which the invisible text behind all texts
was originally generated.

It is from this perspective that one encounters the hermeneutics
of kabbalistic interpretation. According to that hermeneutics, the
kabbalist penetrates to the source of all utterance by means of the
fourfold method of interpretation common to medieval biblical
exegesis. In keeping with that method, exegesis moves from the
literal (*peshat*), to the allegorical (*remez*), to the homiletical (*derash*),
and finally to the mystical (*sod*) level of interpretation. For the
exegetes the *peshat* or literal level involved not only "the factual
and historical content of the Torah but also the authoritative Oral
Law of rabbinic tradition." The *derash* or homiletical level followed
"the path of ethical and aggadic commentary." The *remez* or allegorical level addressed "the body of philosophical truths that
the Torah contained." The *sod* or mystical level, finally, represented "the totality of possible kabbalistic commentaries which
interpreted the words of the Torah as references to events in the
world of the *Sefirot*." From the kabbalistic perspective "the *peshat*,
therefore, which was taken to include the corpus of talmudic law
as well, was only the Torah's outermost 'husk' that first met the
eye of the reader. The other layers revealed themselves only to
that more penetrating and latitudinous power of insight which
was able to discover in the Torah general truths that were in no

14. Scholem, *On the Kabbalah and Its Symbolism*, p. 50. The entire chapter, entitled "The
Meaning of the Torah in Jewish Mysticism" (pp. 32–86), should be consulted.

way dependent on their immediate literal context. Only on the level of *sod* did the Torah become a body of mystical symbols which unveiled the hidden life-processes of the Godhead and their connections with human life."[15]

For our purposes this fourfold method of interpretation (*peshat, remez, derash, sod*) becomes particularly germane, because it redefines the world of the *merkabah* in hermeneutical terms. The very acronym of the fourfold method, in fact, becomes in kabbalistic interpretation a mnemonic device (*PaRDeS*) that suggests the centrality of the *ma'aseh merkabah* as hermeneutical enterprise to the elucidation of the secrets of *kabbalah*.[16] From this perspective it should come as no surprise, then, that the *merkabah* itself is of crucial importance to the kabbalistic world-view. Indeed, in the formulation of the doctrine of emanation the *merkabah* was looked upon as a symbol of the *sefirot* themselves.[17]

If such is the case, this is a *merkabah* of an entirely different order from the one encountered in the writings and practices of the old *merkabah* mystics. As Scholem observes,

> The world of the Merkabah, with its celestial throne, its heavenly household, and its palaces through which the wanderer passes, is for the Kabbalist no longer of supreme importance, though its core, frequently clothed in new disguise, never ceases to attract his interest. All knowledge concerning it is, for him, merely provisional. Indeed, some Kabbalists go so far as to refer to Ezekiel's Merkabah as the *second Merkabah*. In other words, the new Kabbalistic Gnosis or cognition of God, which in the Hekhaloth tracts is not even mentioned, is related to a deeper layer of mystical reality, an "inner Merkabah," as it were, which can be visualized only in a symbolic way, if at all. Briefly, this gnosis concerns God Himself. Where pre-

---

15. Scholem, *Kabbalah*, pp. 172–174. See also Scholem, *Major Trends*, p. 210. For a full and enlightening discussion of the fourfold method, see Frank Talmage, "Apples of Gold: The Inner Meaning of Sacred Texts in Medieval Judaism," *Jewish Spirituality from the Bible through the Middle Ages*, ed. Arthur Green (New York: Crossroad, 1986), I, 313–355 (vol. 13 of the series World Spirituality: An Encyclopedic History of the Religious Quest). See also Michael Fishbane, *The Garments of Torah: Essays in Biblical Hermeneutics* (Bloomington: Indiana University Press, 1989), pp. 112–120.

16. Scholem, *On the Kabbalah and Its Symbolism*, p. 57.

17. Scholem, *Kabbalah*, p. 118. Distinctions were even made between the *merkabah* and what became known as the *mirkebet ha-mishneh* or "second chariot," which "represented the domain that came after the Sefirah Malkut, and was itself divided into ten *Sefirot* of its own" (p. 118).

viously the vision could go no farther than to the perception of the glory of his appearance on the throne, it is now a question, if the expression may be permitted, of the inside of this glory.[18]

It is, concludes Scholem, at the roots of the impulse of *kabbalah* to penetrate into this new field of contemplation beyond the sphere of the throne. Precisely the way this impulse manifests itself in the reformulation of the *merkabah* portrayed by *kabbalah* will represent the focus of the account that follows. In order to understand the nature of that reformulation, we address some of the crucial works that constitute the traditions of *kabbalah*.

II

As scholars generally concur, any consideration of these traditions must take account of two early but seminal texts that formed the basis of much kabbalistic speculation in the later Middle Ages. These two texts are the *Shiʿur Komah* (ca. second century ?) and the *Sefer Yetsirah* (ca. third to sixth century?).[19] A brief analysis of these texts, particularly as they draw upon and transform the inaugural vision of Ezekiel, will provide an introduction to the kabbalistic works that fostered the concepts discussed above.

"Hailed by the Kabbalists of the Middle Ages as the profound

18. *Major Trends*, pp. 206–207.

19. The dating, provenance, transmission, and meaning of these works are very problematical. For discussions of such matters with regard to the *Shiʿur Komah*, see, in particular, Scholem's *Major Trends*, pp. 63–67; *Kabbalah*, pp. 16–18; and "The Age of *Shiur Komah* Speculation and a Passage in Origen," in Gershom Scholem, *Jewish Gnosticism, Merkabah Mysticism, and Talmudic Tradition* (New York: Jewish Theological Seminary of America, 1960), pp. 36–42; Ithamar Gruenwald, *Apocalyptic and Merkavah Mysticism* (Leiden: E. J. Brill, 1980), pp. 213–218; and the extensive and illuminating introduction in Martin Samuel Cohen's edition and translation *The Shiʿur Qomah: Liturgy and Theurgy in Pre-Kabbalistic Jewish Mysticism* (New York: University Press of America, 1983). For corresponding treatments of the *Sefer Yetsirah*, see Scholem's *Major Trends*, pp. 75–78; and *Kabbalah*, pp. 23–30; Gruenwald, *A Preliminary Critical Edition of the S. Yezira*, in *Israel Oriental Studies* 1 (1971): 132–177. See also the editions and translations of Carlo Suarès, *The Sepher Yetsira* (1968), trans. Micheline and Vincent Stuart (Boulder, Colo.: Shambala, 1976); Knut Stenring, *Sepher Yetsirah: The Book of Formation* (1923; rpt. New York: Ktav, 1970); and *Sefer Yetsira: Text and Commentary*, in David Blumenthal's *Understanding Jewish Mysticism* (New York: Ktav, 1978).

symbolic expression of the mysteries of what could be called the Kabbalistic *pleroma*," the *Shiʿur Komah* (Measure of the Height) is really part of the traditions of ancient *merkabah* mysticism, particularly those manifested in the *hekhalot* writings.[20] Putatively deriving its immediate inspiration from such texts as the the Song of Songs (esp. 5:11–16), it moves beyond the framework of generally accepted midrashic exegesis by reformulating its sources to accord with its view of the Bible as an esoteric text that contains "sublime and tremendous mysteries regarding God in His appearance upon the throne of the Merkabah."[21] As a result of the revelations afforded by the *Shiʿur Komah*, the *merkabah* mystic was able to gain the most profound of insights into the true nature of the Enthroned Figure depicted in the inaugural vision of Ezekiel (1:26–28).[22]

From the very outset the *Shiʿur Komah* makes it clear that its concern is with "the [Divine] Body [and] Varia Regarding the Chariot-Throne."[23] Engaging in its own liturgy in celebration of the Enthroned Figure, it exalts God as He resides on the Throne of Glory, supported by the *ḥayyot*. This figure, the *Shiʿur Komah* refers to as *Yotser Bereʾshit*, the Creator of the world, a designation that attests to the sense of power and majesty embodied in the subject it extols.[24] "You are fire," the text proclaims, "and Your throne is fire, and your [celestial] creatures [*ḥayyot*] and servants are fire. You are fire consuming fire. You are prince over the princes and your *markabot* are on the *ʿofannim*'" (A: 5–7). God's body, the *Shiʿur Komah* later observes, "is like *tarshish*," the substance that underlies the wheels of the *merkabah* (Ezek. 1:16).[25] "His splendor is luminous, [and] awesome from within [the] darkness; cloud and fog surround

20. Scholem, *Jewish Gnosticism*, p. 36. One finds actual recensions of the *Shiʿur Komah* in the various *merkabah* texts. See the discussion in Cohen, *The Shiʿur Qomah*, pp. 68, 167, 169, and elsewhere.

21. Scholem, *Jewish Gnosticism*, pp. 36–40. In an appendix to Scholem, *Jewish Gnosticism*, Saul Lieberman analyzes the rabbinic texts regarding the esoteric meaning of the Song of Songs, pp. 118–126. Cohen, *The Shiʿur Qomah*, has argued that the putative significance of the passage from the Song of Songs is questionable (p. 19).

22. Scholem, "The Age of *Shiur Komah*," *Jewish Gnosticism*, pp. 36–40.

23. References by section and line number to the *Shiʿur Komah* in my discussion are to the Cohen edition.

24. Scholem, *Major Trends*, p. 65.

25. For *tarshish*, compare Song of Songs 5:14, Ezek. 1:16, and Dan. 10:6. The word *tarshish* has been variously interpreted. See Cohen, *The Shiʿur Qomah*, p. 209, n. 41; and Gruenwald, *Apocalyptic*, p. 215.

Him, and all the princes of the presence [supplicate] before Him" (D:80–82). In short, the Enthroned Figure is resplendent and absolutely unknowable.

Acceding to (and, in fact, celebrating) this unknowability, the *Shi'ur Komah*, then proceeds to violate fundamental strictures (both biblical and mishnaic) that interdict any attempts to disclose the secret things of God, especially those concerning His appearance (cf Exod. 33:20) and His name (cf. Exod. 3:13–14; Gen. 32:29), as well, of course, as His manifestation in the *merkabah*. What emerges from this violation is a remarkable gnosis, one that recalls corresponding tendencies in the *hekhalot* tracts but also one distinguished by its own unique characteristics. In keeping with the *hekhalot* tracts, its spokesmen for this gnosis are the famed mystics Rabbis Akiba and Ishmael, as well as Rabbi Ishmael's student Rabbi Nathan. In their encounter with the Enthroned Figure they reveal graphically and minutely not only the dimensions of God's body but the designations of its various parts.

"What is the measure of the body of the Holy One, blessed be He [?]" asks the mystic (in this case, Rabbi Ishmael), who then responds to his own question with detailed measurements and secret names.[26] As one who approaches the Enthroned Figure from the most abject of postures, Rabbi Ishmael begins his account from the feet of the Holy One and then proceeds to the head. Whereas God's "feet fill the entire universe," the height of His soles, the mystic informs us, "is 30,000,000 parasangs." Moreover,

> the name of His right ankle is Atarqam, and [the name] of the left [one] is Ava Tarqam. From His ankles until His knees is 190,000,000 parasangs. Qanangi is its name. The name of His right calf is Qangi; the name of the left [calf] is Mehariah. From His knees until His thighs is 120,000,000 parasangs. The name of His right knee is Setamnegatz, and the name of the left [knee] is Pedangas. The name of the right thigh is Vihmai, and the name of the left [thigh] is Partmai. From His thighs until His neck is 240,000,000 parasangs. The name of the innermost part of His loins is Asasnigiyahu. And on His heart are seventy names: sas, tzedeq, tzehu'el, tzur, tzevi, tzadiq...[etc.]. (D:47–72)

26. The measurements are in parasangs, a Persian unit of distance of varying length, anciently, something over three miles. According to the *Shi'ur Komah* itself, "each parasang is four mils, and each mil is ten thousand cubits, and each cubit is three *zeratot* [an ambiguous term, possibly equivalent to a handspan]. And His *zeret* fills the entire universe" (E: 107–108). See Cohen's glosses, pp. 215–216.

Moving upward toward the higher parts of the Enthroned Figure, Rabbi Ishmael next measures and names the head and the parts of the head, such as the beard (called Hadarqamsiah) and the nose (called Mag Bag Ve'akhargag), each of gigantic size.[27] So large are the parts of the head, in fact, that the tongue alone stretches "from one end of the universe to the other" (D:74–84). These ideas receive further elaboration later in the text, when the legs of the throne and even the individual *ḥayyot* themselves are named (J:136–150). "Whoever knows this measurement of his Creator and the glory of the Holy One," it is asserted, "is secure in this world and [in] the world to come" (G:120–123). In short, he has attained to a divine gnosis that only the *Shiʿur Komah* is able to provide.

Needless to say, the *Shiʿur Komah* generated a great deal of controversy both in its own time and, more recently, in our own.[28] At the center of this controversy is the question of what one is to make of the blatant anthropomorphisms that surround the conception of deity and the graphic and detailed manner in which those anthropomorphisms are expressed. As a way of justifying the anthropomorphic focus of the work, scholars have suggested that one must distinguish between the appearance of God the creator, on the one hand, and His indefinable essence, on the other. While adhering in principle to the fact of God's essential unknowability, the *Shiʿur Komah*, it is argued, does not hesitate to elaborate upon the anthropomorphic aspect of His appearance, especially as it is grounded in Ezekiel's concept of the Enthroned Figure manifested in the likeness of "a human form" (1:26).[29] It is the tropology implicit in the idea of the human form as the defining characteristic of God's appearance that the *Shiʿur Komah* causes to become the basis of its own anthropomorphic outlook.

If such is true, one is prompted to respond that the reason the

27. In the manuscript sources the dimensions of the nose are either not given or, as Cohen suggests, have "fallen out." As for the name of the nose, Cohen conjectures that this may be a veiled reference to the divine 'eybar or penis (p. 211, n. 47).

28. Although the kabbalists hailed the *Shiʿur Komah*, it is a work that elicited much criticism. The Karaites attacked it, and although Maimonides endorsed the book in his youth, he rejected it in his later years. For a discussion of the medieval controversies surrounding the work, see Alexander Altmann, "Moses Narboni's Epistle on Shiʿur Qoma," *Jewish Medieval and Renaissance Studies*, ed. A. Altmann (Cambridge: Harvard University Press, 1967). For an account of recent scholarship, see Cohen, *The Shiʿur Qomah*, pp. 13–41.

29. The suggestion is Scholem's, *Major Trends*, p. 85.

Shi'ur Komah proceeds in this manner is not to emphasize the distinction between the appearance of God and His indefinable essence. To do so would be to compromise the fact of God's unknowableness by emphasizing the anthropomorphisms implicit in His appearance. Quite the contrary is the case. In its insistence upon those anthropomorphisms, the *Shi'ur Komah* paradoxically reinforces the fact of God's essential unknowableness.[30] This is made clear in the graphic and detailed manner in which the *Shi'ur Komah* portrays the anthropomorphisms that distinguish God's appearance, for, as enumerated, the dimensions of God's bodily parts are so vast that, by their very nature, they defy perception. The more that the *Shi'ur Komah* literalizes trope with precise numeration, the greater our sense of the mystery that numeration would presume to disclose. Tropology reasserts its indefinableness in the very act of attempting to embody it in numerical form: the obverse of the *via negativa* is a *via positiva* that enacts its own paradoxical attestation to the unknowableness of the divine. It is the fact of this unknowableness, expressed through a hyperbolic numeration of the known, that underscores the gnosis disclosed by the *Shi'ur Komah*.

Corresponding to this act of numeration is that of designation or naming. One way of attesting to the unnamable quality of the divine is paradoxically through the same modus operandi that underscores the practice of numeration. In this instance the *via positiva* is expressed through the attribution of names. Just as numeration in the *Shi'ur Komah* defies understanding, so does designation. As most scholars agree in their attempts to come to terms with the plethora of names that appear in the *Shi'ur Komah*, few, if any, of the words used to designate the bodily parts of the Enthroned Figure are intelligible. Most of the names simply defy attempts at etymological analysis. What results is a complex series of designations (Atarqam, Ava Tarqam, Qanangi, Qangi, Mehariah, Setamnegatz, Pedangas, Vihmai, Partmai, and the like) that amount (in "rational" terms) to "non-sense." As such, this practice of designation performs the same function as that of numeration.

30. According to Joseph Dan ("The Religious Experience of the *Merkavah*," *Jewish Spirituality from the Bible through the Middle Ages*, ed. Arthur Green [New York: Crossroad, 1986], p. 296), "It is quite clear that the mystics who evolved this concept of the divine figure did not intend to describe in measurement that could be understood by human beings; quite to the contrary, they presented a picture which, in its time and place, was completely beyond human comprehension."

In the process of literalizing trope, of bestowing upon the visionary a local habitation and a name, designation, like numeration,
paradoxically heightens the mystery that surrounds the divine.
Although practices of this sort are hardly foreign to the *hekhalot*
tradition, in the *Shi'ur Komah* they are carried to the extreme. This
fact causes the *Shi'ur Komah* to assume its remarkable quality.

In conjunction with the idea of employing numeration and designation to reinforce the sense of paradox implicit in a *via positiva*
is another dimension that must be taken into account in any attempt to understand the *Shi'ur Komah*. This dimension is one that
draws upon those very numerations and designations, not as speculative devices for expressing God's unknowability, but as practical
means of achieving a state of ecstasis through which that unknowability may at once be celebrated and encountered as fully
as possible. In this case the numerations and designations possess
a special meaning to the mystic, who recites them in a fashion that
distinguishes his unique mode of *praxis*. Engaging in that *praxis*,
the mystic receives a gnosis that only an acquaintance with the
secret significations of the numerations and designations will reveal. From this perspective the *Shi'ur Komah* fulfills its original
function as a text that sets forth magic numbers and names as a
way of allowing the mystic who would recite the text to acquire
the rewards associated with the experience of encountering the
merkabah.[31]

Conceived in such a manner, the *Shi'ur Komah* must be looked
upon as a magic text, a source of theurgy and theosophy, manifested in the pronouncement of special numerations and designations that take on a life of their own.[32] Reformulated in
theurgical and theosophical terms, the *merkabah* thereby comes to
possess very special properties, ones that allow the *merkabah* mystic

31. According to Cohen, this was, in fact, the purpose of the *ur*-text of the *Shi'ur Komah*.
"It seems that the author of that original text derived those mystic names and dimensions
from some already existent fund of information, if he did not actually derive them from
his own personal mystic experiences. Regardless of whether they were the product of his
own or another's experiences, they presumably derived from a real mystic revelation. The
author of the Urtext used his own (or another's) information and made it the basis of his
theurgy" (pp. 167–168).

32. In this regard, Cohen observes that "the author of our text was a precursor both
of the speculative and practical kabbalists of the medieval period. In later generations,
the two styles of kabbalah separated." The *Shi'ur Komah*, however, "recalls a simpler time,
when the act of meditation on the godhead according to a set of esoteric principles was
considered enough to produce real results" (p. 69). For further discussions of the distinction between speculative and practical kabbalah, see Scholem, *Kabbalah*, pp. 182–189.

not only to speculate on the nature of godhead but indeed to possess the powers associated with godhead. The *merkabah* mystic becomes not just a divine seer but a divine doer or magus, a veritable *Yotser Bere'shit*, and the *merkabah* itself becomes not just a source of divine vision but a vehicle of divine enactment. As portrayed in the *Shi'ur Komah*, the power to engage in that enactment resides in the theurgical recitation of numbers and names.[33] These represent the objective correlative of all that is associated with the special gnosis that the *Shi'ur Komah* is able to bestow.

In its particular concern with the significance of numerations and designations as sources of gnosis and power, the *Shi'ur Komah*, in turn, finds its counterpart in that prekabbalistic work of immense importance, the *Sefer Yetsirah* (The Book of Formation).[34] Generating a multitude of commentaries in the later Middle Ages, this work, along with the *Shi'ur Komah*, assumed crucial importance to the traditions of *kabbalah*.[35] As what Gershom Scholem terms "the earliest extant speculative text written in the Hebrew language," the *Sefer Yetsirah* is, in effect, a work in the tradition of the *ma'aseh bere'shit*.[36] As such, it casts its discourse in the form of pronouncements concerning the esoteric principles of creation implicit in the Genesis account. These principles are formulated according to the "thirty-two paths of wisdom," by means of which God created the world. As the foundations of all creation, the thirty-two paths of wisdom are divided into ten *sefirot* or numerations (the subject of the first chapter) and *'otiot* or the twenty-

33. For examples of works in the same tradition, among others, see the *Sefer ha-Razim* (ca. fourth century C.E.?). This work has recently been translated into English by Michael A. Morgan, *Sepher ha-Razim: The Book of the Mysteries* (Chico, Calif.: Scholars Press, 1983).

34. Cohen suggests the possibility that the author of the *Sefer Yetsirah* knew the *Shi'ur Komah* and was perhaps influenced by it (*The Shi'ur Qomah*, pp. 179–180). The *Sefer Yetsirah* is extant in two versions, a shorter and a longer one. In both versions the book is divided into six chapters of *mishnayot*. References in my text (by chapter and mishnah) are to the Blumenthal edition, augmented by those of Stenring (*Sepher Yetsirah*) and Suarès (*The Sepher Yetsira*). These have been compared with the editions of Lazarus Goldschmidt, *Das Buch der Schöpfung* (Frankfurt am Main: J. Kauffmann, 1894), and Gruenwald, *A Preliminary Critical Edition*.

35. According to Scholem (*Kabbalah*, pp. 28–30), "the number of commentaries [on the *Sefer Yetsirah*] written in the spirit of the Kabbalah" comes to about fifty. Although first printed in Mantua in 1562, the *Sefer Yetsirah* was translated into Latin by Guillaume Postel and printed (Paris, 1552) even before the Hebrew edition. Other editions (notably that by Rittangelius in 1652) followed.

36. Scholem, *Major Trends*, p. 75. The summary that follows is derived largely from that provided by Scholem, *Kabbalah*, pp. 23–25.

two elemental letters of the Hebrew alphabet (the subject of the remaining five chapters).

The ten *sefirot* fall into two categories: that of generation (represented by the first four *sefirot*) and that of dimension (represented by the next six *sefirot*). From the first *sefirah*, as prime generative spirit, spring the next three, each successively manifesting itself in the elements of air, water, and fire. The next six *sefirot* represent dimensions or "extremities" of space (height, depth, and the four points of the compass). As a totality, the *sefirot* constitute a closed, self-contained unit, one in which their end is in their beginning and their beginning is in their end. So conceived, they revolve like circles and wheels within each other. The counterpart of the *sefirot* are the *'otiot*. By means of the secret combinations of these letters to form occult terms, the world comes into existence. The world-process thus becomes a linguistic phenomenon (a speech-act, as it were), grounded in the unlimited combinations of the *'otiot*.

The letters themselves are divided into three groups, according to the phonetic system adopted by the text. The first group contains three matrices or "mothers" (*'alef, mem, shin*), which are, in turn, the sources of the elements of air, water, and fire, mentioned above. These three matrices likewise generate all the other letters. The second group consists of seven "double" letters or "fathers" (consonants written with or without a *dagesh*). By means of these letters are created the seven planets, the seven heavens, the seven days of the week, and the seven orifices of the head (eyes, ears, nostrils, mouth). The twelve remaining "simple" letters or "progeny" correspond to such phenomena as the twelve signs of the zodiac and the twelve months of the year. In the "linguistic-mystical cosmogony" portrayed in the *Sefer Yetsirah*, one finds the roots of all things.

The precise bearing that all this has on the *merkabah* is apparent from the very outset, for the *sefirot* are immediately described in terms that are reminiscent of Ezekiel's description of the throne-chariot:

> There are ten intangible sefirot whose appearance is like lightning and whose limits are infinite. His word is in them in their to-and-fro movement, and they run at His command like the whirlwind, and before His Throne they bow down.

There are ten intangible sefirot whose end is fixed in their beginning, as the flame is bound to the coal. Know, count, and form.
For the Lord is the Only One, and the Former is One. He has no
second, and before one what can you count?

There are ten intangible sefirot. Shut your mouth from speaking
and your heart from thinking. And if your mouth runs to speak
and your heart to reflect, return to the place, for thus it is said: "And
the living creatures ran and returned," and upon this word a covenant is cut. (I.6–8)

Resorting to the inaugural vision, the author of the *Sefer Yetsirah*
focuses in particular upon the appearance and movement of the
ḥayyot in order to suggest the nature and dynamics of the *sefirot*.
Like the *ḥayyot*, the *sefirot* are surrounded by fire and have the
appearance of lightning; implicitly in the midst of the *sefirot*, moreover, is something that resembles "burning coals of fire." In keeping with this description, one finds that the *sefirot*, like the *ḥayyot*,
dart "to and fro" (Ezek. 1:13–14). To prevent any misunderstand-
ing of the biblical context from which the concept of the *sefirot* is
drawn, the *Sefer Yetsirah* even refers specifically to the *ḥayyot* and
their movement: "And the living creatures ran and returned."
Essential to the idea as a whole is the sense of circularity, moving
to and fro, running from and returning to the place of origin,
the dynamic source of all energy and movement. (" Their end is
in their beginning, and their beginning is in their end.")[37] Coupled
with the sense of return is that of devotion, an idea that extends
the biblical context to include later elements of the *merkabah* tradition itself: "they run at His command like the whirlwind, and
before His Throne they bow down."

What renders the process as a whole of such great interest,
however, is the way in which the author of the *Sefer Yetsirah* reconceptualizes the *merkabah* in general and the *ḥayyot* in particular
to agree with his own theosophical outlook. Implicit in that outlook
is the transformation of visionary experience into the esoterica of
that which requires one to "shut...[his] mouth from speaking
and...[his] heart from thinking," that is, of divulging the profound gnosis embodied in the *sefirot*. This gnosis involves the act
of seeing in the *ḥayyot* and in their movement how God drew upon
His ten essential attributes, the "intangible" or "ineffable" *sefirot*

---

37. Compare Stenring, *Sepher Yetsirah*, p. 18 (*Sefer Yetsirah* [I.7]).

("*sefirot belimah*") (I.3–4), to create the universe.[38] As suggested by the root of the term *sefirah* (*samekh, peh, resh*), the act of divine creation is consummated through delineation or numeration, declaration or expression, and recording or decreeing. "He created His universe by three forms of expression [*sefarim*]," the text declares: "numbers, letters, and words" (I.1).[39] These three forms underlie that process by which the *sefirot* become sources of knowing, counting, and forming for those able to penetrate the secrets embodied in the *hayyot*. The ability to penetrate those secrets enables one to gain profound insights into the processes by which the world came into being.

The result of a remarkable transformation of the visionary substratum of the *merkabah* into forms of divine utterance and vocalization, these processes foster a mystical linguistics that causes the *sefirot* to assume a distinct interpretive life. From a hermeneutical perspective, one is able to discern in the *sefirot* an entirely new way of comprehending the nature of the visionary mode, one that textualizes the visionary, embodies it in numbers, letters, and words that represent the basis of a unique system of esoteric thought and expression.

If such is true of the *sefirot*, it is no less true of the *'otiot* (the twenty-two elemental letters of the Hebrew alphabet). They, too, are a fundamental aspect of the textualizing of the visionary that underlies the *Sefer Yetsirah*. Like the *sefirot*, the *'otiot* are founded upon the concept of the *merkabah*. The manifestation of utterance in its most elemental form, the *'otiot* are, in fact, referred to as "the foundation" (*ha-yesod*). God "engraved them through sounds, He hewed them out in Spiritual Air, He set them through the mouth in five places":

> Alef, Chet, Hey, and Ayin in the throat,
> Gimel, Yod, Kaf, and Kof on the palate,
> Dalet, Tet, Lamed, Nun, and Tav with the tongue,
> Zayin, Samech, Shin, Resh, and Tzade with the teeth,
> Bet, Vav, Mem, and Pey with the lips. (II.3)

38. The term *belimah* as a modifier of *sefirot* is subject to a number of interpretations. Literally, it implies "without" (*beli*), "what," or "any thing" (*mah*). See further Scholem, *Kabbalah*, pp. 24–25.

39. The translation is Stenring's. (For alternate renderings, see Stenring, *Sepher Yetsirah*, p. 33). Blumenthal has "by border and letter and number." As Blumenthal suggests, "the last three terms can be translated in many ways" (*Understanding Jewish Mysticism*, p. 15).

These utterances, avers the *Sefer Yetsirah*, are set in "a wheel" (*galgal*) that rotates in a circular motion, forward and backward, to and fro. Within that wheel "they return in a circular movement (turn by turn) to where all that is formed and uttered is found coming out of the One Name" (II.5), that is, the Divine Name that seals all.[40]

Just as the *sefirot* represent the esoteric reformulation of the *ḥayyot*, the *'otiot*, then, represent the esoteric reformulation of the wheels (*'ofannim* and especially *galgalim*) that accompany the *ḥayyot* in the *merkabah* (cf. Ezek. 1:15–21, 10:13). These are the "whirling wheels," conceived as wheels within wheels as they revolve one within the other to suggest the sense of energy and dynamism that propels the chariot-like vehicle of God. As with the *sefirot*, so with the *'otiot*: one experiences a remarkable transformation of the visionary substratum of the *merkabah* into forms of divine utterance and vocalization. The mystical linguistics initiated in the *sefirot* is recapitulated and reformulated in the *'otiot*, which, like their counterparts, similarly assume an interpretive life all their own. Once again, the visionary is textualized in a form that inspires unique systems of thought, ones in which the *merkabah* is "enacted" through magical utterances to produce new worlds. Corresponding expressions of a fundamental process of reconceptualization, the *sefirot* and the *'otiot* provide yet another perspective through which the visionary mode is able to be understood. Theosophical and finally theurgic in focus, that perspective is what underlies the *merkabah* as an esoteric phenomenon.

III

As that phenomenon is reformulated in the later traditions of *kabbalah*, it assumes renewed impetus in the theosophical speculations of those for whom the *merkabah* remained a source of profound significance. The *Sefer ha-Bahir* (The Book of Brightness) is a case in point. Appearing in Provence (but not composed there) at some point between 1150 and 1200, the *Sefer ha-Bahir* has been designated "the earliest work of kabbalistic literature." Such an ascription is more nearly in keeping with the spirit of the *Sefer ha-Bahir* than with the letter, for the work does not actually

40. The translation is that of Suarès, *The Sepher Yetsira*, p. 97.

adopt the term *kabbalah* to characterize its teachings. Rather, it introduces its teachings significantly as *ma'aseh merkabah* and its putative spokesman as the famed *merkabah* mystic Nechunyah ben Hakkanah. Portrayed as an ancient midrash, the *Bahir* is cast in the form of interpretations of scriptural verses through which it "transforms the Merkabah tradition into a gnostic tradition concerning the powers of God that lie within the Divine Glory (*Kavod*), whose activity at the creation is alluded to through symbolic interpretation of the Bible and the *aggadah*."[41] According to Gershom Scholem, the symbolic dimensions of the *Bahir* as a compendium of gnostic thought are all pervasive. "Every word, every phrase it [the *Bahir*] introduces becomes an allusion to some secret."[42]

At the forefront of this esoteric symbolism are the *sefirot*, which the *Bahir* reinterprets to accord with its own point of view. Drawing upon the terminology of the *Sefer Yetsirah*, the *Bahir* appropriates the concept of the *sefirot* in order to provide a new gnostic rendering of their meaning and significance. Implicit in this rendering is a formulation of the *sefirot* that associates them not just with *safar* but with *sappir*. Becoming commonplace in later kabbalistic literature, this mystical etymology causes the *sefirot* to assume at once a celestial and visionary bearing that suggests "the sapphirine reflections of the divinity." As such, the *sefirot* in the *Bahir* become the expression of divine attributes, lights, and powers, each of which performs a particular function and over which God Himself reigns as supreme Master. In the highly symbolical language that constitutes the delineation of the *sefirot*, one is given access to the secrets of the divine realm, the fundamental core of the teachings of the *Bahir*.

What results is "a new conception of the divinity exhibiting gnostic components that enter almost everywhere into the contexture of the work and determine its religious physiognomy." In this new conception God is "no longer the holy king of the Merkabah gnosis and the writings of the Hekhaloth who sits upon his throne in the innermost rooms of the Temple of Silence and is conceived as utterly transcendent." Rather, the God of the *Bahir* is a theosophical conception that is "the bearer of cosmic potencies, the source of the internal movement in his attributes, hypostatized

---

41. Scholem, *Kabbalah*, pp. 42–43, 313–316. For a full treatment of the *Bahir*, see Scholem, *Origins*, esp. pp. 49–198.

42. Scholem, *Origins*, p. 58.

as aeons." It is this notion that underlies the sefirotic symbolism through which the divine realm is cast.[43] That such is the case will be seen upon an analysis of the sefirotic dimensions of the *Bahir* and the relations of those dimensions to the concept of the *mer-kabah*.[44]

"What are the ten logoi [*ma'amarot*, literally, "sayings" or "ut-terances"]?" asks the *Bahir* and then offers its own delineation of the *sefirot*. The first is the "highest crown"; the second, "wisdom"; the third, the "quarry of the Torah, the treasure-house of 'wis-dom' "; the fourth, God's rewards and kindness (*ḥesed*) to the world, symbolized by His right hand; the fifth, God's terrible, all-consuming fire, symbolized by His left hand (*geburah*); the sixth, the throne of glory (*kisse' ha-kabod*); the seventh, the heaven called *'arabot*; the eighth, the single righteous one (*tsadik*) who maintains the world and is its foundation; the ninth and the tenth, finally, are like two wheels (*'ofannim*), one leaning northward and the other westward. With the ninth logos five hundred years higher than the tenth, they both extend to the lowest earth and represent the furthest reaches of the *Shekhinah* (96, 102, 103–105, 114–115).

Among the many meanings implicit in this delineation, that of the *merkabah* is of crucial importance. For example, the fifth logos (which is the dreadful counterpart of the fourth) is specifically associated with the holy *ḥayyot* and the holy *serafim* that stand to the right and left of the Enthroned Figure. These, comments the *Bahir*, "are the gracious ones who are extremely high, and of whom it is written (Ezek. 1:18): 'They were high, and they were fearful,' and they are full of eyes, for . . . their backs were full of eyes round about them four." As the seat of glory upon which the Enthroned Figure resides, the sixth logos suggests the unitary nature of the fourth, fifth, and sixth logoi. Those logoi, in turn, are preceded by the delineation of the crowned head of the Enthroned Figure (the first logos), followed by an account of His generative powers

43. Ibid., pp. 58, 67, 81–82.
44. References to the *Sefer ha-Bahir* by section number in my text are to the translation in *The Secret Garden: An Anthology in the Kabbalah*, ed. David Meltzer (New York: The Seabury Press, 1976), pp. 49–96. The translation is based on the edition of Gershom Scholem, *Das Buch Bahir* (Leipzig: W. Druckulin, 1923). Scholem's version derives from the oldest and relatively best extant manuscript (see Scholem, *Origins*, p. 49, n. 1). References likewise take into account the *Sefer ha-Bahir*, ed. Reuben Margaliot (Jerusalem: Massad Ha-Rav Kook, 1950–1951), based on corresponding manuscripts. This edition serves as the basis of Aryeh Kaplan's version of the *Sefer ha-ahir* (New York: Samuel Weiser, 1979), which provides both the English and the Hebrew, as well as commentary.

as they are manifested in His Wisdom as a source of creativity (the second logos) and in His Torah as the fundamental record of creativity (the third logos) (96). Designated *'arabot*, the seventh logos recalls the traditions of the *hekhalot* and, in fact, is specifically referred to as "the hall of holiness [*hekhlah ha-kadosh*]" (102). At the same time, the seventh, as an embodiment of the first six, carries through and continues the concept of the divine body of the Enthroned Figure (104).

Below the seventh logoi are the remaining three. Maintaining that all the logoi are to be conceived as concentric spheres (*gal-galim*) (122) (cf. Ezek. 10:13), the *Bahir* associates the final three most specifically with what amounts to a lower *merkabah*, that is, a Chariot manifested in this world (115). This is seen as a driving force with wheels that are constantly spinning in various directions to indicate God's multidirectional potency in all realms of the universe (north, south, northwest, southwest, left, right, front, rear, center, high, low, and so forth). Made evident in the last two logoi, these wheels are "the carriers of the world." As a symbol of divine power, the eighth logos (the righteous one who maintains the world and is its foundation), in turn, propels the other two. So, the *Bahir* observes that whereas the second potency (the ninth logos) "stands behind the *Merkabah*," the first potency (the tenth logos) stands in front of it, and the "righteous one, the foundation of the world," is in the center as the prince of these two others. Holding the souls of all living things, he is the "eternally living," and all "creating" occurs through him (123).

In its logos-centered conception of the *sefirot*, then, the *Bahir* provides its own multidirectional correspondences as they are structured spatially through an image of wheels within wheels or spheres within spheres that are constantly in motion. What is true of the last three spheres is true of the conception as a whole: the vehicle through which the entire structure is set in motion is the Chariot, which is propelled by the powers infusing the *sefirot* in their various forms. Corresponding to these powers, in turn, is that "fullness" through which the universe was created and continues to be sustained. What is "the fullness [*ha-male'*]?" the *Bahir* asks. It is not only the place from which the world emerged; it is that ray which infuses everything in the universe.[45] In the midst

---

45. See Scholem, *Origins*, pp. 68–70, for the implications of *ha-male'* as a technical ren-

of the fullness is God's throne placed over the earth, which, in turn, is surrounded by the sea. The sea reflects the firmament, and the firmament is like the throne of glory. As the centerpiece of the universe, the throne of glory has the appearance of the "sapphire stone," which is the basis of Ezekiel's vision of the *merkabah* (65). All emanates from it, and all leads back to it.

Accordingly, through the *Bahir*, one is made to view the Chariot from a multitude of perspectives. Whether as a manifestation of the multidirectional notion of the powers that infuse the *sefirot* or of the fullness that permeates all, the one idea that underscores the theosophical foundations of the *Sefer ha-Bahir* is that of the *merkabah*. The *Bahir* is unequivocal on this point. Theosophical speculation is *merkabah* speculation, the primary activity of which is the formulation of new structures of thinking. This is the journey upon which the kabbalistic *yored merkabah* embarks. It is a journey not of ecstasis to the celestial realms but of conceptualization in a new key. Its destination is a renewed understanding of the kabbalistic implications of the *merkabah*. Employing the language familiar to the *yordei merkabah*, the *Bahir* provides its own rendering of this idea.

Thus, the text asks, "What is thinking [*maḥshabah*]?" and then responds: It is "the king who is needed by everything" created in the world, both above and below (59). The idea recalls a question of crucial importance to the *hekhalot* literature:

> Why do we employ [in Hebrew] the expression "it arose in thought" [in the sense of: it came to mind], and we do not say: "it descends," while we do say [in the "Greater Hekhaloth"]: whoever plunges into the vision of the Merkabah descends and [only] afterwards ascends? There [it is written "descend"], because we say: whoever plunges into the vision of the Merkabah . . . but here, in the *maḥshabah*, the thought, there is no longer any vision or any end. And everything which has neither end nor conlusion suffers no descent, as people [indeed] say: someone descended [that is, penetrated] to the end of the opinion of his companion; but not: to the end of his thought (60).[46]

---

dering of the concept of the *pleroma* in gnostic thought. In the *Bahir*, see in particular sec. 4 and 65.

46. As rendered by Scholem, *Origins*, pp. 129–130.

The implications are clear enough: the *ma'aseh merkabah* of the *Sefer ha-Bahir* dispenses with vision or at least with that kind characteristic of the old *yordei merkabah*.[47] In lieu of vision the *Bahir* extols thought (*mahshabah*). For that reason one no longer needs to "descend" to the Chariot in preparation to "ascend," for descent implies limit. Because thought is without limit, it does not entail descent. Ascent through thought is limitless. The theosophical reformulation of the *merkabah* delineated in the *Bahir*, therefore, is without limit in the complexities and nuances of its formulations. Those formulations create a new *merkabah*, one free of the trammels imposed upon it by the old visionary renderings. Appropriating earlier conceptions of the *merkabah*, the *Sefer ha-Bahir*, then, forges its own theosophy, one in which the visionary mode assumes a new meaning in keeping with the decidedly speculative and theosophic foundations of a text that was to assume a status of seminal importance in the history of *kabbalah*.

Among the writers in whom these speculative and theosophic foundations received profound expression in later kabbalistic thought, Rabbi Jacob ben Jacob ha-Kohen of Castille (second half of the thirteenth century) is particularly apposite. Assimilating the outlook of the *Bahir* and anticipating the concerns of generations that were to follow, Rabbi Jacob ben Jacob reveals the importance of the *merkabah* to his interpretive outlook, one that is especially concerned with the esoteric dimensions of the Hebrew alphabet.[48] Reflecting a theosophic interest in the *'otiot* that extends back to the *Sefer Yetsirah* and is rearticulated in the *Sefer ha-Bahir*, these speculations transform the visionary dimensions of the *merkabah* into a linguistic trope. This transformation, in turn, amounts to a theology of utterance.

47. Scholem's explanation is particularly illuminating: "The *mahshabah* is therefore the object of a vision and a contemplative immersion, *histakluth*; indeed, it is the last and the most profound object of all such contemplation. The vision finds its limit in the object contemplated. It can therefore be said that these old mystics 'descend toward the Merkabah.'" *Origins*, p. 130.

48. Parenthetical references by page number in my text are to the work entitled "Explanation of the Letters," in *The Early Kabbalah*, ed. Joseph Dan (New York: Paulist Press, 1986), pp. 153–164. The works of the Kohen circle, which also includes Rabbi Jacob ben Jacob's brother Isaac ben Jacob, were published by Scholem in *Mada'ey ha-Yahadut* 2 (1927): 165–293, under the title "Qabbalot R. Ya'aqov ve-R. Yitshaq." The present selection is from pp. 201–219 of the writings of Rabbi Jacob ben Jacob as published by Scholem in *Mada'ey ha-Yahadut*. For a discussion of the Kohen brothers, see Dan, pp. 36–37, in *The Early Kabbalah*, and Scholem, *Kabbalah*, passim, esp. pp. 55–56, as well as *Tarbiz* 2–4 (1931–1934), passim.

Beginning with the letter 'alef, Rabbi Jacob thus advises us to concentrate on the image of the letter itself in order to behold there what amounts to the hiddenness of God. "Just as the 'alef is pronounced in a hidden and concealed spot at the back of the tongue," observes Jacob, "so the Holy One, blessed be He, is hidden from visible sight. Similarly, just as the 'alef is ethereal and imperceptible, so the Holy One, blessed be He, denied to all creatures the ability to comprehend Him, save by means of thought, for thought is pure and unblemished and subtle as the ether. But not even thought can grasp the Holy One, blessed be He, so hidden that He is" (p. 153). By means of the individual letter, then, one has access to the *Deus absconditus*, the fact of whose hiddenness is revealed not only in the shape of the letter but in the manner of its pronunciation. At the forefront of this revelation is thought, the exercise of which in the act of concentration yields insight into the nature of the divine.

Extending his analysis further, Rabbi Jacob distinguishes in the form of the 'alef between what he calls an "inner white form" and an "external black form." In what amounts to a kind of Neoplatonic discourse on the theory of forms, Rabbi Jacob observes that the inner form "corresponds to the Holy One, blessed be He, completely hidden from the sight of all creatures and unbounded in His interiorness." The outer form, on the other hand, "corresponds to the world." Rabbi Jacob elaborates this distinction through the metaphor of clothing. The white form, he says, corresponds to a white robe, as the sages maintain that God "wrapped Himself in a white robe whose sparks shone forth from one end of the world to the other" (cf. Ps. 104:2; Dan. 2:22). The inner white form, in turn, encircles the outer form and encompasses all the directions of the outer form. What are these directions? Rabbi Jacob answers this question specifically in terms that provide a multiplicity of contexts for understanding the significance of the 'alef. Among those contexts and, in fact, representing a culminating moment in the enumeration of them is the *merkabah*: "When you observe the four directions from which the letter 'alef extends forth from the center point, know that they correspond to the four directions of the heavens and the four letters of His great and holy name and the four holy animals and the four encampments of the Chariot" (pp. 154–155).

All these meanings, in turn, are summed up in the figure of man, who, for Rabbi Jacob, is a microcosm of the entire universe.

So, Rabbi Jacob observes of the letter 'alef that the tip recalls *yod*, which is associated with the ten parts of the human head, that is, "the four temples of the head, the two ears, two eyes, and two nostrils. The 'alef also corresponds to the ten fingers in the human hand. So the middle stroke resembles *vav*, which corresponds to the six directions of man. "For man is a microcosm, and just as the world possesses six directions, so too does man possess six directions, [including] front, back, left, right, head, and feet." The front signifies the east, the back the west, left the north, right the south; the head symbolizes upward movement, the feet downward. The foot of 'alef, in turn, resembles *yod* and reflects the ten toes of man (p. 156).

For Rabbi Jacob, then, the human figure encapsulates all the other meanings. Included in those meanings are the physical universe, the Tetragrammation, and the divine Chariot of God with its angelic creatures and its encampments. These dimensions emerge in the very letters that constitute the Hebrew alphabet (letters that are themselves contained in the 'alef) and are part of the secret language that the alphabet discloses in the shapes of the letters themselves. To view those letters, to pronounce them, to understand the occult significations that they embody is to gain access into the nature of the *Deus absconditus*, a phenomenon that reveals itself in thought and encompasses in its interiority all that lies without.

If such is true of the letter mysticism that Rabbi Jacob applies to the 'alef, this outlook is discernible in his treatment of the other letters as well. Of paramount importance to this treatment are the theosophical implications of the *merkabah*. Those implications make themselves apparent throughout Rabbi Jacob's analysis. In his discussion of the *dalet*, for example, he maintains that the significance of this letter resides in part in its numerical value as that which corresponds to the four holy creatures. Engaging in a *gematria* of numerical signification here, as elsewhere, Rabbi Jacob invokes the *merkabah* with its accoutrements as the centerpiece of his discourse.[49] Having done so, he then proceeds to other aspects of his alphabetical analysis.

49. In the literature of *kabbalah* distinctions are customarily drawn among the following: (1) *gematria*, "the calculation of the numerical value of Hebrew words and the search for connections with other words or phrases of equal value"; (2) *notarikon*, "the interpretation of the letters of a word as abbreviations of whole sentences"; and (3) *temurah*, "the inter-

Like the 'alef, the dalet becomes a pictogram of the merkabah. The yod-like appearance of the upper stroke of the dalet, observes Rabbi Jacob, is like the Holy One riding upon the Chariot. Because the dalet does not turn toward the yod in the sequence of the letters, this implies that, even though the Holy One rides upon the four holy creatures, they are unable to behold the face of the divine Presence (Shekhinah), for that sight causes fear and trembling. They are accordingly "equipped with wings so that they may shield their eyes and thus avoid viewing the face of the divine Presence" (p. 157). In his analysis of both the shape and directional place-ment of the dalet within the alphabet, then, Rabbi Jacob discerns the secrets of the divine realm as those secrets bear upon the mystical significance of individual letters. The outlook here is at once highly serious (after all, celestial matters are involved) and sublimely playful (ingenuity underscores one's ability to discover as much as possible within the visual representations of the letters). Both qualities bear upon the analysis as it proceeds to discover additional correspondences.

Focusing once again upon the directional significance raised earlier, for instance, Rabbi Jacob observes:

> When you notice that the yod-shape is behind the dalet and not before the dalet, you learn that the Throne and Presence of the Holy One, blessed be He, are in the west. West is called "back"; therefore Scripture states: "And you shall see My back, but My face shall not be seen" [Exod. 33:23], which is on the western side. Thus you will find that man's brain is toward the back of the head and the spirit is in the brain. The brain represents the Throne of Glory while the soul... corresponds to the divine Presence in the West. The enlightened will understand. (pp. 157–158)

The passage represents a triumph of kabbalistic reasoning con-cerning the merkabah and its associations. Drawing once again upon the pictorial significance of the letters, Rabbi Jacob makes much of the fact that the dalet embodies the shape of the yod on its upper portion, which, viewed spatially, faces west. Correspond-ingly, comments Rabbi Jacob, the Enthroned Figure upon the Chariot faces west as a symbol of the fact that the hinderparts of

_____

change of letters according to certain systematic rules." Among others, Rabbi Jacob ben Jacob ha-Kohen made marked use of these techniques. Scholem, Major Trends, p. 100.

God may be seen but that His face may not. This idea is reinter-
preted in terms of the all-important image of the human figure,
specifically, the head as the seat of thought and the residence of
the spirit.

Moving from *dalet* to *he'*, Rabbi Jacob continues to relate the
'otiot to the *merkabah*. The form of the letter *he'*, Rabbi Jacob
observes, contains the shape of *dalet* and *vav*. *Dalet* corresponds
to the four holy creatures, and *vav* represents the six directions
of the world. One of the four creatures is named Israel, who rules
over the six directions of the world. Just as the top of the *he'*,
which resembles the *dalet*, rules and rises above the lower *vav*
stroke, so this creature whose name is Israel is the judge of the
entire world. "In response we say HEAR O ISRAEL—here meaning:
Hear O Israel who is inscribed upon the Chariot." Standing at
the head of the four holy creatures, the creature called Israel
"leads and guides the others" (p. 159).

As leader and guide, this creature reflects the pictograph of the
he' as that which has an opening between the upper and lower
strokes of the letter. This opening takes the shape of the opening
in the human eye, an idea that supports what was said in the *Sefer
Yetsirah*: "*he'* is vision," and "there can be no sight except with an
eye." This creature, then, "sees everything that man does, according to the Will of the Holy One, blessed be He" Corresponding to sight is hearing, an element that is likewise integral to the
letter *he'*. So Rabbi Jacob observes that the *vav*, which may be
observed in the inner part of *he'*, assumes the form of "the inner
heads which reside in the ear." Because there cannot be hearing
without an ear, the *Sefer Yetsirah* says: "*vav* is hearing." This "creature" hears the prayers of Israel and "brings them before the King
of all kings, the high and lofty God" (p. 159). As a result of this
analysis, one is able to discern still further how Rabbi Jacob not
only associates the individual letters with the *merkabah* and its
traditions but finds essential correspondences between the occult
dimensions of the Chariot and the physiognomy of the human
form, a motif that runs throughout his commentary.

To penetrate the secret of the letters is to behold the *merkabah*
as a theosophical phenomenon that finds its counterpart in a range
of significations, human as well as divine. In the process of discerning hidden significations, kabbalistic reasoning does not hesitate to engage in metaphysical speculations of the most extreme
sort nor to refrain from discovering the most radical of corre-

spondences in areas that might otherwise defy such comparisons. With the locus of its pronouncements in the visual depictions of the letters of the Hebrew alphabet, this kind of reasoning transforms the visionary into a unique system of theosophical endeavor, at the forefront of which is the *merkabah* with its accoutrements. Moving from one letter to the next in his discourse upon the Hebrew alphabet, Rabbi Jacob discovers new correspondences and new relationships that suggest how intricately, as well as how harmoniously, the multiple structures of the divine world are embedded in the *'otiot*, which become sources of profound insight into the secrets of God's ways.[50] "The enlightened will understand," declares Rabbi Jacob. To understand is to penetrate the veil of thought, to move from the external form into the internal form, from the black form into the white. Delighting in the correspondences to which that movement gives rise, Rabbi Jacob embarks upon his own journey to the realm of the visionary. At the center of that realm resides the *merkabah* as an object of speculative pursuit and as a well-spring of esoteric, as well as figurative, revelation.[51]

IV

The foregoing suggests how the concept of the *merkabah* was developed in works ranging from the *Sefer ha-Bahir* to those of Jacob ben Jacob ha-Kohen, but no account of the esoteric dimensions of the visionary experience can afford to overlook the *Sefer ha-Zohar* (The Book of Splendor), the central document of medieval *kabbalah*.[52] Attributed to Moses ben Shem Tob de León of

50. Corresponding interpretations are discernible in Rabbi Jacob's analysis of *tet, pe'*, and *zayyin*, all of which are related to the *merkabah*. In his commentary on *tet*, Rabbi Jacob speaks of a first Chariot and a second Chariot. He also incorporates into his *merkabah* analysis a discussion of the *sefirot* (pp. 159–163).

51. Limitations of space do not permit consideration of the immensely important work of Abraham ben Samuel Abulafia of Saragosa (1240–1291), one of the most important exponents of letter mysticism in the late thirteenth century. For an illuminating discussion of Abulafia, see Scholem, *Major Trends*, pp. 119–155. More recently, see the fascinating study of Moshe Idel, *The Mystical Experience in Abraham Abulafia* (Albany, N.Y.: State University of New York Press, 1988), which offers not only a new reading of the major works but translations of sections of previously unavailable material.

52. For detailed and illuminating accounts of the *Zohar*, its authorship, dates of composition, manuscript versions, editions, and doctrines, see Scholem, *Major Trends*, pp. 156–243, and *Kabbalah*, pp. 57–61, 213–243; and Daniel Chanan Matt's introduction to his

Guadalajara (d. 1305), the *Zohar* was produced largely between 1280 and 1286. Pseudepigraphal in nature, it adopts the persona of Rabbi Simeon ben Yochai, the famous second-century *tanna*, who is portrayed as wandering about a Palestinian setting with his son Eleazar, his friends, and his disciples, and discoursing with them on a full range of topics both human and divine. Written primarily in Aramaic (or pseudo-Aramaic), the *Zohar* adopts the language of the Talmud in order to bestow upon its teachings the force of authority and the aura of tradition and authenticity. In form and content the *Zohar* is a vast work, indeed, a veritable library of writings, many of them differing in character and in focus and suggesting varying periods of composition.[53] Nonetheless, the work exhibits an essential unity, as well as an underlying approach.

Midrashic at its core, the main portion of the *Zohar* is conceived as a kabbalistic commentary on the Torah, combined with short statements, long expositions, and stories concerning Rabbi Simeon ben Yochai and his disciples. In this section of the *Zohar*, as well as in the others, the Torah is looked upon as a vast *corpus symbolicum* in which every word, every phrase, is not only polysemous but capable of revealing the most profound and occult insights into the hidden life of God. What results from such an approach is an outlook that views the biblical text as a reservoir of infinite meanings. It is this outlook that distinguishes the mind and art

---

translation *Zohar: The Book of Enlightenment* (New York: Paulist Press, 1983), pp. 1–39. Many of my own summary comments are drawn from their accounts. All sections of the *Zohar* were published in the complete edition of Yehudah Ashlag (Jerusalem: Chevrah Le-Hotsa'at ha-Zohar, 1945–1958), 22 vols., with a Hebrew translation of the Aramaic. An accurate English translation by Harry Sperling and Maurice Simon of the main parts of the *Zohar* appeared under the title *The Zohar*, 5 vols. (London: Soncino Press, 1949). Large sections of the *Zohar*, along with commentary, may be found in Isaiah Tishby, *The Wisdom of the Zohar: An Anthology of Texts*, trans. David Goldstein, 3 vols. (Oxford: Oxford University Press, 1989). Other portions were also translated into English by Roy Rosenberg under the title *The Anatomy of God: The Book of Concealment, the Greater Holy Assembly, and the Lesser Holy Assembly of the Zohar, with the Assembly of the Tabernacle* (New York: Ktav, 1973). Unless otherwise noted, parenthetical references in my text are to the Sperling and Simon edition, which has been compared with that of Ashlag.

53. For an account of the various complex strata of the *Zohar*, see Scholem, *Major Trends*, pp. 159–163, and *Kabbalah*, pp. 214–220. Scholem comments that "in the 16th century the legend grew up that the present *Zohar*, which contains about 2,000 closely printed pages, was only a tiny remnant of the original work, which was some 40 camel loads in weight. These ideas are not sustained by a critical examination of the Zohar." *Kabbalah*, p. 20.

of Moses ben Shem Tob de León. So Scholem comments: "For the peculiar speculative genius which discovers in the Torah layer upon layer of hidden meaning, there is in principle no limit. In the last resort, the whole of the Torah, as is often stressed by the author, is nothing but the one great and holy Name of God. Seen that way, it [the Torah] cannot be 'understood'; it can only be 'interpreted' in an approximate manner." Indeed, for the author of the *Zohar*, the Torah has "seventy faces" shining forth to the initiate, an idea that later kabbalists transformed into six hundred thousand faces.[54] Be that as it may, this view of the biblical text as a multifaceted *corpus symbolicum* is one that permeates the *Zohar* and its method of interpretation. In no instance does such an idea become more compelling than in the Zoharic treatment of the vision of Ezekiel. That vision and all it implies are of crucial importance to the *Zohar* as among the most profound expressions of *kabbalah* in the Middle Ages.

In its interpretation of the vision the *Zohar* initially adopts the perspective of the biblical hermeneut who examines the text qua text, that is, what the text says, what Ezekiel sees, what his motives are in sharing his revelation, and the way in which one is to understand Ezekiel's vision in the context of corresponding visions. The approach is very much in keeping with traditional midrash. So consistent is the *Zohar* with earlier exegetical accounts, in fact, that it even exhibits some of the long-standing ambivalence toward and indeed distrust of what the prophet purports to have beheld. Actually calling into question the significance of the vision, the *Zohar* goes so far as to invoke the commonplace idea that "the Israelites at Mount Sinai saw more of the Divine than the prophet Ezekiel." Whereas the Israelites through Moses encountered God, as it were, "face to face," Ezekiel saw only a "likeness," as one who looks through a partition. Unlike Moses (and, through him, the Israelites), Ezekiel "both saw and did not see, heard and did not hear"; as he says, "he saw something *like ḥashmal*, but not actually *ḥashmal* itself." On Sinai the "Head" and the "Body" of God were revealed to Moses, but to Ezekiel it was only the "Hand" that was shown. Extending the comparison still further, the *Zohar* maintains that Moses, according to tradition, "derived his prophetic vision from a bright mirror, whereas the other prophets [like

54. *Major Trends*, pp. 209–210.

Ezekiel] derived their vision from a dull mirror."[55] Finally, in comparison with Moses, all the prophets are like females in comparison with males. The Lord did not speak to Moses in "riddles" but showed him everything clearly. "Blessed indeed," exclaims the *Zohar*, "was the generation in whose midst this prophet [Moses] lived!" (*Jethro* 81b–82b).

Viewed from such a perspective, the vision of Ezekiel, then, is actually seen to be a lesser form of revelation than that afforded Moses, the greatest of all prophets. For Moses had access to the white fire that constituted the original Torah. But this primal vision is lost: what remains now is the black fire that constitutes the vision of Ezekiel. It is through this vision that one must regain access to the source of the white fire, the source of all vision. Aligning himself with the exiled generation of Ezekiel's time, the author of the *Zohar* speaks through the persona of the *tanna* Rabbi Simeon ben Yochai in order to effect such an event. Doing so, the author of the *Zohar* would provide the means by which a true restoration of vision might occur. This restoration is possible only if the vision of Ezekiel is subjected to the most intense form of scrutiny. Approaching the vision from as many perspectives as possible, the author of the *Zohar* does not hesitate to interrogate both the prophet and the vision he beholds.

In his discussion of the prophet's method of disclosing his prophecy, for example, the author of the *Zohar* begins by expressing some understandable concerns: "If Ezekiel was indeed a faithful prophet, why did he disclose the whole of his vision?" Is it appropriate, that is, for one who has beheld as much as Ezekiel has "to reveal all the secrets which he has seen there?" Ezekiel was indeed a faithful prophet, we are assured, and "whatever he revealed he revealed by permission of the Holy One, blessed be He, and for proper reasons." The question nonetheless remains: What are the reasons? The answer lies in the fact that, at the time of the vision, the Babylonian exiles to whom Ezekiel prophesied were so hardened in their despair that only a full account of what Ezekiel saw would move them in the direction of renewed hope. The *Zohar* describes the event in the following terms:

> When the celestial Company arrived in Babylon, the heavens opened, and the holy spirit of prophecy descended upon Ezekiel,

55. Compare the statement in *Vayetze* 149b: "A 'vision' [*mar'eh*] is so called because it is like a mirror, in which all images are reflected."

and he saw his wonderful vision, and proclaimed to the exiles: "Behold, your Master is here, and all the celestial beings have come down to be your companions." But they believed it not, and so he was compelled to disclose to them the whole of his heavenly vision. Then their joy was exceedingly great, and they recked not of the exile, knowing that the Lord Himself was in their midst. They were all filled with a perfect love of Him, ready to sacrifice themselves for the holiness of the All-Holy, blessed be He! This is the reason why the prophet disclosed to them all that he saw. (*Shemoth* 2a–2b)

From the perspective that this explanation embodies, the vision is seen as the occasion of renewal, hope, and joy to a people otherwise completely lost to despair. Because of the extent of their loss and the shock of their exilic condition, however, a full account of the vision is necessary to alleviate their suffering. Accordingly, those in exile are permitted to know all, to behold all, as a means of allowing them to experience that sense of communion they enjoyed as true children of Israel before their exile. It is the quality of revivification even in exile that underscores the interpretation at this point.

If the vision is seen as a source of renewal for the faithful, it likewise functions as a source of destruction for God's enemies. Here, the vision embodies the quality of "Power" (*geburah*) reflected in the terrifying movement of the vision from the realms of the north. "And what do we read of Ezekiel when he saw the Presence? 'And I looked, and, behold, a whirlwind came out of the north, a great cloud, and a fire infolding itself.' " The whirlwind, states the *Zohar*, symbolizes the breaking of the power of the enemy by the power of God. This whirlwind was "stirred from the side of celestial Power" that came from the north, a hidden region out of which justice emanates (*Jethro* 82a).

In addressing the concept of power, the *Zohar* distinguishes between God's right hand and His left. The right hand of God dashes in pieces His enemies. When Israel neglects God's teachings, however, the left hand of God predominates, and with it the power of heathendom (*Beshalah* 58b). This power of heathendom embodied in the left hand, the author of the *Zohar* associates with the chariots of Pharaoh. Although these chariots as symbols of Egyptian power originally enjoy divine protection, they lose that protection after the Egyptians fall into evil ways. At that point the Egyptians become subject to destruction. Accordingly, when God desires to bring the hosts of Pharaoh down "even unto the depths,"

He removes that "supernal influence" that guides their chariots and destroys them in the Red Sea (*Beshalaḥ* 48b–49a).

The conception is of particular interest because, from the perspective of God's right hand and His left, the *Zohar* envisions a complex interlinking of chariots both in the realms above and in the realms below. "Behold, how many chariots, how many hosts, the Holy One has formed above!" declares the *Zohar*. "And all of them are linked to one another, all are chariots one to another, manifold grades, diverse and yet united!" What is true of the right hand is true of the left:

> From the left side the chariots of the unholy principalities rise up. They also are linked one with the other, grade to grade, the greatest of them being ... "the first-born of Pharaoh," whom the Holy One killed. All of these unholy powers are delivered unto the judgment of the Kingdom, the which is called "the great sea," in order that they may be uprooted each in his own grade, and be utterly cast down, and when they are broken above, all their counterparts below are also broken and lost in the "lower sea." (*Beshalaḥ* 56a–56b)

Such is the fate of what the *Zohar* calls the "other side" (*sitra' 'aḥra'*), the domain of evil. If this domain as a manifestation of the left hand was originally associated with the attributes of God, in its corrupt form it is no longer part of the world of holiness.[56] So divorced from holiness, it is ultimately destroyed, as God comes forth with His hosts from the region of power to overwhelm His enemies. Essential to this conception is the vision of Ezekiel, one in which the Chariot assumes a decidedly military bearing.

In its concern with what amounts to the military aspects of the Chariot, this approach, in turn, is further reflected in the discussion of Ezekiel's vision as a manifestation of the encampments of the Israelites. Recalling similar treatments in the *Midrash Rabbah* and elsewhere, the vision of Ezekiel undergoes an elaborate taxonomy that associates the *ḥayyot* in particular with the arrangement of the Israelite military forces in the wilderness. Those forces, suggests the *Zohar*, are organized into four camps, comprising the twelve tribes that constitute the twelve boundaries enclosing the com-

56. For an illuminating discussion of the *sitra' 'aḥra'* and the problem of evil in the *Zohar* and traditions of *kabbalah*, see Scholem, *Kabbalah*, pp. 122–128. See also Rabbi Isaac ben Jacob ha-Kohen's *Treatise on the Left Emanation* in Dan, *The Early Kabbalah*, pp. 165–182.

munity of Israel. These encampments, in turn, are founded on the celestial model, the source of which is Ezekiel's vision as manifested in the *ḥayyot*. In that vision the faces of the *ḥayyot* turn toward the four cardinal points, each with its own likeness, but all summed up in the likeness of man, which subsumes them all.[57]

Recalling the traditions of earlier midrashic commentary, each of the *ḥayyot* has its angelic counterpart, its direction, its image, and its camps: Michael is on the right (toward the south), represented by the image of the lion on his standard and signifying the camps of Reuben, Simeon, and Gad; Gabriel is on the left (toward the north), represented by the image of the ox on his standard and signifying the camps of Dan, Asher, and Naphtali; Uriel is in front (toward the east), represented by the image of the eagle on his standard and signifying the camps of Judah, Issachar, and Zabulon; and Raphael is behind (toward the west), represented by the image of man on his standard and signifying the camps of Ephraim, Manasseh, and Benjamin. Over them all hovers the *Shekhinah*, which resides in the eastward-facing ark in the center of the encampments. The whole, in turn, is unified by the letters of the Tetragrammaton, the Divine Name in which resides all power. Because of the divine nature of the entire conception, the encampments are figured forth in the celestial firmaments themselves (*Bemidbar* 118b–119a; *Behaʿalothekha* 153b–155a).

In his treatment of this idea, the author of the *Zohar* creates his own mythology surrounding the *ḥayyot*. The wings of the *ḥayyot*, for example, are formed of white flaming fire, and their faces are illumined by the white light of the sun. As the encampments set forth for the battle, the spirit of the *ḥayyot* propels the wheels (*ʾofannim*) of the Tabernacle through which the processions move. Two heralds march in front of the Tabernacle, and at their proclamation all hosts and legions assemble, and all the firmaments move forward along with the hosts. Each of the *ḥayyot*, in turn, exhibits its own behavior. The lion puts forth its right hand and summons to itself an entire host of lions. When the lion roars, all the firmaments quiver and shake. Then the lion puts forth its left hand, and its enemies quake with fear. Gathering to itself all its forces, the eagle next arises, puts forth its pinions, and all the

---

57. Compare the statement in *Jethro* 80b: Discussing the *ḥayyot*, the *Zohar* concludes: "As for 'man,' he comprises all."

winged forces move in unison. The description of the lion and the eagle is followed by that of the ox, a truly imposing creature. Goring and trampling ruthlessly with its feet, the ox has eyes that flame with burning fire. When the ox moos, "there emerge out of the hollow of the great abyss numerous spirits of wrath who proceed in front in a chorus of shrieking." In front of the ox seven fiery rivers flow, and, when thirsty, the ox draws up an entire riverfull at one gulp. The man, finally, brings up the rear of the procession. Although the *Zohar* does not elaborate on his appearance or his behavior, one is no doubt to assume that he is the manifestation of all that is represented by the other *ḥayyot* (*Beha'alothekha* 153b–155a; cf. *Pinḥas* 240b–241a).

If the foregoing suggests some of the contexts that distinguish the *Zohar*'s interpretation of Ezekiel's vision, others are equally compelling. Not the least of these contexts is that which locates the *merkabah* at the center of all conceptions embodied in the *Zohar*'s multilayered interpretive structures. The *merkabah*, in fact, becomes the "foundation stone" (*'eben shetiah*) of these structures. As the "foundation stone," the *merkabah* for the *Zohar* is "the central point of the universe," the place of the Holy of Holies. Drawing upon the concept of the foundation stone, the *Zohar* extends its exegesis still further by reformulating the *ma'aseh merkabah* into a myth of creation. When God was about to create the world, the *Zohar* comments, "He detached one precious stone from underneath His Throne of Glory and plunged it into the Abyss, one end of it remaining fastened therein whilst the other end stood out above." That which stood out above "constituted the nucleus of the world, the point out of which the world started, spreading itself to right and left and into all directions." The starting point of the world, this nucleus is the foundation stone.

Elaborating still further upon this notion of the foundation stone as the central point of generation, the *Zohar* devises a spatial construct through which the concept as a whole can be understood. That construct assumes the form of three concentric rings, as of wheels within wheels that encircle and expand outward from the central point: "The first expansion embraces the Sanctuary and all its courts and enclosures and all its appurtenances, as well as the whole city of Jerusalem bounded by the wall; the second expansion embraces the whole of the Land of Israel, the Land which was declared holy; the third expansion comprehends the rest of the earth, the dwelling-place of all the other nations."

Surrounding this spatial construct, the universe that emanates from the cental point or foundation stone, is the great ocean.

The whole arrangement, suggests the *Zohar*, can be conceived in optical terms through an understanding of the structure of the human eye: "For just as in the human eye there are three concentric layers surrounding a central point, which forms the focus of vision, so is the world's vision focused in the central point, consisting of the Holy of Holies and the Ark and the Mercy Seat" (*P'qudé* 222a–222b). In visionary terms, of course, the image in its entirety resolves itself into a generative, cosmic, and finally sacral interpretation of the *merkabah*, the center of centers and foundation of foundations from which all concepts emerge (cf. *P'qudé* 237b–238a).

Having surveyed a number of approaches that the *Zohar* adopts in its interpretation of the vision of Ezekiel, we have seen how the author devises his own network of midrashim fashioned to disclose the many layers of meaning implicit in the biblical text. Moving from this hermeneutical posture to one that is distinctly theosophic in focus, we may now explore that dimension of the *Zohar*'s multifaceted interpretation of the *merkabah*. From this perspective we discover that what the *Zohar* creates in its treatment of the vision is an elaborate theosophy that assimilates and transforms the major traditions of *kabbalah*.

That theosophy expresses itself in a number of ways. Among them is that which demonstrates how the figure of man as *hayyah* is a consummate expression of all that is represented by the other *hayyot*. Engaging in an elaborate process of physiognomy and chiromancy in its examination of the parts of man, the *Zohar* anatomizes the hair, the forehead, the eyes, the lips, the ears, the lineaments of the countenance, and the lines of the hands. In its analysis of the lineaments of the countenance, for example, it penetrates to what it calls "the inner wisdom" of the face. There, it finds "the four prototypes—Man, Lion, Bull, and Eagle, in the Supernal Chariot." Although these forms are hidden, they are discerned by the "masters of the inner wisdom." Elaborating upon the significance of each of these from a theosophic perspective, the *Zohar* observes: "To penetrate through these reflections to the inner symbols and to decipher those symbols aright is the privilege of the wise alone, that they may finally attain to knowledge of the spirit of which the symbols are the manifestation (*Jethro* 70b–78a)."

Moving from physiognomy to chiromancy, the *Zohar* invokes Ezek. 1:8: "And they [the *ḥayyot*] had the hands of a man under their wings." The phrase "the hands of a man," observes the *Zohar*, signifies "all those forms and supernal mysteries which the Holy One has stamped upon man and ordered in his fingers outwardly and inwardly and in the 'palm.' When the Holy One created man, He set in him all the images of the supernal mysteries of the world above, and all the images of the lower mysteries of the world below, and all are designed in man, who stands in the image of God, because he is called 'the creation of the palm.'" To read the palm, that is, the *ḥayyot* embodied in the palm, then, is to understand the mysteries of God. Doing so is to penetrate beneath flesh, skin, bones, and sinews to the soul itself, for flesh, skin, bones, and sinews are but the outward covering, the mere garments of the soul. They "merely symbolize the Chariots and the celestials Hosts, which are inward." This is the mystery of the Supernal Man, who is "innermost" and whose true origins are to be found above. Distinguishing in Neoplatonic fashion between upper and lower worlds, the *Zohar* discovers that essential correspondence between the two: "esoterically, the man below corresponds entirely to the Man above" (*Jethro* 70b–78a). Moving from one to the other in its discussion of the vision of Ezekiel, the *Zohar* embarks upon its own contemplative journey to the realm of the *merkabah*.

In its treatment of the Chariot the *Zohar* accordingly provides a detailed account of the experience that the mystic undergoes in his ascent to the *merkabah*. In its own way the account is reminiscent of the narratives that portray the journeys of the *yordei merkabah* to the celestial halls. As it is rendered, the account assumes an almost lyrical form. In effect, it is a hymn of celebration:

> In the hour when the morning breaks, the Hind [i.e., the *Shekhinah*] rises and starts from her place in order to enter the two hundred palaces of the King. When a man studies the Torah in solitude at midnight, at the hour when the north wind springs up and the Hind desires to be astir, he is taken with her into spiritual realms, to appear before the King. When dawn brightens and he recites his prayers, and unifies the Holy Name in manner due, he is encircled with a thread of grace; he looks into the firmament and a

light of holy knowledge rests upon him. As the man is thus adorned
and shrouded with light all things tremble before him, for he is
called the son of the Holy One, the son of the King's Palace. (*Be-shalaḥ* 57a)

With its establishment of a time frame (midnight-morning), an
appropriate context and setting (study of the Torah in solitude),
a recourse to the elements of trope (the hind, the north wind,
light, and the like), a portrayal of action (movement to the supernal realms, recitation of prayers), the account becomes a self-
conscious literary artifact, a poem commemorating the experience
of the mystic sojourn to the King's Palace (*hekhal*), there to worship
before the *merkabah*. As a result of this experience the mystic
assumes new knowledge and a new identity as Metatron, son of
the Holy One. In one form or another the *topoi* have all been
encountered before, but here they assume renewed significance
within the kabbalistic framework established by the author of the
Zohar.

According to that framework, the purpose of the journey is to
ascend by means of prayer and concentration to the highest of
the supernal realms, an experience that the author of the *Zohar*
describes in some detail, although such an experience finally defies
description. "The 'wise' is he who by the power of his own contemplation attains to the perception of profound mysteries which
cannot be expressed in words," the *Zohar* comments (*Waera* 23a).
Nonetheless, the *Zohar* does venture something of a description.
When praying, the mystic, we are told, raises his hand on high
and concentrates his mind on that realm "which can never be
known or grasped, the starting-point that is absolutely concealed,
that produced what it produced while remaining unknowable, and
irradiated what it irradiated while remaining undisclosed." As
discussed above, this is the *ein-sof*, that which is without limit, and
the source of all the *sefirot*. "It is the desire of the upward-striving
thought," observes the *Zohar*, "to pursue after this and to be illumined by it." In the process the upward-striving thought is illumined by a light undisclosed and unknowable from the *ein-sof*.[58]
So illumined, the mystic's thought is fused with that light into a

58. To have some idea of how these illuminations (which are actually multicolored)
appear, the *Zohar* offers some practical advice: "close thine eye and press thine eyeball,
and thou wilt discern radiating and luminous colours which can only be seen with closed
eyes" (*Waera* 23b).

light from which are formed nine palaces (*hekhalot*). "All the mysteries of faith," the *Zohar* comments, "are contained in those palaces, and all those lights which proceed from the mystic supreme thought are called *ein-sof*." Up to the point of the *ein-sof* "the lights reach and yet do not reach: this is beyond the attainment of mind and thought" (*Noah* 65a).

In its portrayal of this experience the *Zohar* offers a fascinating and detailed commentary on the mystic's journey of contemplation through the spheres of the *sefirot*. This commentary is cast in the form of an elaborate mythology concerning the ascent of the soul through the firmaments in order to appear before the divine Throne. The mythology itself is founded on the notion of the *sefirot* conceived as ten lower heavens and ten upper heavens. Counterparts of each other, the one embodies lower grades of emanation, the other upper grades of emanation, as in successive and interlinking chains of light from lower to higher. Each set of heavens has its own paradise, a lower Eden and an upper Eden, and the topography of one Eden is reflected in that of the other. These Edens are conceived as possessing central points of light from which flow four rivers of light that water the gardens and emanate to the other grades.

In both Edens this central point of light "is not given to any to see or know, but only the light radiating from it, before which the righteous...prostrate themselves." It is the desire of the aspiring soul to enter first the lower paradise and, once having achieved that state of bliss, to ascend to the upper paradise. In order to do so, however, the soul, as an act of penance, must be purged of all impurities by passing through the infernal fires of Gehinnom. Having sustained this rite of passage, the soul is then brought into the lower paradise. "Oh, how broken is that soul after her ordeal in the infernal fire!" the *Zohar* exclaims. Because its ultimate quest is to ascend to the upper paradise, however, it must once more pass through the river of fire in order to cleanse it of any remaining residue of impurity. As a result of this second ordeal it emerges entirely purified. In that state it appears bathed in light, dressed in new raiment, and adorned with crowns before the presence of the King of the universe (*Vayaqhel* 209a–212a). Such is one of the ways in which the *Zohar* mythologizes the mystic's journey of ascent to the *ein-sof* through the spheres of the *sefirot*.

From the perspective of Ezekiel's vision the account of this journey assumes compelling significance in the mythology that it associates with the *merkabah*. As the *Zohar* delineates that mythology, there are in fact two *markabot*, a lower one and an upper one. Whereas the lower one supports the lower firmaments, the upper one supports the upper firmaments. Each set of firmaments rests on its own *ḥayyot*. These *ḥayyot*, in turn, are stationed respectively in the lower Eden, on the one hand, and the upper Eden, on the other. The four heads of the *ḥayyot* correspond to the four rivers of paradise (the light emanations) that flow in both the lower and upper realms. Upholding the firmaments, the *ḥayyot* likewise support the divine throne in each realm, and as a result of the weight of that burden, the *ḥayyot* "ooze perspiration." Out of this perspiration is formed that very river of fire which the souls of aspiring mystics must traverse in their quest for access to the highest realms (*Vayaqhel* 211a–211b).

As remarkable as this mythologizing of the *merkabah* might appear to be, there is even a more fascinating dimension that is given full expression in the *Zohar*. Once again centered in the *merkabah*, this dimension has to do with the gender distinctions the *Zohar* draws between the masculine and feminine elements in God. Those elements are manifested in the *markabot* that uphold the two sets of firmaments (lower and upper) discussed above. According to the *Zohar*, "there is a lower firmament that rests upon the four lower Holy Beasts, whence it extends and begins to take on the form of a female figure behind a male figure: this is esoterically implied in the passage, saying, 'and thou shalt see my back, but my face shall not be seen' [Exod. 33:23], also in 'Thou hast formed me aft and fore' [Ps. 139:5], and again in the words, 'and he took one of his ribs' [Gen. 2:21]." As a counterpart to this feminine aspect, one finds the masculine aspect: "there is an upper firmament resting on the four upper Holy Beasts, whence it extends and takes on the figure of a male, very recondite" (*Vayaqhel* 211a–211b).

In its account of the *merkabah* the *Zohar* makes a great deal of these masculine and feminine figures. The masculine figure, of course, is the Enthroned Figure who dwells in the upper reaches and represents the ultimate manifestation of that godhead toward which the visionary strives, a motif shared by the long traditions of the *hekhalot* upon which the author of the *Zohar* draws in his own depictions of the *merkabah*. The manner in which this masculine Enthroned Figure becomes crucial to the outlook reflected in the *Zohar* is discernible in those sections that detail "the anatomy of God," an anatomy that rivals the *Shiʿur Komah* itself in its delineation of the various parts of God's body.[59]

As far as the feminine figure is concerned, she, too, becomes crucial to the outlook reflected in the *Zohar*. Assuming the form of the *Shekhinah*, she is revealed in her Chariot to Ezekiel as a lower manifestation of the true Presence that dwells above (*Jethro* 82a–82b). In his portrayal of the *Shekhinah* the author of the *Zohar* devises an entire mythology in which the *Shekhinah*, also known as *Matrona*, is ornately dressed in beautiful garments and wears a splendid crown, all in preparation for her ultimate betrothal to the King (*Balak* 208b–209b). Taken together, these two figures, male and female, are what the *Zohar* refers to as "the Masculine world above" and "the Feminine world below," the union of which results in a new form, the members of whose body create a supernal mystery of the most profound sort (*Terumah* 165b). According to Scholem, this emphasis upon gender in the *Zohar* (and, in particular, the representation of the feminine element in God through the auspices of the *Shekhinah*) is "one of the most important and lasting innovations in Kabbalism."[60] As such, this dimension represents yet one more instance through which the *merkabah* assumes renewed and complex expression in the *Zohar*. No matter how the *merkabah* is conceived, it is of central importance to the *Zohar* as both hermeneutic and kabbalistic enterprise.

The foregoing discussion of the *Sefer ha-Zohar* brings to a close our exploration of the esoteric dimensions of the visionary mode as a Judaic phenomenon in the Middle Ages. That exploration has encompassed a number of texts dating back to the earlier prekabbalistic phases of Judaic thought and extending into the later periods that witnessed the flourishing of *kabbalah* as an endeavor fully conscious of its own vocation. Analyzing some of the assumptions and ideas underlying that vocation, we have witnessed the versatility of *kabbalah* in accommodating itself to the transformative nature of the visionary. Once again, the adage that underscores the visionary in its various aspects is true of its esoteric character as well: "*Gestaltung, Umgestaltung, / Des ewigen Sinnes ewige Unterhaltung.*"

---

59. For an account of the *Zohar's* concern with this dimension, see the tracts included in Rosenberg's *The Anatomy of God*.

60. Scholem, *Major Trends*, pp. 229–230. For the presence of the idea in the *Bahir*, see Scholem, *Origins*, pp. 162–180.

In the archetypal form through which such an idea manifests itself in the traditions of *kabbalah*, one recalls Jung's observation that the visionary mode is subsumed into the lore of every culture as a systematic body of secret teaching (*System der Geheim- und Weisheitslehre*). It is this systematic body of secret teaching with which we have been concerned in our investigation of the esoteric dimensions of the visionary mode. As a category of apperception, the esoteric point of view has been seen to represent one of a number of categories that constitute the visionary mode. Complementing the apocalyptic and mystical, on the one hand, and the speculative, on the other, the esoteric provides additional insight into the visionary as an experience of crucial import to Judaism. Having explored those traditions in some depth, we may now proceed to an investigation of the visionary mode from the perspective of its assimilation into the Christian traditions.

~ *Part II*

THE CHRISTOCENTRIC FRAME

⌒ *Five*

The Gnosis of Vision

I

Focusing upon Ezekiel's *visio Dei* as an originary event, we shall now examine the Christocentric contexts of the *Urerlebnis*. In our treatment of this idea we shall be concerned with the *merkabah* as a phenomenon that assumed renewed impetus from the perspective of the dispensation accorded by the Christian traditions. Specifically, we shall attempt to determine the extent to which one is empowered to speak of a Christocentric *merkabah*. Our point of departure will be the "gnostic" foundations of this concept. Given the nature of the material discussed thus far, such an approach is only natural, if not inevitable. As Gershom Scholem would maintain, this is in fact what we have been doing all along in our consideration of the Judaic traditions that underlie the *merkabah*. All of Scholem's works reflect a long-standing belief in the affinity between gnostic systems of thought and the traditions of Jewish mysticism and *kabbalah*. As an expression of this belief, Scholem looked upon the *ma'aseh merkabah* as a form of what he called "Jewish gnosticism."[1] Although Scholem's conclusions in this regard have been debated and indeed contested on a number of fronts, the association of the *merkabah* with gnosticism is one that continues to engage the attention of scholars.[2] In light of this

1. See, for example, Gershom Scholem's *Major Trends in Jewish Mysticism* (New York: Schocken Books, 1954), and *Jewish Gnosticism, Merkabah Mysticism, and Talmudic Tradition* (New York: Jewish Theological Seminary of America, 1960), passim. The idea of Jewish gnosticism (treated disparagingly) can be found as early as Heinrich Graetz, *Gnosticismus und Judenthum* [sic] (Krotoschin: B. L. Monasch and Son, 1846). Graetz actually coined the phrase *"eine jüdische Gnosis,"* which suggested for Scholem a direction in his own study of the *merkabah*.

2. Among those who have called into question the association, see in particular Gruenwald's important studies, " 'Knowledge' and 'Vision': Towards a Clarification of Two 'Gnos-

attention, an examination of the *merkabah* as a manifestation of
what is customarily termed Christian gnosticism seems entirely
appropriate at this juncture.

In order to carry out such an examination, however, we must
say something about the nature of gnosticism in general and Christian gnosticism in particular. It hardly needs to be observed that
there is as much debate about the meanings associated with the
term *gnosticism* as there is about the origins of those movements
thought to constitute it.[3] For the sake of convenience, the observation of Hans Jonas will suffice:

> The *name* "Gnosticism," which has come to serve as a collective
> heading for a manifoldness of sectarian doctrines appearing within
> and around Christianity during its critical first centuries, is derived
> from *gnōsis*, the Greek word for "knowledge." The emphasis on
> *knowledge* as the means for the attainment of salvation, or even as
> the form of salvation itself, and the claim to the possession of this
> knowledge in one's own articulate doctrine, are common features
> of the numerous sects in which the gnostic movement historically
> expressed itself.[4]

tic' Concepts in the Light of Their Alleged Origins," *Israel Oriental Studies* 3 (1973): 63–
107; "The Problems of Anti-Gnostic Polemic in Rabbinic Literature," *Studies in Gnosticism
and Hellenistic Religions*, ed. R. van den Broek and M. J. Vermaseren (Leiden: Brill, 1981),
pp. 171–189; and "Aspects of the Jewish-Gnostic Controversy," *The Rediscovery of Gnosticism: Proceedings of the International Conference on Gnosticism at Yale, New Haven, Connecticut,
March 28–31, 1978*, ed. Bentley Layton, 2 vols. (Leiden: E. J. Brill, 1980–1981), II, 713–
723. See also P. Alexander, "Comparing *Merkavah* Mysticism and Gnosticism: An Essay
in Method," *Journal of Jewish Studies* 5 (1984): 1–17. Among those who continue to pursue
the association, see Gedaliahu G. Stroumsa, "Acher: A Gnostic," in Layton, *The Rediscovery
of Gnosticism*, II, 808–818. For an extended study of the dualistic dimensions implicit in
the association, see A. F. Segal, *Two Powers in Heaven: Early Rabbinic Reports about Christianity
and Gnosticism* (Leiden: Brill, 1977).

3. For problems with definition, see Morton Smith, "The History of the Term Gnos-
tikos," in Layton, *The Rediscovery of Gnosticism*, II, 796–807; and Rudolf Bultmann, *Gnosis*
(London: Adam and Charles Black, 1952). According to Alexander, "It is well known that
it is difficult to achieve a satisfactory definition of Gnosticism. In many ways, 'Gnosticism'
is an artificial modern construct imposed by scholars on a set of diverse phenomena which
are perceived to have some sort of family likeness." Though Greek in formation, *gnosticism*
as a term is of fairly recent coinage, dating to the mid-seventeenth century ("Comparing
Mysticism and Gnosticism," p. 3, n. 6).

4. Hans Jonas, *The Gnostic Religion: The Message of the Alien God and the Beginnings of
Christianity* (Boston: Beacon Press, 1958), pp. 32–33. See also Robert M. Grant, *Gnosticism
and Early Christianity*, 2d ed. (New York: Columbia University Press, 1966); *Gnosticism: A
Source Book of Heretical Writings from the Early Christian Period*, ed. Robert M. Grant (New
York: Harper, 1961); E. R. Dodds, *Pagan and Christian in an Age of Anxiety* (Cambridge:
Cambridge University Press, 1965); and G. Van Groningen, *First Century Gnosticism: Its
Origins and Motifs* (Leiden: Brill, 1967). Addressing the origins of gnosticism, Grant sum-

As a Christian formulation, then, *gnosticism* is a term generally used to describe those heterodox systems of belief a number of the early church fathers found inimical to the teachings of Christianity. Accordingly, the church fathers viewed gnosticism as essentially a Christian heresy and geared their commentaries and refutations to systems that either had arisen already from the foundations of Christianity (for example, the Valentinian system), or had in some way assimilated the figure of Christ into their otherwise heterogeneous teaching (for example, that of the Phrygian Naassenes), or else through a corresponding Judaic milieu were sufficiently proximate to be viewed as challenging and distorting the Christian message (for example, that of Simon Magus). Responding to such polemic, modern research, suggests Jonas, has progressively broadened this traditional range to include other areas of thought as well (pre-Christian Jewish, Hellenistic pagan, Mandaean, and the like).[5]

In keeping with this larger perspective, Jonas treats gnosticism as a "class-concept" having to do with "knowledge" (*gnōsis*) of an emphatically "religious" or "supernatural" kind. Viewed in this way, *gnōsis* means "pre-eminently knowledge *of God.*" The objects of such knowledge "include everything that belongs to the divine realm of being, namely, the order and history of the upper worlds." Closely bound up with the knowledge of these worlds is "revelationary experience," disclosed either through "sacred and secret lore or through inner illumination" that is essentially redemptive. In this respect gnosis has an eminently practical function: it brings about salvation. If the ultimate object of gnosis is God, the experience of gnosis is one that "transforms the knower himself by making him a partaker in the divine existence." In that manner, he is redeemed. This redemption is one in which "knowledge and the attainment of the known by the soul are claimed to coincide—the claim of all true mysticism." Such, observes Jonas, is also the claim of Greek *theōria*, the foundation of philosophical knowledge. But there, the object of knowing is the universal, and the cognitive relation is "optical," that is, "an analogue of the visual relation to objective form that remains unaffected by the relation." Gnostic "knowledge," on the other hand, concerns the particular

---

marizes four principal explanations that have emerged in modern times: (1) Hellenistic philosophy, (2) oriental religion, i.e., Iranian, (3) Christianity, (4) heterodox Judaism. *Gnosticism and Early Christianity*, p. 13.

5. Jonas, *The Gnostic Religion*, p. 33.

as embodied in the transcendent deity, and the relation of knowing is mutual, that is, "a being known at the same time, and involving active self-divulgence on the part of the 'known.' " As a result of this reciprocity of knowing, "the mind is 'informed' with the forms it beholds and while it beholds (thinks) them: here, the subject is 'transformed' (from 'soul' to 'spirit') by the union with a reality that in truth is itself the supreme subject in the situation and strictly speaking never an object at all."[6] This transformative dimension is the basis of the gnostic experience.

If such is true of gnosticism as a "class-concept," it is no less true of the *merkabah* as an expression of gnosis so conceived. A visionary phenomenon that evinces close ties with gnosticism as a "religious" form of apperception, the *merkabah* is very much the product of a gnostic point of view. As gnostic enterprise, the *merkabah* provides the occasion by which the visionary not only gains knowledge of God but undergoes a "revelationary experience" that veritably transforms the knower himself. So transformed, he becomes a "partaker in the divine existence." Already suggested in the Judaic renderings we have examined, this idea is of fundamental importance to the Christocentric perspective. Such is discernible in the New Testament itself as a source of *merkabah* speculation.[7] It is here that the *merkabah* is first canonized as a Christocentric phenomenon.[8] The validity of this observation has been amply demonstrated by a number of scholars, all of

6. Ibid., pp. 34–35.

7. In keeping with the traditions of gnostic thought, a number of scholars have discovered in the New Testament what might be called an "incipient gnosticism." See, for example, Grant, *Gnosticism and Early Christianity*, esp. pp. 151–181. Significantly, New Testament gnosticism is seen to have particular affinities with the sources of the *merkabah*. According to Gilles Quispel, for example, the New Testament attributes of Christ as "the Glory of God, which comes from heaven, touches the earth for a moment, is incarnated in the man Jesus, and eventually returns to the heavenly realm" embodies a perspective not only in accord with gnostic thought but ultimately indebted to "the personified Glory of the Lord" beheld by the prophet Ezekiel in his inaugural *visio Dei* ("Gnosticism from Its Origins to the Middle Ages," *The Encyclopedia of Religion*, ed. Mircea Eliade, 16 vols. [New York: Macmillan, 1987], V, 567; see also Quispel, "Gnosticism and the New Testament," *Vigiliae Christianae* 22 [1968]: 81–93). In short, the very well-spring of Christian gnosticism as a New Testament phenomenon is that vision from which emerge the traditions of the *merkabah* in its various forms. Given these circumstances, an investigation of the New Testament foundations of the *merkabah* as a form of gnosticism is entirely justified.

8. References in English are to the RSV, and Greek interpolations are to the Novum Testamentum Graece, ed. Eberhard Nestle (Stuttgart: Württembergische Bibelanstalt, 1953), which has been consulted as the base text throughout.

whom attest to the assimilation of *merkabah* material into the New Testament outlook.[9]

The seminal work of Morton Smith is a case in point. According to Smith, the paradigm of *merkabah* lore is already discernible in the figure of Jesus as one thoroughly conversant in the implications of ascent. Resorting to the gospel narratives and the Pauline epistles, Smith demonstrates the manner in which Jesus is conceived as a well-spring of *merkabah* thought, especially that bearing on the culture of the *hekhalot*, a concept encoded in the New Testament as Christocentric phenomenon. Reflecting the disposition of the *yored merkabah*, Jesus may be seen, in his own way, as a *hekhalot* mystic who actually "practiced" the "techniques for ascent to the heavens" and imparted these techniques to those with whom he shared the divine gnosis. A magus who communicated the *disciplina arcani* of a transcendent heterodoxy, Jesus thereby provided the impetus of all that is to be found in the *merkabah* teachings of his followers.[10] Smith finds evidence for this idea in a number of texts but principally those that address themselves to such events in the life and ministry of Christ as the Transfiguration and related accounts of the Baptism, the scene in Geth-

9. In this regard, see Christopher Rowland's doctoral dissertation, "The Influence of the First Chapter of Ezekiel on Jewish and Early Christian Literature" (University of Cambridge, 1974), as well as his book *The Open Heaven: A Study of Apocalyptic in Judaism and Early Christianity* (New York: Crossroad, 1982), passim. See also J. W. Bowker, *The Targums and Rabbinic Literature* (Cambridge: Cambridge University Press, 1969), p. 38, and " 'Merkabah' Visions and the Visions of Paul," *Journal of Semitic Studies* 16 (1971): 157–173; Gershom Scholem, "The Four Who Entered Paradise and Paul's Ascension to Paradise," *Jewish Gnosticism*, pp. 14–19; Peter Borgen, *Bread from Heaven: An Exegetical Study of the Concept of Manna in the Gospel of John and the Writings of Philo* (Leiden: Brill, 1965), p. 3; Gedaliahu G. Stroumsa, "Form(s) of God: Some Notes on Metatron and Christ," *HTR* 76 (1983): 269–288; Jacob Neusner, *A Life of Rabban Yoḥanan ben Zakkai* (Leiden: Brill, 1962), pp. 100ff.; Morton Smith, *Clement of Alexandria and a Secret Gospel of Mark* (Cambridge: Harvard University Press, 1973); and, most recently, James Tabor, *Things Unutterable: Paul's Ascent to Paradise in Its Greco-Roman, Judaic, and Early Christian Contexts* (Lanham, Md.: University Press of America, 1986). As Christopher Rowland aptly points out, one does not need a throne-chariot vision per se to describe a visionary event as having been influenced by *merkabah* speculation. Although the New Testament might at first appear generally indifferent to the throne-chariot vision, the *merkabah* assumes a number of different forms, depending upon the circumstances in which the vision is portrayed (*Open Heaven*, pp. 358–374).

10. Smith, *Clement of Alexandria and a Secret Gospel of Mark*, pp. 203, 213–216, 225–226, 237–248. The arguments here are reiterated in a popular but fascinating form in Smith's *The Secret Gospel: The Discovery and Interpretation of the Secret Gospel According to Mark* (Clearlake, Calif.: Dawn Horse Press, 1982), esp. pp. 89–138. See also Smith's *Jesus the Magician* (San Francisco: Harper & Row, 1978), passim.

semane, the Resurrection, and the Ascension."[11] The "deliberately secretive reflections" that these accounts encode emphasize "the mystery of the kingdom of God" as that which is acquired through an "ecstatic experience" in which the visionary beholds the heavens opened and is possessed by the spirit. This visionary is Jesus himself. As *yored merkabah*, he adopted "the magical discipline of his day" and developed that gift "into a technique by which he was able to ascend to the heavens and also give others the same experience and similar spiritual powers."[12] If such is the case, then the New Testament may be seen as a text that embodies a gnosis as remarkable as any that the Judaic traditions centered on the *merkabah* ever produced. Consistent with those traditions and incorporating their outlook, the New Testament reformulated the culture of the *merkabah* in its own terms. As a result of that reformulation, one is indeed authorized to speak of a Christocentric *merkabah*, a new chariot with its own distinguishing characteristics.

Founded in the notion of Jesus as paradigm of the *yored merkabah*, those characteristics are likewise discernible in the experiences of his followers. At issue are the writings of the apostle Paul, on the one hand, and the seer Saint John the Divine, on the other. Both may be said to reinterpret the *merkabah* to accord with their own points of view, and both suggest still further how the *merkabah* was assimilated as visionary event into the Christology of New Testament teaching.

According to J. W. Bowker, Paul, as an émigré from a Judaic past and as a "true descendant of Abraham," gives every evidence of familiarity with the traditions and practices that constitute not only the ways of his own former heritage but of the culture of such institutions as the *ma'aseh merkabah*. An almost exact contemporary of Jochanan ben Zakkai, the great *merkabah* mystic, Paul reveals ties with this school of mysticism. Indeed, observes Bowker, Paul might have actually been "trained to the point of contemplating the meaning of the 'chariot' chapters."[13] At least two of

11. See, in particular, Matt. 3:16, 17:2; Mark 1:10, 14:32–51; Luke 3:21; 9:29, among others. Rowland is fully in agreement and cites, in addition to these texts, that having to do with the Pentecost (Acts 2:3) (*Open Heaven*, pp. 358–374; cf. David J. Halperin, *The Faces of the Chariot: Early Jewish Responses to Ezekiel's Vision* [Tübingen: J. C. B. Mohr, 1988], p. 17). A plethora of New Testament texts, in fact, draw upon the language and concepts of Ezekiel's vision to portray the events involved.

12. Smith, *Clement of Alexandria and a Secret Gospel of Mark*, p. 244, and passim.

13. Bowker, " 'Merkabah' Visions and the Visions of Paul," pp. 158–159. Cf. among

Paul's visions suggest the possibility that they arose from a base of *merkabah* contemplation. These are the vision on the road to Damascus (Acts 9:1–19; 22:4–16; 26:9–18; cf. Gal. 1:13–17) and the account of the ascent to the third heaven (2 Cor. 12:1–4).[14] Both visions are likewise in accord with the kind of "knowing" we have come to associate with the concept of gnosis.

The vision on the road to Damascus is variously related both by the author of Acts and by Paul himself as part of the narrative. As the event is described, Paul né Saul (cf. Acts 13:9), in hatred of those who are disciples of the Way, is commissioned to travel to the synagogues of Damascus in order to bring these disciples bound to Jerusalem. As Saul is on the road to Damascus, a light from heaven ("*phōs apo tou ouranou*") flashes about him; he falls to the ground and is accosted by a voice that identifies itself as that of Jesus, whom Saul has been persecuting (Acts 9:3–4). The voice then commands Saul to arise from the ground and go to Damascus no longer as the persecutor he was but as "a chosen instrument" (*skeuos ekloges*, lit. "a vessel of election") to carry Christ's name "before the Gentiles and kings and the sons of Israel" (Acts 9:15). Although initially blinded by the vision, the converted sinner finally regains his sight.

Drawing upon the biblical and rabbinical sources, Bowker demonstrates how the New Testament accounts accord with the *merkabah* narratives portrayed in the Judaic material. Such elements as the setting (travel along the road), the nature of the vision itself (revelation of light as of fire from heaven, the voice that addresses the visionary), the conditions surrounding the trance (temporary blindness), the receipt of the commission to prophesy as an "instrument" of God (a particular thrust of Ezekiel 2), and indeed the very language in which the Pauline renderings are cast all have affinities with *merkabah* speculation. In short, the account of Paul's conversion on the road to Damascus is, according to Bowker, conceived and executed within the context of the *maʿaseh merkabah*.

If such is true, then what results is a reformulation of *merkabah* material in order to accommodate an entirely new perspective,

---

many other passages, Gal. 1:14: "I advanced in Judaism beyond many of my own age among my people, so extremely zealous was I for the traditions of my fathers."

14. In addition to the foregoing, such epistles as that to the Colossians adopt the language and insights of *merkabah* mysticism. See Rowland, "The Influence of the First Chapter of Ezekiel," esp. pp. 239–242.

one that is revolutionary in its implications and that places Christ
himself at the center of the visionary experience. In Christocentric
terms, to encounter the *merkabah* is to undergo a conversion undreamt of in the annals of earlier *merkabah* discourse. Christ is
thereby seen to operate by means of the *merkabah*, and those who
have access to the message of Christ through Christ's "instruments" or "vessels" gain a new understanding, indeed, a gnostic
appreciation, of the meaning of the mysteries surrounding the
maʿaseh merkabah.

Corresponding to the Pauline conversion on the road to Damascus is Paul's account of his ascent to the third heaven, a highly
personal portrayal of the apostle's experience of "visions [*optasias*]
and revelations [*apokalypseis*] of the Lord" (2 Cor. 12:1). Paradoxically intensifying the personal nature of that experience by referring to himself in the third person as alter ego, Paul avers that
he knows "a man in Christ" who was "caught up [*arpagenta*] to the
third heaven," where "he heard things that cannot be told" and
that may not be uttered (2 Cor. 12:2). Paul's account is part of
the same milieu as the pseudepigraphical accounts that portray
the way such figures as Enoch and Abraham were caught up to
the higher realms. Although it refuses to specify the precise nature
of the ecstasis ("whether in the body or out of the body I do not
know") or of what was experienced during the period of ecstasis,
the account nonetheless represents a New Testament version of
corresponding portrayals that underlie the culture of the *yordei
merkabah*.

Paul's account establishes its connection with this culture in a
number of ways. In keeping with *merkabah* lore, it suggests, for
example, the inexpressibility of the experience in the sense of
encountering that which not only defies but prohibits utterance.
In addition to emphasizing this dimension, Paul identifies the
third heaven as "paradise [*paradeison*]" (2 Cor. 12:4), a term that
specifically recalls the *pardes* ascription in the talmudic versions.
As Gershom Scholem has demonstrated in his study of the text,
Paul is consciously employing the language of *merkabah* mysticism
as a means of reinforcing the Christological content of his message.[15] As Paul adopts the *topos* of the *merkabah* ascent, the visionary

---

15. Scholem, "The Four Who Entered Paradise and Paul's Ascension to Paradise," *Jewish Gnosticism*, pp. 14–19. In his "New Testament and Hekhalot Literature: The Journey into Heaven in Paul and in Merkavah Mysticism," *Hekhalot-Studien* (Tübingen: J. C. B. Mohr, 1988), pp. 234–249, Peter Schäfer calls into question Scholem's argument, as well as some

alludes to his experience not as a sign of his superiority or power over those who have not witnessed what the apostle has but as an emblem of his own frailty in the face of the overwhelming power embodied in Christ. So Paul comments upon his *merkabah* experience in a manner that ironically devalues it (or at least any attempt to claim a personal elevation as the result of it): "And to keep me from being too elated by the abundance of revelations, a thorn was given me in the flesh, a messenger of Satan, to harass me, to keep me from being too elated" (2 Cor. 12:7). In Christocentric terms, what is to be learned from the experience is the fact of our own limitations and the need to place one's entire faith in Christ, through whose power one's weakness is ultimately perfected (2 Cor. 12:8–10). Paul's *merkabah* account, then, once again constitutes a new understanding of vision, one totally in accord his Christocentric point of view. At the same time, it ironically devalues gnosis as a means of claiming undue superiority over those who do not possess it.[16]

As one in whom the traditions of the *merkabah* find their own unique expression, Saint John the Divine, in turn, offers a reading of Ezekiel's vision that reveals how extensively the *maʿaseh merkabah* as apocalyptic enterprise assumes a distinctly Christocentric bearing in the New Testament. Although the *merkabah* in various way is discernible throughout Revelation, the locus classicus of the Johannine rendering is the fourth chapter. According to Christopher Rowland, this chapter portrays a vision that is "entirely Jewish in its inspiration."[17] As such, the fourth chapter embodies a Christocentric form of the *maʿaseh merkabah*. In keeping with this idea, John provides more than "a mere interpretation of the

---

of the methodological premises upon which it is based, but Schäfer does allow for the possibility of "other points of contact between the New Testament and Hekhalot literature." Tabor, on the other hand, strongly endorses the association of Paul's ascent with the traditions of the *merkabah* (*Things Unutterable*, see esp. pp. 116–123).

16. So in another context, Paul advocates doing battle against those sources of pride that might incline one to embrace a false gnosis: "For we are not contending against flesh and blood, but against the principalities, against the powers, against the world rulers of this present darkness, against the spiritual hosts of wickedness in the heavenly places " (Ephes. 6:12). According to Grant, this suggests gnostic influence (*Gnosticism and Early Christianity*, p. 161). The idea of warring against the evil "powers" that rule the heavens reinforces the notion of not taking false pride in one's ability to achieve the celestial realms.

17. Rowland, *Open Heaven*, p. 222. See also A. Vanhoye, "L'utilisation du livre d'Ezéchiel dans l'Apocalypse," *Biblica* 43 (1962): 436–476. For a corresponding discussion of Revelation 4 in the context of the *merkabah* traditions, see Ithamar Gruenwald, *Apocalyptic and Merkavah Mysticism* (Leiden: E. J. Brill, 1980), pp. 63–69.

biblical original," as depicted in the inaugural vision of Ezekiel. Addressing the visions that underscore Revelation as a whole, Rowland observes: "The variety which we find in the contents of the visions suggests that, while Ezekiel may have been the starting-point for what we have in these chapters, the order and detail of the original have been left behind in favour of a more elaborate view of the nature of God's dwelling in heaven." It seems plausible, therefore, to assume that the visions in Revelation are in fact what they purport to be: the visions of one who believed it possible to "pierce the vault of heaven and be shown the most intimate secrets of God and his world." Such visions "would have arisen within a situation, where an individual started with the scriptural description of God's glory in Ezekiel 1 and, on the basis of this passage, believed that he saw again the vision which had once appeared to the prophet Ezekiel by the banks of the river Chebar. Thus although the details of Ezekiel's vision marked the launching-pad for this new vision, the imagination of the visionary enabled him to transcend the original" and create his own version of the *maʿaseh merkabah*.[18] The force of this statement will be seen upon an analysis of Revelation 4 in the context of the prophecy as a whole.

As John delineates his vision, he first asserts not that the *visio Dei* descends to him, as in the case of Ezekiel, but that he is invited, much as in the manner of the Enoch pseudepigrapha, to ascend to it. In short, Revelation already includes the concept of ascent so characteristic of the intertestamental apocalypses, an element, as we have seen, familiar to Paul. In the Johannine version the ascent is conceived in "architectural terms": a door opens in heaven (4:1). This detail suggests that in John's ascent, as in that of Enoch (*I Enoch* 14:15), the visionary is to be led through portals of a celestial temple enclosure to the inmost presence of God (cf. Ezekiel 40–48).[19] The ascent itself is accompanied by a voice that instructs the prophet to "come up hither," so that he may be shown "what must take place after this" (4:1). What John is to behold, then, is a vision not only of the celestial world but of future events:

18. Rowland, *Open Heaven*, pp. 226–227. Anticipating Rowland and fully in agreement with his thesis, J. Massyngberde Ford sees the fourth chapter of Revelation entirely within the context of the *merkabah* traditions, which she summarizes in commentary. See her edition *Revelation* (Garden City, N.Y.: Doubleday, 1975), esp. pp. 76–81 (volume 38 of The Anchor Bible).

19. According to Gruenwald, the reference to the opening of a door in heaven suggests, on John's part, the use of "technical terminology" consistent with the language of the *merkabah* (*Apocalyptic*, p. 63).

in its depiction of the *visio Dei* apocalypse moves toward its consummation in finality, in a time out of time. The ascent embodies both a spatial and a temporal movement toward last things, a movement reminiscent of those experienced by the *yordei merkabah* in their various journeys not only to behold God but to be instructed in apocalyptic matters. In short, the experience portrayed in Revelation is directly in keeping with the narratives of ascent that underlie the *merkabah* texts in the Judaic traditions and that form the basis of the gnostic disclosures that these texts embody.

As John describes his experience, he finds himself at once in the Spirit ("*eutheōs egenomen en pneumati*"), overcome, that is, with the divine breath and transported in ecstasy to the realm of the throne (4:2; cf. Ezek. 8:1–4, 11:1–2). On the throne John beholds a figure whose glory is described in terms of precious stones (jasper and carnelian) and whose throne is surrounded by a rainbow that has the appearance of an emerald (4:3; cf. Rev. 10:1). Like His counterpart in Ezekiel, the Enthroned Figure of John is the embodiment of "otherness," a quality reinforced by the references to the exotic gems as artifacts that distance the seer from the seen (cf. Exod. 28:17–21). Surrounded by the rainbow as in Ezekiel (1:28; cf. Gen. 9:13–16), the Enthroned Figure of John, however, also suggests that binding characteristic of the covenant, although in John, of course, it is a totally new kind of covenant that is emblematized. The nature of that covenant is suggested in part in the next reference: "Round the throne were twenty-four thrones, and seated on the thrones were twenty-four elders, clad in white garments, with golden crowns upon their heads" (4:4; cf. Rev. 7:9, 13, 14).

Within the new context of the throne-room that John provides for the *merkabah*, the scene suggests how extensively Ezekiel's inaugural vision in the first chapter, coupled with the return of the vision to the restored Temple in the forty-third chapter, promotes a reenvisioning or reenactment of what was already a staple of Judaic biblical and even postbiblical thought. In John this reenactment assumes a form that is in effect an interpretation that harmonizes earlier texts with the new text that John is creating in his prophecy. Drawing upon such ideas as the twelve patriarchs (cf. Acts 7:8) and twelve tribes (cf. Matt. 19:28) that underscore New Testament renderings of Old Testament ideas, John harmonizes this outlook with such New Testament commonplaces as the twelve apostles (cf. Matt. 10:1–4). Doing so, he invites one to see in the twenty-four elders upon their thrones a harmonizing of Old and New Testament concepts that reinforce his view of the new covenant, the new dispensation as that which distinguishes his rendering of the throne-room and its attendants, here cast in the form of a kind of celestial ecclesiology that transforms the angelic hosts into elders and the temple vision into a divine church.

Ballasting this dimension still further is the description of the throne itself and those creatures that accompany it. "From the throne issue flashes of lightning, and voices and peals of thunder, and before the throne burn seven torches of fire, which are the seven spirits of God; and before the throne there is as it were a sea of glass, like crystal" (4:5–6). Recalling the thunder and lightning that surround the enthroned figures not only of Ezekiel (1:4, 27) and Daniel (7:10) but that of *I Enoch* (14:18–19), among others, John's description places his throne directly within the context of the *merkabah* conceived as an awesome and terrifying theophany of divine power and regal authority. Reinforcing this idea are "the seven torches of fire, which are the seven spirits of God" that burn before the throne. Drawn both from Ezekiel's vision of the "torches" moving to and fro (1:13) and from Zechariah's vision of the "candlesticks" that are also the eyes of the Lord "which range through the whole earth" (4:2–10), John's image combines the seven golden lampstands of his preparatory vision (1:12–16) with the ecclesiological dimension portrayed as the seven churches to which John preaches (cf. Rev. 1:4).

Accompanying these details is that concerning the sea of glass like crystal that extends before the throne (cf. Rev. 15:2). The image returns us, of course, directly to "the awesome crystal" of Ezekiel's vision (1:22): constituting the firmament that supports the throne of the seated figure and separates Him from the world below, the crystalline substance in Ezekiel is an integral part of the visionary rendering (cf. Gen. 1:7; 1 Kings 7:23–26; *I Enoch* 14:9). In John this substance is later associated both with the New Jerusalem (21:11) and the river of the water of life that regenerates eternally (22:1), a suggestion of the transformative powers implicit in the New Dispensation.

If the foregoing images underscore the throne and its accoutrements, that which associates it indisputably with the complex of traditions surrounding the *merkabah* is the description of the creatures that accompany it:

And round the throne, on each side of the throne, are four living creatures [*tessara zōa*], full of eyes in front and behind: the first living creature like a lion, the second living creature like an ox, the third living creature with the face of a man, and the fourth living creature like a flying eagle. And the four living creatures, each of them with six wings, are full of eyes all round and within, and day and night they never cease to sing, "Holy, holy, holy, is the Lord God Almighty, who was and is and is to come!" (4:6–8).

As many have noted before, the description combines elements of the *hayyot* in Ezekiel 1 with the seraphim in Isaiah 6. The fusion of anthropomorphic and theriomorphic characteristics is a hallmark of Ezekiel, whereas the six wings and the celebration of God through the *trisagion* is a hallmark of Isaiah.[20] In the *zōa* are consummated Ezekiel's terrifying vision of otherworldly creatures that are the moving force of what the prophet beholds and Isaiah's awesome account of presiding and ministering spirits that celebrate the Enthroned Figure with a divine liturgy. Combining Ezekiel and Isaiah, John portrays a celestial environment distinguished both by the sense of the "otherness" embodied in the *hayyot* and by the sense of liturgical jubilation embodied in the seraphim. As our earlier discussions of celestial visions have made clear, both aspects are crucial to the traditions of the *maʿaseh merkabah*.

In the implied ecclesiology that distinguishes John's account, however, the mystifications that surround Ezekiel's *hayyot* have been removed: as they now appear, the *hayyot*-become-*zōa* lose all those ambiguous and indeed baffling characteristics that the inaugural vision ascribes to them. They are denuded of such qualities as their truly fourfold aspect. Although four in number, each *zōan* has one face rather than four; directional considerations (either in terms of placement of the faces or in the movement of the *zōa* themselves) are no longer an issue; nor do the *zōa* dart to and fro like their forebears; essentially stationary, indeed, almost iconic, the *zōa* represent votive presences that have been elevated to the level of the throne as an expression of divine worship; finally, the wheels that accompany the *hayyot* in the inaugural

20. Recapitulating the *kedushah* ("Holy, holy, holy is the Lord of hosts") of Isa. 6:3, the *trisagion* of Rev. 4:8 recalls the liturgical dimension that is so crucial to the traditions of the *merkabah* with its *piyyutim*. This liturgical dimension is likewise of importance to the early church. See Lucetta Mowry, "Revelation 4–5 and Early Christian Liturgical Usage," *JBL* 71 (1952): 75–84.

vision have been completely removed. No longer is there the same kind of ambiguity, the same emphasis upon sudden, unexpected, darting movement: all is controlled, all put to the service of a unifying conception centered in the throne itself and worshiped as such by all that surround it:

> And whenever the living creatures give glory and honor and thanks to him who is seated on the throne, who lives for ever and ever, the twenty-four elders fall down before him who is seated on the throne and worship him who lives for ever and ever; they cast their crowns before the throne, singing, "Worthy art thou, our Lord and God, to receive glory and honor and power, for thou didst create all things, and by thy will they existed and were created." (4:11)

In the divine ecclesiology that John envisions, the underlying theme of the vision is the liturgical: this is a solemn, indeed, antiphonal celebration by elder and *zōan* alike of that central, divine figure seated on his throne. Such is the *ma'aseh merkabah* of Saint John the Divine. In that vision of the *merkabah* it is no longer a question of seeing the Enthroned Figure only at multiple removes ("the appearance of the likeness of the glory"). As complex and indeed mysterious as John's vision is, he does provide the occasion for an enactment in which the Enthroned Figure is seen as much as possible in His full resplendence.

Reinforcing this sense of visual and indeed liturgical enactment is the spatial arrangement of the entire scene. As others have noted before, that arrangement suggests the quality of a kind of amphitheater in which the Enthroned Figure, surrounded by the elders and the living creatures, becomes the focus of high drama. Conceived in this manner, John's *merkabah* portrayal becomes the occasion for grand theater. In the spatial construct represented by that theater, one finds enacted drama of the most compelling sort.[21] The pivotal place that the fourth chapter occupies in Saint John the Divine's prophecy allows this visionary drama to embrace the entire temporal spectrum of past, present, and future, as the *zōa* themselves celebrate Him "who was and is and is to come" in their *trisagion*. As suggested by the wording of the *trisagion*, John's drama of the *merkabah* becomes the matrix not only of the spatial

---

21. For an examination of this dimension, see R. R. Brewer, "Revelation 4, 6 and the Translation Thereof," *JBL* 71 (1952): 227–231, as well as Ford's summary note (*Revelation*, p. 74).

coordinate but of the temporal coordinate as well. Such is exactly as it should be considering that the figure in the drama of apocalyptic enactment is one who is both first and last, alpha and omega (1:17–18). This is the "son of man," the new *ben 'adam* (cf. Ezek. 2:1–3; Dan. 7:13–14; *I Enoch* 48:2; Mark 2:10), attired in a long robe and a golden girdle surrounding his breast; his head and hair white as wool; his eyes ablaze like a flame of fire, his feet appearing like polished bronze, and his voice like the sound of many waters (1:13–16). The veritable product of earlier throne visions (cf. Ezek. 1:7, 24; Dan. 7:9), this messianic figure dominates John's reenactment of the experience of the *merkabah* and provides the Christocentric focus that experience is made to assume. It is John himself as *merkabah* visionary who is the official transcriber of this experience (1:11, 19).

The significance of this idea makes itself especially apparent in the divine drama enacted in the theatrical setting of the celestial court. Although anything like a detailed description of this drama lies well beyond the purview of the present undertaking, it does need to be emphasized that the Christocentrism of John's vision assumes its full expression only as a result of the unfolding drama that occurs here. Having described the accoutrements of the Enthroned Figure in the fourth chapter, John proceeds in the chapters that follow to delineate the sublime events of his apocalyptic drama.

Recalling the scroll that is handed to Ezekiel in the second and third chapters of his prophecy (2:8–3:3), a corresponding document makes its appearance in the fifth chapter of Revelation (5:1, cf. 20:12). Like Ezekiel's scroll, that of Saint John the Divine is in effect written on the front and on the back with words of lamentation and mourning and woe.[22] Unlike Ezekiel's scroll, however, John's is sealed with seven seals as a symbol of the multiple mysteries it embodies. Both prophecies reflect that all-consuming concern with the text of the vision as that which is at once occlusive and revelatory and as that which is self-consciously and self-reflexively focused upon the mode of its own dissemination. What is true of Ezekiel's vision is true of John's: this is a prophecy that conceives of itself as a text that emerges from the very vision it

---

22. Like Ezekiel, John is later said to eat a scroll (Rev. 10:9–10), but this is apparently a different one from that which he describes in ch. 5, although it may indeed be a veiled reference to the same scroll (cf. Ford, *Revelation*, pp. 163–166).

portrays. If the text generates the vision, the vision generates the
text. Like the prophecy of Ezekiel, the apocalypse of Saint John
the Divine is a work about the way in which the visionary experience resolves itself in the creation of a text that is at once part
of the drama that the prophet beholds and a transcription of the
drama that the prophet shares with all those who receive his message. The Apocalypse of Saint John the Divine appears as a scroll
to be opened and consumed in the context of the throne-vision
that John himself is made to see. Text within text, vision within
vision: such is the basis of the visionary mode as an experience
that is forever replicating itself, (re)generating itself, transforming
itself, seeing itself again. As such, it embodies a gnosis disclosed
only to those capable of understanding the mysteries contained
in its secret text. This text, in short, is a gnostic document par
excellence.

In the drama that Saint John the Divine portrays in the context
of his throne-vision, the process of reenactment is presented as a
challenge. " 'Who is worthy to open the scroll and break its seals?' "
proclaims a mighty angel with a loud voice. The silence is deaf-
ening: "And no one in heaven or on earth or under the earth was
able to open the scroll or to look into it" (5:2–4). Such a challenge
has all the qualities that one associates with the genre of romance,
a mode we have already seen to be consistent with the traditions
of the *merkabah*.[23] In the context of Revelation the challenge provides the opportunity for the previously unnoticed hero to make
his mark. " 'Who is worthy to open the scroll and break its seal?' "
From the perspective of the romances, one thinks of the task that
distinguishes the most famous of all such heroes: Who is worthy
to draw the sword from the stone?[24] It will require a truly remarkable being to do so, and it is just such a being who is introduced into the apocalyptic drama at this pivotal moment.

A figure who appears to emerge out of the "mythos of romance," one who is called "the Lion of the tribe of Judah, the
Root of David" suddenly comes forth to perform this seemingly

23. See, for example, the earlier discussion of *III Enoch* in the context of Northrop
Frye's discussion of the "mythos of romance." *The Anatomy of Criticism* (Princeton: Princeton
University Press, 1975), pp. 186–206.

24. Although the Arthurian dimension of the idea comes immediately to mind, such a
challenge finds its correspondence in a multitude of analogues. The book of Revelation
is replete with what might be called romance (or proto-romance) elements: the dragon
(12:3), the figure Faithful and True upon the white horse (19:11), the divinely adorned
bride (19:7–9, 21:2), and so forth. See Frye, *Anatomy*, p. 189.

impossible task. Having been encountered earlier in his roles as the son of man (1:13–16), this messianic figure now emerges as a new member of the celestial court. Representing in effect John's version of Metatron, he is beheld as "a Lamb, standing, as if it had been slain, with seven horns and with seven eyes, which are the seven spirits of God sent out into all the earth" (5:6). Like that of his previous appearance, the bearing that he assumes here is equally remarkable, as well as intensely symbolic. Although the nature of the symbolism lies beyond the purview of our present concerns, suffice it to say that it suggests not only the power and the providential knowledge required to carry forth God's mission (cf. Dan. 7:8, 20; Zech. 1:18–21) but the willingness to offer oneself as a divine sacrifice on behalf of mankind (cf. John 1:29; Acts 8:32; 1 Pet. 1:19). Only such a being is worthy to open the seals.

It is this worthiness that both the four living creatures and the twenty-four elders celebrate in their "new song" of adoration before the throne: "Worthy art thou to take the scroll and to open its seals, for thou wast slain and by thy blood didst ransom men for God from every tribe and tongue and people and nation, and hast made them a kingdom and priests to our God, and they shall reign on earth" (5:1–12; cf. Exod. 19:6). Such is the new liturgy, the new *trisagion* enacted as a sign of adoration in the high drama that takes place before the Enthroned Figure and the Lamb in the Book of Revelation. Providing both an occasion and a locus by which the spatial and the temporal meet, the drama enacted before those present in the celestial court transforms the *ma'aseh merkabah* into an imposing drama. The celestial court thereby becomes a theater of vision, one in which the Christocentrism of Johannine theology manifests itself in the sudden emergence of that mysterious figure conceived as "a Lamb, standing, as if it had been slain, with seven horns and with seven eyes." It is this figure who, because of his sacrifice, is worthy to "receive power and wealth and wisdom and might and honor and glory and blessing!" (5:12). It is this figure who is worthy to open the seals of the scroll that is itself the Apocalypse of John and to reveal the secrets inscribed within his text.

Embodying the multitude of divine events that culminate in the creation of a new heaven and a new earth, these secrets represent the core of apocalyptic history as John understood it. The narrative of disclosure that underlies the revelatory method of John's text is what the seer as *yored merkabah* portrays. The horsemen, the trumpets, the plagues, the judgments, the warfare, the creatures, the destruction of the profane kingdom, the establishment of the divine kingdom, the sacred marriage, the promised coming of the eschaton: such is the apocalyptic panorama of redemptive history that constitutes the *ma'aseh merkabah* of Saint John the Divine. In it, the drama of the *merkabah* is transformed to accord with the Christocentric bearing of the new text, the new song, that John creates. It is a soteriological drama, one in which the elements associated with the *ma'aseh merkabah* in the Judaic tradition assume renewed meaning centered in the figure of the savior as he, along with the Enthroned Figure, is worshiped in the celestial court. "And I heard every creature in heaven and on earth and under the earth and in the sea, and all therein, saying, 'To him who sits upon the throne and to the Lamb be blessing and honor and glory and might for ever and ever!' And the four living creatures said, 'Amen!' and the elders fell down and worshiped" (5:13–14). Such is the nature of John's "new song," his new *ma'aseh merkabah* as it is reconceived and reenvisioned within the Christocentric and finally apocalyptic context he establishes for it.

II

If the foregoing suggests how the *merkabah* was canonized within the New Testament, its presence in the extracanonical renderings is no less engaging. A glance at this literature will reveal how familiar the early Christian apocalypticists were with the traditions of the *merkabah* and how inclined they were to integrate these traditions into their outlook. In this respect, two foundation texts are particularly significant: *The Ascension of Isaiah* and *The Apocalypse of Paul*.[25] Such texts, as Ithamar Gruenwald has demonstrated, not only "lean heavily on Jewish material" but reflect the content and spirit of the *merkabah*.[26] The literary dimensions of this content and this spirit will concern us here.

25. References to these works are to *New Testament Apocrypha*, ed. Edgar Hennecke and trans. R. McL. Wilson, 2 vols. (Philadelphia: Westminster Press, 1964).

26. Gruenwald, *Apocalyptic*, pp. 70–72. For corresponding texts, see *The Gospel of Peter* (10:38–42) and *The Shepherd of Hermas* (I, 4: 4). Addressing concepts of ascension in such texts, Jean Daniélou sees *merkabah* influence throughout. See Daniélou's *The Theology of Jewish Christianity*, trans. John A. Baker (London: Darton, Longman and Todd, 1964), esp. pp. 248–263.

Originating in the second century C.E., *The Ascension of Isaiah* is the obvious product of the confluence of Jewish-Christian thinking that distinguishes the earlier periods. Apparently composite in nature, *The Ascension* falls into two distinct (but related) parts, which differ in their contents. Whereas the first part (chs. 1–5) concerns the so-called martyrdom of Isaiah, the second part (chs. 6–11) describes a celestial journey or vision of the prophet.[27] It is with the second part that we shall be concerned. A remarkable piece of writing, this section of the work not only reveals a full awareness of the *merkabah* traditions but is distinguished by genuine artistry.

The narrative itself is divisible into three parts. Whereas the first and third parts (6:1–17 and 11:36–43, respectively) establish a setting for the vision, the second part (7:1–11:35) concerns the vision itself. Framing the vision, the first and third parts are written in third-person narrative. Providing an account of the vision, the second part is written in first-person narrative. The protagonist is Isaiah. After the fashion of Old Testament pseudepigraphal accounts, Isaiah relates his vision to reveal the *kerygma* of New Testament teaching to those of his compatriots wise enough to understand the dispensational significance of his message. Considering how Isaiah as prophet is traditionally looked upon as the harbinger of the Redeemer (cf. Isa. ll:1–16; 49: 5–7), the choice of such a protagonist for this account is entirely appropriate. What renders the account so interesting is its appropriation of *merkabah* material in its kergymatic delineation of Isaiah's vision.

27. According to J. Flemming and H. Duensing, the editors of *The Ascension of Isaiah* in *New Testament Apocrypha* , "the martyrdom narrated in the first section is a Jewish writing of uncertain date, the substance of which was known, according to Heb. 11:37, in the first Christian century. The vision which describes the ascension of Isaiah through the seven heavens and the revelation of the future redemption through Christ may have originated in the 2nd century A.D." Within this composite text there are also extraneous units of Christian origin, notably 3.13–15, in the first section, and 11.2–22, in the second. There are those, however, who continue to argue for the unity of the text as a whole (Hennecke, *New Testament Apocrypha*, II, 642–643). In addition to the various forms (Greek, old Slavonic, Coptic, Ethiopic) in which the work, either in whole or in part, has been transmitted, a Latin text of the vision (chs. 6–11) was printed in Venice in 1522. For additional treatments of *The Ascension*, see Gruenwald, *Apocalyptic*, pp. 57–62; Martha Himmelfarb, *Tours of Hell: An Apocalyptic Form in Jewish and Christian Literature* (Philadelphia: University of Pennsylvania Press, 1983), pp. 64–66; D. Flusser, "The Apocryphal Book of *Ascensio Isaiae* and the Dead Sea Sect," *Israel Exploration Journal* 3 (1953): 30–47; Vacher Burch, "The Literary Unity of the Ascensio Isaiae," *JTS* 20 (1919): 17–23, and "Materials for the Interpretation of the Ascensio Isaiae," *JTS* 21 (1920): 249–265; and R. H. Charles, trans., *The Ascension of Isaiah* (London: A. & C. Black, 1900).

The motifs commonly associated with visionary encounters with the *merkabah* are all-pervasive. Such is true from the very outset, which describes Isaiah's audience with Hezekiah, king of Judah. Presumably called before Hezekiah to prophesy, Isaiah takes up a position befitting his station: refusing to sit on the chair that is offered him, he insists on placing himself on the king's couch, no doubt as a reflection of the posture of the One who resides above. So seated, Isaiah is surrounded not only by all the princes of Israel with their eunuchs and counselors but by prophets and sons of prophets who had come from afar to hear him (6:1–5). One is reminded here of the Judaic traditions of the accounts of the *yordei merkabah* surrounded by their attendants in preparation for the visionary ascent. That aura is reinforced by what follows in the first section of the narrative.

As if a door has been opened, the voice of the Holy Spirit suddenly enters and overwhelms all those sensitive to its presence, particularly Isaiah, the center of focus. Overwhelmed by the Holy Spirit (cf. Acts 2:1–21), "he suddenly became quiet and his consciousness was taken from him and he saw no (more) the men who were standing before him: his eyes were open, but his mouth was silent and the consciousness in his body was taken from him; but his breath was (still) in him, for he saw a vision" (6:6–12). The posture is that of the mystic, the visionary, who becomes oblivious to his surroundings as he transcends all bodily awareness and becomes totally involved in "seeing" his vision. Corresponding to the experience of the *yordei merkabah*, the vision that he beholds is of a secret world, one that is hidden from all flesh and can be imparted only to those capable of understanding its significance (6:14–17). This all-important dimension of "hiddenness" and the nature of its disclosure underlies the focus of the second part of the account, in which Isaiah narrates what he has seen.

Conceived and orchestrated with consummate skill, this part traces the process of growth and maturation that the prophet undergoes in his exposure to the secrets of the other world. That gnostic process is signaled from the very outset of Isaiah's visionary experience. Characteristic of *merkabah* ascents in general, a glorious, indeed, indescribable, angel appears to Isaiah in order to transport the prophet and interpret for the prophet what is witnessed in the other world. Isaiah's immediate reaction to the sudden appearance of the angel is quite natural: "What is thy name, and wherefore dost thou lead me on high?" The angel's response to this question brings into focus the major issues that the work as a whole develops during the course of the narrative. "When I have led thee on high by degrees and have shown thee the vision for which I have been sent to thee, then wilt thou know who I am, but my name thou shalt not find out, since thou must return to this thy body. But whither I would raise thee on high, thou shalt see, since for this purpose I have been sent" (7:1–5). The entire thrust of the apocalypse is gnostic: how and under what circumstances is knowledge disclosed. Although the concept of requesting the secret name of a divine being has ample biblical precedence (cf. Gen. 32:39; Exod. 3:13–15; Judg. 13:17–18), here the idea takes on a special meaning in its association with what might be called the heuristic dimension of the account.

As a narrative of discovery, of gnosis in all its forms, *The Ascension of Isaiah* empasizes above all else the significance of learning the secrets of the other world.[28] That process, however, occurs only "by degrees," to adopt the language of the angelic guide, and even then full disclosure is not to be realized in this life: Isaiah, after all, must be returned to his body. To those fortunate enough to receive it, complete knowledge occurs only after death. For the time being, then, the full identity of the angel is not disclosed, just as the full nature of the other world is not communicated. Enough is known, however, to share with those assembled the startling revelations that Isaiah's vision embodies. These revelations are contained in the account itself.

According to that account, the angelic interpreter transports Isaiah first to the firmament, where the prophet beholds the satanic hosts fighting among one another, a struggle, the angel informs Isaiah, that will continue until "he whom thou shalt see shall come and destroy him (Satan)" (7:9–12). Given the heuristic nature of the narrative, this promise is interesting, for it establishes in the context of the promise of an apocalyptic battle, the coming forth of one about whom Isaiah still has to learn (cf. Rev. 12). The chord is sounded here, only to be taken up later as the narrative develops. Having ascended to the firmament, Isaiah is then led through the seven heavens, each of which is described in some detail.

28. See especially in this regard, N. K. Helmbold, "Gnostic Elements in the 'Ascension of Isaiah,'" *NTS* 18 (1972): 222–227, which emphasizes the relationship between *The Ascension* and the thematic and literary forms of the gnostic documents discovered at Nag Hammadi.

Sharing the same characteristics, the first five heavens are conceived as a unit. In the midst of each is a throne occupied by a seated figure, and each throne is surrounded by angels on the left and on the right, with those on the right more glorious than those on the left.[29] From one heaven to the next, these angels sing praises to God and His Beloved seated on their respective thrones in the seventh heaven. Upon seeing the enthroned figures, Isaiah desires to worship them. He is stopped by his angelic guide, however, because all such worship is to be saved for the Most High and His Beloved, through whom Isaiah is able to ascend first in vision and ultimately after death. As Isaiah proceeds up the five heavens, he becomes aware, moreover, that both the angels and their songs of praise grow more glorious and splendid. The growing intensity of his own understanding and illumination, in short, finds its correspondence in the increasing brilliance of his surroundings. This fact is reinforced by the transformative power of his own visionary experience, for, as he moves by degrees to the higher heavens, he finds that the glory of his countenance is similarly being transformed. This transformative dimension is crucial to the experience as a whole. Isaiah is becoming a new person, assuming, as it were, a new identity in the purification and intensification of his ability to see and know. He responds to the experience of transformation with a doxology that reflects both his superior knowledge and his ultimate inability to fathom the mysteries of the divine: "And I praised the unnamed one and the only one, who dwells in the heavens, whose name is unfathomable for all flesh, who has bestowed such a glory from heaven to heaven, who makes great the glory of the angels and makes greater the glory of him who sits on the throne" (7:13–37).

The first five heavens are conceived as a unit, but the sixth and seventh are *sui generis*. For the author of *The Ascension* the sixth heaven is a transitional realm, one in which the prophet is made to reevaluate who he is, what he is, and how far he is capable of understanding the nature of the divine. Approaching the sixth heaven, Isaiah begins with a question, the formulation of which immediately puts him in error: "What is this that I see, my Lord?" The request to know what he sees is appropriate, but the form

29. Recalling such works as the *Re'iyyot Yeḥezk'el*, the idea of having a throne in each of the heavens suggests the extent to which *The Ascension of Isaiah* draws upon and manipulates the *topoi* of the *merkabah*. See Gruenwald, *Apocalyptic*, p. 59, for a discussion of this motif in *The Ascension of Isaiah*.

of address is not. The angel responds with the needed correction: "I am not thy Lord, but thy companion" (8:1–5). As with all such texts of this sort, protocol is important, and as one who is only first being introduced to the protocol of a world that is entirely new to him, Isaiah needs much correction. He must learn about whom he is to worship and in what manner he is to address those he thinks are of superior status to his own. As a crucial aspect of the process of transformation that the apocalypse as a whole embodies, the prophet is constantly learning, constantly made to reevaluate his own identity in relation to the identity of others.

Now that he is made aware of the appropriate form of address, he may proceed with his questions. Why, he wants to know, are the angels no longer in two groups? The answer of his angelic companion moves the prophet's perception a step forward toward an understanding of the larger revelation that the apocalypse as Christocentric document embraces. By means of the answer, Isaiah begins to receive a lesson in the *kerygma* of the New Testament. Initially, however, that lesson is as mysterious in its terms as the vision that Isaiah beholds. From the sixth heaven to the seventh, the companion observes, there is no longer a division of angels with a throne in the midst. Rather, the "arrangement" of the sixth heaven is totally dependent upon the nature of the seventh heaven, "where the unnamed one dwells and his Elect one whose name is unfathomable and cannot be known by the whole heaven" (8:7). By answering Isaiah's question, the angelic guide has in effect deepened the mystery still further. The response obfuscates as much as it clarifies.

But the companion does not stop there: he complicates matters by providing even more information of a mysterious sort: "Thus I have been empowered and sent to bring thee up here to see the glory, and to see the Lord of all those heavens and these thrones being transformed till he comes to your image and likeness." No one, concludes the guide, has ever beheld such things. The answer, of course, points to what Isaiah as Old Testament prophet can know only by types and shadows, that is, the fulfillment of Isaiah's own message of the coming of the Redeemer in the image and likeness of man (cf. Phil. 2:7). As Isaiah of *The Ascension* will learn, this event is to be articulated through that all-important process of transformation that he himself is experiencing in his visionary encounter with the other world. If that process of transformation is occurring in vision now, the angelic guide observes, ultimately it will occur in fact, when Isaiah, after death, will through God's grace ascend to the highest heaven "in body" and "receive the garment" that has been stored up for him. Then he will undergo a true transformation and resemble the angels in the seventh heaven (8:14–15).

Imbued with this promise, Isaiah with his guide enters the sixth heaven, where "there was no one on the left and no throne in the midst, but all had one appearance and their song of praise was the same." In this new environment Isaiah accompanies the angelic hosts in their song of praise, a song that reveals his ability at last to name the unnamable: "And (power) was given to me and I sang praise with them [the hosts], and that angel also, and our praise was like theirs. And there they all named the primal Father and his Beloved, Christ, and the Holy Spirit, all with one voice" (8:16–18). The event is remarkable, for it at once recalls the biblical context of Isaiah's original throne-vision (6:1–6) and at the same time refashions that context to accord with its new point of view. Characteristic of that point of view is the idea that the old throne-world of the biblical Isaiah has been replaced by a new throne-world, one in which the throne as originally conceived is obliterated. In its place is a totally spiritualized and ultimately Christocentric conception, one toward which the apocalypse has been moving all along (cf. Rev. 21:22–23). Although the nature of that conception is not fully clarified until Isaiah ascends to the seventh heaven, its meaning is already signaled by the liturgy in which Isaiah engages in the sixth heaven. There, the *kedushah* of the biblical Isaiah assumes the form of the Trinitarian liturgy, a new *sanctus*, in which the earlier "holy, holy, holy" of the old throne-world now represents the Father, Son, and Holy Spirit of the new. As the prophet of this *sanctus*, Isaiah is empowered to participate in it as a culminating moment of celebration in his own vision.

Having traversed the sixth heaven as a transitional moment in the movement to the seventh, Isaiah approaches the highest point of all. Here, for the first time, he is immediately challenged by a presiding presence: "How far shall he ascend who dwells among aliens?" Reminiscent of the experience of *yordei merkabah* who are constantly challenged in their attempts to ascend to higher realms, this challenge is answered by none other than one whom the text calls "thy Lord, God, the Lord Christ, who will be called Jesus on earth." The answer is formulated appropriately in the language of transformation, the ultimate assumption of a new identity. As suggested by the answer, that assumption recalls the commonplace association of the transformation of the *yordei merkabah* with the donning of new garments: "It is permitted to the holy Isaiah to ascend hither, for his garment is here" (9:1–5). Both the answer and the identity of the one who answers recapitulate the all-important transformative motif that underlies the action of the apocalypse. Even now, Isaiah is unaware of the full meaning of all that transformation implies: his knowledge of the divine name, in fact, will not be complete until he has ascended out of his body (9:5). Nonetheless, his perception at this point is at a much higher stage than it was formerly. For this reason he is prepared to be admitted to the highest of the heavens. There he sees not only the angelic hosts but all the righteous from Adam, including that *yored merkabah* Enoch himself, "stripped of the garment of flesh" and attired in his "higher garment" (9:7–9).

Having witnessed these figures, as well as the heavenly hosts, Isaiah returns to the all-important question of thrones and their regalia. Why, he asks, have the righteous "received their garments, but are without their thrones and their crowns?" These appurtenances of office, the guide responds, are not to be bestowed until the Beloved descends in human form and undergoes his redemptive and sacrificial mission on earth, after which he will reascend to the seventh heaven. Only then will thrones and crowns be bestowed upon the righteous. As Isaiah will see, this descent and subsequent ascent are now "hidden from the heavens so that it remains unperceived who he is" (9:12–18). Like the other responses of the angelic guide, this one as well is cloaked in mystery. At the same time the response becomes part of the unfolding revelation of the meaning of the New Dispensation to which the Old Testament prophet as announcer of the Redeemer is progressively introduced.

Having received this answer, Isaiah then beholds that very figure about whom he has heard so much and regarding whom he has himself prophesied: this is the Redeemer, the Beloved Lord, "whose glory surpassed that of all, and his glory was great and wonderful." It is this figure that Isaiah sees *standing*, that is, not yet enthroned, a posture that reflects the transitional moment symbolized by the obliteration of the old throne-world embodied in the sixth heaven. Like those he will be commissioned to save, the Beloved shares the fate of his worshipers. The appurtenances of

his office await the glorious outcome of his future acts (cf. Rev.
5:6). It is this messianic figure in whose presence Isaiah is transformed. Celebrating the Beloved, Isaiah, along with the heavenly
hosts, engages in devout worship, after which he beholds another
glorious one situated on the left of the Beloved. This new figure
is the angel of the Holy Spirit, whom Isaiah also worships. The
splendor of the theophany is so great that the prophet is unable
to see, even though the eyes of his spirit are opened (9:27–42).

Moving progressively from the Beloved to the Spirit, Isaiah is
now empowered to behold God, the recipient of all praise from
all the heavens. So great is the glory of the Most High that Isaiah
is unable to bear the vision. In the presence of God the prophet
is informed: "This is the Most High of the High ones, who dwells
in the holy world and rests with the holy ones, who will be called
by the holy Spirit, through the mouth of the righteous, the Father
of the Lord" (10:1–6). Encountering this figure, Isaiah is now
prepared to come to a full awareness of the meaning of the *kerygma*
to which he has been introduced in stages and by degrees from
one heaven to the next. In keeping with the transformative nature
of the visionary experience, that awareness assumes the form of
the adoption of a new identity on the part of the Beloved himself.
The way in which this process occurs suggests the primacy of the
concept of visionary transformation to the theology of the New
Dispensation, as formulated by the author of *The Ascension.*

Accordingly, the Most High directs His son the Lord Christ to
descend through all the heavens, including the firmament, to the
world below. The manner of this descent will be remarkable, for
having traversed the sixth heaven, Christ is to assume the form
of the angels in each of the respective lower five heavens, so that
he will not be recognized as "the Lord of the seven heavens." As
that process occurs, Isaiah is summoned to behold "the transformation of the Lord and his descent." So Isaiah observes:

> "And I beheld and when the angels who are in the sixth heaven
> saw him they praised and extolled him, for he had not yet been
> transformed into the form of the angels there, and they praised
> him, and I also praised with them. And I saw how he descended
> into the fifth heaven, and in the fifth heaven took the appearance
> of the angels there, and they did not praise him, for his appearance
> was like theirs." (10:8–12)

This pattern is followed in almost formulaic fashion throughout all the heavens, including the firmament below, until his descent to earth. Because he is not recognized for the divine being he really is, he is not praised in any of the heavens, and, like any other being making his way either upward or downward through the celestial kingdoms, he is required to give the "pass-word" to the "door-keepers" at each of the gates (10:18–28).[30]

What makes this mode of descent so remarkable is the way it draws upon motifs familiar to the literature of visionary transport (especially that associated with the traditions of the *merkabah*) in order to portray what ultimately amounts, of course, to Christ's assumption of the form of a servant in the Incarnation (cf. Phil. 2:5–11). These motifs include the act of transformation so fundamental to *The Ascension* as a whole, as well as the concept of secret knowledge arising out of that act. In Christ's descent the transformative dimension of Isaiah's ascent is effectively and ironically reversed, as the Beloved, assuming a progressively diminished stature, undergoes an *occultatio Dei* that subverts knowledge rather than deepens it. In effect, Christ fulfills the concept of "descent" implicit in the term *yored* of *yored merkabah*. It is the self-consciousness of the *merkabah* tracts that is at work here, in this case, put to the service of delineating an entirely new theologoumenon, one that sets the concept of the *merkabah* on its heels and causes it to undergo a radical reassessment.

The *occultatio Dei* implicit in that reassessment underscores not only the narrative of descent but the account of Christ's earthly ministry during the period of his Incarnation, a period that Isaiah as Old Testament prophet of the Redeemer in the midst of an unbelieving world learns about for the first time here as he is introduced to the events of the future. Accordingly, the prophet is exposed to the matter of the gospel accounts, the circumstances surrounding the birth of Christ, the course of his life, his crucifixion, his resurrection and ascension. What distinguishes the account throughout is its emphasis upon the idea of occultation (cf. Matt. 8:4, 17:9). The nature of the birth is kept hidden. Even before he is born, Mary and Joseph have a vision of the future

---

30. When he assumes the form of the angels of the air in the firmament below, however, he gives no password, for in this place ruled by the powers of evil, there is too much fighting for anyone to take notice of him (10:29–31).

child, but both she and her husband are instructed by a voice not
to reveal the vision to any one. After Christ is born a report is
noised abroad in Bethlehem, but, even though the people know
of him, all are in the dark concerning him and the manner of his
conception and birth. During his infancy the mystery of his divine
nature continues to be kept hidden: "In Nazareth he sucked the
breast like a baby, as was customary, so that he would not be
recognized." Despite his performance of great signs and wonders
in Israel after he grows up, he is not acknowledged by the unbelievers, who deliver him to the king and crucify him (11:1–21).

It is only after he ascends as deity that he is recognized by those
in the heavens. Lamenting their failure to perceive his true identity during his descent, they exclaim, "How did our Lord descend
in our midst and we perceived not the glory [which was upon
him]." Returning in his ascent to the seventh heaven, he assumes
his position as an enthroned figure: "And then," Isaiah says, "I
saw how he sat down on the right hand of that great glory. . . .
And I also saw the angel of the holy Spirit sitting on the left"
(11:22–33). The holy Trinity is now complete. Concluding the
second part of the narrative is a reassertion of the transformative
and revelatory nature of all that the prophet has seen. So the
angel of the holy Spirit addresses the prophet: "Thou hast seen
what none born of flesh has yet seen, and thou wilt return into thy
garment till thy days are fulfilled: then thou wilt come hither"
(11:34–35).

The third part, finally, embodies a return to the present context
of the frame narrative and, along with it, a reassertion of the
third-person point of view. In this return to the present Isaiah,
now out of his trance and seated before those assembled to witness
the vision, promises that what he has beheld will be "consummated
in the last generation." The historical present and the apocalyptic
future are thereby seen to constitute one continuum in the transition from the old dispensation to the new and the Old Testament
to the New. Arising from the deployment of the frame narrative
through which the account is conceived, the establishment of this
continuum occurs within the context of the traditions of the *merkabah* of which *The Ascension* is an integral part. In keeping with
those traditions, as well as with the secret nature of the account
as a whole, Isaiah enjoins King Hezekiah from revealing the vision
in any form to the unbelieving masses but prophesies that those

who are faithful and capable of understanding will "be in the holy
Spirit so that ye may receive your garments and the thrones and
crowns of glory which are preserved in the seventh heaven"
(11:36–40). As with all such visions and the prophets who are the
source of them, the unbelievers prevail: Isaiah is martyred, and
his vision goes unheeded (11:41–43). Nonetheless, *The Ascension
of Isaiah* itself remains as a remarkable document that demonstrates how the traditions of the *merkabah* are integral to the Christocentrism of New Testament apocalyptic.

A corresponding perspective is discernible in *The Apocalypse of
Paul*, a crucial and immensely influential text that dates back to the
third century or possibly later.[31] Using Paul's reference to his being
caught up to the third heaven in 2 Corinthians 12 as the motive
force for the apocalyptic account, the narrative relates what might
be called the "adventures" of the apostle in the other world, here,
transformed into the realm beyond death. According to the narrative, these adventures are described in an account or revelation
discovered in a marble box by a man living in Tarsus in the very
house that had once belonged to Paul himself (1–10). As it portrays
Paul's experiences in the other world, the account describes in
detail how the apostle is introduced not only to the bliss of the
saved but to the torments of the damned. Paul is permitted to
witness both as a result of his having been "caught up in the Holy
Spirit" and carried by an angelic being "up to the third part of
Heaven, which is the third heaven" (11). In short, the narrative
emends the New Testament account to include an angelic con-
veyor who also acts as an interpreter of what the apostle beholds
both in the celestial realms and in the abyss.

For our purposes, Paul's experience in the celestial realm is of
most immediate interest.[32] The terms in which this experience is

31. *The Apocalypse of Paul* was written in Greek, probably by an Egyptian, as early as the
third century, possibly the end of the fourth or beginning of the fifth century. For the
definitive study see Theodore Silverstein, *Visio Sancti Pauli: The History of the Apocalypse in
Latin Together with Nine Texts* (London: Christophers, 1935), as well as Silverstein's "The
Vision of St. Paul: New Links and Patterns in the Western Tradition," *Archives d'Histoire
Doctrinale et Littéraire du Moyen Âge* 34 (1959): 199–248.

32. On the other hand, what Paul beholds in the abyss is likewise of interest from the
perspective of the *merkabah*. In their terrifying presence, the angelic guards there are
reminiscent of the guards that the *yored merkabah* encounters in his celestial journey: "And
again I looked and I saw angels who were pitiless, who had no compassion; their faces
were full of wrath and their teeth projected from their mouths; their eyes flashed like the
morning star in the east, and from the hairs of their head and out of their mouth went

described find their counterpart in characteristics that are commonplace to the experience of the *merkabah* in Judaic thought but
that are here recast in a uniquely Christian form. Examples
abound. Transported to the third heaven, Paul encounters "the
door of a gate" that provides entrance into the paradisal realm
of the righteous (19). As suggested above, the liminal aperture
through which the visionary enters into *pardes* is already a staple
of at least certain kinds of *merkabah* texts. Here as elsewhere,
movement through this aperture suggests a step in the attainment
of gnosis. Once within the enclosure of *pardes*, Paul first encounters "an old man whose face shone as the sun" (20). Transfigur-
ative in nature, the reference combines Old and New Testament
mountain theophanies often associated with the experience of the
merkabah: the first concerns Moses, whose face shone brilliantly as
a result of his encounter with God in the mount (Exod. 24:29–
35); the second, Jesus, whose face indeed "shone like the sun" in
his transfiguration (Matt. 17:2; cf. Rev. 10:1). Such theophanies,
we recall, are hardly foreign to Paul himself: being overwhelmed
by such light is crucial to his conversion (Acts 22:6; cf. Rev. 12:1).

In the context of *The Apocalypse of Paul* the identity of the "old
man whose face shone as the sun" is particularly apposite, for, as
in *The Ascension of Isaiah*, this figure is "Enoch, the scribe of righteousness." A personage of fundamental importance to the literature of the *merkabah*, Enoch, enveloped in the aura of his own
transfigured nature, welcomes Paul into the visionary realm of
pardes where the apostle is to behold the secrets of the other world.
These are secrets, of course, "which it is not lawful for a man to
speak" (21). Despite this injunction, Paul is empowered to report
(and indeed does report) what he beholds in the realm of vision.
What he sees there is very much in keeping with the experience
of the *merkabah*, here assimilated into the Christocentric and finally
gnostic outlook of the apocalypse as a whole.

In *The Apocalypse of Paul* that outlook assumes an "architectural"
bearing that recalls visionary accounts of the Temple (cf. Ezek.
40–48; Rev. 11:1, 21:10–15). Entering the City of Christ, Paul is
allowed to examine its twelve walls, which appear to be arranged
in such a manner that one is higher and more glorious than the

---

forth sparks of fire" (11). These angelic figures have much greater affinity with the traditions of the *merkabah* than the benevolent creatures that Paul discovers in the realm of
the blessed.

next as Paul and his interpreter move toward the mid-point of the city itself. At the gates to each of these walls is placed a golden throne upon which is seated a man attired in golden throne upon which is seated a man attired in golden diadems and gems. Although suggesting at once the visionary temple of Ezekiel and the New Jerusalem of Saint John the Divine, the spatial construct of the conception is reminiscent of the traditions of *hekhalot* literature in which the seer, in his pursuit of the Enthroned Figure, traverses one palace after the next, each palace equipped with its respective guards.

Unlike the guards of the *hekhalot* literature, however, the enthroned figures of *The Apocalypse of Paul* do not challenge the approach of the seer, nor are they frightening and threatening. Symbols of those innocents upon whom divine grace has been bestowed, they are, rather, figures of humility and selflessness who have "made themselves fools for the Lord God's sake" (cf. 1 Cor. 4:10). They embody the spirit of the new dispensation that infuses the *merkabah* and all it represents. Finding himself in the mid-point of the city, Paul as seer now beholds "a great and very high altar; and there was standing alongside the altar one whose face shone like sun." Recalling the figure of Enoch encountered earlier, the individual standing beside the altar is David, who celebrates God with a "Hallelujah" that is, in the manner of Isaiah's *kedushah* and Saint John the Divine's *trisagion*, answered antiphonally by those who are present in this center of holiness. As Gruenwald has observed, the particularly Judaic basis of the conception is made evident by the fact that, when Paul asks the angelic interpreter, "What is 'Hallelujah'?" the angel responds, "Hallelujah is a word in Hebrew, the language of God and angels." Because it implies the act of praising God all together, those in the presence of God celebrate Him in the singing of Hallelujah (29–30).[33]

Characteristic of the *piyyutim* found in such works as the *Hekhalot Rabbati* (ch. 30), this idea is reinforced by the later description of the court of God, a description that recapitulates the throne-vision of Revelation 4:

> And they [those in attendance] suddenly threw themselves on their faces before the throne; and I [Paul] saw the 24 elders and the 4 beasts worshipping God, and I saw the altar and the veil and the

33. Gruenwald, *Apocalyptic*, pp. 70–72.

throne, and all were rejoicing; and the smoke of a good odour rose up beside the altar of the throne of God, and I heard the voice of one who said: For what reason do you pray, angels and ministers of ours? And they cried out and said: We pray because we see thy great goodness to the race of men. (44)

Culminating in a vision of the throne, its attendants, and its liturgy, *The Apocalypse of Paul* offers its own reading of the traditions of the *merkabah*, one in which the Pauline account of the ascent of the apostle to the third heaven is fused with the Johannine account of the ascent of the prophet to the celestial court of God. At the center of the conception is the figure of Christ, the Son of God, who is seen "coming down from heaven" with a diadem on his head (44). The Christocentrism of the New Testament renderings reiterated in later apocalyptic reinscribes the throne-vision of the *merkabah* into the setting of a full-scale narrative concerning the "adventures" of Paul in the other world. These adventures, in turn, suggest how pervasively the gnostic dimensions of the visionary mode were adaptable to a wide variety of literary forms and points of view.

III

This variety of forms and perspectives, however, is not confined to the Christocentrism of the New Testament and related postcanonical texts alone. The gnostic dimensions of the *merkabah* are likewise discernible in the plethora of so-called heretical accounts against which such early church fathers as Irenaeus and Origen wrote.[34] Suggesting the nature of the outlook that the church as an emerging institution held to be anathema, these accounts afford insight into dimensions of the visionary experience that were thought to run counter to prevailing belief. Fascinating in their own right, such dimensions are the embodiment of forces that the church apparently felt it necessary to guard itself against in

34. Among the more important church fathers who discussed gnosticism are Justin at Rome (ca. 150–165), Irenaeus at Lyons (ca. 120–202); Clement of Alexandria (ca. 150–215); Origen (ca. 185–254); Hippolytus at Rome (ca. 230); and Epiphanius in Cyprus (ca. 315–403). In addition, one finds pagan opposition to gnostic thought, especially among such Neoplatonists as Plotinus (204–270) and Porphyry (234–301/5). Selections from the writings of a number of these figures are conveniently anthologized in Grant's *Gnosticism: A Source Book*.

order to preserve its stability. In his superb study *Faces of the Chariot* David Halperin has coined the phrase "anti-*merkabah*" to suggest the perception of the *merkabah* as "evil" entity. Looking upon the misappropriation of the *merkabah* by those ill equipped to understand its true meanings, the rabbis "directed their fears, and hence their disapproval, toward texts or statements that might serve as starting points for lines of thought leading toward" heretical assumptions. This is what Halperin calls "the dark side of the *merkabah*."[35] In rabbinical circles its contexts reside in gnostic modes of thought. One thinks of the figure of Acher (putatively the apostate Elisha ben Abuyah) in the *pardes* account.

What is true of the concept of anti-*merkabah* in rabbinical circles is no less true of the concept in patristic circles. There the anti-*merkabah* also functions to describe that which the early church looked upon as decidedly "other" (that is, *aḥer*), in its delineation of the dangers of apostasy. Counterbalancing this view of heretical gnosticism on the part of figures like Irenaeus and Origen is a sublime gnosticism toward which the truly religious person should strive. Expressed in the figure of Clement of Alexandria, this form of gnosticism suggests the way in which the anti-*merkabah* of heretical gnosticism finds its counterpart in a visionary perspective that asserts the positive aspects of a true pursuit of the divine. Moving from negative to positive notions of gnosis among the church fathers, we shall conclude this aspect of our exploration with a glance at Irenaeus and Origen, on the one hand, and Clement of Alexandria, on the other.

Irenaeus represents a fitting point of departure. In his *Adversus Haereses* he discusses at great length the major tenets of an entire range of gnostic heretics and their sects, a number of whose doctrines have an affinity with the visionary material we have been discussing.[36] Irenaeus's account of the beliefs of the gnostic Mar-

---

35. Halperin, *Faces*, pp. 238–247.

36. These include the Valentinians, as well as Simon Magus, Menander, Satornil, Basilides, Carpocrates, Cerinthus, the Ebionites, the Nicolaites, Cerdon, Marcion, Tatian, and the Encratites. Originally written in Greek, this work bears the full title: *Detection and Overthrow of the Pretended but False Gnosis*. For a convenient summary of the work in the context of the patristic traditions, see Johannes Quasten, *Patrology*, 3 vols. (Westminster, Md.: Newman Press, 1950–1960), I, 288–313. References to the *Adversus Haereses* in my text are from the translation in *The Ante-Nicene Fathers*, ed. Alexander Roberts and James Donaldson, 10 vols. (Grand Rapids: Wm. B. Eerdmans, 1950), I, 309–567. This edition is used in conjunction with *Adversus Haereses* in the *Sources chrétiennes* (Paris: Éditions du Cerf, 1965), vol. 264.

cus and his followers is a case in point (I.xii–xxi).[37] According to Irenaeus, the Marcosians believed that redemption might be accomplished in a number of ways, one of which includes the act of anointing the head of the initiate with oil and water in preparation for a divine ascent to the Demiurge who dwells in the celestial realms. Involving the flight of the soul from the body, the ascent is a dangerous one. In his pursuit of the redemptive knowledge of the other world, the gnostic runs the risk of being seized upon and destroyed by the "principalities and powers," that is, the archons, that lie in wait. Like the *yored merkabah* in his visionary quest for the Enthroned Figure, the Marcosian must accordingly be prepared to recite complicated formulas along the various stages of his journey in order to appease the fearsome warders.

Irenaeus appears to be well acquainted with these formulas, for he provides a detailed account of them. In his encounter with the powers the gnostic is thus instructed to repeat the following formula:

> "I am a son from the Father—the Father who had a pre-existence, and a son in Him who is pre-existent. I have come to behold all things, both those things which belong to myself and others. . . . For I derive being from Him who is pre-existent, and I come again to my own place whence I went forth."

Having successfully recited this formula (to the great consternation of the warders), the gnostic is then able to advance to the presence of the Demiurge himself. There the gnostic recites yet another formula of admission before the companions of the Demiurge (I.xxi.5).[38] Both formulas are revealing because they establish the basis upon which the gnostic feels himself authorized to undertake such a journey: his is a direct lineage from that preexistent divinity with which he seeks to reassert a connection.

37. This Marcus was thought to have taught in Asia Proconsularis as a member of the Oriental school of Valentinus. Sharing the doctrines of Valentinus, Marcus, according to Irenaeus, "celebrated a Eucharist by means of magic and fraud" and "seduced many women." The disciples of Marcus preached near the Rhone in Gaul and some were known to Irenaeus personally (Quasten, *Patrology*, I, 265).

38. The formulas addressed to both the powers and the companions of the Demiurge involve a complex mythology having to do with conceptions of an androgynous God that suggests the importance of the female principle to gnostic conceptions of deity. For a fascinating discussion of this topic see Elaine Pagels, *The Gnostic Gospels* (New York: Random House, 1981), esp. the chapter entitled "God the Father / God the Mother," pp. 57–83.

He is returning to a place of origins that he wishes to behold both for his own sake and for the sake of others. That is the purpose of his gnostic quest: it is to gain redemptive knowledge. So Irenaeus observes: "The redemption must therefore be of a spiritual nature; for they [the Marcosians] affirm that the inner and spiritual man is redeemed by means of knowledge, and that they, having acquired the knowledge of all things, stand therefore in need of nothing else. This, then, is the true redemption" (I.xxi.4–5).

It is a redemption the foundations of which are epistemological. What the gnostic beholds in his redeemed state is the highest truth, the source of all power and the basis of all knowing. As one who recites the formulas that will protect him on his journey to this truth, the gnostic finally understands the nature of that phenomenon through which he is able to recite his formulas in the first place. He beholds in truth the very origins of utterance. In terms that reflect the emphasis upon the primacy of language in kabbalistic lore, Marcus conceives truth as a kind of *'adam kadmon*.[39] The very embodiment of utterance itself, this being is at once male and female. On the one hand, it is Anthropos, "the fountain of all speech, and the beginning of all sound, and the expression of all that is unspeakable." On the other hand, it is Aletheia, the beauty of whose female form is revealed in all its splendor to the gnostic.

To him is disclosed not only the unveiled form of Aletheia but the names of her various parts. Reflecting the fundamental importance of language in the Marcosian system, each part is a letter of the alphabet. So he is told:

> "Behold, then, her head on high, *Alpha* and *Omega*; her neck *Beta* and *Psi*; her shoulders with her hands, *Gamma* and *Chi*; her breast *Delta* and *Phi*; her diaphragm, *Epsilon* and *Upsilon*; her back, *Zeta* and *Tau*; her belly *Eta* and and *Sigma*; her thighs, *Theta* and *Rho*; her knees, *Iota* and *Pi*; her legs, *Kappa* and *Omicron*; her ankles *Lambda* and *Xi*; her feet, *Mu* and *Nu*."

Such, according to Marcus, is "the body of Truth." Dwelling in absolute silence, this originary source of utterance gives voice to the unknowable through the enunciation of her own bodily parts.

39. See Scholem's comments in *Jewish Gnosticism*, p. 37.

Doing so, she utters the word in which is contained the secrets of
all gnosis. That word is "Christ Jesus," the Logos himself (I.xiv.2–
4).

In this gnostic reformulation of visionary motifs that find apt
correspondence in the esoterica of *merkabah* mysticism, one discovers a renewed emphasis upon the primacy of utterance, the
word made flesh. Here, that word is conceived as the Logos Christ
Jesus. To pronounce this word with a full understanding of its
meanings is to be in possession of all power. In such a manner
language redeems. Possessing a knowledge of the secrets embedded in the word, the gnostic is able to work miracles. Like his
progenitor Marcus, he becomes a magus in his own right (cf. I.xii–
xiii). As a manifestation of the kinds of beliefs formative Christianity found repugnant to its tenets, such a heterodox outlook is
of crucial importance to an awareness of the transformations the
visionary mode is made to undergo in the early traditions of the
church. Embodying its own systems of thought, heretical gnosticism reconceptualizes the *visio Dei* into a syncretistic and linguist-
ically based mythology of utterance as fascinating in its own right
as the corresponding systems of *kabbalah* with which it offers fit
comparison. Such is only one of a number of manifestations of
the gnostic outlook made evident in the *Adversus Haereses* of Irenaeus.

Of comparable importance to an understanding of that outlook
is Origen. Reflecting an intimate acquaintance with the assumptions
of heretical gnosticism, Origen addresses the foundations of gnostic belief in *Contra Celsum*, his major statement on the subject.[40]
Origen's point of view is discernible in his discussion of the larger
issue of the essential unknowability of God. Faulting Celsus for
his exclusive dependence upon pagan sources as a means of deriving the concept of deity, Origen extols the biblical text as the

40. References are to *Contra Celsum*, trans. Henry Chadwick (Cambridge: Cambridge
University Press, 1953). This edition of *Contra Celsum* is used in conjunction with that in
Origenes Werke, ed. Paul Koetschau et al., 12 vols. (Leipzig: J. C. Hinrichs'sche Buchhandlung, 1899–1919), vols. I and II. Written in eight books, the *Contra Celsum* is a refutation
of the *True Discourse* that the pagan philosopher Celsus directed against the Christians ca.
178. Although Celsus's work has been lost, Origen quotes sufficient amounts of it to provide
a detailed idea of what Celsus said. His aim was to convert the Christians by showing them
the folly of their beliefs, a subject in which Celsus, as a learned and widely read scholar,
was deeply versed. He knew not only the pagan philosophers but the Bible, the Christian
writings, and the works of the gnostics (Quasten, *Patrology*, II, 52). See also Chadwick's
excellent introduction to his edition (pp. ix–xxxii).

true repository of such concepts. The Bible makes entirely clear the idea that God cannot be known. Hiding Himself as if in darkness from those unable to bear the radiance of the knowledge of Him, God reveals Himself only to those who are divinely appointed, such as the prophets and, of course, His own son (VI:17).

As examples of the profundity surrounding the *occultatio Dei*, Origen invokes the visions of God portrayed by Isaiah and Ezekiel. His observation provides a context for the discussions that follow:

> I could quote the statements about the seraphim, as they are called by the Hebrews, described by Isaiah as hiding the face and the feet of God, and about what are called cherubim, which Ezekiel portrayed, and of their shapes, as it were, and of the way in which God is said to be carried upon the cherubim. But, as these things are expressed in a very obscure form because of the unworthy and irreligious who are not able to understand the deep meaning and sacredness of the doctrine of God, I have not thought it right to discuss these matters in this book. (VI:18)

The observation is interesting for a number of reasons. In order to support its outlook, it makes a point of resorting to those crucial loci that represent the foundation of the the visionary mode. To understand the nature of the *occultatio Dei*, Origen implies, is to encounter the sources of the *merkabah*, embodied here in the seraphim of Isaiah and the cherubim of Ezekiel. These are the sources of true gnosis to those fully initiated into the secrets of God. In the fashion of the rabbinical commentators, however, Origen resorts to that disclaimer with which any commentator on the *merkabah* would be entirely familiar: Because only the most religious and worthy are capable of understanding the secret doctrines to which he alludes, he as a true cognoscente has elected not to discuss "these matters" here. By issuing such a disclaimer, Origen immediately places himself in that select religious and rhetorical community of those qualified to discuss what he and the members of this society know to be the *maʿaseh merkabah*. In the very refusal to discuss such matters, Origen, like his rabbinical counterparts, brings them to the fore. They become in effect the subtext of the gnostic speculations that follow.

Accordingly, Origen continues his treatment of the *occultatio Dei* by attempting to "place" God, to suggest where He resides. Drawing upon biblical accounts, Origen argues that the idea of situating the Deity above the highest of heavens, as well as the desire to ascend to those realms, is discernible in figures ranging from David to Paul. Although the Bible does not specify any number to the heavens above which God dwells, "Moses, our most ancient prophet, says that in a divine dream our forefather Jacob had a vision in which he saw a ladder reaching to heaven and angels of God ascending and descending upon it, and the Lord standing still at its top; perhaps in this story of the ladder Moses was hinting at these truths or at yet more profound doctrines" (VI:19–22).[41] Reflected in the account of Jacob's dream, these "more profound doctrines" are apparent in those traditions associated with the *merkabah*. So Origen observes: "If anyone should want to have suggestions of the deeper truths about the way in which the soul enters into the divine realm," let him "read the visions seen by the prophet Ezekiel at the end of his prophecy where different gates are depicted, conveying in veiled form certain doctrines about the various ways in which the more divine souls enter into the higher life" (VI:23).

The allusion is fascinating, for what it does is to look upon Ezekiel's vision of the Temple (40–48) as an originary symbol of the soul's ascent through the celestial realms to attain the highest sphere, that in which the Enthroned Figure dwells. In order to achieve that sphere, Origen implies, the visionary must pass through the various "gates" that serve to keep the uninitiated at bay. As his reference to the idea of "conveying in veiled form certain doctrines about the various ways in which the more divine souls enter into the higher life" suggests, this is Origen's version of the *ma'aseh merkabah*, one fully in accord with the idea of ascent through the *hekhalot*. Associating Ezekiel's vision with corresponding biblical texts, Origen enacts his own reading of the *merkabah*.

That reading, in turn, provides a context for Origen's consideration of heretical gnosticism. At issue is the sect known as the Ophites.[42] According to the teachings of this sect, there are seven

41. Origen associates these doctrines specifically with Philo's commentary *De Somniis*, but, Jacob's ladder, we recall, is also a staple of *merkabah* speculation. See Alexander Altmann, "The Ladder of Ascension," *Studies in Religious Philosophy and Mysticism* (Ithaca, N.Y.: Cornell University Press, 1969), pp. 41–72.

42. The Ophites (from the Greek *ophis*, "serpent") were an early gnostic sect, probably associated with the Naassenes. As suggested by their name, they incorporated the serpent into their rituals. Epiphanius, for example, describes a eucharistic ritual in which they released a serpent to entwine itself around the elements. According to the anti-gnostic

powers or *"archontic daemons"* that guard the gates of each realm in the ascent of the visionary to the highest realm, there to obtain full gnosis. In keeping with the theriomorphic thrust of Ezekiel's vision, these archons are conceived as beasts. The first is formed in the shape of a lion, the second in the shape of a bull, the third in the shape of a serpent, the fourth in the shape of an eagle, the fifth in the shape of a bear, the sixth in the shape of a dog, and the seventh in the shape of an ass. Corresponding to each of these forms is an angelic figure: Michael, Suriel (or Uriel), Raphael, Gabriel, Thauthabaoth, Erathaoth, and Thaphabaoth or Onoel. The names of the archons are likewise given variously (and in ascending order) as Ailoaeus, Astaphaeus, Adonaeus, Sabaoth, Iao, and Ialdabaoth (VI:31).[43]

To persuade the archons to allow him to pass, the gnostic must address them by name, recite the correct formula, and present to each a "symbol" or "seal." Having successfully traversed the realms of the seven archons, the gnostic achieves the eighth sphere, the Ogdoad, which lies within the realm of the Father and the Son and is presided over by a nameless being called the "First Power." At this juncture the gnostic has achieved his goal of transcendent awareness. Enveloped in the light of the Father and the Son, he may now be sent forth in complete purity. Whatever the significance of the specific characteristics of the ascent and the manner in which it conducted, one point is clear: Origen's account is very much in keeping with the spirit of the *merkabah* made evident in the *hekhalot* treatises.[44]

---

literature, they denigrated the God of the Old Testament. *Encyclopedic Dictionary of Religion*, ed. Paul Kevin Meagher et al., 3 vols. (Washington, D.C.: Corpus Publications, 1979), III, 2605.

43. Corresponding to the names in the *hekhalot* literature, these names likewise have special meanings upon which Origen refuses to elaborate. Having given them, in fact, he then dismisses them. He cites these names, he says, so that "the sorcerers may not, by claiming to know something more than we do, succeed in deceiving those who are swept off their feet by the parading of names." Nonetheless, he does suggest that such names as Ialdabaoth, Astaphaeus, and Horaeus come from the realm of "magic" and that such names as Iao, Sabaoth, Adonai, and Elaeus come from "the Hebrew scriptures," where they are all "titles of one and the same God" (VI:32). Similar names are alluded to by Irenaeus in the *Adversus Haereses* (I.xxx.11), and they appear in a number of the gnostic documents in the Nag Hammadi codex. See Chadwick, *Contra Celsum*, p. 349, n. 2, as well as R. Van Den Broek, "The Creation of Adam's Psychic Body in the Apocryphon of John," *Studies in Gnosticism and Hellenistic Religions*, ed. R. Van Den Broek and M. J. Vermaseren (Leiden: Brill, 1981), pp. 39–57.

44. The summary of the ascent is indebted to the concise and useful description in

The similarity is discernible in a number of respects, among them, the requirement that the visionary recite passwords to appease the archontic guards. Like Irenaeus, Origen makes a point of emphasizing the nature of the secret language employed by the Ophites as an essential constituent of the ritual of ascent. As one of a number cited by Origen, the following liturgy will serve as an example of what the gnostic says after he has traversed the so-called Barrier of Evil and stands before "the eternally chained gates of the Archons":

> Solitary King, bond of blindness, unconscious oblivion, I hail thee, the supreme Power, preserved by the spirit of providence and wisdom; from thee I am sent in purity, being already part of the light of Son and Father. May grace be with me; yea, father, let it be with me. (VI:31)

As what is probably the final recitation in the ascent, this liturgy suggests how the experience of receiving gnostic illumination and purification is essential to the conception as a whole.[45] In the ultimate realm the gnostic, like the *yored merkabah*, issues his "hail" in celebration of the "power" whose realm he has successfully achieved. As an expression of this success, he is able to utter words that themselves embody power. In that act the gnostic, like the *merkabah* mystic, reveals his ability to appropriate the secrets of the other world and to make those secrets distinctly his own. He becomes the authorized purveyor of gnosis: in him, language encapsulates vision, and through him, it is the source of power. Inspired by the esoteric traditions, the mythology of recitation, then, is as important to Origen as it is to Irenaeus. As much as each looked upon heretical gnosticism as anathema, the kind of perspective that was the very stuff of the *yordei merkabah* infused their points of view as well. Responding to the tenets of heretical gnosticism, they created their own mythology of ascent indebted to the *merkabah* as generative source of the visionary mode.

Irenaeus and Origen are only two of a number of sources that

Alexander, who concludes by noting the similarities of the gnostic ascent described by Origen with the literature of the *merkabah* ("Comparing *Merkavah* Mysticism and Gnosticism," pp. 2–3).

45. Although Origen cites this liturgy first, Chadwick feels that Origen's list of passwords "starts at the top with the eighth and supreme sphere, not at the bottom, so that he has the Ophite liturgy in the reverse order" (*Contra Celsum*, p. 346, n. 3).

might be examined to suggest the primacy of the *merkabah* to gnostic modes of thought.[46] If they represent the kind of reaction to heretical gnosticism made evident in the writings of the early church fathers, it should not be forgotten that those same fathers endorsed a form of gnosticism entirely in keeping with the tenets of the early church. Alluded to above as Christian gnosticism, this idea is fully articulated in the writings of Clement of Alexandria, the putative instructor of Origen himself. Among Clement's works, that which offers most dramatic evidence of the worth of Christian gnosticism is the *Stromata*.[47] There, in the very act of confuting heretical gnosticism, Clement forges a gnosticism based upon a Hellenistic outlook that extols a true Christian faith in God and the ardent desire to know and worship Him fully, worthily, and chastely. "He is the Gnostic," Clement observes, "who is after the image and likeness of God, who imitates God as far as possible, deficient in none of the things which contribute to the likeness as far as compatible, practising self-restraint and endurance, living righteously, reigning over the passions, bestowing of what he has as far as possible, and doing good both by word and deed" (II.xix). The emphasis here is distinctly moral: the true gnostic is, before all else, a good person, one whose behavior is absolutely impeccable. Disciplining himself in all areas that bear upon his conduct in this world, the gnostic becomes an example for others to follow. Approaching the concept of gnosticism in this manner, Clement broadens the range of interpretations available to those who seek to know its true meaning.

The gnostic, however, is not simply a good man: he is also one determined to behold God through a complex process of self-purification and contemplation. In order for the gnostic soul to fulfill this quest, he must be "consecrated to the light, stripped of the integuments of matter, devoid of the frivolousness of the body

46. Space does not permit an examination of the documents in the Nag Hammadi codex (discovered in 1945). As Francis T. Fallon has demonstrated in his discussion of the codex, two documents in particular reflect extensive *merkabah* influence: *The Hypostasis of the Archon* and the untitled work to which has been assigned the name *The Origin of the World*. See Fallon's *The Enthronement of Sabaoth: Jewish Elements in Gnostic Creation Myths* (Leiden: Brill, 1978), passim; and Segal, *Two Powers in Heaven*, pp. 251–253.

47. According to Eusebius and Photius, the full title is "Titus Flavius Clement's miscellaneous collections of speculative [*gnosticon*] notes bearing upon the true philosophy." References in my text are to the translation in *The Ante-Nicene Fathers*, II, 299–568. This edition has been used in conjunction with the edition of the *Stromata* by Otto Stählin, 2 vols. (Berlin: Akademie-Verlag, 1960).

and of all the passions" (V.xi). Only then will he be brought up
to the highest of heavens. Clement expostulates on this process
in a number of ways, including an analysis of Moses' ascent of
Sinai as a symbol of the contemplative process and Saint Paul's
ascent to the third heaven, where he is initiated "in the mysteries"
(V.xii).[48] His most detailed description, however, may be found
in his mystical analysis of Genesis 22:3–4: "Abraham, when he
came to the place which God told him of on the third day, looking
up, saw the place afar off." Responding to this text, Clement
observes: "For the first day is that which is constituted by the sight
of good things; and the second is the soul's best desire; on the
third, the mind perceives spiritual things, the eyes of the understanding being opened by the Teacher who rose on the third day."
The *visio Dei* for Clement is assimilated into the context of the
Paschal Triduum culminating in the Resurrection and Ascension
of Christ. Correspondingly, the *visio Dei* is conceived as the realm
of God that Plato called "the region of ideas, having learned from
Moses that it was a place which contained all things universally."
The ultimate quest of the gnostic who ascends in contemplation
to this realm is to understand the way biblical and Platonic concepts of vision are fused to embrace a larger perspective. Having
ascended to the highest realms, the gnostic will no longer be made
to participate in that event "afar off" but will eventually experience it "face to face" (V.xii). Such is the gnosticism of Clement of
Alexandria. His is a form of divine knowing that attempts to
reconcile pagan and Christian concepts within a harmonious
frame. Forging that frame, Clement bestows upon gnosticism a
new legitimacy and a new receptivity to a wide variety of interpretations.

It is to this variety of interpretations that the foregoing discussion has itself attempted to be receptive. Basing its outlook on the
transformative concept of gnosticism suggested by Hans Jonas,
the discussion has traced the course of the gnostic impulse not
only in the canonical accounts portrayed in the New Testament
but in the extracanonical narratives that underlie New Testament
apocalyptic. Moving beyond these texts, the discussion has undertaken to explore the assumptions of heretical gnosticism de-

---

48. This view of Moses is no doubt indebted to Philo's discussion of the subject in his
work *On the Life of Moses* (II.xii–xxx). Clement, like Origen, reflects the Philonic influence
throughout.

lineated in the literature of the early church fathers. The purpose of the discussion has been to approach the visionary mode from another point of view, one that suggests the way in which the dynamics that distinguish the *merkabah* are as compellingly expressed in the traditions of early Christianity as they were in the Judaic traditions. Interpenetrating, these two modes of thought indicate how the transformative nature of the visionary mode assumes a vital presence in an entire spectrum of texts. Doing so, it emerges as a crucial determinant of interpretive response in the manifold traditions of hermeneutics from its point of origin in the Bible to its later formulations in the early Middle Ages and beyond.

∼ Six

The Spirituality of Vision

I

The foregoing discussion has suggested how Ezekiel's *visio Dei* was appropriated as a gnostic phenomenon both in the New Testament and in the earliest traditions of the church. The present discussion explores a subject of comparable importance to an understanding of the visionary mode as a reflection of the Christocentric point of view. This subject falls under the heading of what might be called the spirituality of vision, a phenomenon that manifests itself in the long and complex traditions of exegesis originating in the early church and extending into the later Middle Ages. In some respects the subject has already been addressed in the earlier treatment of such figures as Irenaeus, Origen, and Clement of Alexandria. As might be expected, however, these figures represent only a few of the many that distinguish the exegetical traditions concerned with the visionary mode as a Christocentric category. Once again, the subject is of a magnitude to preclude an exhaustive consideration. Nonetheless, the nature of Christian spirituality is such that, like its counterpart in the Judaic sphere, it is receptive to the treatment of representative figures and significant trends. Such a treatment should go far toward elucidating the exegetical dimensions of the visionary mode among the early church fathers and beyond.

Although lines of demarcation overlap, one is able to discern at least two major trends in the traditions of exegesis that constitute the spirituality of vision among the church fathers. These trends are distinguished more nearly by the emphasis they bestow upon certain meanings than by categorical differences in approach or outlook. Whereas the first emphasizes what might be called the mystical or phenomenological dimensions of a given text, the second stresses what might be termed the interpretive or hermeneutical dimensions. Subscribing roughly to the distinctions addressed in the earlier treatment of the Judaic traditions, these trends exhibit identifiable characteristics that reveal a good deal about the exegetical practices of the church.

The mystical or phenomenological dimension is characterized by a concern with contemplative modes of thought and the cultivation of prescribed norms of behavior as a means of achieving communion with godhead. Focusing upon the experience of "seeing God," this trend has its closest affinities with the traditions of gnosticism discussed in the previous chapter and might well, in fact, have been treated under that very heading. The interpretive or hermeneutical dimension is characterized by a concern with the various meanings that a particular text yields in the course of a given exegesis. Its focus is not so much experiential as elucidative. That is, it concerns itself more nearly with the constellations of meaning inherent in texts that portray the *visio Dei* than with the act of embarking upon such a vision and the experience of having one. In the process of elucidating a given text, it establishes interpretive structures through which that text can be better understood. It does so by establishing a contextual framework through the citation of corresponding biblical passages or through allusions to works outside the biblical canon. Overlapping and interconnected, both trends often find complementary expression in the same exegesis, distinguished at once by an interest in the experience associated with the idea of seeing God and by a concern with the texts in which the *visio Dei* is portrayed.[1] In either case the vision that inaugurates the prophecy of Ezekiel is at the forefront of patristic exegesis from the earliest times.[2] Having begun the exploration of this idea in the last chapter, we further examine

1. Here, as elsewhere, of course, the term *mysticism* must be used with utmost caution. As Louise Bouyer points out, *mystikos* as spiritual phenomenon assumes among the church fathers the form of *theōria*, that which involves the act of seeing (mystical visions are quite literally *theōrēmata*). *The Spirituality of the New Testament and the Fathers*, trans. Mary P. Ryan et al., 2 vols. (New York: Desclee, 1960–1961), I, 405–410.

2. Evidence of this fact is made abundantly clear in the seminal study of Wilhelm Neuss, *Das Buch Ezechiel in Theologie und Kunst bis zum Ende des XII. Jahrhunderts* (Münster: Aschendorffsche Verlagsbuchhandlung, 1912). See also Neuss's *Die Apokalypse des Johannes in der altspanischen und altchristlichen Bibel-Illustration*, 2 vols. (Münster: Aschendorffsche Verlagsbuchhandlung, 1931), which contains a wealth of related material.

the course of its history here. Doing so, we concern ourselves with
its manifestation as both a mystical and an exegetical phenomenon.[3]

In accord with the approach adopted throughout this study, we
focus on representative figures through whom the mystical and
exegetical dimensions of the visionary mode found expression.
Addressing this issue, we might well return to the Alexandrian
milieu invoked in the previous chapter. As already suggested in
the discussion of Clement of Alexandria, contemplation underlies
the attainment of gnosis in its various forms. For Clement, "the
Christian goal is to know or see God. In its perfection gnosis is
an *aidios theōria*, a perpetual contemplation." By means of contemplation or *theōria*, one is able to ascend like Moses to the summit
of Sinai, there to behold God in all His splendor. In his extolling
of contemplation as the most supreme form of devotion, Clement
endorses a "super-intellectualistic mysticism," in which the contemplation of God is presented as the "highest bliss." For Clement,
"knowledge is beatitude." In this respect Clement serves as the
basis by which the contemplative process assumes not only a renewed legitimacy as a philosophical activity but a profound urgency as a religious endeavor of the most exalted kind.[4] If such
is true of Clement, it is no less so of Origen, in whom the different
stages of the contemplative life were fully codified. These stages
include the spiritual struggle within the self (*praktikē*), the attainment of the knowledge of the mysteries of creation (*physikē theōria*),
and the realization of the vision of God in the Logos (*theologia*).
The goal in Origen is to rise from *praktikē* through *theōria* to *theologia*.[5]

3. The literature on the subject is vast. Among more recent works, see the excellent
essays in *Understanding Mysticism*, ed. Richard Woods, O.P. (Garden City, N.Y.: Doubleday,
1980), as well as the important individual studies by Andrew Louth, *The Origins of the
Mystical Tradition: From Plato to Denys* (Oxford: Clarendon Press, 1981), and Harvey D.
Egan, S.J., *Christian Mysticism: The Future of a Tradition* (New York: Pueblo Publishing,
1984). For the treatment of mysticism among the eastern fathers, the essential work is
Vladimir Lossky's *The Vision of God*, trans. Asheleigh Moorhouse, 2d ed. (Bedfordshire:
Faith Press, 1973). Correspondingly important for the western fathers is Dom Cuthbert
Butler's *Western Mysticism: The Teaching of Augustine, Gregory and Bernard on Contemplation
and the Contemplative Life* (1922), 2d ed. (New York: Harper and Row, 1966).
4. Lossky, *Vision of God*, pp. 39–43. See further, Bouyer, *Spirituality*, I, 271: "Clement
develops these themes by having recourse to philosophic expression of *theōria* and *epistēmē*."
In the second book of the *Stromata*, according to Bouyer, Clement says that "to know God
is the greatest *theōria*," one that involves "the science of being itself [*to onti epistēmē*]."
5. Lossky, *Vision of God*, pp. 46–60. Origen elaborates this idea of ascent in his twenty-

Following in Origen's footsteps and developing this mystical or contemplative perspective still further is the figure of Gregory of Nyssa (ca. 332–ca. 395), the philosophical spokesman for Cappadocian monasticism.[6] In him, one discovers the "final development of Alexandrian gnosis which would lead it towards what the following periods would call, precisely, mysticism."[7] Among Gregory's works, that which develops the contemplative approach most compellingly is his treatise *The Life of Moses*.[8] Assuming the form of a logos, that is, a formal treatise, Gregory's *Life* is divisible into four sections: "(1) the Preface, or covering letter of introduction; (2) the History (*historia*), or paraphrase of the Biblical story; (3) the Contemplation (*theōria*), or spiritual meaning of the Scriptural narrative, which is his main concern; and (4) the Conclusion."[9] Whereas the second part (*historia*) selectively summarizes the events of the life of Moses from the account in Exodus and Numbers, the third part (*theōria*) derives spiritual lessons from the first part as a means by which one is able to realize (as the complete title of the work indicates) "Perfection in Virtue."[10]

As such, the work establishes ties with and elaborates upon a long exegetical tradition in which the life of Moses was viewed as

seventh homily on Numbers, in which he interprets the "stations" of the Israelites in the wilderness as stages on the journey toward the vision of God. See *Homily XXVII on Numbers* in *Origen*, trans. Rowan A. Greer (New York: Paulist Press, 1979), pp. 249–269, as well as the Latin version of Rufinus in *Origenes Werke*, vol. VII. David J. Halperin sees in Origen's *Homilies* (both on Numbers and on Joshua) certain parallels to the Judaic myth underlying the *hekhalot; Faces of the Chariot: Early Jewish Responses to Ezekiel's Vision* (Tübingen: J. C. B. Mohr, 1988), p. 453.

6. According to Louth, "the pattern for Gregory's treatment of mystical theology is, inevitably, Origen" (p. 81). See Louth's discussion of Gregory, *Origins*, pp. 80–97.

7. Bouyer, *Spirituality*, I, 351. Among other studies of this dimension, see Walther Völker, *Gregor von Nyssa als Mystiker* (Wiesbaden: F. Steiner, 1955), H. F. Cherniss, *The Platonism of Gregory of Nyssa* (Berkeley: University of California Press, 1930), and Jean Daniélou, *Platonisme et théologie mystique* (Paris: Aubier Editions Montaigne, 1944), esp. pp. 171–182.

8. References are to Gregory of Nyssa, *The Life of Moses or Concerning Perfection in Virtue*, trans. Abraham J. Malherbe and Everett Ferguson (New York: Paulist Press, 1978) (hereafter cited in notes as Malherbe and Ferguson), in conjunction with *Grégoire de Nysse, La vie de Moïse*, ed. Jean Daniélou, *Sources chrétiennes* (Paris: Éditions du Cerf, 1955), and the edition of Herbert Musurillo, *Gregorii Nysseni, De Vita Moysis*, in *Gregorii Nysseni, Opera*, ed. Werner Jaeger and Hermann Langerbeck, 9 vols. (Leiden: E. J. Brill, 1960–1967), vol. VII, part 1.

9. This summary of the structure and exegetical tradition is derived from Malherbe and Ferguson's excellent Introduction to the Paulist Press edition, pp. 3–7.

10. Gregory's work is a manual of asceticism, one that emphasizes on behalf of the Cappadocian monks the virtues of the ascetic life (Malherbe and Ferguson, pp. 3, 10).

exemplary in the cultivation of the highest virtues.[11] Of immense importance in this regard is Philo, whose two-part *Life of Moses* first presents a "historical" account of the life and then provides a treatment of the character in the roles of lawgiver, priest, and prophet.[12] In a somewhat different vein Philo addresses corresponding issues in his *Questions and Answers on Exodus*, which considers both the literal meanings of passages and the "deeper" or "underlying" significance.[13] In the Christian appropriation of Philo, Clement of Alexandria incorporates a "life of Moses" into the *Stromata* (I:23–26), and Origen in his *Commentary on Lamentations* follows the method of Philo's *Questions and Answers* in first addressing the literal meaning and then considering the inner or underlying meaning.[14] Both in subject matter and in method, then, earlier traditions of exegesis represented the occasion by which Gregory of Nyssa was able to offer his own reading of the life of Moses. In Gregory's account this fact assumes great importance for an understanding of the visionary renderings that one encounters.

Among those renderings, that which shall engage us here is the interpretation of Moses' ascent of Sinai and the *visio Dei* that he experiences in that realm. For our purposes the subject is particularly appropriate because it offers fit correspondence not just to those various ascents that we have noted in the Judaic treatments but to the concept of Moses himself as prototype of the *yored merkabah*, a subject of the first importance to the *merkabah* literature.[15] In keeping with the traditions that Gregory inherited, the ascent of Sinai culminating in the theophany on the mountain top is at the very center of the present meditation. Receiving elaborate attention in the contemplative part of the account (Book II), the Sinai theophany fulfills what has been anticipated in the historical

11. Among the treatments of this subject, see John G. Gager, *Moses in Greco-Roman Paganism*, Society of Biblical Literature Monograph Series, vol. 16 (Nashville: Abingdon Press, 1972); and Moses Hadas, *Hellenistic Culture* (New York: Norton, 1972).

12. In vol. 6 of *Philo*, trans. F. H. Colson and G. H. Whitaker, 10 vols. and 2 supplementary vols. (Cambridge: Harvard University Press, 1956–1979).

13. In supplementary vol. 2 of *Philo*. Correspondingly, see the *Questions and Answers on Genesis* in supplementary vol. 2. In his *Life of Moses* Gregory uses a number of interpretive terms in reference to the nonliteral meaning, including *anagōgē*, *uponoia*, and *tropikos*. See Malherbe and Ferguson, p. 145, n. 47.

14. Malherbe and Ferguson, pp. 5–7.

15. See earlier references (in Chapter 3, note 22) to the *Pesikta Rabbati*, especially the *parashah* dealing with the giving of the Torah (*Piska* 20), as well as the Ascension of Moses in the *Gedullat Mosheh*.

part (Book I). There, Gregory asserts that having ascended the mount, Moses "boldly approached the very darkness itself." Within that darkness "he entered the inner sanctuary of the divine mystical doctrine [*to adytontes theias mystagōgias*]," where "he was in company of the Invisible" (I:46).[16]

Precisely what Gregory means by such an observation is made apparent in the second book (secs. 152–188), which focuses upon the ascent of the mount. As Gregory makes clear, that ascent is undertaken only after Moses has been successful in overcoming the travails of the wilderness. These include that process of purification which occurs by passing through dangerous waters, by sustaining the assaults of the enemy, and by continued faith in the sustenance of God. Only then is the votary prepared to "hear the sound of the trumpets [and] to enter into the darkness where God is" (secs. 152–153). Both in outlook and in focus, the portrayal of Moses' experience is very much in keeping with the milieu that distinguishes the culture of the *merkabah* mystic. Like the *yored merkabah* in his pursuit of the Throne of God, the Moses of Gregory embarks upon his own vision of the Chariot.

Addressing himself to the rituals of purification involved in such an enterprise, Gregory makes a great deal of the baptismal dimensions of the idea. Those dimensions are already sounded in the earlier discussion of the overthrow of the Egyptians in the Red Sea (secs. 121–125). Gregory interprets this event as a cleansing of the passions through "the mystery of the water." For who is not aware, he asks rhetorically, that the Egyptian army, with their horses, chariots, and drivers are "the various passions of the soul by which man is enslaved?" Among the passions, the need for pleasure is to be seen in the horses that "with irresistible drive pull the chariot." In the chariot itself, moreover, there are three drivers who are carried along by the chariot. These, observes Gregory, are to be interpreted as "the tripartite division of the soul, meaning the rational, the appetitive, and the spirited" (secs. 122–123).

16. Gregory adopts the language of Hellenistic mystery religions. According to Malherbe and Ferguson, "the terminology of mystery initiation was employed by Hellenistic philosophers to express learning philosophical doctrines" (p. 153, n. 74). In Philo the idea is already associated with Moses as priest of the mysteries. See in particular *Questions and Answers on Exodus* (11.44–49). See Goodenough's treatment of the "mystic Moses" in *By Light, Light: The Mystic Gospel of Hellenistic Judaism* (Amsterdam: Philo Press, 1969), pp. 199–234.

The context, of course, is Platonic: as a means of conceiving the composite nature of the soul, it combines the fable of the chariot with its horses and charioteer in the *Phaedrus* (246–255) with the discourse on the principles that govern the soul in the *Republic* (IV.439–442; cf. VI.511; IX.588–589).[17] In both respects the soul is to be cleansed and purified before embarking on the ascent of the mount. Such purification assumes both a spiritual and a ritual bearing.[18] So Gregory observes that both the body and the clothing are to be washed in preparation for the ascent. He who would approach "the contemplation of Being," says Gregory, "must be pure in all things so as to be pure in soul and body, washed stainless of every spot in both parts, in order that he might appear pure to the One who sees what is hidden and that visible respectability might correspond to the inward condition of the soul" (II:154–157). Externals accord with internals, clothing and body with the parts of the soul. For Gregory, clothing and body represent as much the "outward pursuits of life" reflected in the external appearance of respectability as they do the actual physical trappings of the individual. Because he who would see will himself be seen, he must, in all respects, be "washed."[19]

Recalling the preparatory rituals for ascent among the *merkabah* mystics, the cleansing of external and internal, in turn, is complemented by another act of preparation. This has to do with what Gregory calls the seer's withdrawal of himself from "customary intercourse with his own companion, that is, with his sense perceptions, which are, as it were, wedded to our nature as its companion" (II:157). In short, the seer is obliged not only to cleanse himself externally and internally of all corruption but to withdraw himself from those senses (such as physical sight and hearing) that bind him to this world. Like the *yordei merkabah* of whom Hai Gaon

17. For further discussion of Gregory's conception of the soul, see Daniélou, *Platonisme et théologie mystique*, pp. 61–71; and J. P. Cavarnos, *St. Gregory of Nyssa on the Origin and Destiny of the Soul* (Belmont, Mass.: Institute for Byzantine and Modern Greek Studies, 1956).

18. Cf. the emphasis upon spiritual and ritual purity in such texts as *The Apocalypse of Abraham* and the *Hekhalot Rabbati*, discussed in Chapter 2.

19. In the *Pesikta Rabbati* (20:4) Moses as *yored merkabah* is rebuked by the angel Kemuel, "What dost thou among the holy ones of the Most High? Thou comest from a place of foulnesses; what wouldst thou in a place of purity? Born of a woman in heat, what wouldst thou in a place of fire that is pure?" (I, 406). As we have seen, the idea is a staple of *hekhalot* literature.

speaks, the seer of Gregory must remove himself completely from all bodily trammels. This act of withdrawal is, as it were, a receding into the self and an obliteration of the self as the physical world of sense perceptions is left entirely behind. With that obliteration, those very sense perceptions from which the seer has withdrawn become increasingly and paradoxically heightened. Such is especially true of hearing and seeing.

With regard to hearing, Gregory makes a great deal of the sounds of the trumpets that Moses was said to have heard in his ascent of the mount (Exod. 19:13, 16, 19; 20:18). These sounds become louder as one advances up the mountain. For Gregory the significance of the trumpet sounds lies in their prefigurative function. Although "the Law and the Prophets trumpeted the divine mystery of the Incarnation," they could not be heard or understood by those unreceptive to their meaning. It required the seer and his ascent to appreciate the true meaning of the increasing sound of the trumpets (II:159; cf. I:44). Withdrawing himself from the physical sense of hearing, Moses is able to appreciate the spiritual significance of the trumpet blast as he ascends. His ascent thereby assumes a decidedly Christocentric bearing. What is true of the trumpets is likewise true of the voice that speaks to him from the heights. "The multitude was not capable of hearing the voice from above but relied on Moses to learn by himself the secrets and to teach the people whatever doctrine he might learn through instruction from above." "Initiated into the divine mysteries," Moses becomes a mediator for the typology of the New Dispensation (II:162).

Corresponding to the act of hearing is that of seeing. For Gregory the withdrawal of the self from the sense of physical sight finds its counterpart in the spiritual illumination that one receives as a result of that withdrawal. The paradox of renewed sight is discernible in the biblical reference to Moses' drawing near to "the thick darkness where God was" (Exod. 20:21). "What does it mean," asks Gregory, "that Moses entered the darkness and then saw God in it?" How can darkness be a source of illumination, and how does this theophany differ from that revealed in the burning bush (Exod. 3:1–6)? The answer to both questions for Gregory lies in the concept of "progress" or increasing intensity. Those who first experience religious knowledge receive it in the form of light; so Moses experienced light from the burning bush, a light that dispelled

the darkness of ignorance. But there is a different kind of
darkness, Gregory avers, a darkness that extends beyond light
or that which appears as darkness when the intensity of light is
so great that the unknowable becomes known. This is what
happens when the mind progresses to the point of apprehend-
ing ultimate reality. In the contemplative progression that constitutes an ever more heightened awareness of *theōria*, that is,
of seeing in its most exalted form, the soul "gains access to the
invisible and incomprehensible, and there it sees God."

Gregory explains this experience paradoxically as the profound
and "luminous darkness" of not seeing, a not seeing that is absolute
sight. "This is the true knowledge of what is sought; this is the
seeing that consists in not seeing, because that which is sought
transcends all knowledge, being separated on all sides by incomprehensibility as by a kind of darkness." Such is the darkness that
Moses beholds after he grows in knowledge. It is the "inner sanctuary" of this luminous darkness into which Moses enters in order
to be initiated into the mysteries that it otherwise occludes (II:
162–163). Having reached this point, Moses has, as it were, passed
from one peak to another in his ascent to the heights. He has left
behind the base of the mountain, where he is separated from all
those too weak for the ascent. Next, he has risen to the point of
hearing the sound of trumpets at their most intense. Finally, he
has penetrated the luminous darkness of divine knowledge in
order to be initiated into its mysteries (II:167). Underlying those
mysteries is an experience that represents the culmination of his
ascent: the *visio Dei* embodied in the celestial tabernacle. It is this
experience toward which all the efforts of the seer are finally
directed. In his account of that experience Gregory examines the
celestial tabernacle in great detail (II:170–183).

As Gregory describes it, the celestial tabernacle is an archetype
or pattern of that which is to be replicated on earth. In ideal form
it contains gold and silver pillars supported by silver and bronze
bases, a seven-branched golden candlestick, a golden altar, and a
golden ark with its throne of mercy and the cherubim whose wings
overshadowed the ark. Dividing the tabernacle in two parts (the
holy place and the holy of holies) are the curtains woven of diverse
colors (cf. Exod. 25:9–40). These will be manifested in the tabernacle made by hands in the world below (II:170–172). In archetypal form they constitute "the mystery of the tabernacle which
encompasses the universe." In short, the archetypal tabernacle is

also a cosmic tabernacle.[20] More than that, however, the archetypal tabernacle is a representation of the spirit of Christ. In fact, Gregory comments, *tabernacle*, like *physician, shepherd, protector, bread, vine, way, door, mansion, water, rock*, and *spring*, is one of the names or designations of Christ "used piously to express the divine power" (cf. Col. 2:9).

In this respect *tabernacle* for Gregory contains a hidden significance, one that implies not only a cosmic meaning but a Christocentric one as well. As a tabernacle, Christ is thereby a universe that both encompasses everything within himself and is in effect that tabernacle not made with hands of which he himself is the high priest (Heb. 9:1–14). Entering the celestial tabernacle, Moses, then, is imbued with a knowledge of all that Christ represents. With the establishment of the Christocentric context, Gregory recasts the idea in Pauline terms by invoking the apostle's account of his ascent to the third heaven (2 Cor. 12:1–4). No doubt, Gregory observes, Paul himself had "a vision of the tabernacle when he entered the supercelestial sanctuary where the mysteries of Paradise were revealed to him by the Spirit."

The cosmic and the paradisal, then, reinforce the overriding image of the tabernacle as the embodiment of Christ, in whom dwells "the fullness of divinity." Elaborating upon this idea of fullness, Gregory sees in the tabernacle that Christ represents the entire angelic hierarchy. To that end Gregory cites Col. 1:16: "in him were created all things, everything visible and everything invisible, Thrones, Dominations, Sovereignties, Powers or forces." By means of this hierarchy the universe itself is supported and guided to accord with the divine will. As such, the angelic hierarchy mirrors God's providential design (III:173–180).

Pursuing the angelic dimension even further, Gregory addresses himself to the cherubim that "cover the mysteries in the ark with their wings." It is with regard to these cherubim that Gregory makes it clear just how abstruse are the mysteries that they conceal. "For," he observes, "we have learned that this is the name of those powers [*dynameōn*] which we see around the divine nature, which powers Isaiah and Ezekiel perceived" (II:180). Such a statement provides evidence of how compellingly the entire ascent moves toward a realization of this crucial moment. Having

---

20. Much of what Gregory says about the cosmic and mystical significance is Philonic. See the *Questions on Exodus* 2.52, 59, 83, 85; *Life of Moses* 2.18.88.

ascended the mountain of knowledge, the seer penetrates the luminous darkness of the tabernacle to find himself before the ark of the covenant upon which reside those cherubim whose significance is to be seen in the respective visions of Isaiah and Ezekiel. Within the tabernacle Gregory's seer beholds his own version of the *merkabah*.

All that is implied in the *serafim* and *ḥayyot* are embodied for Gregory in the cherubim that overshadow the ark of the covenant in the archetypal tabernacle. Surrounding the "divine nature," those cherubim are the "powers" that not only support the universe, of which the tabernacle is a symbol, but cover the mysteries in the ark with their wings.[21] For Gregory, the sacrosanct nature of those mysteries is reinforced by the interpretation of the ark not only as a repository of the laws of God but as a manifestation of the Divine Presence itself. Accordingly, Gregory comments that the ark is on occasion referred to as "the Face," a designation that in the Judaic traditions is looked upon as one of the names of God. To cover the ark is thereby to cover the Divine Presence embodied in the Face. Such an act suggests what Gregory calls "the incomprehensibility of contemplating the ineffable secrets" (II:181).

Encountering the ark with the cherubim in the holy of holies, Moses as seer is given access to those secrets, an experience that finds consummate expression for Gregory in the vision of Isaiah, on the one hand, and Ezekiel, on the other. These texts represent a locus classicus in Gregory for the kind of visionary enactment that expressed what Moses was made to undergo in his ascent of the mount. Such texts and their corresponding traditions underlie Gregory's awareness that what the ineffable secrets conceal (that is, the ultimate truth of the divine nature) is "incomprehensible and inaccessible to the multitude." Because this truth "is set in the secret and ineffable areas of the tabernacle of mystery," Gregory observes, "the apprehension of the realities above comprehension should not be meddled with" (I:188). Like the *merkabah* itself, that which is enclosed in the holy of holies may be understood only by one deemed worthy. Once the experience is undergone, the hierophant is "transformed to such a degree of glory" that the "mortal eye" is incapable of beholding him (cf. Exod. 34:29), for

21. In both respects, the thought is indebted to Philo. Cf. *Questions and Answers on Exodus* (II:62–66).

"in his surpassing glory he becomes inaccessible to these who would look upon him" (II: 217). Such is the *visio Dei* as Gregory portrays it. Drawing upon earlier traditions of ascent, Gregory assimilated the Alexandrian influence and made it distinctly his own.

II

In the history of monastic spirituality, the influence of Gregory of Nyssa appears to have been wide-reaching. Indeed, scholars have traced the impact of his thought on a number of fronts.[22] For our purposes, two areas are of particular interest. The first has to do with a body of writings attributed to a figure known as Macarius the Egyptian (fourth century) and the second with a corresponding body of writings attributed to the so-called Dionysius the Areopagite (fifth or sixth century). Because of the importance of Ezekiel's vision to both figures, each will receive due attention in our treatment of the mystical dimensions of the visionary mode.

There are putatively two Macariuses in Egyptian monasticism: Macarius of Alexandria and Macarius called the Egyptian. Although a number of apothegms have been ascribed to both, an entire literature has been attributed to the second. The most important part of this literature is comprised of fifty homilies, which appear to be "spiritual conversations directed by the master to answer the questions of his disciples."[23] Throughout the homilies one finds an emphasis upon "the fire of grace kindled by the Holy Spirit in the hearts of men, making them burn like candles before the Son of God." This fervor is responsive to the fluctuations of the human will: "now it is shining brilliantly as it embraces the

22. See Bouyer, *Spirituality*, I, 369.
23. Ibid., p. 370. There has been much debate about the provenance and dating of the Macarian corpus. In some circles the works of Macarius (in particular, the homilies) are associated with the Euchite or Messalian sects, the disciples of Symeon of Mesopotamia (fourth century), who maintained that the entire existence of a monk should be taken up with prayer. The influence of Gregory on Macarius has been established by Werner Jaeger, *Two Rediscovered Works of Ancient Christian Literature: Gregory of Nyssa and Macarius* (Leiden: Brill, 1954). The connection, however, has been questioned by Louth, *Origins*, p. 115, n. 29. For an endorsement of the Messalian view, see ibid., pp. 113–125, esp. p. 115, n. 29. For an endorsement of the traditional view, see Bouyer, *Spirituality*, I, 370–371; and Lossky, *Vision of God*, pp. 91–95.

entire being; now it diminishes and no longer sheds its radiance in hearts that are darkened by passions." The purpose of those fully devoted to the worship of God is to intensify the radiance of the fire. In that process the soul becomes fully enveloped in light. Macarius's spirituality is founded on a theology of light, and participants in the divine glory progress in the true vision of unspeakable light.[24]

How compellingly this theology draws upon the *visio Dei* that inaugurates the prophecy of Ezekiel may be seen in an examination of the first homily in the Macarian corpus of homilies.[25] *Homily I* is in effect a meditation on Ezekiel's vision as a vehicle of transcendence that embodies the soul's aspirations to ascend to the realm of the divine. The homily begins with an account of the vision that emphasizes both its ineffable nature and its chariot-like appearance. "Full of unspeakable mysteries," the vision, says Macarius, is that of the "chariot of Cherubim [*harma kheroubim*]." Propelling the chariot are "four spiritual living creatures," described by Macarius in a manner at once consistent with the biblical text and selective in the details it emphasizes.

Among the details are those having to do with faces and eyes. Accordingly, we find that the creatures are equipped with fourfold faces (including those of a lion, an eagle, a calf, and a human being) and wings to every face, "so that there were no hinder parts to any of them." The faces are constantly in view. Correspondingly, there are the eyes, a detail that assumes particular prominence in Macarius's rendering. Referring to the living creatures, he says: "their backs were full of eyes; their bellies likewise were thick set with eyes; there was no part about them that was not full of eyes." This visionary emphasis upon faces and eyes, in turn, is reinforced by an emphasis upon the spiritual, for these are, above all, "spiritual creatures," the spirituality of which is manifested in the wheels. So Macarius observes: "There were also wheels to every face, wheel within wheel. In the wheels there was a Spirit." Finally, Macarius calls attention not only the chariot-like bearing

---

24. Lossky, *Vision of God*, pp. 94–95.

25. References by section number are to Saint Macarius the Egyptian, *Fifty Spiritual Homilies of St. Macarius the Egyptian*, trans. A. J. Mason (New York: Macmillan, 1921), pp. 284–289, in conjunction with the *Opera Omnia*, ed. J.-P. Migne, ed. *Patrologiae Cursus Completus, Series Graeca*, 161 vols. in 166 (Paris: n.p., 1857–1891), XXXIV, 449–463; hereafter cited as *PG*.

of the vision but to the charioteer, who is the Master that guides
the divine vehicle (1:1).

Having set the motifs in order, Macarius examines their implications in detail. The first concern is with what the "unspeakable
mysteries" of the chariot signify. Drawing upon New Testament
texts, Macarius maintains that although what the prophet saw was
"in substance true and certain," the vision itself "signified and
foreshadowed something else, mysterious and divine—a *mystery
hidden* verily *from ages and from generations* [Col. 1:26], but *in the
last times made manifest* [1 Pet. 1:20] at the appearing of Christ."
Establishing the specifically Christocentric context of the chariot,
these New Testament allusions provide insight into how the vision
is to be interpreted in Macarian terms.

From the perspective of Colossians, the vision for Macarius
embodies that mystery which is the presence of Christ in every
individual, for in Christ himself "are hid all the treasures of wisdom and knowledge." Aware of this mystery formerly hidden
"from ages and generations but now made manifest to his saints,"
the true Christian as saint follows the example of Christ and, by
suffering on behalf of Christ, rejoices in those sufferings (Col.
1:24–2:3). Complementing the allusion to Colossians is that to 1
Peter. In the context of that allusion the reference to "ages" and
"generations" in Colossians assumes both a providential and eschatological bearing. From the providential perspective, Christ is
seen to have been "destined before the foundation of the world"
to make his appearance. Now, in what is an anticipation of "the
end of the times," he has appeared for the sake of those who
believe in him. For that reason (both providential and eschatological), the believers in Christ are counseled to "have confidence
in God, who raised him [Christ] from the dead and gave him
glory" (1:2; see Pet. 1:20–21).

In the intertextual network implicit in the allusion to Colossians,
on the one hand, and Peter, on the other, the cherubim-chariot
of Ezekiel moves through a range of meanings that cast the vision
in a specifically Christocentric form. Beginning with its mysterious
nature, the allusions establish the vision as a phenomenon that
exists within every individual who patterns himself after Christ,
has faith in God's providence through Christ, is aware of the
eschatology implicit in the making known of Christ at "the end
of the times," and finally exalts in the glory of Christ's resurrection.

Such is the typological, as well as theological, bearing of Ezekiel's *visio Dei* as Macarius understood it. The peculiarly mystical bearing of that event, in turn, represents the primary focus of the remainder of the homily.

Assimilating the typological and theological into the mystical, Macarius begins by addressing himself to the "mystery" embodied in the chariot. For Macarius, this mystery is that of the soul prepared "to receive her Lord and to become a *throne of glory* for Him" (1:2). The reference to the throne of glory recalls Matt. 25:31: "When the Son of man comes in his glory, and all the angels with him, then he will sit on his glorious throne." The eschatology here, of course, carries forth that of the earlier reference to 1 Peter. At the same time, it refocuses the *parousia* to suggest that the Second Coming of Christ is what occurs within the soul, itself a throne of glory upon which the eschaton is to reside.

For Macarius, this remarkably internalized event is an experience replete with the joy, indeed, the ecstasy of fulfilled communion with the Spirit of God in a *visio Dei* of the profoundest sort. It is an experience in which the soul, beholding all, is irradiated with the unspeakable light of the Divine Presence:

> For the soul that is privileged to be in communion with the Spirit of His light, and is irradiated by the beauty of the unspeakable glory of Him who has prepared her to be a seat and a dwelling for Himself, becomes all light, all face, all eye; and there is no part of her that is not full of the spiritual eyes of light. (1:2)

In the mystical theology of Macarius the *parousia* is a transformative experience in which the soul becomes that which it beholds: all light, all face, all eye. Becoming these things, it partakes rapturously not only of the glory but of the beauty of the event. It is the aesthetics of the mystical that contributes a uniquely poetic flavor to Macarius's understanding of the *visio Dei*. In the making or remaking of the vision that occurs within the context of the account that Macarius provides, the soul itself is seen to be the very chariot that Ezekiel is said to have beheld. Like the chariot with its creatures, the soul of the seer is replete with eyes, "has no such thing as a back part, but in every direction is face forward," and as it moves, it is guided by "the unspeakable beauty of the glory of the light of Christ mounted and riding upon her."

The presence of the whole, finally, is likened to the sun, in which the brilliance of the fires through which it burns obliterates all distinctions of form and extension. "As the sun is one of likeness all over, without any part behind or inferior, but is all glorified with light throughout, and is, indeed, all light, with no difference between the parts," so it is with the soul. "Perfectly irradiated by the unspeakable beauty" of Christ's face, "perfectly in communion with the Holy Ghost," and "privileged to be the dwelling-place and throne of God," the soul undergoes a glorious transformation by which it becomes "all eye, all light, all face, all glory, all spirit, being made so by Christ, who drives, and guides, and carries, and bears her about, and graces and adorns her thus with spiritual beauty" (1:2). Such are the remarkable effects of the transformative experience that the soul undergoes in its communion with the Spirit of God. In his account of that experience Macarius engages in a poetic theology that bestows upon his mysticism an aesthetic brilliance as finally wrought as any encountered in the traditions that constitute the visionary mode.

Having concentrated on this transformative dimension of Ezekiel's *visio Dei*, Macarius next attends to corresponding aspects that reinforce and deepen the sense of mystery and complexity surrounding the chariot. In keeping with his emphasis upon the soul as the matrix of his discourse, he offers a range of interpretations through which the chariot as a kind of psycho-vehicle may be more fully understood. Fundamental to the movement as well as the constitution of this psycho-vehicle are the four living creatures. Macarius interprets these creatures as symbols of what he calls "the ruling factors" or *logismoi* of the soul. For Macarius, then, the creatures, as psychocentric entities or factors, possess a certain regal significance. So Macarius observes that "as the eagle is the king of the birds, and the lion of wild beasts, and the bull of tame ones, and man of creatures in general, so the soul has its ruling factors." These factors are, respectively, the will, the conscience, the intelligence, and the faculty of love. "By these the chariot of the soul is controlled, and upon these God rests" (1:3).

So ensconced, God as Christ becomes the charioteer of the soul: "The Rider, then, is conveyed and carried by the chariot or throne of the living creatures which are all eye, or, in other words, by every soul that has become His throne and seat, and is now eye and light." As a charioteer, God governs the psycho-vehicle with the reins of the Spirit and the guidance of His understanding.

Under His tutelage the soul travels in thought through both the
terrestrial and celestial realms.[26] "Oh, the noble and good and
only true Charioteer!" Macarius declares; "in like manner shall
our bodies also be privileged at the Resurrection, the soul being
thus pre-glorified even now, and mingled with the Spirit" (1:3).

True to the context of 1 Peter, Macarius views the translation
of the soul to the higher realms in resurrectional terms: the Resurrection is the greatest of all mysteries, a fulfillment of the translation that the soul undergoes in its preglorified state as it patterns
itself after Christ, who is, after all its charioteer and guiding spirit.
In order to experience such preglorification, then, the soul must
subject itself to (and rejoice in) that Christ-like suffering through
which it will be fully purified. In that suffering it will rid itself of
the element of darkness that would otherwise drag it down and
prohibit it from undergoing a celestial translation. In the spirit of
Colossians, Macarius accordingly admonishes the soul to be "slain
through His [God's] power, and die to the world of wickedness,"
so that the spirit of sin will be destroyed. Then the soul will "be
translated from the wickedness of darkness into the light of Christ,
and may rest in life through world after world" (1:3).

In its entirety the process is compared by Macarius to a chariot-
race. When the thought of sin gets the upper hand, this is comparable to a race in which the terrestrial chariot gets the upper
hand over that chariot which aspires to the celestial spheres. "But
where the Lord mounts and takes the reins of the soul into His
own hands, He always wins, skilfully managing and guiding the
chariot of the soul into a heavenly and inspired mind for ever."
When this occurs, the living creatures or factors of the soul are
driven, "not where they are inclined of themselves to go, but where
the Rider or Charioteer directs." "Where He wills, they go; and
He supports them." So transported, the redeemed soul ascends
to the "land of the living" (cf. Ps. 27:13), where it draws spiritual
nourishment and makes increase, "growing up unto the Lord,"
and "arrayed with the ineffable raiment of heavenly beauty" (1:8–
11). As the foregoing suggests, Macarius, like Gregory of Nyssa,
knew and did not hesitate to draw upon the Platonic myth of the

26. The idea finds its correspondence in a long tradition of philosophical and religious
thought extending back to the pre-Socratics. In its pagan antecedents it assumes the form
of the Logos as a pilot that steers the universe. In Jewish Hellenistic thinking one discovers
it in Philo's *Who Is the Heir of Divine Things* (LX:301–303) and in *Of Flight and Finding*
(XIX:100–101).

Phaedran charioteer in order to suggest the nature of the ascent of the redeemed soul conceived as a chariot that is guided and sustained by the Spirit of Christ. Like the chariot of the Phaedran myth, the psycho-vehicle of Gregory is pulled in opposite directions, and like its Platonic forebear, the soul that is represented in the image of the chariot desires to be replenished in the ideal realm.

In Macarius that desire is ultimately fulfilled in Christocentric terms, a fact that the seer celebrates at the conclusion of his sermon. Addressing those who aspire to the celestial experience, Macarius proclaims:

> If then thou art become a throne of God, and the heavenly Charioteer has mounted thee, and thy whole soul has become a spiritual eye, and thy whole soul light; and if thou hast been nourished with that nourishment of the Spirit, and if thou hast been made to drink of the Living Water, and if thou hast put on the garments of the ineffable light; if thine inward man is established in the experience and full assurance of all these things, behold, thou livest, thou livest the eternal life indeed, and thy soul from henceforth is at rest with the Lord. (1:12)

In the form of a peroration, this passage brings together all the issues that the homily as a whole addresses. Doing so, it reveals the self-conscious artistry of Macarian homiletics, an artistry reflected as well in the remaining sermons that constitute the corpus. Combining biblical exegesis with mystical transport, Macarius thereby offers his own interpretation of Ezekiel's *visio Dei*, an interpretation as compelling in its own way as any that had gone before.[27]

27. Limitations of space will not permit consideration of Saint Ephrem the Syrian (fourth century), who founded the seminary "School of the Persians." Although he hated the Jews, his writings reflect an awareness of *'aggadot*. For discussion of Ephrem, see Abraham Levene, *The Early Syrian Fathers on Genesis, from a Syriac Ms. on the Pentateuch in the Mingana Collection* (London: Taylor's Foreign Press, 1951), pp. 6–10; and Lossky, *Vision of God*, p. 75. Of importance to Ezekiel's *visio Dei* is Saint Ephrem's work *Rhythms*, composed of homiletic poems in celebration of the mystical experience. In this regard *Rhythm the Fifty-Fifth*, which focuses specifically on the Chariot of God, is apposite; in *Select Works*, trans. J. B. Morris (Oxford: John Henry Parker, 1847), pp. 285–288. The same image of the Chariot is to be found in Ephrem's commentary on Ezekiel: *In Ezechielem Prophetam Explanatio, Ephraem Syri Opera Omnia*, 6 vols. (Rome, 1732–1746), II, 165–167.

III

If the writings attributed to Macarius the Egyptian represent one direction suggested by the influence of Gregory of Nyssa, the writings ascribed to the so-called Dionysius the Areopagite represent another.[28] Revered in the Middle Ages as the Athenian who had been converted by Saint Paul's speech on the Areopagus (Acts 17:34), the author of the Dionysian corpus ensured the authority and legitimacy of his utterances through the appropriation of a "canonical" voice. If his writings are now considered in effect pseudonymous, they are not for that any the less relevant. Exerting an immense influence on later writers, the Pseudo-Dionysius is a figure of paramount importance to the traditions through which the visionary mode embodied in Ezekiel's *visio Dei* was given eloquent expression both as an exegetical and as a mystical enterprise.[29] The force of this observation will be seen upon an examination of two of the Pseudo-Dionysius's most important works: *The Mystical Theology* and *The Celestial Hierarchy*.

The Mystical Theology represents a *clavis* of sorts to the Pseudo-Dionysian method. Addressing his friend Timothy, the Pseudo-Dionysius reveals how one is to ascend to the highest peak of "mystic scripture," where "the mysteries of God's Word lie simple, absolute and unchangeable in the brilliant darkness of a hidden silence." Transcending all that is known in this world, the ascent is one in which the seer leaves behind him every voice, every word, every understanding and plunges into the darkness where dwells the One who is beyond all things. In this realm of luminous darkness, all knowing and all perceiving fail. What remains is that

---

28. References are to *The Complete Works*, trans. Colm Luibheid (New York: Paulist Press, 1987), in conjunction with the *Opera Omnia* in J.-P. Migne, *PG*, III. *La hiérarchie céleste*, ed. R. Roques and G. Heil, *Sources chrétiennes* (Paris: Les Éditions du Cerf, 1958), LVIII, has also been consulted.

29. For a brief but informative discussion of these matters, see the prefatory essays of Jean Leclercq and Karlfried Froehlich in *The Complete Works*, pp. 25–32 and 33–46, respectively. For a technical account of the philosophical influence, see Stephen Gersh, *From Iamblichus to Eriugena: An Investigation of the Prehistory and Evolution of the Pseudo-Dionysian Tradition* (Leiden: E. J. Brill, 1978). Important for an understanding of the mystical bearing of the works is Walther Völker, *Kontemplation und Ekstase bei Pseudo-Dionysius Areopagitica* (Weisbaden: Franz Steiner, 1958). Likewise of importance are René Roques, *L'univers dionysien, structure hiérarchique du monde selon pseudo-Denys* (Paris: Aubier, 1954), and Paul Rorem, *Biblical and Liturgical Symbols within the Pseudo-Dionysian Synthesis* (Toronto: Pontifical Institute of Medieval Studies, 1984). See also Vladimir Lossky's discussion in *The Mystical Theology of the Eastern Church* (London: James Clarke, 1957), esp. pp. 23–43.

silent union with the mystery toward which every hierophant strives (I:997 A–1001 A 1–3).

Both in content and in outlook, of course, such an ascent recalls and indeed rearticulates the teachings of Gregory of Nyssa's discourse *The Life of Moses*. The seer upon whom the Pseudo-Dionysius models his own hierophant is the Moses of Gregory of Nyssa. Like Gregory's Moses, the Pseudo-Dionysius's seer does not reveal his knowledge to the multitude, which is incapable of grasping the mysteries into which all such seers have been initiated (I:1000 A–1000 B 2). In his account of the initiation and subsequent ascent, the Pseudo-Dionysius makes it clear that it is precisely the Moses of Gregory that is implied. Recalling Gregory, the Pseudo-Dionysius accordingly observes that "it is not for nothing that the blessed Moses is commanded to submit first to purification and then to depart from those who have not undergone this. When every purification is complete, he hears the many-voiced trumpets." Having heard these sounds, he pushes ahead to "the summit of the divine ascents," where he is able to contemplate the dwelling place of God. In that divine state of ultimate contemplation the seer "plunges into the truly mysterious darkness of unknowing." Knowing nothing, "he belongs completely to him who is beyond everything." With his own identity utterly obliterated, the seer is "supremely united by a completely unknowing inactivity of all knowledge, and knows beyond the mind by knowing nothing" (I: 1000 C–1001 A 3). As such statements indicate, the methodology of the Pseudo-Dionysius is that of paradox: his is a language, indeed, a theology of self-obliterative trope. To know God is not to know Him; to see Him is not to see Him; to hear Him is not to hear Him; His articulation is that of the unspoken; His language that of nonlanguage; His utterance that of silence. In the language of the rabbis, He fulfills that "silent-speaking" through which the meanings of the unknowable *hashmal* are revealed.

It is this methodology that the Pseudo-Dionysius develops in *The Mystical Theology*. With an awareness of the play that constitutes all metaphor, he utters one paradox after the next in what amounts to a kind of cleansing of utterance from the blemish of the literal: "If only we lacked sight and knowledge so as to see, so as to know, unseeing and unknowing, that which lies beyond all vision and knowledge," then such an act of cleansing would be truly to see and know by means of "the denial of all beings." That theology of denial (*aphairesis*) is at the center of the Pseudo-Dionysian point of view, one that makes the all-important distinction between cataphatic or affirmative theology, on the one hand, and apophatic or negative theology, on the other.[30] The Pseudo-Dionysius sounds the distinction cryptically at first but then elaborates upon it further during the course of his argument. We ought, he says, to acknowledge the denials in quite a different manner from the way we do the assertions. When we venture assertions, we begin with the first things, then move downward through intermediate terms until we reach the last things. But now as we climb from the last things up to the most primary, we deny all things that we may "unhiddenly know that unknowing which itself is hidden from all those possessed of knowing amid all beings." In this way, we may "see above being that darkness concealed from all the light among beings" (II:1025 A–1025 B). Precisely what is meant by the foregoing remarks is clarified in the remainder of the treatise.

Distinguishing between cataphatic and apophatic theology, the Pseudo-Dionysius maintains that the former embodies a descent from first things to last, that is, from the most abstruse conceptions of deity to their concretization in symbolic form. This is essentially an affirmative act of delineating deity in perceptible terms. It is a "symbolic theology" in which God is analogized through "the images we have of him, of the forms, figures, and instruments proper to him, of the places in which he lives and of the ornaments he wears." So conceived, God is portrayed in His "beingness" as experiencing "anger, grief, and rage," as sleeping and waking, as possessing certain characteristics such as names and bodily parts. These are all "images shaped by the workings of the symbolic representations of God."[31] Such a symbology is in effect a rhetoricizing or troping of God's presence in order to engage in philosophical or theological arguments about the nature of His existence. Moving from what it conceives as the divine world of first things (deity in its essence), this theology travels "downward from the most exalted to the humblest categories, taking in on this downward path an ever-increasing number of ideas" that

---

30. See the full discussion of these distinctions, as well as the writings of Pseudo-Dionysius in general, in Louth, *Origins*, pp. 159–178.

31. For a detailed explanation of this symbolic theology, which is indeed the title of the Pseudo-Dionysius's putative but presumably lost work, see his letter to Titus the hierarch (Letter 9).

proliferate "with every state of the descent" (III:1032 D–1033 C).
Such is affirmative or cataphatic theology. In Pseudo-Dionysian
terms, it reflects a downward procession or *proodos* into knowing,
understanding, naming, speech, and language.[32] Its purpose is
essentially discursive: it seeks to conceptualize in order to provide
demonstrable evidence, to build structures, to systematize, to engage in proofs, to enlighten.

The counterpart of affirmative or cataphatic theology is negative or apophatic theology. Rather than a procession or *proodos*
downward from first to last things, this theology involves a return
or *epistrophē* upward from last to first things. In this return we
discover an obliteration of knowing, understanding, naming,
speech, and language as the seer travels into the realm of unknowing, divine ignorance, the nameless, the speechless, and the
silent. This is a deconstructive, obliterative act, one in which seeing
or *theōria* is not seeing.[33] It is an act in which interpretation denies
itself in the "mystical" pursuit of the uninterpretable, undemon-
stratable. Its purpose is not so much philosophical or constructive
enactment through conceptualization as it is the experience of
that which cannot be conceptualized or construed. Its mode is
nondiscursive rather than discursive, nonconceptual rather than
conceptual. Embodying a *theologia negativa*, it is known only by
that which it is not.

Deconceptualizing as well as derhetoricizing deity, the Pseudo-
Dionysius thereby deconstructs all symbolical representations of
God. Because "the supreme Cause of every perceptible thing is
not itself perceptible," the Pseudo-Dionysius maintains that "it is
not a material body, and hence has neither shape nor form, quality, quantity, or weight. It is not in any place and can neither be
seen nor touched. It is neither perceived nor is it perceptible"
(IV:1040 D). Correspondingly, "the supreme Cause of every conceptual thing is not itself conceptual." This is to say, "it is not soul
or mind, nor does it possess imagination, conviction, speech, or
understanding." Not only can it not be spoken of, but it cannot
be grasped by understanding. It is not number, order, greatness,

---

32. See Rorem, *Biblical and Liturgical Symbols*, pp. 58–65.

33. From the deconstructive point of view, the Pseudo-Dionysius appropriately employs
an image of construction and deconstruction to suggest the idea: "We would be like
sculptors who set out to carve a statue. They remove every obstacle to the pure view of
the hidden image, and simply by this act of clearing aside [*aphairesis*] they show up the
beauty of what is hidden" (II:1025 B).

smallness, power, light, or any of those other attributes that one associates with deity. There is simply no speaking of it, nor is there naming of it, nor knowledge of it. It is beyond not just assertion but denial as well (V:1045 D–1048 B). As that which is beyond denial, it denies that very act of *aphairesis* through which its ineffability is experienced.

Such is the nature of the Pseudo-Dionysius's concept of apophatic theology. Manifesting itself through the profoundest of paradoxes, it represents for the Pseudo-Dionysius the mystical response to affirmative or cataphatic theology. Doing so, it completes that sense of return in the dialectic of *proodos* and *epistrophē* that constitutes the Pseudo-Dionysian outlook. Such, in brief, is the methodology upon which the works of the Pseudo-Dionysius are based. From the perspective of that methodology, one is in a better position to understand the articulation of the visionary mode in *The Celestial Hierarchy*, a work in which Ezekiel's *visio Dei* assumes paramount importance.

Beginning with an allusion to James 1:17 ("Every good endowment and every perfect gift is from above, coming down from the Father of lights"), the Pseudo-Dionysius places *The Celestial Hierarchy* in precisely the processional context established in *The Mystical Theology*. Once again we discover not only a cataphatic movement downward (*proodos*) into diversity but an apophatic movement upward (*epistrophē*) into unity. Citing Rom. 11:36 ("from him and to him are all things"), the Pseudo-Dionysius accordingly observes: "Inspired by the Father, each procession of the Light spreads itself generously towards us, and, in its power to unify, it stirs us by lifting us up. It returns us back to the oneness and deifying simplicity of the Father who gathers us in" (I:120 A–121 A).

By means of such a processional idea, the Pseudo-Dionysius constructs the elaborate angelology that serves as the basis of *The Celestial Hierarchy*. As he makes clear, the inspiration for this angelology derives from his reading of Scriptures. That reading involves an "uplifting" or a process of interpretive anagogy by which the reader moves from the text of the Bible with its perceptible images to the imperceptible realm of the hierarchies. Thus, the Pseudo-Dionysius maintains that God revealed the hierarchies to us "in the sacred pictures of the Scriptures so that he might lift us in spirit up through the perceptible to the conceptual, from sacred shapes and symbols to the simple peaks of the hierarchies of heaven" (I:124 A). An encounter with the text, then, becomes an education in the process of ascent. The nature of that education is that to which the Pseudo-Dionysius addresses himself in the remainder of his treatise.

As a means of being "lifted up" or moving anagogically from the biblical text to the "utter simplicity" of the hierarchies themselves, the Pseudo-Dionysius accordingly begins with a description of the sacred forms bestowed by Scriptures upon the heavenly ranks. His procedure in doing so is essentially apophatic: it cites the details of "the sacred pictures of the Scriptures" in order to demonstrate what these pictures do *not* signify. The locus classicus for this mode of demonstration is Ezekiel's *visio Dei* portrayed within the framework of corresponding visions:

> We cannot, as mad people do, profanely visualize these heavenly and godlike intelligences as actually having numerous feet and faces. They are not shaped to resemble the brutishness of oxen or to display the wildness of lions. They do not have the curved beak of the eagle or the wings and feathers of birds. We must not have pictures of flaming wheels whirling in the skies, of material thrones made ready to provide a reception for the Deity, of multicolored horses, or of spear-carrying lieutenants, or any of those shapes handed on to us amid all the variety of the revealing symbols of Scripture. (II:136 D–137 B)

Such "poetic imagery," the Pseudo-Dionysius maintains, is made use of by the Word of God not for aesthetic reasons but as a means of accommodating the unknowable to that which can be understood. Responding to this imagery, we are enabled "to uplift our mind in a manner suitable to our nature." Drawing principally upon the imagery of Ezekiel's vision, the Pseudo-Dionysius alludes as well to corresponding texts from Daniel (7:9), Zechariah (1:8, 6:2), and Revelation (4:2, 6:1–9) to suggest the biblical contexts out of which his systematizing of the angelic hierarchies is to arise.

To do so, however, he emphasizes repeatedly that such descriptions are not to be read literally. A literal reading results in both an entangling of the reader in the web of the text and a misleading of the reader into false notions concerning the celestial realms. As a result of such a reading, "one would likely then imagine that the heavens beyond really are filled with bands of lions and horses, that the divine praises are, in effect, great moos, that flocks of birds take wing there or that there are other kinds of creatures all about"

(II:137 C–137 D). In order to avoid such absurdities, we must be trained in the proper reading of Scriptures in general and visionary material in particular. In both respects the biblical text is to be seen as a reservoir of shapes and forms that provide access to that which cannot be conceptualized or imagined in sensible terms. Moreover, there are certain descriptions in the Bible that are shrouded in such mystery that, by their very nature, they will be forever hidden to the uninitiated. For the Pseudo-Dionysius, Ezekiel's *visio Dei*, of course, is the prime example of such a description (II:140 A–140 B).

This fact leads the Pseudo-Dionysius to distinguish two modes of revelation in the Bible. Corresponding to his cataphatic and apophatic views of mystical theology, these modes articulate a theoretics of scriptural interpretation. Whereas the first mode "proceeds naturally through sacred images in which like represents like," the second mode uses "formations which are dissimilar and even entirely inadequate and ridiculous." According to the first mode, the sacred blessedness of the transcendent Deity is manifested conceptually under such forms as "Word," "Mind," and "Being"; through such attributes as rationality and wisdom; and by means of such images as light. Although the first mode might appear to be superior to that which reveals Deity through "images drawn from the world," it provides no better access than what the Pseudo-Dionysius describes as the second mode. According to this mode, the Deity is manifested through "dissimilar shapes" that embody an essential paradox: the more *unlike* God and the celestial realms they appear to be, the more they lead us to a knowledge of the unknowable. "So it is that scriptural writings, far from demeaning the ranks of heaven, actually pay them honor by describing them with dissimilar shapes so completely at variance with what they really are that we come to discover how those ranks, so far removed from us, transcend all materiality" (II:140 C–141 C). It is this second mode of which Ezekiel's *visio Dei* is the prime example. We are to read that vision apophatically by distancing ourselves from, indeed, denying (*aphairesis*), "the sheer crassness of the signs" in order to understand what the signs truly signify. This is essentially a deconstructive reading, one that resorts to the materiality of the biblical text in order to ascend by negation to the spirituality of the celestial realms.

For the Pseudo-Dionysius such a reading is not a profaning of Scriptures. Quite the contrary: by interpreting the biblical text negatively, one is actually performing a reverential act of honoring the hidden and indeed supernal meanings embedded in the text, those meanings to which a proper reading of the text leads. Indeed, an apophatic interpretation in effect sets the "Holy of Holies" apart from the defilement of a literalistic reading and protects it from the eyes of those who would defile it. Proponents of an apopathic interpretation thereby "honor the dissimilar shape so that the divine things remain inaccessible to the profane and so that all those with a real wish to see the sacred imagery may not dwell on the types as true." Fulfilling that wish, the true readers of the scriptural text will undergo "an initiation into inspired things." So initiated, they will become hierarchs of the holy, readers who will "keep these holy truths a secret in...[their] hidden mind." Like the *merkabah* mystics, they will guard the truths from the profane, knowing that they must not throw before swine "that pure, shining and splendid harmony of the conceptual pearls" (II:141 D–145 C; cf. Matt. 7:6). Within the unique context of his own apophatic reading of Ezekiel's *visio Dei*, the Pseudo-Dionysius thereby creates his own version of the *ma'aseh merkabah*.

Consistent with his approach to biblical interpretation, he constructs an angelological system worthy of the most detailed and complex of the *merkabah* treatises. This system is hierarchical. Extolling the very concept of hierarchy, the Pseudo-Dionysius avers that through it one is enabled to be as much like God as one possibly can be. "A hierarchy bears in itself the mark of God. Hierarchy causes its members to be images of God in all respects, to be clear and spotless mirrors reflecting the glow of primordial light and indeed of God himself" (III:165 A). Systematizing and reconstructing the visionary at the very point of deconstructing the biblical text in the act of *aphairesis*, the Pseudo-Dionysius defines hierarchy as a "perfect arrangement, an image of the beauty of God which sacredly works out the mysteries of its own enlightenment in the orders and levels of understanding of the hierarchy, and which is likened toward its own source as much as is permitted" (III:165 B–165 C).

Underlying the hierarchical system of the Pseudo-Dionysius, the three categories of order, understanding, and activity find their correspondence in the threefold process of purification, illumination, and perfection. As the Pseudo-Dionysius describes this process,

> purification, illumination, and perfection are all three the reception of an understanding of the Godhead, namely, being completely

purified of ignorance by the proportionately granted knowledge of the more perfect initiations, being illuminated by the same divine knowledge..., and being also perfected by this light in the understanding of the most lustrous initiations. (VII:209 D)

Embodying the concept of perfect order, the threefold process involves the activity of rising to greater levels of spiritual knowledge through an initiatory purification from the dross of the material world, followed by a higher degree of illumination until one achieves the highest stages of luminous perfection in the realm of absolute light. Having achieved this state, one becomes a truly fulfilled hierarch (cf. X:272 D–273 A).

Corresponding to the threefold process is the ordering of the angelic hierarchies. In the thought of the Pseudo-Dionysius, this ordering is also triadic. In fact, the triadic systemization of the angelic forms is conceived as three groups of three, each group consisting of three types of angelic being and each ranked hierarchically. The first rank is composed hierarchically of seraphim, cherubim, and thrones; the second of dominations, powers, and authorities; the third of principalities, archangels, and angels (VI:200 C–201 A). During the course of his *Celestial Hierarchy* the Pseudo-Dionysius discourses upon each of these ranks and the angelic forms that constitute them. The first group, for example, is closest to godhead. Circling in immediate proximity to God, it "simply and ceaselessly dances around an eternal knowledge of him." Filled with the divine nourishment of God's light-stream, it experiences pure vision. In keeping with this experience, it intones its own *piyyutim* in a manner reminiscent of the visions of both Ezekiel and Isaiah. Whereas some of the hymns are like the "sound of many waters" (Ezek. 1:24; cf. Rev. 14:2, 19:6), others assume the form of "that famous and venerable song": "holy, holy, holy is the Lord of hosts. The whole earth is full of his glory" (VII:212 A–212 B; see Isa. 6:3; cf. Rev. 4:8). Addressing the nature of the angelic forms that constitute the first group, the Pseudo-Dionysius associates the seraphim with the idea of fire ("fire-makers," "carriers of warmth"); the cherubim with the idea of knowledge ("fullness of knowledge," "outpouring of wisdom"); and the thrones with the idea of transcendence ("upward-bearing toward the ultimate heights") (VII:205 B–205 D). Such analysis is characteristic of the handling of the other groups as well.

For our purposes, this treatment of the hierarchies is significant because of the way it refocuses and reintegrates the visionary contexts of Ezekiel and Isaiah within a new framework. In keeping with that framework, the prophet Isaiah in particular assumes the role of consummate prophet and seer. Fulfilling that role, Isaiah is viewed as a kind of *yored merkabah* who achieves a true vision of the seraphim. So conceived, he is able to behold "the summit, beyond every source, enthroned amid the subordinate powers." Instructed in the divine powers of the holy seraphim, he, more than any, understands the true meaning of the seraphim, all aspects of which assume a renewed significance in the discourse of the Pseudo-Dionysius:

> The sacred image of their six wings signifies an endless, marvelous upward thrust toward God by the first, middle, and lower conceptions. Seeing the limitless number of feet, the multitude of faces, those wings blocking out the contemplation of their faces above and their feet below, and the unending beat of the middle set of wings, the sacred theologian was uplifted to a conceptual knowledge of the things seen. There were shown to him the many facets of the most exalted of the intelligent minds, the power of their multifarious vision. He witnessed that sacred caution of theirs which, in an unearthly fashion, they maintain regarding any brash, bold, and unpermitted search of the highest and the deepest things. (XIII:304 C–305 A)

Assuming the aura of the *ma'aseh merkabah*, such a description consolidates the *topoi* of the *merkabah* traditions and assimilates them into the conceptual and and contemplative structures of Pseudo-Dionysian thought.

From the perspective of such an undertaking, the Pseudo-Dionysius concludes his work with a full discourse on what is signified by the myriad of details surrounding the portrayal of the angelic beings. The discourse represents something of a coda to the work as a whole. Averring that he will now descend from "the solitary heights of contemplation" to "the plains of distinction and multiplicity," he maintains that his treatment will concern itself with "the many variegated forms and shapes adopted by the angels" (XV:328 A). In short, the final chapter of *The Celestial Hierarchy* provides the Pseudo-Dionysius with the opportunity to address the significance of the attributes of the angelic figures that constitute those crucial biblical texts (principally, Ezekiel, Isaiah, Daniel, and Revelation) that underlie the visionary mode.

Addressing these attributes, he commences with a discourse on the nature of fire as that element with which the angelic forms are most often associated and in which these forms are traditionally seen to be enveloped. Why, asks the Pseudo-Dionysius, does the Word of God honor the depiction of fire above all others? This question he substantiates with a series of rhetorical flourishes that conflate the depictions in which fire appears. His citation of examples is in effect a celebration of fire as visionary element. It is depicted, he observes, not only in flaming wheels (Dan. 7:9) but burning animals (Ezek. 1:13; cf. 2 Kings 2:11), as well as human-like forms that are aflame (Ezek. 1:4–7; Dan. 10:1; cf. Matt. 28:3; Luke 24:4). Enveloping the celestial creatures of the prophets (cf. Ezek. 1:13, 10:2), it emanates like roaring rivers from divine thrones (cf. Dan. 7:10). It constitutes in fact the angelic forms known as "fiery thrones" (cf. Dan. 7:9) and "seraphim" (Isa. 6:6). Whether the reference is high or low within the hierarchy, the Word of God, then, "always honors the representation of fire" (XV:329 A).

Having cited his examples, he answers his question by maintaining that God does indeed honor the representation of fire because the image of fire reflects many of the characteristics of deity. Like God, fire is not only in everything but passes undiluted through all things and yet continues to be beyond them. It both illuminates all things and remains hidden at the same time. Undetectable in itself, it manifests its presence through its workings on matter. "It is unstoppable. It cannot be looked upon. Yet it is master of everything. Wherever it is it changes things toward its own activity." Pure and undiluted in itself, it regenerates and illuminates others. The source of dynamic movement in itself, it causes others to move. Appearing suddenly and without warning, it "rises up irresistible and, losing nothing of itself, it communes joyfully with everything" (XV:329 B–329 C). Taking obvious delight in the attribute of fire as a crucial element through which one gains a greater understanding of godhead, the Pseudo-Dionysius isolates this one aspect of the visionary in what amounts to cataphatic account of the angelic beings. In effect, the coda to *The Celestial Hierarchy* is, to use the terminology of the Pseudo-Dionysius, a kind of "symbolic theology."

In keeping with his symbolic theology, the Pseudo-Dionysius moves from fire as attribute to a consideration of the therianthropic dimension of the descriptions. A major preoccupation of the interpreters, this dimension represents a crucial aspect of the symbolic theology through which the coda to *The Celestial Hierarchy* is sounded. At the forefront of this symbolic theology are the fourfold creatures of Ezekiel, conceived therianthropically as man, lion, ox, and eagle, a paradigm that the Pseudo-Dionysius both adopts and alters radically to suit his needs. His first concern is with the anthropomorphic basis of the fourfold creatures (Ezek. 1:5–10). To this end, he focuses on the "parts of the human body" and what they signify. Beginning with the senses, he addresses himself to seeing, hearing, smelling, tasting, and touching. Whereas seeing suggests the ability to gaze upward toward the lights of God, hearing indicates the ability to apprehend divine inspiration. Through the sense of smell, one welcomes the fragrances of divinity; by means of taste, one is able to be nourished on the celestial streams; and employing touch, one is equipped to distinguish the profitable from the harmful. Corresponding significations are assigned to eyelids and eyebrows, teeth, shoulders, arms, hands, the breast, and the feet. Emphasizing the hermeneutical basis of his concerns, the Pseudo-Dionysius suggests that teeth are particularly appropriate, for through them we are able to make conceptual distinctions in the mode of spiritual nourishment we receive. "For," he says, "it is a fact that every intelligent being, having received from one which is more divine the gift of a unified conception, proceeds to divine it and to make provision for its diffusion in order that an inferior may be lifted up as far as possible" (XV:332 A–332 D).

Implicit here is the communicative and mediatorial nature of the hierarchies, which disseminate information from higher to lower ranks. In possession of that information, the lower ranks analyze and digest it in order to understand its true meaning. The cataphatic movement from higher to lower is as much a hermeneutical event as it is a spiritual one. Integral to the interpretive process, the anthropomorphic dimensions of the visionary are accorded a hermeneutical status. Having considered these anthropomorphic attributes, the Pseudo-Dionysius concludes this aspect of his symbolic theology with observations on the significance of the accoutrements of the angelic forms, including their sacred vestments and sacred instruments (XV: 333 A–333 C). These observations reinforce still further how inclined the Pseudo-Dionysius is to integrate what he calls "the plains of distinction and multiplicity" into his overall scheme.

His concern with the anthropomorphic dimension of the angelic creatures appropriately finds its correspondence in the theriomorphic dimension (Ezek. 1:10). Like its anthropomorphic counterpart, this dimension reflects "the hiddenness of the unspeakable Deity" by paradoxically "covering the tracts of their own intellects," that is, by disclosing their meanings only to those wise enough to understand them. In that process of paradoxical concealment and disclosure, they humbly and mysteriously "draw a veil over the upward journey of divine enlightenment." For those wise enough to be initiated into the meanings of the symbolic theology, however, the significance of the theriomorphic basis of the creatures will become clear. Accordingly, the Pseudo-Dionysius explores the meanings inherent in the lion, ox, and eagle. Whereas the lion represents the "powerful indomitable command" of the angelic creatures, the ox is "a token of strength and of might, of the capacity to plough deeply the furrows of knowledge on which the fertile rains of heaven will fall." The horns of the ox, in turn, are a sign of the capacity to protect and to be invincible. The eagle suggests "regal might," the "thrust to the pinnacle," alacrity, agility, readiness, cunning to locate nourishing food, and, finally, "the contemplation which is freely, directly, and unswervingly turned in stout elevations of the optical powers toward those generously abundant rays of the divine sunshine" (XV:336 C–337 B). With its ability to behold the brilliance of light, the eagle, in short, is the consummate expression of the contemplative process by which the mystic moves upward toward God.

The Pseudo-Dionysius does not confine his discussion of the theriomorphic dimension of the visionary to an analysis of the lion, the ox, and the eagle, however. He likewise incorporates the image of the horse into his symbolic theology (cf. 2 Kings 2:11, 6:17; Zech. 1:8–10, 6:1–5; Rev. 6:1–8, 19:14). Having earlier alluded to the "multi-colored horses" that contribute to the dazzling panoply of the hierarchy (II:136 D–137 B), he makes a point of including them in his consideration of the fourfold creatures. Doing so, he alters the original conception to suit his own needs. Restructuring Ezekiel's vision, he dislocates the anthropomorphic from the theriomorphic, so that the human dimension is fully removed: it stands on its own. The fourfold nature of the vision is now totally theriomorphic. Encompassing the lion, the ox, the eagle, and the horse, it becomes an entity unto itself, one that complements the anthropomorphic and adds a new dimension to the therianthropic idea.

Focusing upon the image of the horse, then, the Pseudo-Dionysius says,

> Horses mean obedience and docility. Their whiteness is the gleam of their kinship with the light of God; their blue color is the sign of hiddenness; the red is the power and sweep of fire; the piebald is the alliance of opposite extremes, and the capacity to move from one to the other, that adaptibility of superior to inferior and inferior to superior which comes of return and providence. (XV: 337 B)

Anticipating the fascination with color symbolism in later kabbalistic texts, the Pseudo-Dionysius offers us a multicolored vision that intensifies the dazzling (indeed, fantastic) nature of his theology.[34] At the same time the movement from higher to lower and lower to higher in the alliance of colors reinforces the processional idea that underlies his mystical hierarchy as a whole.

What emerges in the analysis of this aspect of the symbolic theology is a visionary metaphysics, indeed a metaphysics of play (like the play of colors) in which opposites are reconciled in one grand scheme. On the "plains of distinction and multiplicity" the Pseudo-Dionysius engages in an act of reconciliation by which he applies "dissimilar similarities to the powers of heaven." This is an apophatic act that moves from dissimilarity to similarity in an anagogical celebration of the ascent to absolute unity and simplicity. It is a "hierarchizing" of the multiple forms as one proceeds from the theriomorphic to the anthropomorphic to the utterly spiritual. The Pseudo-Dionysius conceives of the process not only in symbolic terms but in distinctly psychological terms as well. "To put the matter briefly," he says, "all the feelings and all the various parts of the irrational animals uplift us to the immaterial conceptions and to the unifying powers of the heavenly beings" (XV:337 B–337 C). This uplifting is what underscores the treatment of the visionary that distinguishes the final passages of the coda.

Here, the Pseudo-Dionysius focuses on "the reason for applying to heavenly beings the titles of rivers, wheels, and chariots." In accord with his earlier discourse on fire, he maintains that the rivers of fire (cf. Ezek. 47:1; Dan 7:10; Rev. 22:1) represent the

---

34. For a full discussion of color symbolism in *kabbalah*, see Moshe Idel, *Kabbalah: New Perspectives* (New Haven: Yale University Press, 1988), pp. 103–116.

"divine channels" that eternally dispense their "generous and un-
checked flow" and thereby nourish with their "life-giving fruitful-
ness." In short, they are restorative and regenerative. Sources of
new life and fruition, they embody that emanative quality so important to the processional dimension of the mystical theology.
Corresponding to the rivers of fire are the chariots (2 Kings 2:11,
6:17; Ps. 104:3; Zech. 6:1–8) and the wheels (Ezek. 1:15–21, 10:1–
13; Dan. 7:9). Essential to the conception of the visionary as a
dynamic experience, both aspects (chariots and wheels) reinforce
the notions of unity and mobility. Thus, the chariots "signify the
fellowship binding together beings of the same order." Each of
the three orders in the hierarchy is, in a sense, a chariot unified
by a particular calling.

Intimately associated with (indeed, crucial to the equipage of)
the chariots, the wheels, in turn, give rise to their own complex
of associations. Moving forward without swerving from their true
course, they reflect the ability to "keep right on along the straight
road, directly and without wandering off" (cf. Matt. 3:3; Mark
1:3; Luke 3:4; John 1:23). Conceived in this manner, the wheels
become spiritual imperatives for right behavior, specifically, the
setting of one's sights on the rewards of the next world. So conceived, they are what the Pseudo-Dionysius calls "the wheels of
the mind" that "uplift" the soul anagogically to the realm of the
spiritual. In that uplifting they fulfill the dual function of both
"revolving [*anakulismous*]" and "revealing [*anakalupseis*]," the two
distinguishing and complementary features of their nature.[35] Revolving about themselves in a "ceaseless movement around the
Good," they concurrently reveal "hidden things" and "lift the
mind from below and carry the most exalted enlightenments down
to the lowliest" (XV:337 C–340 A).[36]

35. Invoking the phrase *"Gelgel"* (i.e., *galgal*), the Pseudo-Dionysius alludes specifically
to the Hebraic formulation of Ezek. 10:13: "As for the wheels, they were called in my
hearing, the whirling wheel [*hagalgal*]," which in the Pseudo-Dionysian economy signifies
both "revolving" and "revealing" (XV:337 D).

36. Compare the discussion of angelic and spiritual movement in *The Divine Names*. The
divine intelligences move in a circle while "they are at one with those illuminations which
without beginning and without end, emerge from the Good and the Beautiful." They also
move in a straight line when, in keeping with providence, "they come to offer unerring
guidance to all those below them." Finally, they move in a spiral, "for even while they are
providing for those beneath them they continue to remain what they are and they turn
unceasingly around the Beautiful and the Good from which all identity comes." Movement,
in short, results in a process of individuation, the realization of identity. Correspondingly,
the soul has its movements too. It moves in a circle when there is an "inner concentration

Reflected in their movement is that very processional idea of *proodos* and *epistrophē* upon which the mystical theology of the Pseudo-Dionysius is founded. The coda to his work appropriately culminates in this dynamic spiritual-psychological image of momentum and revelation. Speaking earlier of the angelic forms "tirelessly circl[ing] about their own identity" (XV:333 B), the Pseudo-Dionysius makes perfectly clear at this culminating moment the way in which his *maʿaseh merkabah* embraces as much a theology of individuation in the establishment of one's own identity as a theology of procession in the attainment of the celestial realms. In both respects his theological outlook draws together an entire complex of associations through which the visionary mode assumes renewed meaning in the traditions of interpretation that distinguish the mysticism, as well as the exegetical foundations, of the early church.[37]

IV

Having focused our attention in some detail on the transmission of the visionary mode as mystical enterprise among such figures as Gregory of Nyssa, on the one hand, and Macarius the Egyptian and Dionysius the Areopagite, on the other, we might now appropriately consider corresponding interpreters whose works provide additional insight into the major trends and movements that distinguish the hermeneutical dimensions of patristic commentary. To that end, we shall conclude our discussion with two major figures for whom Ezekiel's *visio Dei* was looked upon as an event of the first importance: Jerome (340–420) and Gregory the Great (ca. 540–604). Devoting immense labors to the explication of Ezekiel, these two fathers suggest how extensively the complex associations surrounding his inaugural vision became a staple of

---

of its intellectual powers." Its motions bring it to "the Beautiful and the Good." It also moves in a spiral and in a straight line, each signifying different aspects of the dynamics of the soul. The goal of all movements is to uplift it from external things, "as from certain variegated and pluralized symbols, to the simple and united contemplations" (IV:704 D–705B).

37. In *The Ecclesiastical Hierarchy* a correspondingly significant emphasis is placed upon the visionary contexts surrounding Ezekiel and Isaiah. From the ecclesiastical perspective that the Pseudo-Dionysius established, these texts are assimilated into a sacramental system of theurgy and theology, especially that having to do with the so-called sacrament of "myron" or the anointing of the altar (see IV: 473 A–481 D).

patristic orthodoxy. From the perspective of that orthodoxy, the inaugural vision was given renewed impetus, one that not only recalled prevailing traditions of interpretation but that set the vision on a new course. This course reconceived the inaugural vision in a number of ways. These included a concern with the vision as a source of generative recreation, as a means of figural and allegorical enactment, as a key to classical rhetorical, philosophical, and poetic thought, and as a paradigm of perfect discipline. Such ideas were summed up in the writings of Jerome and Gregory the Great, both of whom represented an interpretive standard for the inaugural vision among succeeding generations.

In order to appreciate Jerome's understanding of Ezekiel, one must be aware of the Origenic dimensions of his thought. Although Jerome denounced Origen as a heretic, he not only appropriated the Alexandrian father's exegetical insights into his commentaries but translated portions of Origen's writings. These include Origen's homilies on Ezekiel, the source of much of what Jerome himself has to say concerning the subject. In preparation for a consideration of Jerome, then, we might provide a preliminary overview of Origen's own thought concerning the matter of Ezekiel's inaugural vision.[38]

Sounding prevailing Judaic themes, Origen emphasizes throughout his exegesis the extreme difficulty surrounding any analysis of the vision, a motif that we have already encountered elsewhere in Origen's works. In keeping with this outlook, Origen views himself in his homilies on Ezekiel as a member of a select society dealing with the mystery ("*mysterium*") manifested in the *maʿaseh merkabah*. The matters addressed there are so hidden ("*abscondere*") that it is tantamount to a heresy to share them with a public unprepared for what is to be disclosed (secs. 881–883). In Origen the mysteries of the *merkabah* assume a decidedly Christocentric bearing. That bearing is discernible in the various aspects of the vision that Origen discusses.

38. References are to *Homiliae XIV in Ezechielem, Patrologiae cursus completus... Series Latinae*, 221 vols. (Paris, n.p., 1844–1880), XXV, 691–707; hereafter cited as *PL*. For an illuminating treatment of Origen's homilies on Ezekiel, particularly from the perspective of the Judaic milieu, see Halperin, *Faces*, pp. 322–354. This expands and develops Halperin's earlier study, "Origen, Ezekiel's Merkabah, and the Ascension of Moses," *Church History* 50 (1981): 261–275. Analyses of Origen's homilies can be found in Johannes Quasten, *Patrology*, 3 vols. (Westminster, Md.: Newman Press, 1950–1960), II, 46–47, as well as in Neuss, *Das Buch Ezechiel*, pp. 35–42. According to Quasten, Origen wrote some twenty-five commentaries on Ezekiel. Those commentaries are now lost (II, 51).

Placing the vision in a typological context, for example, Origen interprets Ezekiel's reference to the fact that God appeared to him in "the thirtieth year" (1:1) as an anticipation of Luke's account of Jesus' assumption of his ministry in his thirtieth year (Luke 3:23; cf. John 8:57). Recalling that Luke's account is followed by a genealogy that traces Jesus' lineage through Joseph to Adam, the Son of God (Luke 3:23–38; cf. Matt. 1:1–17), Origen reminds us that Ezekiel, too, holds the title *ben 'adam* ("son of man") (Ezek. 2:3). These associations, among others, allow Origen to view the entire vision from a Christocentric perspective, one that focuses upon the events of the life of Christ, including his Incarnation, his Nativity, his Baptism, his Passion and Crucifixion, followed by his Resurrection and Ascension (sec. 885; cf. sec. 896).

The vision embodies a full account of Christ as a manifestation of what Origen calls the "*imperium Dei*" (sec. 885). So conceived, Christ as the charioteer of God ("*auriga Dei*") within his own chariot of fire is granted supreme authority over the operations of the entire universe. Under him, God's troops are marshaled in appropriate order and array (sec. 895), and through his auspices the workings of providence, made evident in the wheels within wheels of the chariot, are executed (sec. 896). This is a cosmic chariot, one that embraces the celestial and terrestrial realms, as well as an allegorical chariot in which the fourfold creatures that propel it represent the faculties of the soul.

As *imperium Dei*, Christ, moreover, is the fulfillment of that promise by which God says through David, "*De fructu lumbi tui ponam super sedem meam*" (Ps. 132:11). Recalling the genealogical dimension associated with Christ as the antitype of the *ben 'adam*, Origen views the vision as a whole in generative (indeed, sexual) terms. Such is particularly true of the Enthroned Figure as the charioteer surrounded by fire. Alluding to Ezekiel 1:27 ("and downward from what had been the appearance of his loins I saw as it were the appearance of fire, and there was brightness round about him"), Origen observes that the loins of the Enthroned Figure signify "*coitus*," for through them (as through the loins of Abraham) will arise a priestly race culminating in the heirs of the New Dispensation (cf. Heb. 7:1–5). Not only will the fires that emanate from this figure punish the sinful, but through them, the righteous will be purified (secs. 881–882). Such in brief is Origen's *ma'aseh merkabah*, one that brings into sharp focus the kerygmatic transformation of Ezekiel's vision into a Christocentric event and that suggests how compellingly Judaic themes were introduced into patristic exegesis and served as the basis of Christian spirituality from the earliest times.

This fact is made apparent in Jerome's own account of Ezekiel's *visio Dei*. Drawing upon and extending Origen's insights, Jerome reveals how the inaugural vision assumed a crucial bearing in his outlook.[39] In accord with Origen, Jerome at the outset reiterates the commonplace idea that there are certain texts that may not be interpreted by anyone who is unprepared. These include the beginning and ending of Ezekiel, the beginning of Genesis, and the Song of Songs.[40] Only an interpreter who is mature enough, that is, one who has reached at least the age of thirty is permitted to address these texts (Prologue, 20–30).[41] Acknowledging the sacrosanct nature of the task, Jerome proceeds to analyze all aspects of Ezekiel's *visio Dei*. Christocentric in focus, the approach that Jerome adopts is particularly fascinating not only because of its polysemous nature but because of its willingness to accom-

39. References are to the *Commentariorum in Hiezechielem Libri XIV, S. Hieronymi Presbyteri Opera* (Pars I, 4, *Opera Exegetica*), in *Corpus Christianorum, Series Latina*, 176 vols. to date (Turnholt, Belgium: Brepols, 1957–), vol. LXXV.

40. In his "Prologue" to the *Commentary on the Song of Songs*, Origen places this biblical book quite appropriately in the context of the *merkabah*. Referring to the Song of Songs, he says: "I give warning and advice to everyone who is not yet free of the vexations of flesh and blood and who has not withdrawn from the desire for corporeal nature that he completely abstain from reading this book and what is said about it. Indeed, they say that the Hebrews observe the rule that unless some one has attained a perfect and mature age, he is not even permitted to hold this book in his hands."

Corresponding to the Song of Songs, three additional texts fall into the same category: "the beginning of Genesis in which the creation of the world is described, the first chapters of Ezekiel the prophet in which mention is made of the cherubim [and] the end of Ezekiel, which includes the building of the Temple" (in *Origen*, trans. Greer, pp. 218–219). For discussions of this passage, see Gershom Scholem, *Jewish Gnosticism, Merkabah Mysticism, and Talmudic Tradition* (New York: Jewish Theological Seminary of America, 1960), pp. 36–42, and Nicholas R. M. De Lange, *Origen and the Jews* (Cambridge: Cambridge University Press, 1976), pp. 59–60. De Lange calls into question the assumption that the passage is entirely Origen's, since it exists only "in a version by Rufinus, who may be suspected of having inserted or doctored the passage himself" (p. 60).

41. Similar views are discernible in Jerome's other writings. See, for example, his "Letter to Paulinus" (Letter LIII), which includes a detailed account of the mysteries contained in Scriptures. "As for Isaiah, Jeremiah, Ezekiel, and Daniel, who can fully understand or adequately explain them?" he asks. "The beginning and ending of Ezekiel . . . are involved in so great obscurity [*obscuritatibus involuta*] that like the commencement of Genesis they are not studied by the Hebrews until they are thirty years old [*annos triginta non legantur*]" (LIII.8). References to the letters are to *The Works of Jerome, A Select Library of Nicene and Post-Nicene Fathers of the Christian Church*, ed. Philip Schaff and Henry Wace, 2nd series, 14 vols. (New York: Christian Literature, 1893), VI, 96–102, in conjunction with *Sancti Eusebii Hieronymi Epistulae*, 3 vols. (Lipsia: G. Freytag, 1910–1918), LIV, 442–465.

modate the vision to a multiplicity of points of view, that to which Jerome himself refers as "*a multis varie exponitur*" (II.1a. 658). In both respects Jerome enhances one's understanding of how the vision takes on a character of its own as a subject of exegesis.

Beginning with the Origenic notion that the reference to "the thirtieth year" in Ezekiel prefigures the time-frame indicated in Luke's account of Jesus' assumption of his ministry, Jerome immediately establishes the Christocentric basis of his analysis (I.1a.1–20). Having already indicated that one cannot study such texts as the first chapter of Ezekiel until one has reached the age of thirty, Jerome assimilates this version of the talmudic commonplace into the typological framework that he establishes. This context is all-pervasive in Jerome's commentary. Such is discernible in his handling of various aspects of the vision. Addressing himself to the opening passages (Ezek. 1:1–5), for example, Jerome interprets the vision as a manifestation of the power and providence of God to liberate the redeemed soul from bondage, just as the Israelites are liberated from the Egyptians. In this respect, the approach of the glory of God in whirlwind, clouds, and fire prefigures the coming of Christ in judgment. Whereas those enveloped in sin are damned, those purged of their sins are saved (I.3b.70–4b.151). In accord with Origen, Jerome likewise interprets the vision as a chariot ("*quadriga*") guided by the Enthroned Figure as charioteer ("*auriga*") (I.8b.300–302). As for the Enthroned Figure Himself, Jerome, like Origen, sees in his limbs that generative dimension of "*coitus*" through which is born the sense of promise and renewal that underlies the New Dispensation (II.1a.620–627). In Christocentric terms, the vision as a whole for Jerome moves toward the realization of this promise and renewal.

Corresponding to this point of view is Jerome's treatment of the fourfold creatures. In that treatment the creatures take on a fully allegorical cast, one that reflects the predilections that so distinguish Jerome's interpretive practices. Consistent with those practices, Jerome schematizes the fourfold creatures in a manner that allows him to view the *ḥayyot* from a multitude of perspectives. These include an evangelical, an elemental, a seasonal, a geographical, a psychological, and an ethical pattern of correspondences, all of which suggest Jerome's reading of the vision as an enterprise that embraces all aspects of life and all areas of learning. In rhetorical terms the *ḥayyot* for Jerome become a marvelous reservoir for the expression of *inventio*: in the fourfold creatures

one can find the very well-spring of *copia* that suggests the con-
currence and harmony of the otherwise apparently disparate aspects of the universe, here coalescing in a wonderfully
orchestrated fourfold scheme.[42] In Jerome this scheme assumes
its own allegorical symmetry.

From the evangelical perspective, for example, the face of the
man for Jerome represents the figure of Matthew; the lion, the figure of Mark; the ox, the figure of Luke; and the eagle, the figure of
John (I.6–8a.182–200).[43] Deriving such correspondences from his
readings of the individual gospels associated with these evangelists,
he bestows upon the fourfold creatures a "bookish" identity, one
that redefines the creatures in terms that find expression in gospel
narrative and that bestows upon each of the portrayers of that narrative his own distinct personality. In various forms such a conceptualization was not only to become a commonplace of patristic
exegesis of both Ezekiel 1 and Revelation 4 but was to find its way
into the complex traditions of iconography that flourished during
the Middle Ages and into the Renaissance.[44]

For Jerome the allegorization of the fourfold creatures in this
manner was, moreover, eminently in accord with his general view
of Ezekiel's vision (and, by implication, Saint John the Divine's)
as a *quadriga* of marvelous proportions. So, he observes in the
Letter to Paulinus:

> Matthew, Mark, Luke and John are the Lord's team of four [*quad-
> riga domini*], the true cherubim or store of knowledge. With them
> the whole body is full of eyes, they glitter as sparks, they run and

42. Jerome's outlook is very much in keeping with medieval interpretive practices. For
a full and fascinating account of those practices, see Anna C. Esmeijer, *Divina Quaternitas:
A Preliminary Study in the Method and Application of Visual Exegesis* (Amsterdam: Van Gorcum
Assen, 1978).

43. For Jerome's explanations of the associations, see the *Commentarium* I.6–8a.190–
202. In his account of the correspondences Jerome differs from Irenaeus, the earliest to
make such associations. In his *Adversus Haereses* (III.xi.8) Irenaeus associates the lion with
John, the ox with Luke, the man with Matthew, and the eagle with Mark. In his works
entitled *The Harmony of the Gospels* (I.vi.9) and *On the Gospel of St. John* (XXXVI.5), Saint
Augustine (354–430), on the other hand, rearranges the order once again. For Augustine
the lion is associated with Matthew, the ox with Luke, the man with Mark, and the eagle
with John. Obviously, the associations were somewhat fluid among the church fathers.
Iconography, however, normally followed the example of Jerome.

44. The literature on this subject is vast. See especially Neuss, *Das Buch Ezechiel* and *Die
Apokalypse des Johannes*, passim, as well as his *Die katalanishce Bibelillustration um die Wende
des ersten Jahrtausends und die altspanische Buchmalerei* (Bonn: Kurt Schroeder Verlag, 1922).

return like lightning, their feet are straight feet, and lifted, their backs also are winged, ready to fly in all directions. They hold together each by each and are interwoven one with another: like wheels within wheels [*rota in rota*] they roll along and go whithersoever the breath of the Holy Spirit wafts them. (LIII.9)

An image of remarkable energy and verve, this reenactment of Ezekiel's *visio Dei* reveals how compellingly the early church fathers were inclined to reconceptualize the visionary to accord with their view of the Scriptures as a "vehicle" for the revelation of God's providential design. Propelled by the evangelists, the *quadriga* moves forth in triumphal procession as a celebration of the power and glory of God. Typologically conceived, it is a celebration in which the wheels within wheels become for Jerome a symbol of the "*duorom junctura Testamentorum*," the Old within the New.[45] This "bookish" formulation is also an interpretive formulation: one testament comments upon, is "involved in," prefigures the other. At the center of this typological notion is the triumphal "*quadriga Dei*," with its own charioteer and its own means of locomotion embodied in the fourfold creatures allegorized as the evangelists.

Corresponding to this "evangelical" interpretation of the *ḥayyot* are the other interpretations alluded to above. As indicated, they are the elemental, the seasonal, the geographical, the psychological, and the ethical. From the elemental point of view, the fourfold creatures for Jerome find their counterparts in the "*elementa mundi*," that is, fire, air, water, and earth. These elements, in turn, have seasonal relations: spring, summer, autumn, and winter. In their revolutions they reenact the idea of the wheels within wheels of the vision. Geographically, the idea is replicated in the directional placement of the four quarters: east, west, north, and south. Such macrocosmic associations are complemented in Jerome's thought by microcosmic ones. The body of the world is replicated in the body of man. From this perspective, the fourfold creatures provide Jerome with the opportunity to internalize the vision.

The *ḥayyot* accordingly manifest the four dispositions of the soul (conscience, will, intelligence, and desire), the four faculties of the brain (reason, cognition, understanding, and deliberation), and the four categories of emotions (joy, grief, greed, and fear). Fi-

45. *Commentariorum* I.18.485–490.

nally, as ethical categories, the fourfold creatures are allegorized
into the four cardinal virtues of prudence, justice, fortitude, and
temperance (I.6–8a.182–305). At the forefront of such correspondences is a concern with the way the divine is reflected in the
human, the larger in the smaller, the external in the internal. *Rota*
in *rota*, the chariot of Jerome's schema is carefully and minutely
constructed. Although presented schematically, the correspondences that constitute his chariot are not static, however: constantly in motion, constantly undergoing processes of
transformation from one identity or state to the next and one
meaning to the next, they reflect the dynamism, as well as the
harmony, that underlies God's providential design. Constituents
of the *"quadriga Dei,"* they "hold together each by each and are
interwoven one with another: like wheels within wheels they roll
along and go whithersoever the breath of the Holy Spirit wafts
them."

Fascinating in itself, such an outlook is made even more so by
the way Jerome contextualizes the vision in terms of the classical
philosophical and poetic traditions to which his sensibility was so
much disposed. In the process the interpretive dimensions of
Ezekiel's vision are immeasurably deepened and enhanced
through a hermeneutics that does not hesitate to "locate" the vision
in the cultural milieu represented by the writings of such figures
as Plato, Cicero, Virgil, and Horace (I.6–9.182–322). Underlying
his discussion of the fourfold creatures as a manifestation of the
dispositions of the soul, for example, is Plato's complex treatment
of the divisions of the soul in *The Republic* (IV.439–442; cf. VI.511;
IX.588–589) and elsewhere. Implicit in Jerome's reference to the
vision as a *quadriga*, moreover, is Plato's correspondingly complex
treatment of the conduct of the soul in *The Phaedrus*. Already
present in the earlier fathers, this contextualizing of Ezekiel's vision suggests once again not only how much Jerome was in accord
with the traditions of interpretive practice that he inherited but
how willing he was to place his own stamp upon prevailing hermeneutics.

This is particularly true of his contextualizing of the vision in
poetic terms. The image of the *rota* in *rota* represents a case in
point. Signifying for Jerome the seasonal idea of spring, summer,
autumn and winter implicit in *"annum in anno,"* the image evokes
in his mind the whole cyclical and bucolic context of Virgil's *Georgics*, in particular that having to do with the dressing of vines (I.

6–8a.250–255).[46] As a gloss of "*rota in rota*," then, Jerome cites a line from the *Georgics* that recalls this activity, as well as the cycle of the seasons that complements it: "*Atque in se vita per vestigia volvitur annus* [as the shuttling year returns on its own track]" (II.402). Part of a larger context, this line recalls Virgil's georgic advice that the dressing of vines is a task that is never completed. Involving the repeated turning of the soil three or four times a year, year after year, the need to perform this task demonstrates that "A farmer's work proceeds in / Cycles, as the shuttling year returns on its own track." With the passing of the years there is a constant revolution of the seasons and the recurring perfor-mance of a corresponding georgic activity (II.397–407).

Such for Jerome are the poetic implications of the *rota in rota* in Ezekiel's vision. From this perspective the visionary mode opens into an entire world of classical poetic thought, a world in which the landscape of biblical prophecy is made suddenly to coexist with the landscape of the pagan imagination. Additional examples could be cited, but the foregoing should be sufficient to indicate the polysemous nature of Jerome's analysis.[47] Embracing an entire spectrum of meanings and a multiplicity of perspectives, that anal-ysis suggests how receptive Ezekiel's vision was to the outlook reflected in Jerome's handling of biblical prophecy. By means of his interpretation of the *visio Dei* that inaugurates the prophecy of Ezekiel, Jerome in effect created his own *maʿaseh merkabah*.

If such is true of Jerome, it is no less so of Gregory the Great, a church father for whom the vision of Ezekiel was immensely important and whose analyses of that vision proved crucial for both the exegetical and the mystical traditions of the western church. Among those works by Gregory in which the vision as-sumed paramount significance, none is more germane than his homilies on Ezekiel.[48] Divided into two books, these homilies con-

46. References to *The Georgics* in my text are to *The Eclogues and Georgics of Virgil*, trans. C. Day Lewis (Garden City, N.Y.: Doubleday, 1964). In other parts of his commentary Jerome also makes reference to Virgil's *Aeneid*, the poems of Horace, and the works of Cicero (I.6–89.250–322).

47. If such is true of Jerome's contextualizing of Ezekiel's vision in poetic terms, it is no less true of his reconceiving the vision in mythological terms. The focus of the reference once again is the *rota in rota*, in this case, the fact that the rims of the wheels "were full of wheels round about" (1:18). This detail Jerome reconceives through the Ovidian allusion to the "*multorum oculorum*" of Argus set by Hera in the tail of a peacock as a warning against adultery (I.18.465–475).

48. References by section and page number in my text are to the *Homiliae in Hiezechihelem Prophetam*, in *Corpus Christianorum, Series Latina*, Vol. CXLII. I have also made use of

cern themselves with the first four chapters of Ezekiel in the first book (homilies 1–12) and the fortieth chapter in the second book (homilies 1–10). The first book will be our primary concern.

Following in Jerome's footsteps in the first book, Gregory allegorizes all aspects of the inaugural vision in order to discover the multiple senses encoded in the references. But he moves even beyond Jerome by emphasizing what he calls the "allegorical mysteries" that await the disclosure of those capable enough and indeed mature enough to penetrate their secrets (I.ii.3). Engaging at the outset of his analysis in his own form of onomastics, Gregory gives free play to this allegorizing impulse. The name "Chebar," for example, is interpreted as weight or heaviness. "Ezekiel" is the strength or courage of God, whereas "Buzi" is one who is despised or held in contempt. "Chaldean," finally, implies that which holds captive and is likened to a kind of demon.[49] Drawing upon these putative meanings, Gregory interprets the entire vision typologically, as well as allegorically, to suggest that Ezekiel's ministry and circumstances prefigure that of Christ. As a manifestation of God's strength or courage, Ezekiel anticipates the way in which Christ is born into a life of hardship but becomes the means by which humankind is purged of the weight of sinfulness that bears it down, with the result that humans are liberated from the demonic captivity of their iniquity (I.ii.6). From the very outset of Gregory's interpretation, then, one is made to see how all senses move toward a realization of the presence of Christ, whose *kerygma* is manifested allegorically in every "sign" of the text. So the vision as a whole prefigures the announcement in Matt. 3:17: "This is my beloved Son, in whom I am well pleased" (I.ii.5).

This allegorization bears upon Gregory's interpretation of the other aspects of the vision as well. His treatment of the fourfold creatures is a case in point. Beginning with the observation that the number four implies perfection, Gregory engages in the traditional associations to which he was heir. The fourfold creatures signify the four evangelists, the four regions of the world, and the four cardinal virtues (I.ii.18; I.iii.7–8). Distinguishing between

---

Grégoire le Grand, *Homélies sur Ézéchiel*, ed. Charles Morel, Sources chrétiennes, vol. 327 (Paris: Les Éditions du Cerf, 1986). For an illuminating discussion of Gregory's treatment, see Neuss, *Das Buch Ezechiel*, pp. 91–100.

49. For the most part Gregory's onomastics is more nearly "creative" than accurate, although "Ezekiel" (*yeḥezk'el*) does imply "God strengthens" (*ḥazak-'el*), and "Buzi" (from *buz*) suggests one who is despised or held in contempt.

the faces and the wings of the creatures, he observes that the faces signify faith and the wings contemplation. By means of faith, we arrive at a true knowledge of God, particularly as embodied in the Incarnation of His Son; by means of contemplation, we ascend to a vision of God, who enlightens the "eyes of the mind" (I.iii.1– 2). If the faces and wings of the creatures suggest faith and contemplation, respectively, the hands of the creatures suggest activity. In this way, Gregory sees reflected in the fourfold creatures symbols of the active and contemplative lives so fundamental to the spiritual and monastic practices of the early church.[50]

Drawing upon his knowledge of such practices, as well as those who discoursed at length upon them, Gregory asserts that the active life is prior to the contemplative, just as good works are a preparation for contemplation. The first pertains to the external ministry of the believing Christian; the second, to his internal well-being. Of the two callings, the contemplative life is of a higher order than the active life. For that reason the hands of the creatures are found beneath the wings. Alluding to Luke 10:38–42, Gregory associates the figure of Martha with the active life and the figure of Mary with the contemplative life.[51] For Gregory, both modes constitute the full experience of the Christian life, and both find apt expression in the visionary conception of the fourfold figures as allegorical imperatives (I.iii.7–9).

Pursuing the allegorical dimensions still further, Gregory compounds his interpretation of the fourfold creatures as a manifes-

---

50. See especially Butler, *Western Mysticism*, esp. pp. 157–167. See also J. F. Conwell's entry "Active Life, Spiritual" in the *New Catholic Encyclopedia*, ed. William T. McDonald et al., 16 vols. (New York: McGraw-Hill, 1967–1974), I, 98–99. In the history of monasticism the distinction proved crucial. Profoundly influencing Benedictine life in subsequent ages, it exerted an impact on clerical life in general. See Gregory's book on the Pastoral Office, the *Regula Pastoralis*, which established the foundations of clerical conduct.

51. The idea is discernible as early as Origen, who identified the active life with Martha and the contemplative life with her sister Mary. "With St. Augustine the term active life became almost synonymous with ascetical striving by making it consist of the practice of virtues, as apart from the contemplation of truth. St. Gregory the Great seconded this doctrine by identifying the active life with the practice of corporal works of mercy and to some extent the spiritual works, and this tradition persisted through St. Thomas and Suárez" (Conwell, "Active Life, Spiritual," I, 98–99). In Augustine, Martha and Mary are prefigured by Leah and Rachel, respectively (Gen. 29–30); Butler, *Western Mysticism*, pp. 159–60. In the second book of his homilies Gregory himself makes much of these distinctions. See in particular II.ii.7–11, which describes in detail the offices of the active and contemplative lives and develops fully the Leah/Martha–Rachel/Mary typology (trans. in Butler, *Western Mysticism*, pp. 171–173). These distinctions will assume greater import in our discussion of Dante.

tation of the active and contemplative lives by associating the creatures with the four mysteries of Christ reflected in the *"via Dei."* In this way, the life of man is consummated in the life of God. The four mysteries of Christ, of course, are the Incarnation, the Crucifixion, the Resurrection, and the Ascension. With the first, Gregory associates the face of the man; with the second, the face of the ox; with the third, the face of the lion; and with the fourth, the face of the eagle. So Christ was born in the form of a man, was crucified with the sacrificial willingness of an ox, was resurrected with the courage and strength of a lion, and ascended with the majesty and sublimity of an eagle (I.iv.1–2).[52]

This Christocentric emphasis on the mysteries surrounding the events in the life of the Savior is fundamental to Gregory's interpretive posture throughout the homilies. Textualizing the wheel within wheel as the Old Testament within the New, for example, Gregory invokes the typological association to demonstrate the means by which one may return to the Genesis account of Eve's birth from Adam (Gen. 2:21–22). In that event one may see how the entire course of redemptive history is generated. With the coming of Christ and the events surrounding his advent (Incarnation, Crucifixion, Resurrection, and Ascension), man is absolved of his sins and is able to reenter the paradise he was made to forfeit in his fall. In that way Christ fulfills his role as mediator for mankind (I.vi.15). The wheels themselves, in turn, are for Gregory a symbol of the divine spirit that inspires and revivifies man with its "sacred eloquence." If mankind is regenerated in Christ, those who understand the full meaning of the import of the vision are correspondingly reborn (I.vii).

With that rebirth comes a vision of the Universal Church that worships before and is sustained by the Only-Begotten (*"Unigenitus"*) who is portrayed as the Enthroned Figure above the firmament. So in his analysis of Ezekiel 1:12 ("and there came a voice from above the firmament over their heads"), Gregory envisions the angelic creatures, accompanied by the congregation of

52. According to Helen J. Dow, "The Rose-Window," *JWCI* 12 (1957), "this theme had been partially developed by Jerome, and fully stated by Ambrose. It was, however, the wording of Augustine that became the prototype not only for Gregory's version, but for those of all succeeding Western commentators: 'Hominem nascentem, vitulum patientem, leonem regnantem, et aquilam ad coelestia remeantem.' (Christ was, being born, a man; being sacrificed, an ox; reigning [raised from the dead] a lion; and ascending into Heaven, an eagle)" (pp. 274–275).

the redeemed, humbling themselves before the divine presence of the Almighty in a posture of abject devotion. Having attained to that supreme moment in the heights of contemplation, they are made aware of the ineffableness of deity, a fact that Gregory underscores by citing 1 Cor. 13:10: "For our knowledge is imperfect and our prophecy is imperfect." Recognizing their limitations, they know the impossibility of penetrating the supreme mystery of godhead, completely enrobed in light (I.vii.17).

For Gregory, the depiction of the Enthroned Figure with his redeemed congregation is an event of profound significance, one toward which the entire vision builds and one concerning which Gregory devotes a good deal of attention. As Gregory conceives the event, this moment of ecstasis is realized only after great suffering. Those who attain to such a realization have been purged of their sinfulness through travail and indeed flagellation ("*flagello*"). The redeemed who achieve this vision do so by reenacting Christ's own suffering and Passion in order to emulate his purity. Only in this way are they able to find themselves in the presence of the Enthroned Figure (I.viii.22).

As the Only-Begotten ("*Unigenitus*"), the Enthroned Figure is also the resurrected Christ who appears both to judge and to reward. In that capacity he is likewise a figure in whom the procreative urge finds complete expression. Addressing himself to that aspect of Ezek. 1:27 that concerns "the appearance of his loins" like "the appearance of fire" round about, Gregory, in keeping with Origen and Jerome, interprets the image in fully generative and even sexual terms.[53] Just as the incarnate Savior, born of the virgin Mary, is the offspring of the limbs of Abraham, so Christ is himself a "*uterus*" through which mankind will be reborn. Consistent with this generative image, Gregory interprets the fires that surround the limbs of the Enthroned Figure in sexual terms. They are the "*amoris flamma*" that envelop the most powerful ("*potentissimus*") thighs of Christ, through whose "ardor" the Holy Spirit ignites the hearts of believers with the desire for salvation.

---

53. Cf. in this regard Gregory Thaumaturgus (ca. 213–ca. 275), a father influenced by Origen. In his second homily "On the Annunciation of the Holy Virgin Mary," he proclaims: "Thou [Mary] hast a mind whiter than snow, and a body made purer than any gold . . . and a womb such as the object which Ezekiel saw." "Clearly, then, did the prophet [Ezekiel] behold in type Him who was born of the holy virgin, whom thou, O holy virgin wouldest have had no strength to bear, hadst thou not beamed forth for that time with all that is glorious and virtuous" (*Ante-Nicene Fathers*, VI, 62).

Such is Gregory's account of Ezekiel's *visio Dei* in the first book of his homilies. For Gregory, it is a vision in which the congregation of the redeemed participate in a glorious and transcendent event, the focus of which is the resurrected Christ (I.viii.26–28). From this perspective Gregory formulates his mystical hermeneutics, one that reveals an intimate awareness of earlier traditions of exegesis and that devises its own unique response to the text that engendered those traditions. As a figure in whom the exegetical and the mystical find apt expression, Gregory suggests how the vision of Ezekiel assumed paramount importance in the developing history of the early church.

Having examined the range of exegesis that underscores this history, we have witnessed in the patristic sphere what was made evident in the Judaic. The visionary mode is a phenomenon adaptable to an entire constellation of interpretive strategies. Whether Judaic or Christocentric in focus, this phenomenon is constantly undergoing a process of assimilation and transformation from one generation to the next. Like its Judaic counterpart, the Christocentric delineation of the vision moves in directions that are at once mystical and hermeneutic. Recalling many of the concerns that characterize the Judaic point of view, the Christocentric outlook formulates its own theory of purification and ascent, conceives its own mystical theology and system of angelology, engages in its own mode of *allegoresis*, all of which extend the visionary into new areas of perception. As a result, acculturation becomes consonant with transformation: the two occur simultaneously in the traditions of interpretation through which Ezekiel's inaugural vision emerges as an event of crucial import in the Middle Ages.

~ *Seven*

The Theosis of Vision

I

The acculturation of the visionary mode into the Christo-centric outlook made evident in the fathers of the early church received ample expression in the later expositors as well. These expositors articulated a visionary hermeneutics as crucial to the understanding of the transformative nature of the *visio Dei* as any that had gone before. Once again, at the forefront of this hermeneutics is the experience manifested in a network of texts of which Ezekiel's vision is the originary event. The source of all visionary experience, the *visio Dei* delineated in Ezekiel is the wheel within the wheel that generates its own interpretive culture. If such is true of the earlier traditions of interpretation that distinguish the church during its formative period, it is no less true of the later traditions of medieval hermeneutics. Ranging from the ninth century to the thirteenth century, these traditions fostered a rich milieu, one in which the visionary mode assumed renewed impetus and significance. This milieu is the focus of our present discussion. Exploring the interpretive traditions that underscore the delineation of the visionary mode during this period, we shall consider a range of exegetes, beginning with Johannes Scotus Eriugena in the ninth century and ending with Saint Bonaventure in the thirteenth. Through an examination of these figures we shall gain a heightened awareness of the centrality of the visionary mode to the traditions of hermeneutics that distinguish the later Middle Ages.

To establish an interpretive context, we begin with an examination of the way the visionary mode was formulated in the works of Johannes Scotus Eriugena (810–877), that *scholasticus et eruditus* whose commentaries and translations of such fathers as Maximus the Confessor and Dionysius the Areopagite made available Greek mystical thought to the Latin West.¹ Reflecting the influence of the Greek and Latin fathers, the writings of Eriugena are rich in their attestation to the importance of both traditions. As Gershom Scholem has suggested, Eriugena may likewise be seen as a possible link to the philosophical suppositions upon which later Jewish mysticism is founded.² For our purposes, however, his works are germane as they provide a philosophical basis for further exploration of the visionary experience. Offering his own version of what is at stake in the attempt to understand the nature of that experience, Eriugena is important not simply because of the traditions that he assimilates or because of his possible impact upon later generations of thinkers but because of his ability to devise a "science of the visionary" that strikes at the heart of the kinds of assumptions we have been exploring throughout.³ In our analysis of his science of the visionary we are concerned primarily with the *Periphyseon* (ca. 864–866), the centerpiece of his philosophical endeavors.⁴

1. Responding to the request of Charles the Bald, Eriugena translated the works of the Pseudo-Dionysius; he also translated the *First Ambigua* and the *Quaestiones ad Thalassium* of Saint Maximus the Confessor, the *De Hominis Opificio* of Saint Gregory of Nyssa, and the *Ancoratus* of Epiphanius. Aside from these translations, he wrote commentaries on Martianus Capella, on *The Celestial Hierarchy* of the Pseudo-Dionysius, on the Gospel of John, and on the subject of predestination. His major work is the *Periphyseon* or *De Diuisione Naturae*. For specific references, see I. P. Sheldon-Williams, "A Bibliography of the Works of Johannes Scottus Eriugena," *Journal of Ecclesiastical History* 10, no. 2 (1960): 198–222. John J. O'Meara provides a chronological bibliography of the works and a select bibliography of secondary literature in *Eriugena* (Oxford: Clarendon Press, 1988), pp. 221–229.

2. Gershom Scholem, *Major Trends in Jewish Mysticism* (New York: Schocken Books, 1954), p. 109, *Kabbalah* (Jerusalem: Keter, 1974), pp. 48, 392–393. In this regard, see also G. Sed-Rajna, "L'influence de Jean Scot sur la doctrine du kabbaliste Azriel de Gérone," *Jean Scot Érigène et l'histoire de la philosophie*, ed. R. Roques (Paris: Centre national de la recherche scientifique, 1977), pp. 453–463.

3. The extent of his influence on the later Middle Ages is open to question. See Jean-Marie Déchanet, "John Scotus Erigena," *Spirituality through the Centuries*, ed. James Walsh (New York: P. J. Kennedy and Sons, n.d.), pp. 83–96; and Rufus M. Jones, *Studies in Mystical Religion* (London: Macmillan, 1936), pp. 113–129; and the Introduction by Jean Potter to Myra L. Uhlfelder's edition and translation of the *Periphyseon* (Indianapolis: Bobbs-Merrill, 1976), pp. ix–xli. See also Henry Bett, *Joannes Scotus Erigena: A Study in Medieval Philosophy* (Cambridge: Cambridge University Press, 1925), pp. 171–196.

4. References to the first three books of the *Periphyseon* are to the edition and translation of I. P. Sheldon-Williams, *Iohannis Scotti Erivgenae Periphyseon (De Diuisione Naturae)*, Scriptores Latini Hiberniae (Dublin: Dublin Institute for Advanced Studies, 1968–1981). References to the final two books in my text are to the edition and translation of Myra L. Uhlfelder, in conjunction with the *Joannis Scoti Opera*, in the *PL*, CXXII.

Conceived as a colloquy between teacher and student, the *Per-iphyseon* is divided into five books that address the nature of God's self-manifestation (theophany) in the universe and how that man-ifestation can be understood. According to Eriugena, divine self-manifestation is divisible into four species or categories, each of which is explored in the four remaining books that follow upon the first or introductory book, which defines the genus Nature and classifies the four categories. The first is "That which creates and is not created" (book II); the second, "That which is created and creates" (book III); the third, "That which is created and does not create" (book IV); and the fourth, "That which neither creates nor is created" (book V). Reflecting earlier concerns with the qua-ternary as a paradigm for the divine, this fourfold idea is at the heart of Eriugena's point of view. The four categories of Eriugena reconceptualize some of the basic assumptions that we have come to associate with the visionary experience.

As "that which creates and is not created," the first category concerns God both as primal and undifferentiated unity and as the ground and principle of all existence. This is God as Alpha, the source of all that is. The true nature of God's essence in this category is impossible to grasp. It is a mystery in the presence of which intellect is dumb. God here has no attributes, for attributes are the product of divine self-manifestation to lower forms, and that does not occur until the subsequent categories, when God proceeds out of unity into differentiation. Within the first category God as principle transcends all such distinctions: He is beyond all that can be said about Him. All attempts to conceptualize an ul-timate truth about Him in positive terms fail. He must be ap-proached apophatically. There is, however, a divine "procession" by which God manifests Himself in an unfolding universe of ideas. This is the second category: "That which is created and creates." In this ideational realm of thought one discovers the perfect pat-tern of things that originate in God as creator. Of this realm Eriugena maintains that God does not know things because they exist; rather, they exist because God knows or thinks them. What He thinks creates the ideas or patterns through which objects in the material world are defined. The conceptual dimension of His self-manifestation, in turn, is itself dynamic. Embodying an energy of its own, it gives expression to God's will. When God thinks, things are.

This process results in the third category: "That which is created and does not create." Such is the visible universe, the realm of time and space. What is conceived as the "real" world, however, is only an appearance or shadow of the true world of changeless patterns, a local and temporal manifestation of eternal essences and primordial causes. Remove this "essential" substratum from the realm of the visible and nothing remains. In and of itself, all matter, therefore, is immaterial. It has no existence outside of or independent of God. Time and space, moreover, are only the product of individual perception. Once the mind rises from sense to pure thought, it discovers within itself the eternal prototypes. Leaving behind the realm of the sensible, it beholds the immutable whole, the "perfect round" of reality.

Such an ascent or return leads to the fourth category: "That which neither creates nor is created." This is God as Omega, the goal of all that is. Essentially, the primal (Alpha) and the ultimate (Omega) are identical: God the source and God the goal are one. Because the reality of all things in the visible universe is God, the final movement is a return to the divine. Just as everything begins in God, everything ends in Him as well. Such is the goal of all things both visible and invisible, whereby all visible things pass into the invisible or intellectual, and the intellectual passes into and reunites with God. The passing into God occurs in the individual soul as the result of contemplation. By means of contemplation, the soul rises above the mutable and becomes that which it beholds. At the height of contemplation, man finds God, because in this state God is also finding Himself in man. Like knows like, and the soul becomes what it sees. Such in brief are the basic assumptions of the *Periphyseon*.[5] The product of a Neoplatonic outlook, these views represent a rereading of the Pseudo-Dionysius, particularly in the distinction that he draws between *proodos* and *epistrophē*, procession and return. Appropriating that distinction as the basis of his philosophy, Eriugena devises his own science of the visionary, one that reconceptualizes and rearticulates Pseudo-Dionysian thought.

From the visionary perspective, Eriugena's system becomes particularly interesting in its mode of argumentation. This mode is one that not only divinizes the act of seeing but conceives it in

5. The summary of these views is drawn from Jones, *Studies*, pp. 124–128. See also O'Meara, *Eriugena*, pp. 80–154; Bett, *Erigena*, pp. 19–149; and Sheldon-Williams, "Johannes Scottus Eriugena," *The Cambridge History of Later Greek and Early Medieval Philosophy*, ed. A. H. Armstrong (Cambridge: Cambridge University Press, 1967).

distinctly dynamic terms. For Eriugena, both aspects are embodied onomastically in the very name of God as *theos*. This name, suggests Eriugena, is derived either from the verb *theōrō*, "I see" (*video*), or from the verb *theō*, "I run" (*curro*), and, what is even more likely, combines both, since the meaning of both is one and the same:

> For when it is *derived* from the verb *theōrō*, *theos* is interpreted to mean "He Who sees," for He sees in Himself all things that are while He looks upon nothing that is outside Himself because outside Him there is nothing. But when *theos* is derived from the verb *theō* it is correctly interpreted "He who runs," for He runs *throughout all things* and never stays but by His running fills out all things, as it is written: "His Word runneth swiftly" [Ps. 147: 15]. (I:12)

God in His essence embodies the concept of divine seeing (*"videns"*), an act conceived as a looking inward within the self as ultimate reality, for outside of that self nothing else exists. This looking inward within the self suggests how the divine being as entity for Eriugena encompasses all. To see is to behold the self: to know God is to look inward as God Himself looks inward. At the same time seeing is creating: it implies not only vision but action. "God's seeing," comments Eriugena, "is the creation of the whole universe. For for Him it is not one thing to see and another to do, but His seeing is His Will and His Will is His operation" (III:28).

That operation is what is implied by the notion of divine running (*"currens"*). Concomitant with the act of *videns*, then, is that of *currens*. In Eriugena, *running*, like *seeing*, assumes a special significance. It involves a circular, processional movement outward, followed by a return (*proodos* and *epistrophē*), as in the revolution of a wheel forever in motion. At the same time that God is the embodiment of motion, He is also ultimate rest, the fulfillment of complete stasis: "For of God it is most truly said that He is motion at rest and rest in motion." Eriugena observes that God is "at rest unchangingly in Himself, never departing from the stability of His nature." For what purpose then is God said to move? He sets Himself in motion throughout Nature so that those things that subsist by Him are able to come into being. If His rest is absolute, His motion is such that He is able to manifest Himself processionally in the act of His creation. "For by His motion all things are made." Such a *currens* is also a *videns*: the two are implied in His very name. So Eriugena concludes: "And thus there is one and the same meaning in the two interpretations of the same name, which is God. For in God to run through all things is not something other than to see all things, but as by His seeing so too by His running all things are made [*sed sicut uidendo ita et currendo fiunt omnia*]" (I:12). With its emphasis upon *videns* and *currens*, then, the visionary metaphysics of Eriugena embodies the essential features of what we have come to associate with Ezekiel's *visio Dei*. This association lies beneath the surface of Eriugena's optical and kinetic science of the divine.

Such an outlook receives further elaboration throughout the *Periphyseon*. In keeping with the concept of circular motion, Eriugena conceives God as the center of a sphere through which the division of the whole universe originates. In that capacity God is the originary central point of all that is. He is the causal beginning of every existence, the essential middle that fulfills every existence, and the end in which every existence is consummated. At the same time God is beyond all that He creates, including nature, being, life, wisdom, power, and all that is perceived by any sense (III: 1). This notion Eriugena envisions in geometrical terms ("*geometricis rationibus*") as a wheel with a central hub from which emanate spokes moving through progressively widening interstices toward a circumference. At the hub of the wheel the spokes are so closely united that they cannot be distinguished from one another, "but as they extend further from the centre the spaces between them begin gradually to widen until they reach the circle which bounds them."

This circle with its center and emanating lines is for Eriugena a perfect representation of the divine.[6] As such, it defies all attempts at precise measurement. "Suppose," observes Eriugena, "you want to discover the number of the intervals and lines and reduce them to some order. Are you able in any specific way to discover some specific interval or line from which, be it interval or line, the natural or proper beginning may be made?" Because of the infinite multiplicity of lines and intervals, the answer is no. So it is in the contemplation of primordial causes. There will be

6. The conception anticipates the definition of God as a sphere whose center is everywhere and whose circumference is nowhere. See George Poulet, *The Metamorphoses of the Circle*, trans. Carley Dawson and Elliott Coleman (Baltimore: Johns Hopkins Press, 1966), esp. pp. 1–10.

as many laws devised for the measurement of these causes as there are theologians to contemplate them. The "modes of divine science" multiply with the number of those who set about to grasp the full nature of this constantly revolving figure. In the realization of the true measurement of primordial causes, "only the gnostic power of their Creator can number, distinguish, multiply, set in order, and divide them" (III:1).

In his account of this divine figure Eriugena is particularly concerned with the nature of its motion. A figure that is constantly in circular motion ("*circularis motus*"), it is without beginning and holds the primacy over all other motions, such as straight and oblique. Moving itself within itself ("*intra se ipsum se ipsum mouet*"), this figure is one in which its very self-generating mobility is an expression of its immutability. So Eriugena observes that "when it moves, it is at rest, and when it is at rest it moves." As the source of all other causes (and therefore all other motions), it both moves within itself and is unmoved. For the motion of the supreme Goodness, "which in Itself is immutable, and the multiplication of Its simplicity, and Its unexhausted diffusion from Itself in Itself back to Itself, is the cause of all things, indeed *is* all things." Knowing all and embodying all, it is that "gnostic power" ("*gnostica uirtus*") which "knows all things before they are, and does not know all things outside Itself because outside It there is nothing, but It possesses all things within Itself." As such, it encircles all things, and there is nothing within It that is not Itself (III:1, 4).

Such is Eriugena's conception of God. It is one that devises a science of the visionary to conceptualize the unknowable. Embodying an essential dynamism, that science reformulates the immutable through a physics of motion that reflects an understanding of the divine as that which sees and that which moves. In both respects its visionary status is constantly redefining itself, constantly giving rise to renewed speculations concerning the nature of its own meanings. Those meanings are at once fixed and in a constant state of change, as Eriugena's treatment embraces that multiplicity of perspectives involved in the attempt to understand that which defies comprehension.

Complementing Eriugena's conception of God is his view of the experience undergone by those who would behold God. Addressing that experience, he speaks of the difficulty of advancing along "the highest ascents of contemplation." Such ascents involve great risk, especially for those who enter upon them without the aid of a "purer mind." These contemplatives "either stray and lose their way, or when they can go no higher, fall back to the lower levels." Despite the dangers of such an enterprise, those who have attained to purity are at least in the enviable position of being able to undertake that ascent with the promise of some success. "Those who are most perfect and are enlightened by the splendours of the divine radiance" are thus transported "to the most sacred shrines of the celestial mysteries [*ad sacratissima caelestium myster-iorum adyta*]." They ascend the "steps of divine contemplation and behold without any error the form and truth without any cloud obscuring it." Although the shrines toward which the contempla-tives strive are ultimately set beyond all powers of penetration, the true mystics are nonetheless exhorted to ascend the steps ("*gradus*") to the full extent of their powers (III:1).[7]

Doing so, they undergo a process of deification by which the divine nature reaches downward in an act of condescension and human nature strives upward in an act of exaltation. In this su-preme moment of reciprocity and love, God reveals Himself to the contemplative in His profound glory. This revelation assumes the form of a "theophany" by which God in His Son and Spirit embodies Himself in a manner that is conformable to the limits of the purified understanding of the contemplative. Condescend-ing Himself in this theophanic manner, God causes the contem-plative to undergo a transformation through which the human participates in the divine.

Such an experience of deification Eriugena terms a "theosis," a transfigurational event tantamount to the assumption of a new personality. The contemplative is no longer what he had been before the ascent was begun (I:9). Like Paul, he is rapt to the third heaven, there to participate in the divine life of God (II:23, 26). Assuming a new identity, he is transfigured by the theophany of God's holocaustal presence. So Eriugena observes that "the Father is light, fire and heat; the Son is light, fire and heat; and the Holy Spirit is light, fire and heat." As such, they not only enlighten the contemplative with knowledge and wisdom but con-

---

7. It is perhaps significant that Eriugena refers to the steps specifically as what he calls "*bimata*" ("*atissima diuinae theoriae bimata, hoc est gradus*"), a term that suggests the concept of the *bima* (stage or platform) in Judaic lore. Eriugena appears to express both an interest in and a knowledge of this lore at various points in the *Periphyseon*. In his discussion of the term "Cherubim" in the *Periphyseon*, for example, he refers specifically to "those who are learned in Hebrew lore" (III:9).

sume him as well: "The Father burns, the Son burns, the Holy Spirit burns, because They consume our sins together and by *theosis*, i.e., 'deification' [*deificationem*], They convert us, as though we were a holocaust, into Their Unity." We, in turn, are fostered and nourished by their "surging tide of love," so that, "as though from the deformity of our imperfection after the fall of the first man, They bring us up to be the perfect man, and train us for the fullness of Christ's time." In Christ as the perfect man all things are fulfilled, and the fullness of his time is "the fulfillment of the universal salvation of the Church, which is composed of angels and men" (IV:1).

Theosis, then, functions on both the personal and the transpersonal levels. On the personal level it represents a return of the individual soul to its beginnings, to its pristine, prelapsarian state. This return is an ecstatic experience that can be viewed only as a dying into life. In that dying, the contemplative crosses over into God Himself and rises above all that is endowed with being (V:7–8). At the same time it is an experience that anticipates a final conflagration when all those who are saved will undergo an ultimate theosis. This dimension of the idea is one that historicizes the experience and bestows upon it an apocalyptic bearing. In either case it is this sense of return that is all important. Whether on the personal or on the transpersonal level, theosis implies a return.

For Eriugena the concept of return assumes both a paradisal and a sacerdotal significance. So Eriugena maintains that in the experience of theosis, the contemplative is able to reenter paradise, there to penetrate to the very center of the garden. By the designation of the center or middle is implied "the most secret and the inmost retreats of that nature, in which the image and likeness of God has been expressed." There, Eriugena declares, "the tree of life, our Lord Jesus Christ, has been planted." Among those able to return to paradise, "none but the purest in faith and action, the most enlightened in knowledge, the most perfect in wisdom and understanding of the divine mysteries [*perfectissimus sapientia et divinorum mysteriorum intelligentia*]" is allowed to enjoy the contemplation of its innermost recesses embodied in the tree of life at its center. "To this tree, removed from all and granted only to the deified, Paul was carried away into the third heaven." Like Paul, we are exhorted to enter into this paradise.

The paradisal dimension, in turn, is complemented by a sac-

erdotal counterpart. "In my opinion," Eriugena avers, "this interpretation has been prefigured in the mystic construction of Solomon's temple [*mystica Salomonis templi aedificatione praefiguratum
est*]" (cf. Ezekiel 40–48). All the nations of the world were permitted to enter into the outermost regions of the temple, "but
only the priests and the Levites entered the portico of the priests
and Solomon's portico." Beyond that, the priests, cleansed in the
brazen sea in Solomon's portico, were permitted into the outer
sanctuary with its loaves of offering and its candelabra. None but
the high priest, however, was permitted to go beyond the veil into
the Holy of Holies, where was to be found the ark of the covenant,
the altar of incense, the place of atonement, and two cherubim.
"From this prefiguration we may understand that all men within
the bounds of the natural paradise, as though within a temple,
are kept in their order; but that only those sanctified in Christ
will enter the inner part." Furthermore, "those who are in the
High Priest, Christ, and are one with Him and have been made
in Him will be introduced into the Holy of Holies, as into the
inmost of the inmost places" (cf. Hebrews 9). For Christ himself
is the ark in which all the treasures of wisdom and knowledge are
hidden. Under his auspices the angelic orders that surround him
pay him homage and do his bidding. To approach him is to penetrate into the Holy of Holies within that secret temple, "the house
of the Lord built on the mountain of supernal contemplation."
To that realm all men are encouraged to ascend "by the steps of
virtues and the heights of speculation" (V:36).

Contextualizing the experience of theosis in this manner, Eriugena provides his own reading of the nature of the divine world.
It is a world in which the angelic orders themselves are the prime
representatives of the contemplative process. Appropriating the
throne vision in Isaiah 6 for the purpose of dramatizing this idea,
Eriugena speaks of "those mystical living creatures [*mystica illa
animalia*]" that "veiled with their wings both their faces and their
feet," fearing to look upon that which is above every created nature, that is, the height and depth of the Divine Power. These
living creatures "do not cease to fly aloft; for lifted up by divine
grace and by the subtlety of their nature they ever look, in so far
as they are able, for the things which are above them, pursuing
their search to infinity." Their desire to behold as much of divinity
as they possibly can, however, is chastened by an awareness that
even they are limited in their powers of perception. Accordingly,

"at the point where they fail they reverently shield their faces, that is to say, the thrust of their contemplation, beaten back by the divine radiance, and withdraw their scriptural feet [*theologicos pedes*], that is, their intellectual advances, from entering upon the incomprehensible mysteries, lest they should incautiously or rashly commit some act of presumption against what is ineffable and passes all understanding." For Eriugena this behavior on the part of the seraphim as divine symbols (*symbola*) should be interpreted as an object lesson in the attempt to behold the divine, for if such exalted figures are aware of the impropriety of extending themselves too far, we as limited beings should be particularly chastened (III:16).

Despite all the admonitory force that such an example from the divine world might possess, the contemplative in Eriugena's thought presses forward in pursuit of an ultimate theosis as God condescends to his level and he ascends to the level of the divine. In that reciprocal movement the contemplative undergoes a transformation tantamount to a deification as he not only beholds the divine world in the Holy of Holies but becomes himself divine in what amounts to an ultimate apocalyptic deification at the end of time. In this manner he participates in the return of the divine to its ultimate source, to its central point, from which all theophanies proceed. So exalted a view of man and of the mystical process itself is a distinguishing characteristic of Eriugena's outlook.

It is precisely this view, in fact, that underlies Eriugena's *Expositiones in Ierarchiam Coelestem* (ca. 865–870).[8] There, he reconceives the entire contemplative process through an analysis of the angelic figures portrayed in Isaiah 6, on the one hand, and Ezekiel 1, on the other. Recalling his discussion of the seraphim of Isaiah in the *Periphyseon*, Eriugena once again conceives them as figures of contemplation through whose eyes the secrets of the celestial world are beheld. The seraphim reflect the capacity, as well as the burning desire, of the intellect to perceive the divine world in all its splendor. Swift of movement, they are possessed of an alacrity that transports them to the highest realms. It is both with this mobility and this ardent zeal that they inspire and sanctify the

---

8. References are to *Iohannis Scoti Eriugenae Expositiones in Ierarchiam Coelestem*, ed. J. Barbet, in the *Corpus Christianorum Continuatio Mediaevalis* (Turnholt: Brepols, 1975), vol. XXXI.

prophet, who correspondingly seeks a way of beholding God
(XV.i.1–159). That figure, in turn, Eriugena delineates in accord
not only with the enthroned being in Isaiah 6 but with the regal
presence in Daniel 7. Here, Eriugena emphasizes in particular the
"*rotas igneas*" of this presence, whose fiery-wheeled throne reinforces both the sense of mobility ("*mobilis*") that Eriugena sees in
the seraphim and the burning ("*ardentes*") quality of their longing.
In both respects the qualities that Eriugena sees in the seraphim
and the fiery-wheeled throne constitute what he calls the "theosophical science" ("*scientes theosophi*") of his pursuit. By means of
this science one is able to understand the inner workings of the
divine world with its "*deiform*" creatures and its Enthroned Figure
(XV.ii.160–291; cf. vi.650–669).

Drawing upon the profound learning that theosophical science
embraces, Eriugena examines all aspects of this world. As Eriugena makes clear, because of the "creature-like" quality of the
angelic forms themselves, it is a world that includes both the fiery
essences of the celestial realm and the bodily characteristics associated with the creaturely world of the "*humaniform*." From the
perspective of the "humaniform," Eriugena explores the meanings not only of the five senses but of the bodily parts, attributing
to each one a mystical or theosophical significance. This suggests
how the "humaniform" leads to the "deiform" in the transfigurational process by which the realm of the human moves in contemplation to the realm of the divine ("AD DIVINA ET MYSTICA
SPECVLAMINA DVCTIVVM") (XV.iii.293–iv.529).

The "deiform"-"humaniform" distinction, in turn, moves Eriugena from the visionary world of Isaiah 6 to the visionary world
of Ezekiel 1. There, the fourfold creatures of Ezekiel afford Eriugena the opportunity to discourse on the allegorical significance
of each. As a prime member of God's retinue, the lion signifies
the strength, indomitableness, and the ineffableness of God. It is
a symbol of the secret power that envelops divinity as it manifests
itself in all its glory to those who would contemplate its hidden
nature. An animal of the plow, the ox, in turn, embodies the
qualities of robustness and endurance, as well as the willingness
to undertake difficult tasks on God's behalf. It is a guardian of
divine power and strength. The eagle is a symbol of divine royalty.
As the bird of God, it has the agility to fly to the heavenly realms.
Distinguished by the highest powers of contemplation, it reflects
the longing of the individual to become part of the divine radiance

that emanates from divinity. Beholding that radiance, it is the very symbol of the contemplative spirit. As aspects of the "humaniform" dimension of the visionary world of Ezekiel, these creatures find expression in the figure of the man, in whom is embodied both the lower and the higher qualities (concupiscible, irrational, intellectual, and spiritual) that are transmuted by divine love in the ascent of the individual to the highest realms (XV.viii.777–944).

The "deiform"-"humaniform" distinction that underlies Eriugena's treatment of the fourfold creatures culminates in his discussion of the divine chariot ("*currus*") so crucial to the visionary world of Ezekiel. For Eriugena all that has been said in the *Periphyseon* about the visionary dynamism that infuses the concept of deity is embodied in the *currus* as divine vehicle. Reflecting the dual notions of *currens* as running and *videns* as seeing, Eriugena's chariot is a *merkabah* in which the force and vitality of circular motion returning to a central beginning point and the transforming power of beholding are realized. Accompanied by its angelic societies, this is a chariot of supercelestial mobility and grandeur.

In his account of the chariot Eriugena emphasizes its fiery nature and its ability to transfigure all that encounter it. The force of the chariot is centered in its wheels ("*rotae*"), which revolve endlessly and in their revolutions reenact the process of contemplation by which the seer desires to become part of the celestial realms. Like wheels within wheels, these realms turn ceaselessly within themselves. The manifestation of the most secret dimensions of godhead, this is the revelation of revelations, that which defies all power of knowing. Such is the significance of the *rotae*, which Eriugena, in keeping with the original vision, makes a point of distinguishing as *galgalim* ("*gal gal*"), to suggest the specifically Hebraic foundations of their conception.[9] Encircled by the *galgalim*, God is conceived anagogically as the most profound of all mysteries. In the presence of these mysteries we are to remain silent as an expression of our reverence and as an indication of our inability to fathom their full meaning (XV.ix.945–1085).

As a science of the visionary, then, Eriugena's system of thought draws upon earlier traditions of the chariot and reformulates them

---

9. Although Eriugena resorts here to Greek sources such as Epiphanius and the Pseudo-Dionysius in his discussion of the *galgalim* (XV.ix.979–995), his interest in the original formulations is significant.

in its own terms. In Eriugena, as in his forebears, the *merkabah*
assumes a position of paramount importance as a "vehicle" in
which the multiple complexities of the visionary mode are articulated. The *merkabah* focuses those complexities and endows them
with a concrete form. Whether conceived in terms of Ezekiel's
throne-chariot or as the systemization of causal relationships in
the theophanic procession of deity, the visionary experience in
Eriugena is at the forefront in the attempt to understand the
nature of the divine. Such is as applicable to the *Periphyseon* as it
is to the *Expositiones in Ierarchiam Coelestem*. In these works, as in
Eriugena's other writings, one encounters a mind sensitive to the
manifold implications of the *visio Dei*. If this is true of Eriugena,
it is no less true of later commentators who bestowed their own
interpretation upon the experience of the visionary.

II

We begin with an examination of the mystical theology that
underlies the writings of the Cistercians and the Victorines in the
twelfth century, the great age of spiritual renewal. Whatever the
possible impact of Eriugena upon these figures, they proved to
be of essential importance in the transmission of the visionary
mode as a crucial phenomenon during the later Middle Ages.[10]
Like Eriugena, they were responsive to the kinds of issues through
which the visionary assumed its unique character and shape
among the twelfth-century monastics. Synthesizing the concerns
made evident in the Latin fathers, on the one hand, and the Greek
fathers, on the other, they forged their own visionary systems.
Integral to those systems was that deification implicit in theosis as
a transformative event. Manifesting itself in speculations on the
nature of divinity or in accounts of spiritual transport, this event
distinguished the outlook of those in whom the visionary mode
flourished anew. Such were the Cistercians and the Victorines.[11]

10. In addition to the references cited earlier regarding Eriugena's possible influence,
see the comments of Etienne Gilson in *The Mystical Theology of Saint Bernard*, trans. A. H.
C. Downes (London: Sheed and Ward, 1940), pp. 25–27, and in *History of Christian Philosophy in the Middle Ages* (New York: Random House, 1955), p. 164.

11. Deriving its name from its first house at Cîteaux, the Cistercian Order was founded
in 1098 by a group of monks under the leadership of Robert of Molesmes. Its avowed
intention was to follow the *Rule of Saint Benedict* more closely than had been the practice
in previous monasteries. The rapid expansion of the Cistercians came only after Bernard

As the major spokesman for the Cistercian point of view, Saint Bernard of Clairvaux (1090–1153) provides ample evidence of the visionary sensibility among the monastics.[12] His *De considera-tione ad Eugenium papam tertiam libri quinque* (1149–1153), addressed to Pope Eugenius III, is particularly apposite.[13] Divided into five sections or books, the work considers the issue of leadership, so germane to the papal office in general and to his fellow Cistercians in particular. Whereas each of the first four books treats a major aspect of papal office and policy, the fifth (by far the longest) considers the theological problem of knowing God and contemplates the nature of the celestial hierarchy. Four books of practical consideration, then, are balanced by one book of theological speculation.[14]

Given the paradigm that Bernard adopts, there is a certain

---

and his companions became monks there in 1112. Two years later Bernard was sent as abbot to the new foundation at Clairvaux. More than five hundred Cistercian abbeys had been founded by the end of the twelfth century. Distinct from the monastic order represented by the Cistercians, the Victorines constituted a group of regular canons (deacons and priests) that lived in a religious community governed by its own ecclesiastical rules, especially that emphasizing poverty. Communities of regular canons first made their appearance in Italy and southern France during the mid-eleventh century, after which they spread rapidly throughout Europe. The twelfth century marks the high point of their development. Among the important foundations of regular canons were those at Pré-montré (near Laon), Arrouaise, Saint Ruf (at Avignon), and Saint Victor (at Paris). See the entries on Cistercian Spirituality and the Victorines in *A Dictionary of Christian Spirit-uality*, ed. Gordon S. Wakefield (London: SCM Press, 1983), pp. 88–89, 386–387; and *Christian Spirituality: Origins to the Twelfth Century*, ed. Bernard McGinn and John Meyendorff (New York: Crossroad, 1985), pp. 205–220. For a study of the impact of the visionary experience on the pivotal twelfth-century period, see Peter Dinzelbacher, *Vision und Visions literatur im Mittelalter* (Stuttgart: Hiersemann, 1981).

12. A prolific writer, Bernard wrote numerous works. During an eighteen-year period ending in his death, he produced some eighty-six sermons on the Song of Songs. Among his other homilies, he also wrote a series of sermons on the liturgical year. His earliest work is his treatise *The Steps of Humility and Pride* (ca. 1124), in effect, a commentary on Benedict's *Rule*. He likewise produced a treatise on the mystical life (*On Loving God*); a dogmatic work (*On Grace and Free Choice*); a work written to the Templars (*In Praise of the New Knighthood*); and a work (*On Consideration*) addressed to Bernard Paganelli, who became pope (Eugenius III) in 1145.

13. References are to the *Five Books on Consideration*, trans. John D. Anderson and Elizabeth T. Kennan, Cistercian Fathers Series: Number 37, in *The Works of Bernard of Clairvaux* (Kalamazoo: Cistercian Publications, 1971–1980). This edition is used in conjunction with the *Sancti Bernardi Opera Omnia*, ed. J. Leclercq et al., 8 vols. (Rome: Editiones Cistercienses, 1957–1977).

14. Within this context, Saint Bernard distinguishes between *consideration* and *contem-plation* by maintaining that, although both terms are often used interchangeably, the first more nearly concerns "thought searching for truth, or the searching of the mind to discover truth," whereas the second reflects "the true and sure intuition of the mind" in the apprehension of "a truth that is known without doubt" (II.ii.5).

inevitability in this movement from the practical to the speculative. Proceeding from a consideration of the papacy in general in the first book, the next four books posit a quadripartite division that treats the pope himself (second book), those below the pope (book three), those around the pope (book four), and those above the pope (book five), that is, *te, sub te, circa te*, and *supra te*. It is the fifth book (*supra te*) that engages us here.[15] In its various forms this quaternary point of view underlies Saint Bernard's thought. The fifth book (*supra te*) of the *De consideratione* is the culminating moment of that point of view.

In the fifth book Bernard addresses himself to the celestial mysteries and the means of ascertaining them. As such, the fifth book is a self-contained discourse on the nature of the visionary, how it is experienced, and what it involves. Its point of focus is the Pauline transport to the celestial spheres and the nature of the ecstasy experienced by Paul as he was caught up to the third heaven (2 Cor. 12:2). Emulating Paul, we, too, shall experience such ecstasies in a return to our homeland from our exile in the lower world. Fellow citizens in the visionary realms, we shall behold the Word as the source of potency and generation. In that moment of beholding we shall have access to the mysteries (V.i.2–3). The fifth book provides the occasion, then, through which the political and social contexts of the earlier books are counterbalanced by the visionary. Here, the practical and investigative dimensions of *te, sub te*, and *circa te* find their counterpart in the quadripartite outlook reflected in *supra te*. As that toward which all consideration moves in its quest to know the ultimate truth, this is a dimension that has always been known and is now reexperienced in speculative form as the contemplative returns in true citizenry to his original homeland.[16] From this vantage point Saint Bernard investigates such matters as the angelic orders and the essence and dimensions of godhead.

Addressing himself to the angelic orders, for example, he en-

15. Although certainly different in outlook and scope from the talmudic perspectives discussed elsewhere in this study, the fourfold spatial structuring of speculation in Saint Bernard brings to mind that which is customarily associated with the *merkabah*, especially as a manifestation of "what is above, what is beneath, what before, what after." The reference, we recall, is to the *Ḥagigah* 2:1.

16. The sense of return to one's homeland involved in Saint Bernard's idea of speculation as that which "recollects itself" has, to be sure, an Augustinean quality about it. Among Augustine's discourses on the subject, see in particular his treatment of memory in the *Confessions* (e.g., X.1–25) and *On the Trinity* (XIV.3–17).

gages in his own speculations on "the Celestial Hierarchy." Conceiving the angels as distinct entities arranged in order of dignity according to rank and dedicated to the praise and service of God, he designates them from lowest to highest as angels, archangels, virtues, powers, principalities, dominions, thrones, cherubim, and seraphim. To each of these he assigns a role and a purpose in accord with its nature. Doing so, he moves from the lowest to the highest ranks as he himself ascends from the angels to the seraphim. In this voyage of ascent he penetrates through a progressive order of increasing illumination into what he calls "the divine mysteries." Like the angelic orders, he becomes a "confidant" of the hidden realms that he discloses. In his ascension toward the Seated Figure on the throne he extols the Lord of Sabbaoth as a deity of utmost tranquility and serenity, as the fulfillment of that desire for peace which surpasses all understanding (Phil. 4:7).

Surrounding Him are the cherubim that "drink from the very font of wisdom, the mouth of the Most High, and pour forth a stream of knowledge to all the citizens of heaven" (Ecclus. 24:5). Above them, in turn, are the seraphim, "spirits totally enkindled with divine fire." In this state of bliss the seraphim enkindle the other citizens with their own fires that burn with love and shine with knowledge. In this ecstatic state of supreme devotion Saint Bernard addresses his fellow traveler, Eugenius, in the words of Peter at the Transfiguration: "How good it is for us to be here" (V.iv.7–9; see Matt. 17:4). The transfigurational context of Saint Bernard's discourse suggests in what manner his meditation on the celestial hierarchies is to be conceived as his own personal experience of contemplative ascent, of what Eriugena would call "theosis" in the presence of the profound theophanies of God.[17]

Undergoing that theosis, Saint Bernard embarks upon a discourse concerning the essence and nature of God (V.xiii.27–32). In its own way this discourse provides a reading of the divine mysteries reminiscent of the kinds of concerns already familiar to the traditions of the visionary mode. Taking his cue from Eph. 3:18 ("You may be able to comprehend, with all the saints, what is the breadth, and length, and height, and depth"), he begins his final portion of the fifth book with the telling question: "What is God?" by which he means "the length, the width, the height and

---

17. Among Saint Bernard's other writings, see also his *On Loving God* (*De Diligendo Deo*) (IV.12), which speaks of seeing God face to face.

the depth." Recalling the anthropomorphic impulse in the mystical traditions to measure the divine body, this concern with the
dimensions of God assumes its own bearing in Bernard's thinking.

Thus length, breadth, height, and depth, he allegorizes as follows: length implies the eternity of God, breadth the charity of
God, height the majesty of God, depth the wisdom of God. All
four dimensions are of equal proportion: they represent that *divina quaternitas* so fundamental to the visionary experience we have
been exploring. Corresponding to this quaternary view of divinity
is that which associates length, breadth, height, and depth with
four modes of contemplation: meditation on the promises of God
(length), remembrance of the blessings of God (breadth), speculation on the majesty of God (height), and examination of the
judgments of God (depth). Such, in effect, is Saint Bernard's anatomization of the dimensions of God and the modes of perception associated with the attempt to determine those dimensions.
In both respects the quaternity as a category of vision underlies
Saint Bernard's delineation of the *supra te*, a fact that aligns him
with those for whom deity invites anatomization (albeit of a decidedly allegorical sort) from a quaternary point of view.

Having ventured such an anatomization, however, Saint Bernard declares at the outset his ambivalence regarding it. God is
essential unity and cannot be anatomized. To engage in anatomization is to undermine the notion of essential unity. Declaring
such a practice anathema to him, Saint Bernard nonetheless defends it by averring that, although "there are various names, many
paths [*voces diversae, semitae multae*]," they all lead to a unity: "one
thing is signified by the names, one is sought by the paths." Such
is Saint Bernard's formulation of the mysteries. Accordingly, in
the adoption of anatomization he maintains that he does not intend division of substance, nor bodily dimension, nor distinction
of person, nor number of properties. Rather, he implies our inability to deal with the simplicity of God in any other terms than
those we know.

As we strive to comprehend Him in His simplicity and oneness,
"he appears to us as fourfold [*quadruplicatum*]." This is because
we view Him through a glass darkly (1 Cor. 13:12). When we
behold Him face to face we shall see Him as He is (1 John 3:2).
"At that time the fragile gaze of our souls, however assiduously
applied, will in no way return or break down into its own multiplicity. It will draw more together, unite, and conform itself to

God's unity, or rather to God who is unity, so one will answer the other face to face." At the very point that Saint Bernard disavows the sense of multiplicity that the quaternary approach implies, then, he endorses the notion that God manifests Himself to our vision as fourfold. Considering the quadripartite nature of the treatise as a whole (*te, sub te, circa te,* and *supra te*), the quaternary basis of the argument at this point is most appropriate. As we have seen repeatedly in our discussions of the visionary mode, the quaternary as a category is crucial to an understanding of the traditions associated with the *visio Dei.*

To reinforce the adoption of such an approach, Saint Bernard invokes precisely the trope that has assumed archetypal status in the quest to achieve full comprehension of the divine. The trope in question is that of the chariot, which in Bernard, comes to symbolize the idea of the journey from the realm of multiplicity to the realm of oneness:

> And because the search is yet going on, let us climb into the four-horse chariot [*ascendamus quadrigam istam*], since we are still weak and feeble and we need such a vehicle [*vehiculo*], if even in this way we can apprehend him by whom we are apprehended [Phil. 3:12], for he is the reason for this vehicle [*vehiculi rationem*]. Now, we have this instruction from the charioteer [*auriga*] and him who first showed us this chariot [*currus*], that we should strive "to comprehend with all the saints what is the length, the width, the height, and the depth [*longitudo, latitudo, sublimitas et profundum*]." (V.xiii.27)[18]

Whatever the precise source of the chariot in question, it is clear that Saint Bernard has established his own context for the ascent to the divine and the achievement of unmediated vision of the absolute. It is a context in which not only the concept of the quaternity but that of the chariot is of central importance. In effect, Saint Bernard conceives of the contemplative as a chariot rider, a *yored merkabah* of sorts, who embarks upon his vehicle to

---

18. In his treatise *The Steps of Humility and Pride* (*The Works*, Cistercian Fathers Series: Number 13), which summarizes his teaching concerning the *Rule* of Saint Benedict, Saint Bernard addresses himself to the question of ascent to the celestial spheres. His observation is interesting in light of the chariot trope at issue here: "Paul was rapt up, Elijah likewise, Enoch was transported. But our Redeemer, as we read, rose by his own power, receiving no help. He was carried by no chariot, assisted by no angel, but through his own power alone, 'A cloud received him from their sight' [Acts 1:9]" (VIII.23).

the celestial realms. In the ascent that such a journey implies, the seer attempts to seek full reciprocity with the seen, to behold as he is beheld in face-to-face union with that which transcends all multiplicity. Such for Saint Bernard is the ultimate vision toward which his treatise moves in its apprehension of the *supra te.*

If that idea is germane to the *De consideratione*, it is no less so to Saint Bernard's other works. The sermons that appear under the heading *Sermones super Cantica Canticorum* (1138–1153) are a case in point.[19] Consistent with earlier commentators on the Song of Songs, Saint Bernard establishes at the outset that this "nuptial song" is so profound that it is not to be studied by novices or the immature. Invoking this commonplace, Saint Bernard associates himself with those in the mystical traditions for whom the Song of Songs was looked upon in conjunction with the Book of Ezekiel as the most holy of texts in its revelation of godhead. Customarily viewed as a *merkabah* text in its own right, the Song of Songs, as we have seen in earlier discussions, represented for both commentators and mystics a means of gaining access to the divine world.[20] Like the Book of Ezekiel, the Song of Songs was therefore designated a text to be interpreted not just as a reflection of advancement in years but as an indication of purity of conduct.

This ethical imperative is reinforced by the nuptial dimension in which the work as a whole is conceived. "Only a mind disciplined by persevering study, only the man whose efforts have borne fruit under God's inspiration, the man whose years, as it were, make him ripe for marriage—years measured out not in time but in merits—only he is truly prepared for nuptial union with the divine partner" (I.vi.12). The uniting of the soul with God, the Bride with the Bridegroom, for Saint Bernard is the underlying theme of the Song of Songs. As might be expected, he interprets that theme in visionary terms as the ascent of the seer to the celestial realms, there to engage in mystical union with deity. Correspondingly known in the traditions of Jewish mysticism and *kabbalah* as *debekut* or "cleaving to God," Saint Bernard's portrayal of the *unio mystica* assumes a bearing very much in keeping with his delineation of the visionary mode.[21]

19. References by sermon and section number are to the sermons *On the Song of Songs,* trans. Kilian Walsh et al., *The Works,* Cistercian Fathers Series: Numbers 4, 7, 31, and 40.
20. See Chapters 3 and 4 for discussions of the *Ḥagigah* (esp. 13a–14a), Eleazar of Worms, and the *Shiʿur Komah.* In patristic commentary, see the references in Origen and Jerome.
21. An enlightening discussion of the various aspects of *debekut,* as well as the various

That delineation emphasizes in particular the bodily and indeed sexual dimensions of the experience as a counterpart to the spiritual. Focusing upon the first verse of the Song of Songs ("Let him kiss me with the kiss of his mouth"), for example, Saint Bernard devotes a series of sermons (notably, the second through the eighth) to the concept of the divine kiss.[22] In these sermons he admonishes the seer to progress to a knowledge of God and finally a union with God in three stages. The first stage involves conversion as the result of repentance; the second, perseverance subsequent to conversion; and the third, perfection as the fruit of perseverance. These stages assume the form of three kisses, that of God's feet, that of God's hand, and that of God's mouth, respectively. In repentance, we cast ourselves at God's feet; in perseverance, we reach out for the hand that will lift us up and steady our trembling knees; in perfection, we raise our eyes to God's mouth, not merely to gaze upon it but to receive its kiss (III.iii.5).

It is particularly with the third stage, embodied in the kiss of the mouth, that the Song of Songs is concerned and that Saint Bernard proposes to comment upon in detail (IV.i.1). For our purposes the commentary is particularly important, first because of its interest in the so-called bodily members of God and second because of its emphasis upon the sexual implications of mystical union. From the first point of view Saint Bernard rearticulates the assumptions regarding God's body made evident in the *De consideratione*. As in his tract, he at once attests to the spirituality of God while adopting the tropes of divine bodily parts (especially, the feet, hands, and mouth of God) in order to drive home the point that union with deity is tantamount to an embrace of the most profound sort, one that is understandable through the immediacy and indeed intimacy associated with the bodily members

---

dimensions of *unio mystica* in Jewish mystical thought, may be found in Moshe Idel, *Kabbalah: New Perspectives* (New Haven: Yale University Press, 1988), pp. 35–111. In his *Mystical Experience in Abraham Abulafia* (Albany: State University of New York Press, 1988), passim, Idel demonstrates the intensely erotic and sexual dimensions that *debekut* assumes in ecstatic kabbalah. As Halperin has demonstrated, something of this idea is already present in the *hekhalot* literature. Thus, the *Hekhalot Rabbati* reveals how the *ḥayyot* themselves undergo a kind of *debekut*, as they "hug and kiss" the Enthroned Figure (David J. Halperin, *The Faces of the Chariot: Early Jewish Responses to Ezekiel's Vision* [Tübingen: J. C. B. Mohr, 1988], p. 394).

22. For the definitive study of the subject in its broader cultural contexts, see Nicolas James Perella, *The Kiss, Sacred and Profane: An Interpretive History of Kiss Symbolism and Related Religio-Erotic Themes* (Berkeley: University of California Press, 1969).

(IV.iii.4). The anthropomorphisms implicit in such a view extend to corresponding aspects of his analysis.

A case in point is the eighth sermon, which addresses itself to "The Kiss of the Mouth [*Osculum Oris Dei*]." According to Saint Bernard, this supreme kiss is the most profound form that the union can assume. Because of its sacrosanct nature, however, it is an experience toward which the seer strives but one which he never experiences in full. In fact, no creature, either angelic or divine, is permitted to fulfill his desire to kiss the mouth of God. Only the Son of God is able to enjoy this kiss fully in a complete embrace. "Thus the Father, when he kisses the Son, pours into him the plenitude of the mysteries of his divine being, breathing forth love's deep delight." The closest that a mere creature can come to such an experience is reflected in the figure of Saint Paul. Although Paul was certainly a great man, "no matter how high he should aim in making the offer of his mouth, even if he were to raise himself right into the third heaven, he would still of necessity find himself remote from the lips of the Most High." Abiding content within the limits of his capacity, he must ask that the unreachable divine countenance lean down to him, so that the kiss might be transmitted from on high. Unlike the Son of God, who is given the kiss of the mouth, as "mouth is joined to mouth," Paul is given "the kiss of the kiss [*osculum de osculo recipit*]." "For Christ therefore, the kiss meant a totality, for Paul only a participation; Christ rejoiced in the kiss of the mouth, Paul only in that he was kissed by the kiss [*Christo igitur osculum est plenitudo, Paulo participatio, ut cum ille de ore, iste tantum de osculo osculatum se glorietur*]" (VIII.i.1–vii.8).

For Saint Bernard, then, full union is qualified by the nature of the creature who desires to participate in it. A tension exists between lover and beloved, one that heightens the sense of fulfillment when the true embrace is finally and ultimately realized as an expression of the divine union between Father and Son. Such is the nature of *debekut* in Saint Bernard. As a delineator of the visionary mode, he was committed to a mystical theology founded upon the notion of an *amor Dei* of the most suggestive and, indeed, erotic sort.[23] In this respect he enunciated a spirit-

23. In fact, the sexual dimensions of this theology are not limited to the nuptial embrace of Bride and Bridegroom. Responsive to that portion of the opening verse of the Song of Songs that refers to the "breasts" that are "better than wine" (1:1), Saint Bernard does not hesitate to perform a kind of role-reversal, in which the masculinity of deity is feminized

uality of love as compelling as any that emerged during a period when this form of spirituality flourished on all fronts.

Such an outlook is discernible throughout Saint Bernard's sermons on the Song of Songs. One thinks in particular of his commentary on the third verse of the first chapter: "The king hath brought me into his storerooms [*cellaria*]." If the kiss of the mouth is Saint Bernard's version of *debekut*, then the storerooms of the king are his version of the *hekhalot*. It is to these *hekhalot* that the seer is drawn in his ascent to the king. In keeping with the Song of Songs itself, Saint Bernard conceives the rooms of the king as exuding a wonderful fragrance, one that reinforces the sensuous quality of the whole experience. These are, he observes, the "perfume-laden places within the Bridegroom's quarters, where varied spices breathe their scents [cf. Rev. 5:8], where delights are manifold." It is to these rooms that the bride runs, "drawn by the fragrance that issues from them." Aflame with love, she desires union with her lover.[24] "The door is promptly opened to her as to one of the family, one highly esteemed, loved with a special love, uniquely favored" (XXIII.i.1).

In his account of the rooms Saint Bernard categorizes them as three sorts. The first assumes the form of a garden, the second of a storeroom, and the third of a bedroom. Each of these, in turn, reflects a sense of Scripture and therefore an aspect of the interpretation of Scripture. The garden represents the plain, unadorned, historical sense of Scripture; the storeroom, the moral sense; and the bedroom, "the mystery of divine contemplation." Movement through these rooms in the mystical ascent is a movement through levels of interpretation from lowest to highest in what for Saint Bernard is a tripartite process (XXIII.ii.3). Corresponding to the threefold stages that the mystic undergoes in his quest for the divine kiss, such a process, in turn, assumes the form of what Bernard calls discipline, nature, and grace, the three qualities necessary to the mystic in the attainment of the mystery of contemplation consummated in the third kind of room, the

---

to accommodate the idea that God Himself has breasts, both of which are "proofs of his native kindness," that is, "his patience in awaiting the sinner" (symbolized by one breast) and "his welcoming mercy for the penitent" (symbolized by the other breast). The breasts of the groom, in turn, find their counterpart in the breasts of the bride (IX.iv.5–6).

24. In a similar vein, see also Saint Bernard's *On Loving God* (*De Diligendo Deo*) (XI.33), which conceives the embrace of Bride and Bridegroom as an experience of intoxication and delight that occurs during the wedding feast of the Lord (Rev. 19:9), consumed at his table in his kingdom (Luke 22:30).

bedroom of the Groom himself (XXIII.iii.6). As the most holy of rooms, this is the place of contemplation in which the King keeps residence. This room, Saint Bernard makes clear, is really not one room but several. Just as the King has more than one queen, He has more than one bedroom, in each of which the Bride has her secret rendezvous with the Bridegroom. In such a manner, "Thomas attained to this mystery of grace in the Savior's side [John 20:27], John on his breast [John 13:25], Peter in the Father's bosom [Matt. 16: 17], and Paul in the third heaven [2 Cor. 12:2]."

The analogies speak for themselves: the rooms are associated at once with parts of the divine body and with the act of ascent to the highest of heavens (associated with the head of the divine body). However these rooms are conceived, they are looked upon as the most remote and secret of places, where the Bride is at liberty "to explore her Bridegroom's secret charms [*et rimari dulcia secreta sponsi*]" (XXIII.iv. 9–11). Whatever form his theological outlook assumes, then, sexual innuendo underlies the overall conception, here, as elsewhere in Saint Bernard's deliberations. Fusing a multitude of associations in his account of the rooms of the King, Saint Bernard enacts his own journey through the *hekhalot*, a journey consistent with the complex dimensions of his mystical theology. Such is the basis of the Cistercian point of view that he represents. As one of the most able and important spokesmen among the Cistercians, Saint Bernard suggests how the visionary mode flourished during the later Middle Ages.

III

The outlook reflected in Saint Bernard of Clairvaux, in turn, finds its correspondence among the Victorines, especially in the writings of Hugh of Saint Victor (1096?–1142), on the one hand, and Richard of Saint Victor (?–1173), on the other. Between them, contemplation became an established discipline bequeathed to future generations of mystics. Systematizing contemplation, they contributed immeasurably to an understanding of the psychological as well as theological dimensions of the contemplative life. At the same time they reinforced the mystical experience through a renewed emphasis upon the practice of exegesis and theories of hermeneutics. For them, the nature of reading assumed paramount importance. As the basis of their systematic approach, each

adopted a symbolic structure through which to articulate a fully
conceived discourse on the nature of the visionary.[25] For Hugh
of Saint Victor, that symbolic structure is the ark of Noah; for
Richard of Saint Victor, the ark of the covenant. In both respects
we find a *lectio divina* or holy reading by which the contemplative
is able to achieve a *visio Dei* consistent with the multiple implications of the visionary mode.

In Hugh of Saint Victor the nature of the *lectio divina* may be
seen in the *Didascalicon* (ca. 1120), Hugh's illuminating introduction to philosophical study and biblical interpretation.[26] There,
Hugh articulates in detail the exegetical methodology through
which the reading of Scripture forms the basis of the contemplative ascent. For Hugh, the biblical text yields three levels of meaning, the historical, the allegorical, and the tropological (VI.2). The
historical level provides "the means through which to admire
God's deeds"; the allegorical, "the means through which to believe
his mysteries"; the tropological, "the means through which to im-
itate his perfection" (VI.3). For Hugh, the whole is conceivable
by means of the construction of a building: the historical is the
foundation of the building; the allegorical is the structure of the
building itself; and the tropological is the color that decorates the
building after the work is completed (VI.2–4). In his analysis of
the levels of meaning Hugh devotes most of his attention to the
historical and the allegorical. With each he associates specific books
of the Bible. With the historical he associates such Old Testament
texts as the historical parts of Genesis, Exodus, Joshua, and Kings,
and such New Testament texts as the Gospels and the Acts of the
Apostles (VI.3). With the allegorical he associates such Old Testament texts as the beginning of Genesis on the works of the six
days, the three last books of Moses on the mysteries of the law,

25. Grover A. Zinn, Jr., "Mandala Symbolism and Use in the Mysticism of Hugh of St.
Victor," *History of Religions* 12 (1973): 317–341, esp. p. 320. Other Victorines include figures
such as Adam of Saint Victor, Thomas Gallus, Achard of Saint Victor, Andrew of Saint
Victor, Godfrey of Saint Victor, and Walter of Saint Victor. For a discussion of the Victorines in general and Hugh, Richard, and Andrew in particular, see Beryl A. Smalley,
The Study of the Bible in the Middle Ages (Notre Dame: University of Notre Dame Press,
1964), pp. 83–195. For a consideration of the apocalyptic dimensions of the "arts of vision"
among not only the Victorines but later figures as well, see the important work of Barbara
Nolan, *The Gothic Visionary Perspective* (Princeton: Princeton University Press, 1977).

26. References by book and chapter are to *The Didascalicon, A Medieval Guide to the Arts*,
trans. Jerome Taylor (New York: Columbia University Press, 1961), in conjunction with
Charles Henry Buttimer, ed. *Hugonis de Sancto Victore Didascalicon de studio legendi: A Critical
Text* (Washington, D.C.: Catholic University of America Press, 1939).

Isaiah, the beginning and end of Ezekiel, and the Song of Songs, and such New Testament texts as the Epistles of Paul, the Canonical Epistles, and Revelation (VI.4).

Significant in this list, of course, are those texts that Hugh singles out for the allegorical level (the beginning of Genesis, the beginning and end of Ezekiel, the Song of Songs, and the like), for they are crucial, as we have seen to the traditions of the *merkabah*. Hugh is particularly sensitive to the role that Ezekiel's *visio Dei* plays in the formulation of the mysteries that constitute the allegorical level.[27] In fact, he sees in that *visio Dei* the energy and dynamism necessary to embark upon an ascent to the higher reaches of contemplation:

> In Ezechiel you read that the wheels [*rotae*] follow the living creatures, not the living creatures the wheels; it says: "When the living creatures went, the wheels also went together by them: and when the living creatures were lifted up from the earth, the wheels also were lifted up with them" [1:19]. So it is with the minds of holy men: the more they advance in virtues or in knowledge, the more they see that the hidden places of the Scriptures are profound [*sanctarum Scripturarum arcana profunda*], so that those places which to simple minds and minds still tied to earth seem worthless, to minds which have been raised aloft seem sublime. (VI.4)

In Hugh as in all those for whom the inaugural vision has assumed paramount importance as hermeneutical enterprise, Ezekiel's *visio Dei* becomes a central event in the act of reading. In order to read the biblical text correctly, one must, in a sense, "do" the Chariot, engage in the *ma'aseh merkabah*. Imbued with the spirit of the Chariot, the hermeneut advances morally and intellectually from one level of meaning to the next as the "hidden places of the Scriptures" are disclosed to him. Once again, the inaugural vision is appropriated as an interpretive trope in the act of reading. Such is the nature of Hugh's portrayal of the *lectio divina*.

It is this approach, in turn, that Hugh applies to his mystical writings, notably *De arca Noe morali* and *De arca Noe mystica* (ca.

---

27. According to Smalley, Hugh, among the other Victorines, was quite familiar with the Judaic traditions, attempted to learn Hebrew, and incorporated Hebrew words into his works (p. 103). The same is true of Richard and Andrew (Smalley, *Study of the Bible*, passim). As Smalley demonstrates, Andrew had a deep interest in the text of Ezekiel and explicated that text in detail (pp. 138–139, 143–199).

1125–1131).[28] Here, Hugh fulfills his role as *doctor ecstaticus*. In his discourses on the ark of Noah, Hugh adopts what is in effect a "psychocosmogram" for the nature of the divine.[29] That psychocosmogram is a symbolic structure or mandala through which the mystical life is realized. Depicted by Hugh in a drawing that no longer exists, the psychocosmogram contains two elements: a symbolic cosmos that surrounds the ark of Noah and a figure of Christ embracing the cosmos. Assuming the form of a truncated pyramid with an area one cubit square at the peak and a central column reaching from base to summit, the ark assumes the form of a mountain, a cosmic center that is at once a Sinai and a Zion (cf. *A. mys.*, VII). As such, the ark itself is conceived as if viewed from above. "The result is a series of nesting rectangles, three in number, one for each of the three stories of the ark, with a square in the center representing both the central column upon which the upper edges of the inward-sloping sides of the vessel rest, and the cubit at the apex of the ark." According to Hugh's interpretation of the ark, the cubit at the summit of the ark represents the "simple oneness, that true simplicity, and everlasting changelessness, that is in God" (*A. mor.*, IV.4). Reaching from the base to the summit, the column in the center of the ark symbolizes Christ the Incarnate Word (*A. mor.*, II.8). "The corners of the rectangles are connected by lines which extend from the base of the vessel to the summit. Along these lines twelve ladders are drawn, linking the three stories of the ark at each of the four corners." Each of the twelve ladders signifies a stage in the advancement of the mystic life, and each series of three ladders signifies one of the four stages (awakening, purgation, illumination, union) into which Hugh divides the contemplative quest (*A. myst.*, VII–X; *A. mor.*, II.9–10).[30]

The figure of Christ that embraces the cosmos, in turn, is described as "Christ seated in majesty" and is accompanied by two six-winged seraphim, in accord with Isaiah's temple vision (Isaiah

28. Texts in *PL*, CLXXVI, 617–680 and 681–704, respectively. Book and chapter references to the *De arca Noe morali* are to *Selected Spiritual Writings*, trans. a Religious of the Community of Saint Mary the Virgin, with an introduction by Aelred Squire, O.P. (London: Faber and Faber, 1962). The *De arca Noe morali* and the *De arca Noe mystica* in my parenthetical references will be indicated as *A. mor.* and *A. mys.*, respectively. References to the *De arca Noe morali* in my text adopt the chapter divisions as indicated in the translation, which differ from those of the *PL*.

29. The term *psychocosmogram* is that of Zinn, in "Mandala Symbolism," pp. 317–341.

30. The details of this description have been derived from ibid., pp. 321–323.

6). A series of vivid iconographical devices serves to relate the Christ-figure to the cosmos and the ark. He implies Creative Word, Providential Orderer, Final Judge, and the Object of Contemplation for the angelic hosts. "From the mouth of Christ six linked disks extend downward into the eastern area of the map of the world and terminate at the bow of the ark. These six disks represent the six days of creation, culminating in a scene of paradise." By means of this set of symbols, Christ becomes the Creative Word. As Providential Orderer, he is seen embracing the cosmos. In his right hand he holds a throne; in his left, a scepter. These extend to his feet, where a scene of the Last Judgment is depicted. This is Christ the Final Judge. As the Object of Angelic Contemplation, he is surrounded by choirs of angels that are arranged hierarchically and that gaze rapturously at the unveiled face of the Lord of the Cosmos (*A. mor.*, I.8, 10, II.13; *A. mys.*, XV).[31]

From the perspective of both the ark itself and the Christ-figure that encompasses it, Hugh's psychocosmogram, then, is replete with resonances that underscore the primacy of the visionary mode in Victorine thought. As a means of ascent, the ark itself becomes a vehicle for the attainment of the celestial realms. As such, it is "the mountain of the house of the Lord established in the top of the mountain, unto which all nations flow [cf. Mic. 4:1], and go up from the ark's four corners, as from the four quarters of the earth" (*A. mor.*, II.9). "Let us go up," Hugh exhorts us, "putting all obstacles behind us. Let us go up with joy, for we are going 'into the house of the Lord' [cf. Ps. 122:1]." We must "lift up our eyes to see the bright paths strewn along the flanks of the eternal mountains and the footpaths that lead upward to the gates of Jerusalem." The doors of the city are open, and its inhabitants welcome us with "Alleluia." Ascending to this city, we find ourselves in the presence of the enthroned King (*A. mor.*, II.9).

This movement leads us both contemplatively and exegetically to the corresponding image that constitutes Hugh's psychocosmogram: the Christ-figure encompassing the ark. Inspired by the temple vision of Isaiah 6, this, as we have seen, is among the major foundation images through which the concept of the visionary mode is articulated. As a counterpart of Ezekiel's vision of the

31. Ibid., pp. 321–324.

Chariot, Isaiah's vision of the Enthroned Figure is a constituent
of that cluster of originary events that constitute the visionary
mode. If Ezekiel is "a villager who saw the king," Isaiah is a "townsman who saw the king."[32] With Hugh, as with others inspired by
this dimension of the visionary mode, we simply move from the
country to the town (and, correspondingly, from the quadripartite
to the tripartite) in the adoption of Isaiah's *visio Dei* as interpretive
focal point. It is a movement in which country and town, quadripartite and tripartite, Ezekiel and Isaiah are resolved within a
visionary spectrum that embraces a full range of perspectives.

In keeping with those perspectives, Hugh applies the interpretive methodology reflected in the *Didascalicon* to the exegesis of
Isaiah's vision that is the basis of his psychocosmogram. Focusing
upon the seraphim that surround the Enthroned Figure of Isaiah,
for example, Hugh accordingly maintains that on one level the
seraphim denote Holy Scripture itself, and the three pairs of wings
that distinguish the seraphim are the three senses of Scripture,
history, allegory, and tropology.[33] Within this scheme "the two
wings which cover the body of the seraph are the historical sense,
which covers mystical meanings beneath the veil of the letter."
Correspondingly, "the two wings which are extended to cover the
head and the feet of the Lord are the allegorical sense." Inculcated
into the mysteries of Holy Scripture by what these wings cover,
we are thereby illuminated in the knowledge of godhead. So illuminated, we are able to take flight with the two wings through
which the seraphim themselves flew. This is the tropological sense.
In all three cases we find ourselves propelled by that same spirit
by means of which the living creatures in Ezekiel "were lifted up
from the earth," as the result of which the more that we advance
in virtues or in knowledge, the more we behold the profundity
of the hidden places of Scripture. Whether through the seraphim
of Isaiah or the living creatures of Ezekiel, then, "the human mind,
enlightened by the knowledge of Holy Scripture, is raised to the
contemplation of heavenly things." Mounting to the throne, it
"climbs above the choirs of angels and attains to the presence of
its Creator" (*A. mor.*, I.9). Such in brief are some of the main lines

32. See the discussion in Chapter 3 of the *Ḥagigah* 13a–b.

33. *Ḥagigah* 13a–b also focuses upon the triadic basis of Isaiah's vision as distinguished
from the quaternary basis of Ezekiel's. The distinction is centered in the wings of the
seraphim as opposed to the wings of the *ḥayyot*.

of thought that underscore the outlook of Hugh of Saint Victor. As a theologian who articulated his own version of the visionary mode, he established the groundwork for succeeding generations.

Complementing the thought of Hugh of Saint Victor is that of Richard of Saint Victor, whose works are equally important in an assessment of the Victorine point of view. Taking his cue from Hugh of Saint Victor, Richard formulated his own system of thought through which the seer might have access to the divine. If Hugh adopted the ark of Noah as his point of focus, Richard adopted the ark of the covenant. Both provided an elaborate spatial structure by means of which his contemplative system might be conceived and implemented. For Richard the spatial structure assumed the form of the temple, on the one hand, and the tabernacle, on the other. The first is most elaborately discussed in Richard's commentary *In Visionem Ezechielis*.[34] Although the main thrust of this work concerns the vision of the Temple that occupies the last eight chapters of Ezekiel's prophecy, it likewise concerns itself with the inaugural vision in the prologue to the commentary as a whole (*Prol.*, cols. 527–534).

The purpose of the prologue is to reassert the primacy of the literal as a means of understanding the significance of the biblical account. Hugh argues that expositors such as Gregory the Great focused on the allegorical or mystical at the expense of the literal in expounding what otherwise appeared to be inexplicable to them. Unwilling to confront the force of the literal, they ran the risk of compromising the higher meanings.[35] It is to rectify this oversight that Richard has undertaken his analysis. Influenced by Hugh of Saint Victor in his emphasis upon the primacy of the literal, Richard expends a good deal of energy explicating the various features of the *animalia* with their quaternary forms and the *rotae* that accompany them. His purpose in doing so is to address the literal on its own terms, to determine the nature and characteristics of the descriptions, to assess their accuracy and cogency and to reconcile apparent discrepancies.

---

34. References are to the *PL*, CXCVI, 527–599.

35. "Lo! blessed Gregory expounds the wonderful vision of celestial creatures [*Ecce mirabilem illam visionem de coelestibus animalibus*], seen by the prophet Ezechiel, according to the mystical sense [*mysticam intelligentiam*]. But what it means literally he does not say. Of the second vision he says that it cannot mean anything according to the letter. This is true, but only according to the way he takes it here. If we decide to consider the same passage in a different way, perhaps we may be able to extract some suitable literal meaning" (*PL*, CXCVI, 527–528; trans. Smalley, *Study of the Bible*, p. 108).

Having accomplished this, he proceeds to the Temple itself. This culminating vision he conceives quite properly as the counterpart to the inaugural vision: the first anticipates and is fulfilled in the second. Once again, Richard's concern is with the literal description. To this he attends with a kind of mathematical precision and enthusiasm, one that prompts him to measure and graph the dimensions of the Temple in the spirit of the prophet himself. Conceiving the Temple spatially as a kind of cosmic structure, he views it as a tripartite edifice through which the seer moves from the realm of the external to that of the internal, from profane to sacred and from one portal to the next in the progressive ascent to the chamber of the Holy of Holies (ch. 1, cols. 534–538). Having achieved this realm, the seer then measures its dimensions by means of a kind of divine "geometry" that allows him to take into account the full significance of its interior dimensions (length, breadth, width, height) (ch. 15, cols. 574–577).

This mathematical investigation of the multiple dimensions of the Temple Richard uses as the basis of the mystical characteristics implicit in the vision. Addressing himself to Ezek. 40:1–2 ("*Facta est super me manus Domini, et adduxit me illuc. In visionibus Dei adduxit me in teram Israel* [The hand of the Lord was upon me, and brought me thither. In the visions of God brought he me into the land of Israel]"), Richard envisions a cosmic mountain upon which the divinely inspired prophet is placed by the hand of God. Like the prophet himself, the seer is led up step by step, "grade" by "grade," to the highest reaches of this mountain. As Richard makes clear, the mountain he has in mind is *"non terrini sed coelestis."* It is in fact the heaven of heavens, conceived as the celestial temple, the New Jerusalem itself, into which the seer is led. Within the innermost chamber of this sacred place resides the Son of man, the object of the seer's quest as he strives to make his way into the Holy of Holies (ch. 3, cols. 537–542). It is here that Ezekiel's inaugural vision is reinstalled upon the ark of the covenant within the most holy place.

If such is true of Richard's conception of the Temple, it is no less true of his conception of the tabernacle. Particularly with respect to the ark of the covenant as crucial symbol, the idea assumes paramount importance in Richard's mystical works, notably *De mystica archa* (*The Mystical Ark*, also known as *Benjamin major*), a treatise customarily seen to complement his work *De duodecim patriarchiis* (*The Twelve Patriarchs*, also called *Benjamin mi-*

nor). More than any other, these works suggest the complexity of Richard's visionary formulations. The treatise *De mystica archa* or *Benjamin major* serves as our primary point of focus.[36]

In the *De mystica archa* one discovers a fully articulated system of thought on the nature of contemplation and how the seer, trained in the intricacies of contemplative theory and practice, might be able to attain to a true vision of God. As such, Richard's treatise establishes at the outset its intention of offering itself as a "key" or *clavis* to unlock the secrets of mystical ascent (I. 1). For Richard the object of that ascent is symbolized in the ark of the covenant within the tabernacle (Exod. 25). Focusing upon the ark as symbolic structure, Richard launches into a detailed and exhaustive treatment of the contemplative process, one that amounts to a discourse on the nature of epistemology. Although an analysis of that discourse lies beyond the purview of the present discussion, some sense of its main outlines will be helpful in discerning the visionary basis of Richard's thought.

According to this discourse, the ark itself and the angelic forms above it symbolize what Richard designates as the six degrees or kinds (genera) of contemplation. These genera are structured hierarchically according to the way in which the object of contemplation (the ark) is known. "The six degrees represent an ascension in being from the sensual world, perceived by the bodily senses and known to the mind through the imagination, through the interior world of reason, to the transcendent world of spiritual realities." The six degrees, then, are divisible into three groups of two each. Corresponding to the six degrees of contemplation are the modes through which it is manifested. The first is the enlargement of the mind; the second, the raising up of the mind; and the third, the alienation of the mind or ecstasy. The process as a whole is conceived appropriately through the image of the ark: in the first stage it is constructed; in the second it is carried forth on supporting shoulders; in the third it is placed within the

36. References to *De mystica archa* are to *The Twelve Patriarchs, the Mystical Ark, Book Three of the Trinity*, trans. Grover A. Zinn (New York: Paulist Press, 1979), in conjunction with the edition in *PL*, CXCVI, 63–202. For illuminating discussions of Richard's works in general and these works in particular, see, among others, Zinn's excellent introduction to his volume, as well as his various essays, including Grover A. Zinn, Jr., "Personification Allegory and Visions of Light in Richard of St. Victor's Teaching on Contemplation," *UTO* 46 (1977): 190–214; and the important studies of Jean Châtillon, especially *Théologie, spiritualité et métaphysique dans l'oeuvre oratoire d'Richard de Saint-Victor*, Études de Philosophie Médiévale 58 (Paris: J. Vrin, 1969).

Holy of Holies. Once within the tabernacle and before the ark of the covenant, the seer, in a state of ecstasy, attains, as nearly as is humanly possible, complete perfection (V.2). Underlying Richard's systemization of the contemplative experience, then, is the triadic structuring that one discovers throughout his works. At the core of that triadic structuring stands the ark of the covenant within the Holy of Holies as a central symbol. For our purposes, the importance of the triadic structuring is to be seen in its relationship to the quaternary structuring of Ezekiel's vision. From the contemplative perspective that Richard embodies, the triadic and the quaternary represent corresponding aspects of the same idea. One aspect is subsumed into the other. In that subsumption, one encounters a visionary sensibility that is all inclusive.

Such is discernible in Richard's association of the six stages of the contemplative process with the six-winged seraphim of Isaiah 6. Addressing those genera of contemplation, he attempts to determine which wings perform which act of contemplation in the flight to the celestial spheres. Of their own accord, the first two do not: "taken up with earthly and corporeal things," they alone are insufficient for such an undertaking and indeed are only preparatory to higher considerations. Intensifying the desire for transcendent flight, these two wings merely indicate how that which is corporeal in us must be mortified before true ascent is possible. This leaves the recognition that if one pair of wings is insufficient, the contemplative must consider the necessity of possessing at least an additional pair of wings in order to achieve his goal. "Yet it should be too little for you that you receive these two wings; but to prove that you are a celestial animal, be zealous and busy about having at least two pairs, and then you will certainly have those with which you can fly up to heavenly things."

Such a recognition moves Richard from the perspective of the seraphim of Isaiah 6 to the fourfold creatures of Ezekiel 1: "The four animals that the prophet Ezechiel saw, and having seen, described, certainly had four wings. By this they showed that they were celestial, not terrestrial. Ezechiel says: 'Four faces for each one, and four wings for each one' (Ezech. 1:6)." But even four wings are not entirely sufficient, for not all four are used for flight. Rather, two of them are used to cover the body as a way of demonstrating that sense of modesty and circumspection through which the seer tempers the brightness of his own sense of worth "in light of the uncertainty of human mutability." For this reason,

Richard observes, "it is good for a person to hide his good things, not take his merits entirely for granted, and keep himself always in humility." Accordingly, even two pairs of wings are still not sufficient. Three pairs are needed.

Moving from two to four and finally to six wings in a progressive ascent, then, Richard conflates the complementary visionary modes of Ezekiel and Isaiah in order to arrive at the supreme conception that underscores his contemplative point of view. Doing so, he culminates this movement in an allusion to the Pauline ascent to the third heaven. If one desires to ascend with Paul to the highest heaven, one should not assume that one can do it with only two pairs of wings. "Without doubt, it is fitting that he who desires and strives to fly up to the secrets of the third heaven and the hidden things of Divinity have all those six wings of contemplations" (I. 10). Although the full possession of these six wings may not be possible in this life, the true contemplative must constantly strive for such possession in the pursuit of ultimate perfection.

In the structuring of that quest, Richard of Saint Victor provided among the most detailed accounts of how the contemplative experience was to be realized and ultimately fulfilled. In the process he fostered an environment in which the manifold complexities of the visionary mode came to the fore in systematic and intricate ways. At the center of his system stood the ark of the covenant, either in the Temple or in the tabernacle. Both places were enhanced by a plethora of corresponding scriptural material drawn from both the Old Testament and the New. In either case the visionary dimensions of the contemplative experience were realized through the use of such texts as those drawn from Ezekiel and Isaiah. Conflating these texts and engaging in his own poetic reenactments of them, Richard enhanced his systematic approach with a creative sensibility. Doing so, he extended the insights of earlier expositors and practitioners and contributed his own insights to the developing traditions of the visionary perspective.

IV

Those traditions, which flourished under the Cistercians and Victorines in the twelfth century, assumed renewed vigor among the Franciscans during the thirteenth century. Of no figure is this more nearly true than that Doctor Seraphicus Saint Bonaventure

(1217–1274), minister general of the Franciscan Order. Subsuming within his large and diverse corpus the multiple strands of medieval theology, philosophy, and spirituality, Bonaventure devised a system of thought that is both rich and integrative in its implications.[37] Inspired at once by the Platonic and Aristotelian points of view, he sought to reconcile the rational with the mystical. His was a synthesis that drew upon both the eastern and the western fathers, the Pseudo-Dionysius as disseminated through such figures as John Scotus Eriugena, on the one hand, and traditions of thought extending from Augustine through the Cistercians and the Victorines, on the other. As a summation of the mystical theology so crucial to the earlier Middle Ages, moreover, Bonaventure's integrative enterprise represents in some sense the culmination, if not the end, of an era, when such considerations took precedence over all others.[38] In this regard Saint Bonaventure is a singular presence in the delineation of those complex and multifaceted issues that distinguish the traditions we have been exploring. Such an idea is most compellingly revealed in Bonaventure's theological writings, on the one hand, and his spiritual writings, on the other, the first represented by his *Breviloquium* (1255–1257?) and the second by his *Itinerarium mentis in Deum* (1259).[39] These works have been chosen because they serve to focus a number of the concerns that underscore the visionary mode as a distinct category of exegesis and representation.

As a work that provides a hermeneutical context for Bonaventure's entire enterprise, the *Breviloquium* is considered first. A compendium of his views regarding such issues as faith and reason, creation, illumination, proofs of God's existence and attributes, grace and free will, the *Breviloquium* is, in Bonaventure's own words, "a *summa* about the truths of theology." In this *summa* he does not "deal with all matters summarily, but treat[s] briefly certain matters that it is more important to know, including at the

37. Ewert H. Cousins, *Bonaventure and the Coincidence of Opposites* (Chicago: Franciscan Herald Press, 1978), pp. 2–5.

38. For further discussion, see John Francis Quinn, *The Historical Constitution of St. Bonaventure's Philosophy* (Toronto: Pontifical Institute, 1973), and Gilson, *History of Christian Philosophy*, esp. pp. 331–340.

39. References to the *Breviloquium* are to the translation of Erwin Esser Nemmers (St. Louis: B. Herder, 1947). References to the other works are to *The Soul's Journey into God, The Tree of Life, The Life of St. Francis*, trans. Ewert Cousins (New York: Paulist Press, 1978). All translations are used in conjunction with the *Opera Omnia*, ed. Studio et Cura PP. Collegii a S. Bonaventura, 11 vols. (Quaracchi: Collegii S. Bonaventurae, 1882–1902).

same time such explanation for their understanding as may come to mind at the moment" (Prologue, 6.v). For our purposes the Prologue to the *Breviloqium* is of most interest, because it is there that Bonaventure establishes a working hermeneutics for the interpretation of the biblical text as the basis for all future analysis. In this respect the *Breviloquium* recalls Hugh of Saint Victor's *Didascalicon*, which similarly provides a *lectio divina* through which the Bible becomes a crucial source of interpretive insight.

Expounding his own *lectio divina*, Bonaventure demonstrates the way certain fundamental structures assume a cosmic significance reflected in the Bible as a divinely inspired work that "proceeds in accord with supernatural light to give man as a wayfarer a sufficient knowledge of things that expedite salvation." From this divinely inspired perspective the Bible is in effect "a summa of the contents of the whole universe." As such, it reveals its dimensions in a quaternary form: breadth and length, height and depth.[40] "The breadth of Scripture consists of the multiplicity of its parts, the length in the description of the times and ages, the height in the description of the hierarchies arranged in different levels, and the depth in the multiplicity of the mystical senses and intelligences" (iii–vi). Taking this quaternary form into account, Bonaventure discourses on each of its aspects. Out of this discourse a fully conceived hermeneutics emerges, one that moves toward a realization of the visionary potential latent in the biblical text as a fundamental source of the *lectio divina*.

Approaching Holy Scripture from the structural point of view that underlies his quaternary approach, Bonaventure first considers the dimension of depth. If Holy Scripture reveals itself cosmically as fourfold, that principle inheres within individual dimensions of the biblical text. So in the case of breadth as that which reflects the multiplity of parts, the Old and the New Testament are themselves divisible into a quaternary. As fourfold, the Old Testament "has the books of laws, of history, of wisdom, and of the prophets." In like manner "the New Testament has books corresponding to these and also arranged in a fourfold division." Accordingly, the gospels find their counterparts in the books of the laws, the Acts of the Apostles in the historical books,

---

40. This quaternary dimension of Bonaventure's thought is reflected not only in the *Breviloquium* but in other works such as the *Commentarii in quattuor libros Petri Lombardi* (1248–1255). See Cousins, *Bonaventure*, pp. 185–190.

the apostolic letters in the books of wisdom, and the Apocalypse in the prophetical books. "Thus," Bonaventure observes, "the remarkable conformity between the Old and the New Testament may be seen not only in consistency of meanings, but also in their fourfold division" (Prologue, I.i).

For Bonaventure, this harmonic patterning assumes a distinctly visionary bearing, one that is founded on Ezekiel's *visio Dei*. In keeping with the exegetical traditions that he inherited, Bonaventure allegorizes that vision to accord with his own concept of *lectio divina*:

> In this grouping and arrangement [*figuram et consignationem*], Ezechiel sees four wheels of faces [*rotas quatuor facierum*] and a wheel in the midst of the wheel [*rotam in medio rotae*], because the Old is in the New, and the New is in the Old [*vetus in novo, et converso*]. In the books of the laws and in the evangelical books is the face of a lion because of his powerful authority [*excellentiam auctoritatis*]. In the historical books is the face of a bull because of his convincing strength [*exempla virtutis*]. In the books of wisdom is the face of a man because of his nice prudence [*prudentiam sagacem*]. In the books of the prophets is the face of the eagle because of his perspicacious insight [*intelligentiam perspicacem*]. (Prologue, I.i)

Beginning with the patristic assumption that the wheels within wheels are a reflection of the figural relationship between Old Testament and New, type and antitype, Bonaventure incorporates his fourfold perspective into an iconic association of the faces of the creatures with the respective books that they are meant to represent. Doing so, he sees in Ezekiel's vision not only a prime source of hermeneutic enlightenment but an originary event through which one is able to discern the fourfold harmonic correspondences reflected in the divisions of the biblical text as a microcosm of the universe. Such an approach legitimates Bonaventure's quaternary outlook and grounds it prophetically in a visionary moment that is conceived as a well-spring of interpretive insight. Such, in part, is Bonaventure's view of the dimension of breadth. This view, in turn, is reinforced and enriched by those concerning the dimensions of length, height, and depth as well.

Addressing the dimension of length, Bonaventure reconceives his approach in temporal terms, one that interprets length as an expression of the way Holy Scripture moves in its account from the beginning of the world to the day of judgment, from alpha to omega. Doing so, he integrates the quaternary basis of his discourse on breadth with what he conceives as the triadic basis of his discourse on length. From the triadic perspective, biblical history is accordingly divided into the time of the law of nature, the time of the written law, and the time of the law of grace. These, in turn, are subdivided into correlative patterns of sixes and sevens to suggest a complex interweaving of numerical symmetry and harmony, whereby the ages of the world find their correspondence in the days of creation and the day of rest, on the one hand, and the stages of a man's life from infancy to old age and death, on the other.

From the historical point of view embodied in the triadic perspective, Bonaventure distinguishes seven ages that fall into a pattern of six plus one. The first age runs from Adam to Noah, the second from Noah to Abraham, the third from Abraham to David, the fourth from David to the transmigration of Babylon, the fifth from the transmigration to Christ, the sixth from Christ to the end of the world. Running concurrently with the sixth, the seventh begins with the repose of Christ in the sepulchre and extends to the universal resurrection. Even this marks the beginning of an eighth age or the combining of two quaternities, an idea upon which Bonaventure does not elaborate.[41] The point is that Scripture is of great length because "it begins with the commencement of the world and of time, in the beginning of Genesis, and extends to the end of the world and of time, namely to the end of the Apocalypse." In this harmonious and well-ordered conception, one discovers a view of scriptural patterning that resembles a "well-designed song." So Bonaventure observes: "One can view, following the sequence of time, the variety, multiplicity and symmetry, order, rectitude and beauty of the many judgments proceeding from the wisdom of God governing the world" (Prologue, II.i–iv). In this sequential approach the quaternary and the triadic become complementary aspects (wheel within wheel) of a

---

41. For full discussions of Bonaventure's views concerning history, see J. Ratzinger, *The Theology of History in St. Bonaventure* (Chicago: Franciscan Herald Press, 1975), and Bernard McGinn, "The Significance of Bonaventure's Theology of History," *Journal of Religion. Special Supplement. The Medieval Religious Heritage, 1274–1974* (Chicago: University of Chicago Press, 1978), pp. 564–581. See also the section on Bonaventure's apocalyptic theology of history in Bernard McGinn, *Visions of the End: Apocalyptic Traditions in the Middle Ages* (New York: Columbia University Press, 1979), pp. 196–221.

symmetrical superstructure, one founded upon the concept of the *coincidentia oppositorum* that underscores Saint Bonaventure's essentially integrative enterprise.

Such an idea is discernible not only in the discourse on breadth and length but in the treatment of height and depth as the fulfillment of the quaternary pattern. The height of Holy Scripture, then, moves upward through Pseudo-Dionysian hierarchies from the ecclesiastical to the angelical to the divine, that is, from subcelestial to celestial to supercelestial. In the process of disclosure Scripture describes the first (subcelestial) clearly, the second (celestial) a bit more obscurely, and the third (supercelestial) more obscurely still. The task of the interpreter is that of ascending in his understanding from the lowest to the highest levels. The triadic movement implied by the height of Scripture, in turn, finds its correspondence in such categories as matter, spirit, and grace. In each case one is able to erect a ladder that at once touches the earth at its base and heaven at its top. By means of this ladder one will be able to attain to the level of grace. "All this is done through that one hierarch, Jesus Christ, who by reason of the human nature He assumed is a hierarch not only in the ecclesiastical hierarchy, but also in the angelic hierarchy, and the middle person in that supercelestial hierarchy of the Most Blessed Trinity" (Prologue, III.i–ii). Out of the quaternary conception of the Bible as a whole, then, rises the triadic conception of ascent to the supercelestial realm.

Such an idea, finally, is fulfilled in the discourse on depth, which subsumes quaternary and triadic considerations within the *coincidentia oppositorum* that distinguishes the Bonaventurean outlook. Recalling the hermeneutic approach adopted in the discourse on breadth, Bonaventure observes that Holy Scripture possesses a depth that reflects a "multiplicity of the mystical intelligences." This multiplicity consists of four senses arranged according to a grouping of one and three. The first, of course, is the literal sense and the second three (conceived as a unit) are the allegorical, moral, and anagogical, respectively. The allegorical occurs when "through one fact another fact is indicated, according to what must be believed." The moral (or tropological) occurs when, "through what took place, we are given to understand something else, which must be done." Finally, the anagogical sense occurs when "we are given to understand what should be sought after, namely, the eternal happiness of the saints" (Prologue, IV.i).

Existing in the biblical text in addition to the literal significance, this threefold meaning satisfies what Bonaventure calls the subject, the reader, the origin, and end of Scripture. It satisfies the subject because its doctrine is concerned with God and Christ, as well as with the works of reparation and matters of faith, all of which reflect the triadic view of three in one. It satisfies the reader to the extent that, as one who has been sufficiently purified of sinful dross, he is able to perceive the mystical and profound meanings under "the bark of the evident." It satisfies the origin because "it is from God through Christ and the Holy Ghost speaking by the mouths of the prophets and the others who wrote the document." Finally, it satisfies the end because "it was given so that through it man may be guided in knowing and doing things to enable him finally to obtain what should be desired" (Prologue, IV.ii–v).

In all these capacities the Holy Scripture reveals the multiplicity of meanings that characterize the dimension of depth. Both quaternary and triadic in conception, this dimension fulfills the fourfold consideration by which Scripture as a text is viewed harmonically and symmetrically. So conceived, this text comes to embody an outlook that is essentially quaternary but in which triadic considerations are integrated to form a unified whole. Within that whole is to be found the all-pervasive principle of the *coincidentia oppositorum.*

The *lectio divina* that characterizes Saint Bonaventure's theological writings as expressed in the *Breviloquium* is no less a part of his spiritual writings, most notably the *Itinerarium mentis in Deum.* A work of pivotal importance to Saint Bonaventure's understanding of the visionary, the *Itinerarium* reconceptualizes the outlook implicit in the *Breviloquium* and casts it in a new form. Because the inspiration for the *Itinerarium* derives from Saint Bonaventure's meditation on the six-winged seraph that appeared to Saint Francis on Mount La Verna in Tuscany some thirty-five years before (that is, 1224), a glance at the earlier event is appropriate to suggest the background to the text at hand. To this end, one need only consult the event as described in the *Legenda maior* (ca. 1263), the longer of Saint Bonaventure's two biographies of Saint Francis.

According to Saint Bonaventure's account, Saint Francis, during one of his vigils on Mount La Verna, "saw a Seraph with six fiery and shining wings descend from the height of heaven." When in the course of its flight the seraph had reached a place near Saint

Francis, "there appeared between the wings the figure of a man crucified, with his hands and feet extended in the form of a cross and fastened to a cross." Precisely as Isaiah had beheld in his *visio Dei*, two of the wings of the seraph were lifted above his head, two were extended for flight, and two covered his body. As a result of this vision, he knew that, as "Christ's lover," he was to be "totally transformed into the likeness of Christ crucified." The fact of that transformation was confirmed by the experience of the stigmata that followed upon the vision itself, for, as the vision faded, it not only infused Saint Francis' heart with a wonderful ardor but left on his body markings that were no less marvelous. "Immediately the marks of nails began to appear in his hands and feet" like those of the crucified figure he had just beheld (XIII.3).

In short, Saint Francis underwent an experience that transformed the seraphic throne-vision of Isaiah into a Christocentric rearticulation of profound significance. In the process of refiguring the visionary event articulated in Isaiah 6, the seer himself assumed a new form, one that was tantamount to a veritable transfiguration (cf. XIII.i). As a result of that transfiguration, he participated both spiritually and physically in the vision he beheld. Such is the nature of the theosis that Saint Francis underwent and that Saint Bonaventure describes in his *Legenda maior*. Responding to this visionary moment in his own meditative experience on Mount La Verna many years later, Saint Bonaventure adopted it as the occasion to embark upon the extended discourse that serves as the basis of his *Itinerarium mentis in Deum*.

As Saint Bonaventure makes clear at the very outset of his work, his purpose is to delineate "the various ways by which the soul ascends into God" (Prologue, 2). The *Itinerarium* is both an "itinerary" of the journey and a description of the journey. From a structural point of view the basis of that *itinerarium* is the seraph with its six wings. Focusing upon this figure, Bonaventure maintains that "just as God completed the world in six days and rested on the seventh, so the smaller world of man is led in a most orderly fashion by six successive stages of illumination to the quiet of contemplation" (I.5). The order of six stages of contemplation, then, finds expression in a seventh or supreme moment of fulfilled union. As indicated by the concerns of the individual chapters, the stages include contemplating God through (1) His vestiges in the universe; (2) His vestiges in the sense world; (3) His image stamped upon our natural powers; (4) His image reformed by the gifts of grace; (5) His divine unity expressed as a category of being; and (6) His manifestation in the Trinity as an expression of His goodness. These chapters, in turn, culminate in a final chapter on spiritual and mystical ecstasy in which we experience ultimate rest in God.

If this suggests something of the sixfold nature (actually six plus one) of Bonaventure's approach, this structure is further divisible into a triadic form in which the six wings of the Seraph are viewed as pairs. So conceived, the wings suggest a triadic movement in the contemplative process, one in which the lower pair represents the natural world; the middle pair, the spiritual world; and the upper pair, the divine world. In either case, the journey that Bonaventure depicts is an ascent from the material realm to God. Having ascended through the six stages (or the three levels into which those stages are further divisible), the soul attains the state of ecstasy, symbolized by the vision as a whole.[42]

In his account of this contemplative movement Saint Bonaventure conceives the experience not simply as an ascent to higher realms but as a penetration into the innermost confines of the sacred.[43] A triadic journey of ascent, then, finds its counterpart in a triadic penetration to the most holy of sites. With this penetration in mind, Saint Bonaventure distinguishes three modes of contemplating God: outside us, within us, and above us. The outside concerns God's vestiges as manifested in the external world; the inside, God's image as manifested within man; and the realm above, the light that shines from God upon our minds. These distinctions assume spatial form in the figure of the tabernacle and the entrance into the Holy of Holies, that which is itself the most quaternary of forms. So, Bonaventure observes that those who have become accustomed to the first mode of contemplation find themselves in the court before the tabernacle; those accustomed to the second mode of contemplation find themselves in the sanctuary itself; and those accustomed to the third mode of contemplation are able to "enter with the high priest into the Holy of Holies where the Cherubim of glory stand over the ark overshadowing the Mercy Seat" (V.i).

This is in effect a penetration to the realm of God as divine

42. See Cousins, *Bonaventure*, pp. 78–79.

43. See Bernard McGinn, "Ascension and Introversion in the *Itinerarium Mentis in Deum*," *S. Bonaventura 1274–1974* (Rome: Grottaferrata, 1974), III, 535–552.

center. As one whose center is everywhere and whose circumference nowhere, He is the still point that, while remaining stable, "gives motion to all things." The source of all motion, this point is itself "most perfect and immense." In that absolute sense it is conceived in quaternary terms as that which is "within all things, but not enclosed; outside all things, but not excluded; above all things, but not aloof; below all things, but not debased." One and all-inclusive, it is, therefore, "all in all" (V.vii). There, the seer experiences God in all His glory. "Passing over" into God, he is correspondingly "transferred and transformed" into deity ("*transferatur et transformetur in Deum*") through a process that is "mystical and most secret" (VII.iii–iv). His theosis is complete. What is true of the hermeneutics underlying the *Breviloquium* is likewise true of the spirituality underlying the *Itinerarium mentis in Deum*: there emerges a *coincidentia oppositorum* that accommodates and reconciles a multiplicity of perspectives by which one is better able to understand the complex nature of the visionary mode.

As an expression of the way in which exegetes extending from Johannes Scotus Eriugena in the ninth century to Saint Bonaventure in the thirteenth century assimilated earlier traditions into their respective outlooks, the writings addressed in the foregoing discussion should demonstrate the range and versatility of those who attempted to provide a renewed understanding of the visionary mode. One discovers in each case not only a concern with the experience of the visionary as that which transforms the seer in the process of ascent but an attempt to provide a structural, even a systematic, account of how that transformative experience is realized. Something like a "science of the visionary" is delineated, one in which there emerges a concern with fundamental forms and structures (arks, temple spaces, wings, and the like) that represent an objective correlative, an archetype, through which a knowledge of the divine world is able to manifest itself. In that knowledge, theosis finds its counterpart in a fascination with the way the visionary may be systematized and objectified as a reflection of the seer's understanding of the realms that constitute the human, the angelic, and the divine. At the forefront of this enterprise is an analytical discernment that distinguishes the impulse not only to see but to know. In this respect the exegetes under consideration are both seers and knowers. In both respects they are responsive to all that the visionary mode comes to imply in the later Middle Ages.

⌒ Eight

The Poetics of Vision

I

Any consideration of the visionary mode as hermeneutical enterprise might well concern itself with a corresponding endeavor, that of poetics. If one recalls that the originary impulse through which the experience of the *visio Dei* received initial expression is indebted to the transformative idea of "making" and "remaking," it will be readily acknowledged that the visionary mode is "poetic" at its core. Ezekiel is as much a poet as he is a prophet, and many of the texts that his prophecy engendered represent to a great extent creative reformulations of an essentially poetic substratum. In their own way these texts, too, are "poems" or are at least "poetic" in the sense that their authors reconstitute the structures of vision to accord with their own habits of seeing.

So conceived, the visionary mode becomes a phenomenon in which hermeneutics and poetics converge: both recreate the originary experience in a new form. In the acculturation of the visionary mode hermeneutics ultimately becomes poetics. The impulse to interpret becomes the impulse to create anew. So in the present context: the consummate interpretation assumes the form of the divine poem, one that engenders what Joseph Anthony Wittreich, Jr., calls a "visionary poetics," according to which the reader, "progressing from vision to vision," discovers "himself continually bursting confines." In that progression each vision is "an exit to another higher vision." The process itself is continuous, "each exit accomplished after a different set of obstacles has been negotiated, each entrance signifying a new stage in the purification of vision." Each portal, in turn, is attained "after more film has been removed from the eyes and opens into a vision that redefines what it succeeds, deepening its significance and purifying our

understanding of its meaning."[1] In effect suggesting the kind of
enterprise upon which we have been embarked all along in our
investigation of the exegetical traditions, this definition of the
poetics of vision is one that will represent the primary focus of
our present discussion as well.

At the center of this discussion will be one of the major poetic
documents of the Middle Ages, *The Divine Comedy* of Dante Alighieri (1265–1321).[2] A work the very nature of which is visionary,
this poem may be said to represent a culminating moment in the
history of the visionary mode both as poetic and as hermeneutic
event. In both respects this poem will be seen as a capstone to
that process of acculturation that the *merkabah* underwent in its
transmission from the time of its formulation to its reenactments
in later medieval thought. Having commenced the study as a
whole with a discussion of the etiology of vision as a manifestation
of the biblical foundations of Ezekiel's *visio Dei*, we shall conclude
the study, then, with an investigation of how that vision is reconceived within the context of a poetic work that self-consciously
adopts it and refashions it in its own terms. Doing so, we shall
have moved from biblical text through hermeneutics to poetic
text. In this movement, we shall have come full circle to encounter
the new vision, that embodied within the visionary fabric of
Dante's great work.

As a way of approaching *The Divine Comedy* from the visionary
perspective delineated throughout, we shall adopt the letter to
Can Grande della Scala as our point of focus.[3] Written as an

1. See Joseph Anthony Wittreich, Jr., *Visionary Poetics: Milton's Tradition and His Legacy*
(San Marino; Calif.: Henry E. Huntington Library, 1979), pp. 32–33. Although the concern
of this book is with later poets such as Milton, the mode of visionary poetics that Wittreich
articulates is very much in accord with the outlook expressed in the study of Dante offered
here. Among Wittreich's other works in the same vein, see also his *Milton and the Line of
Vision* (Madison: University of Wisconsin Press, 1975). Of corresponding importance to
the establishment of a visionary poetics, especially a poetics traceable to Ezekiel's vision,
are the works of Harold Bloom. See his book *Shelley's Mythmaking* (New Haven: Yale
University Press, 1959), and his essay "Shelley and His Precursors," *Poetry and Repression:
Revisionism from Blake to Stevens* (New Haven: Yale University Press, 1976), pp. 83–111. Of
corresponding importance is Bloom's *The Visionary Company: A Reading of English Romantic
Poetry*, rev. ed. (Ithaca: Cornell University Press, 1971).

2. References are to *The Divine Comedy*, Italian text, with translation and commentary
by Charles S. Singleton, 6 vols. in 3, Bollingen Series 80 (Princeton: Princeton University
Press, 1970–1975). Citations of Singleton's commentary in these volumes will be noted by
volume, part, and page number.

3. References to Dante's letter to Can Grande della Scala (*Epistola X*) in particular and
to his letters in general are to *Dantis Alagherii Epistolae*, ed. and trans. by Paget Toynbee

exposition of the third canticle of the *Commedia* to commemorate
the formal dedication of the *Paradiso* to the Lord of Verona and
Vicenza, this letter suggests how extensively Dante's outlook was
permeated with the kinds of concerns that distinguish the visionary mode as a phenomenon of crucial import. Of particular significance in establishing the nature of these concerns, that aspect
of the letter which addresses itself to the meaning of the transcendent experience embodied in the *Paradiso* will be of most
immediate interest here. In his exposition of that experience
Dante is especially concerned with explicating the opening verses
of the first canto of the *Paradiso* (I.5–9), in which the poet expresses
his inability to relate what he has beheld in the celestial realms.
To understand such matters, Dante observes, one must recognize
that when the human intellect is "exalted [*elevatur*]" to such a
degree, memory fails after its return to itself because it has "tran-
scended [*transcendisse*] the range of human faculty" (sec. 28).

In order to provide an appropriate context for the understanding of this idea, Dante cites three biblical passages that, as we have
seen, are of fundamental importance to the concept of the visionary mode. The first has to do with Paul's ascent to the third
heaven, where he hears "unspeakable words, which it is not lawful
for a man to utter" (2 Cor. 12:2–4); the second has to do with the
three disciples who fall on their faces after the Transfiguration
and "record nothing thereafter, as though memory had failed
them" (Matt. 17:1–8); and the third has to do with the experience
of Ezekiel, who "falls upon his face" after beholding the *visio Dei*
(Ezek. 1:28; Vulg. 2:1).[4] What Dante observes of the first passage
is applicable to all three: "Behold, after the intellect has passed
beyond the bounds of human faculty in its exaltation [*ascensione*],
it could not recall what took place outside of its range" (sec. 28).

Given the nature of the experience that Dante is explicating,
this collocation of prooftexts is especially apposite, for they suggest
that the nature of the ascent to the celestial realms is one that

(Oxford: Clarendon Press, 1920). For the letter to Can Grande, the translations and
commentaries in Charles Sterret Latham's *A Translation of Dante's Eleven Letters*, ed. George
Rice Carpenter (Boston: Houghton Mifflin, 1892), and *Essays on Dante*, ed. Mark Musa
(Bloomington: Indiana University Press, 1964), have also been consulted. Although the
authenticity of the letter to Can Grande has been much debated, we shall assume for the
purposes of discussion that the document in whole or in part is Dante's.

4. References to the Vulgate are to the *Biblia Sacra Iuxta Vulgatam Versionem*, ed.
Robert Weber (Stuttgart: Deutsche Bibelgesellschaft, 1969). Translations are from the
Douay-Rheims version of *The Holy Bible* (Rockford, Ill.: Tan Books, n.d.).

finds its basis not only in Pauline transport as a fundamental locus classicus for this kind of event but in visionary moments that in themselves do not necessarily suggest the experience of ascension. Those moments are at once transfigurational, as in the case of the reference to Matthew, and theophanic, as in the case of the reference to Ezekiel. In both cases the transfigurational and the theophanic combine to underscore the meaning of the ascent, a *topos* that, as we have seen, traditionally underlies the conceptualization of this idea in the earlier accounts.

It is, however, particularly with respect to the experience of Ezekiel that the contextualizing of the poet's own experience in the *Commedia* becomes most interesting. For in the citing of the prooftexts, the reference to Ezekiel assumes a climactic position that suggests the great importance this particular event had for Dante. Even the way it is cited assumes significance, for nothing more is invoked than the fact that in beholding the vision of God, the prophet fell upon his face: "*Vidi et cecidi in faceam meam.*" The nature of the vision itself and our knowledge of it are taken for granted: at issue only is the prophet's response to the vision, that is, the culminating moment of the vision at its most personal and overwhelming point. As heir of this vision, Dante cites it as the culminating moment of that collocation of prooftexts through which the experience of the *Paradiso* is to be understood. Doing so, he aligns himself at once with Saint Paul in his ascent to the third heaven, with the disciples in their witness to the Transfiguration, and, climactically, with Ezekiel in his act of beholding the vision of God, an event that both climaxes and encompasses the others. In all three respects Dante defines and contextualizes the visionary mode to reflect his own disposition as exegete and as poet.

Dante's citation of biblical prooftexts, moreover, is even further bolstered by additional appeals to authority. Adopting the stance of one who has been called upon to respond to the resentment of those who would cast aspersion on his claims, Dante declares: "And should these [prooftexts] not satisfy the cavillers [*Et ubi ista invidis non sufficiant*], let them read Richard of Saint Victor in his book *On Contemplation* [*De Contemplatione*], let them read Bernard in his book *On Consideration* [*De Consideratione*], let them read Augustine in his book *On the Capacity of the Soul* [*De Quantitate Animae*]; and they will cease from their cavilling" (sec. 28). Interesting as a reflection of the kinds of works Dante had in mind to suggest how his own poem should be viewed, these references are equally revealing as the product of an individual who cites them in order to "satisfy the cavillers," that is, to stop the mouths of those who would call into doubt the experience of transcendence that the poet would presume to delineate in poetic form.

From the first point of view the works in question, of course, place Dante squarely in the contemplative traditions examined in the previous chapter and earlier. Whether one considers such works as the *De Contemplatione*, the *De Consideratione*, or the *De Quantitate Animae*, the modes of contemplative theory and practice that these texts portray are very much in agreement with the visionary milieu that Dante invokes through the collocation of biblical prooftexts to underscore the experience depicted through his poem.[5] For Dante as for the medieval world that he inhabited, the systemization of the visionary by means of the contemplative was an inevitable consequence of those transcendent moments experienced by Saint Paul, on the one hand, and, from a transfigurational and epiphanic point of view, respectively, the disciples and the prophet Ezekiel, on the other. All were of a kind; all were fundamental to the traditions of contemplation that underscored medieval culture; and all were crucial to that grand poem in which such visionary moments were most fully realized.

If this suggests something of the contemplative perspective that Dante adopted in his appeals to authority, it is interesting to note the tone in which such appeals are cast. Judging by Dante's implied reference to those who would call his enterprise into doubt, one receives the distinct impression that he conceives himself as a figure who must be prepared to defend himself against all possible

5. The *De Contemplatione* (*On Contemplation*) by Richard of Saint Victor refers to the *De mystica archa* (*The Mystical Ark*) or *Benjamin major* (*Benjamin Major*), and the *De Consideratione* (*On Consideration*) by Saint Bernard refers to *De consideratione ad Eugenium papam tertiam libri quinque*, both discussed in the previous chapter. The *De Quantitate Animae* (*On the Capacity of the Soul*) by Saint Augustine refers to *De Quantitate animae liber unus*. According to Edmund G. Gardner, "the association together in this connection of these three mystics is not peculiar to Dante. We find it similarly in the *Summa Theologiae* of St. Thomas Aquinas, in two articles of the question *De Vita Contemplativa* [II.180.ii–iii]" (*Dante and the Mystics: A Study of the Mystical Aspects of the Divina Commedia and Its Relations with Some of the Mediaeval Sources* [London: J. M. Dent, 1913], pp. 42–43, and passim). In the *De Quantitate Animae* (ca. 388), Saint Augustine offers an account of the seven stages in the progress of the soul "from mere animation, through the life of the senses, rational life . . . , virtue, tranquility or complete trust in God, and the desire of knowing what is true in the supreme degree, to the very vision and contemplation of truth" (Gardner, *Dante and the Mystics*, pp. 44–45; see *PL*, XXXII–XXXIII, esp. 1033–1080).

recrimination. A posture that is consistent with his own personal circumstances as exile, it informs his outlook regarding the visionary contexts of his poem. As one who is constantly aware of the cavillers that beset him, Dante is one for whom both the biblical visionaries and the medieval contemplatives assume in this portion of the letter to Can Grande Della Scala not only exegetical importance but also profound personal significance.

It is this personal dimension that Edmund G. Gardner emphasizes in his discussion of Dante's biblical and postbiblical references at this point in his letter. Addressing himself in particular to the mystical basis of Dante's thought, Gardner suggests that Dante adopts so personal a posture here not only because of his ethical convictions but because of something that he as a visionary actually did experience at a particular point in his career and in which he had an immense personal stake. Such an experience, Gardner argues, determined not only the ethical foundations of Dante's poem but its mystical basis as well. From the ethical point of view, the visionary experience upon which the poem is based was "a sudden realisation of the hideousness of vice and the beauty of virtue, the universality and omnipotence of love, so intense and overwhelming that it came upon Dante with all the force of a special and personal revelation."

Beyond this, however, Gardner argues that the passage of Dante's letter in question clearly implies that more is at stake, that, in fact, Dante (like Saint Paul) is "claiming some ineffable spiritual experience of which he feels himself unworthy, and which he is utterly unable adequately to relate." Elaborating further, Gardner conjectures that the experience might have been

> some momentary flash of spiritual intuition, in which his mind *fu percossa da un fulgore, in che sua voglia venne,* "was smitten by a flash, in which it [his will] was fulfilled" [*Par.* 33:140–141]; in which time and space were annihilated, and the apprehension of the suprasensible, the divine and the eternal was all in all.

If such an event actually did occur, then what Dante says in the letter to Can Grande della Scala about the visions of others is the testimony of an individual who "believed that he himself had experienced one of those contacts with the Divine that are attributed to the great saints and mystics of all creeds." That experience or revelation, Gardner concludes, was "undoubtedly the supreme event of Dante's inner life."[6]

Assuming that the truth of these observations will never be borne out beyond what we are inclined to derive from a reading of the letter as "personal testimony," then the most immediate corroboration for such an idea is, of course, *The Divine Comedy* itself. As the poetic embodiment of the revelations of "the great saints and mystics" to which Dante refers in the letter to Can Grande della Scala, the *Commedia* is at once Dante's most intimate and most dramatic account of the experience that Gardner has in mind. Although the letter adopts the *Paradiso* as its point of focus in the delineation of the visionary experience as both a biblical and postbiblical phenomenon, for our purposes the one text that will provide particularly compelling evidence of the assimilation of the visionary into Dante's thought is the *Purgatorio*, especially those cantos that dramatize the events at the summit of the purgatorial mount (cantos 27–33). Within the environs of this realm the visionary mode, as we have defined it, assumes particular cogency.

II

As an anticipation of the full glory that Dante will experience in the paradisal realms, the events that occur at the summit of the purgatorial mount prepare us for the transcendent experience that will be realized in the third canticle of the *Commedia*. In this respect the last seven cantos of the *Purgatorio* are pivotal, for through the context they establish Dante is able to embark upon his celestial ascent. These seven cantos can be considered a unit that enacts in small the theophanic and transfigurational experience Dante will undergo in the final phase of his pilgrimage. Underlying the visionary circumstances of that enactment are the assumptions that Dante articulates in the letter to Can Grande. Embodying those assumptions, the experience that Dante undergoes within the framework of the seven cantos in which the *Pur-*

6. Gardner, *Dante and the Mystics*, pp. 34–36. With respect to the *Paradiso* itself, this experience is conceived precisely in terms that draw upon and transform aspects of Ezekiel's vision. See John Freccero, "The Final Image: *Paradiso* XXXIII, 144," in *Dante, The Poetics of Conversion*, ed. Rachel Jacoff (Cambridge: Harvard University Press, 1986), pp. 245–257. With respect to the final image, Freccero explores the contexts of the *rota*.

gatorio culminates is one in which the spirit is exalted to the paradisal realms. If those realms find their locus within the terrestrial (as opposed to the celestial) sphere, they are not for that any the less profoundly significant. Prefiguring events in the heaven of heavens, they offer a foretaste of the *Paradisus Dei*. Conceived as a unit, these cantos are replete with associations that have come to assume decisive importance in the delineation of the visionary mode. In order to isolate and comment upon these associations, we might well venture an overview of the events that occur in the last seven cantos. Doing so will establish a basis for the discussion that follows and provide a sense of order in the attempt to assess the structural principles underlying the narrative as a whole.

The narrative falls into three main divisions: (1) the preparation for the vision (cantos 27–28); (2) the vision proper (cantos 29–31); (3) the aftermath of vision (cantos 32–33).[7] In the first division Dante passes through the wall of fire, dreams of Leah and Rachel, enters the sacred wood of the earthly paradise, and encounters Matelda. In the second division Dante beholds the procession of the triumphal chariot, is united with Beatrice, suffers her reproaches, and is immersed in the waters of Lethe. In the third division Dante is confronted with a series of seven visions, witnesses the corresponding metamorphoses of the chariot, hears the mysterious prophecy of the coming savior, and is immersed in the waters of Eunoe.

Within this framework each division might be said to function according to a controlling literary mode. The first division draws heavily upon concepts of pastoral; the second division is indebted to conventions of apocalyptic; and the third division transforms apocalyptic into prophetic history. Although such modal designations overlap, they are useful in suggesting how the action of the narrative is to be understood. A glance at each division and the mode through which it is conceived establishes additional con-

---

7. There have been a number of attempts to determine the structural principles underlying the final cantos. Normally, the last five or six cantos (28 [or 29]–33) are conceived as a unit, but I am convinced that the organizing principle here includes all seven. In agreement is Peter Dronke, *Dante and the Medieval Latin Traditions* (Cambridge: Cambridge University Press, 1986), p. 61. For earlier views, see, among others, Edward Moore, *Studies in Dante*, 3d ser. (Oxford: Clarendon Press, 1903), pp. 178–220, and John S. Carroll, *Prisoners of Hope: An Exposition of Dante's Purgatorio* (London: Hodder and Stoughton, 1906), pp. 390–392.

texts for appreciating how Dante rearticulates the visionary in poetic terms.

Those cantos that constitute the preparation for the vision are crucial in establishing the setting against which the vision itself is beheld. As the action of the twenty-seventh canto makes clear, the preparation for the vision is not undertaken without tribulation and, in fact, its own kind of torment. The purgative process is an ongoing experience, even at the point of greatest consummation. Having already undergone a purificatory journey symbolized by the erasure of the *peccati* in the ascent up the Mount of Purgatory, Dante culminates this part of his *itinerarium mentis in Deum* with a trial by fire. At the limit of the seventh cornice just before sunset of the third day on the Mountain, he faces the prospect of suffering what those confined to this cornice must endure in their quest for the earthly paradise.

The fire represents both the penance of that particular cornice (assigned here to the lustful) and the boundary that separates the earthly paradise from what lies below. In order to enter this paradisal realm, one must be purified in the flames. In this respect the fire recalls the flaming sword of the cherubim placed before paradise and turning every way to prohibit access to the realm that Adam has lost (cf. Gen. 3:24). In anticipation of the reentry into the terrestrial paradise, Dante is made to traverse the barrier of fire. This reentry, however, is to be encouraged rather than denied. The visionary context of that fact is established at the very outset of the canto, when the angel of the cornice appears to the pilgrims outside the flames and sings a portion of the sixth beatitude from the Sermon on the Mount: *"Beati mundo corde"* (27:8), the full statement of which is "Blessed are the clean of heart: for they shall see God [*Beati mundo corde, quoniam ipsi Deum videbunt*]" (Matt. 5:8). It is as much the experience of "seeing God [*Deum videbunt*]" as the purified state requisite to this experience that is at issue here. The *Beati mundo corde* anticipates and is fulfilled responsively by its resolution in the *quoniam ipsi Deum videbunt*.

If such is the framework in which the trial by fire is cast, the visionary implications of this idea are even further reinforced by the drama that follows, for Dante the pilgrim is at first (understandably) terrified at the prospect of subjecting himself to the torment of the flame and must be convinced by Virgil to proceed. As Dante repeatedly resists the admonitions of his guide, the scene assumes a touching and indeed even somewhat comic quality

(27:19–33). The argument that finally convinces Dante to undergo the trial by fire, of course, is that Beatrice awaits him on the other side (27:34–36). As an inducement to Dante not to flag in his determination to complete his passage through the flames, Virgil declares: "Already I seem to behold her eyes [*Li occhi suoi già veder parmi*]" (27:54), a declaration that reinforces this movement toward vision, as if the entire journey has been predicated on the idea that the pilgrim is moving toward that point of supreme sight, supreme illumination, represented by the eyes of his loved one. The *visio Dei* toward which Dante strives is one embodied in the "sight" of Beatrice herself, an idea that is acknowledged at this moment of the passage through the flames.

This visionary context, moreover, is underscored by the apocalyptic dimension it assumes at the culmination of the passage. So Dante relates that, emerging from the flames, he hears an angelic voice singing, "'*Venite, benedicti Patris mei,*' [which was] sounded from within a light that was there, such that it overcame me and I could not look on it" (27:58–60). The allusion, of course, is to Matt. 25:34: "*Tunc dicet Rex his qui a dextris eius erunt: Venite, benedicti Patris mei, possidete paratum vobis regnum, a constitutione mundi* [Then the king will say to those on his right hand, 'Come, blessed of my Father, take possession of the kingdom prepared for you from the foundation of the world']." As Dante expected his readers to know, the allusion is part of Christ's larger declaration that "the Son of man shall come in his majesty, and all the angels with him," as he is seated upon his throne in a posture of judgment. In this triumphant moment all the nations shall be gathered together before him, as he separates (respectively, to the right and to the left) the righteous and the unrighteous (Matt. 25:31–34). Having made his way successfully through the purifying flames, Dante is assured that he, like those to whom the "*Venite, benedicti Patris mei*" is sung, stands ready in that apocalyptic moment of ultimate judgment to "take possession of the kingdom prepared for . . . [him] from the foundation of the world." It is this apocalyptic moment in which all vision eventuates and for which Dante's pilgrimage is a preparation.

The passage through fire, then, operates on a number of levels, both personal and apocalyptic. As such, these levels include the immediate circumstances surrounding Dante's need to overcome all obstacles in his quest to reunite with Beatrice, on the one hand, and the future circumstances surrounding the ultimate experience of those who are to be confronted with their just rewards at the end of time, on the other. At the center of this multileveled (or, to use Dante's term, "polysemous") event is the idea of "seeing," knowing, being illuminated by that vision which is progressively clarified.[8] In this very moment of clarification, however, Dante is made aware that his voyage is still incomplete: he is to remain a *viator* until he is given access to ultimate sight, that point at which he will become a *comprehensor* (compare *Par.* 33:140–141).[9] Until that time his journey must continue. Having emerged from the flames and hearing the promise of what awaits those who have sustained the passage, Dante is accordingly overcome by the light and unable to endure its brilliance.[10] Looking forward to the time when such brilliance will be endured, Dante as seer is prepared to make the transition to ever higher levels of awareness until he is able to behold deity face to face (cf. 1 Cor. 13:12).[11]

Addressing this transitional stage in the seer's maturation, the twenty-seventh canto concludes with Dante's dream of Leah and Rachel (27:94–108). The third and final in the series of dreams that Dante experiences in the course of his pilgrimage through Purgatory (cf. 9:13–18, 19:1–6), this dream, which comes to him just before dawn, brings into focus his concern with the nature of the active and contemplative lives with which the figures of Leah and Rachel are respectively associated in the traditions of

8. See Dante's discussion of the "polysemous" nature of his work in the letter to Can Grande (sec. 7): "*Ad evidentiam itaque dicendorum, sciendum est quod istius operis non est simplex sensus, immo dici potest polysemos, hoc plurium sensuum* [For the elucidation, therefore, of what we have to say, it must be understood that the meaning of this work is not of one kind only; rather the work may be described as 'polysemous,' that is, having several meanings]." This polysemous nature is then discussed according to the fourfold method of interpretation. For elaboration, see, in particular, H. Flanders Dunbar, *Symbolism in Medieval Thought and Its Consummation in the Divine Comedy* (New Haven: Yale University Press, 1929), p. 19; William Anderson, *Dante the Maker* (London: Routledge and Kegan Paul, 1980), pp. 320–345; and T. K. Seung, *Cultural Thematics: The Formation of the Faustian Ethos* (New Haven: Yale University Press, 1976), pp. 21–27.

9. See Singleton's discussion of this distinction in his commentary on the *Paradiso*, III [ii], 585–589.

10. For an exploration of this idea with respect to the concept of light, see Joseph Mazzeo, *Structure and Thought in the Paradiso* (Ithaca, N.Y.: Cornell University Press, 1958), pp. 141–166, and *Medieval Cultural Tradition in Dante's Comedy* (Ithaca, N.Y.: Cornell University Press, 1968), pp. 56–132.

11. See Aquinas's discussion of this point in the *Summa*: "Whether in this life the contemplative life can attain the vision of the divine essence" (II.180.v), as well as his full analysis of contemplation in general (II.180.i–viii), in Saint Thomas Aquinas, *Summa Theologiae*, ed. Dominican Fathers, 60 vols. (Manchester: Blackfriars, 1964), XLVI, 30–31, and passim.

patristic exegesis. The form in which the dream is cast is proleptic: in its depiction of Leah and Rachel it anticipates the figures that Dante will encounter in the cantos that follow.

Accordingly, Dante dreams that he sees a young and beautiful lady going through a meadow gathering flowers and singing. Identifying herself as Leah, who is using her hands to make herself a garland, she compares herself and her activities with those of her sister Rachel:

> "Per piacermi a lo specchio, qui m'addorno;
>   ma mia suora Rachel mai non si smaga
>   dal suo miraglio, e side tutto giorno.
> Ell' è d'i suoi belli occhi veder vaga
>   com' io de l'addornarmi con le mani;
>   lei lo vedere, e me l'ovrare appaga." (27:103–108)

["To please me at the glass I adorn me here, but my sister Rachel never leaves her mirror and sits all day. She is fain to behold her fair eyes, as I am to deck me with my hands: she with seeing, I with doing am satisfied."]

As types of the active and contemplative lives, the figures in this dream represent not only Leah and Rachel (cf. Gen. 29:16–17) but Martha and Mary (cf. Luke 10:38–42).[12] In anticipation of what Dante will encounter in the terrestrial paradise, these figures, of course, also look forward to Matelda and Beatrice, respectively.

Taking into account such configurations, the symbolism implicit in the dream and the form in which it is cast reinforce the visionary dimensions that Dante has been developing throughout. As that which comes to him just before dawn, the dream itself is associated by Dante with the figure of Cytherea, "who seems always burning with the fire of love," a fire that not only recalls the flames that Dante has just traversed but looks forward to that moment of union toward which he has been striving all along (cf. *Purg.* 1:19–21). It is this amatory aspect that underscores the symbolism im-

12. Thus, according to Aquinas, "these two modes of life [the active and contemplative] are exemplified by the two wives of Jacob—the active life by Leah and the contemplative by Rachel—and by the two women who received Christ as a guest—the contemplative life by Mary and the active life by Martha, as Gregory teaches. These symbols would not match the case were there more than two kinds of life. Therefore the division into active and contemplative life is complete" (*Summa* II.179.ii). In addition to our earlier discussion of this distinction, see Dante's own discourse on the active and contemplative lives in the *Convivio* (IV.17), the first associated with Martha, the second with Mary. *The Convivio of Dante Alighieri*, Temple Classics (London: J. M. Dent, 1903).

plicit in the dream. Prefiguring the paradisal environment in which Dante will find himself in the concluding cantos of the *Purgatorio*, the dream projects a bucolic realm of innocence and love, one in which figures delight in their own activities. Leah's activities are those of cultivation and song: in a symphony of voice and movement she gathers flowers to bedeck herself before her glass. This busy world of self-adornment is certain to fulfill the amatory impulse to the extent that it delights in the fruits of its own labors, but it is insufficient in itself to realize the full significance of union. The function performed by the hands must finally be consummated in that performed by the eyes: "she with seeing, I with doing am satisfied [*lei lo vedere, e me l'ovrare appaga*]," observes Leah. As Dante was well aware, the biblical Leah was "bleareyed [*sed Lia lippis erat oculis*]" (Gen. 29:17).[13] Although there is no suggestion of this in Dante's dream, one might observe that as much as Leah may admire herself before her glass, her vision leaves in darkness the full import of what the seer would behold. For that, the seeing of a Rachel is required.

Accordingly, the figure of Rachel is depicted as one totally consumed with the act of seeing. Nor is this a seeing in the physical sense that is suggested in the self-adornments that Leah beholds before her *specchio*. Rachel's seeing is of a decidedly higher order: spiritual, rather than physical, it concerns matters that transcend the trappings (as delightful as they might be) of her immediate surroundings, that is, of the accoutrements of self. In her mode of seeing these accoutrements are entirely obliterated. Never leaving her *miraglio*, she is occupied with the vision of her "fair eyes [*belli occhi*]": that is, she beholds the vehicle of sight, the means of seeing.[14] In a kind of metaphysical flourish Dante portrays the visionary through the trope of eyes that behold eyes. In this way Rachel contemplates not only herself but contemplation itself: she

13. Signifying eyes that are sore, *lippus* can even imply blindness.

14. In this context it is appropriate to distinguish between *specchio* as that which implies the physical reflection of an image and *miraglio* (cf. Provençal *miralh*) as that which implies the act of considering with the intellect. The latter meaning has that about it which suggests *contemplazione spirituale*. Unwilling to turn from her mirror, Rachel is likewise one who is entranced by what she beholds (cf. the various meanings associated with *smagare* and *dismagare*). See the *Grande dizionario della lingua italiana*, comp. Salvatore Battaglia, 13 vols. (Torino: Unione Tipografico-Editrice Torimese, 1978), s.v.; *Dizionario della lingua italiana*, comp. Giacomo Devoto and Gian Carlo Oli (Florence: Felice le Monnier, 1971), s.v.; and *The Cambridge Italian Dictionary*, ed. Barbara Reynolds, 2 vols. (Cambridge: Cambridge University Press, 1962), s.v.

is the essence of the act of contemplation, symbolized in the figure of the eyes that she beholds and that, in turn, behold her as in a mirror.

The idea is one that Dante had anticipated in the *Convivio*. There, he depicts philosophy as contemplating herself "when the beauty of her eyes is revealed to herself." What else is this, asks Dante, "but to say that the philosophising soul not only contemplates the truth, but also contemplates its own contemplation, turning upon itself and enamouring itself of itself by reason of the beauty of its direct contemplation [*ma ancora contempla lo suo contemplare medisimo e la bellezza di quello, rivolgendosi sovra se stessa e di se stessa innamorando per la bellezza del suo primo guardare*]?" (IV.2).[15] Although the context is different, the sense of reciprocity implicit in the act of contemplating contemplation obtains in the idea of Rachel's act of seeing her own eyes in the mirror through which the higher reaches of the contemplative process are realized. In Dante the visionary mode constantly reasserts itself through that act of reciprocal seeing by means of which one undergoes a turning upon oneself (*rivolgendosi*). That supreme moment of reciprocity involves at once the experience of heightened seeing and profound love. Anticipated in the dream of Leah and Rachel, this visionary idea finds expression in the drama that follows.

Awakening to see Virgil and Statius already risen, Dante desires more than all else "to be above." As he stands on the "*grado superno*" of his ascent toward the earthly paradise, Virgil fixes his eyes upon Dante, whom he symbolically "crowns and miters" to indicate the freedom, rectitude, and wholeness that his pupil's will has achieved (27:113–142). In that posture of self-sufficiency Dante is prepared to meet his loved one, a figure whose advent Virgil proclaims in a manner that encompasses all that has gone before: "See the sun that shines on your brow, see the tender grass, the flowers, the shrubs, which here the earth of itself alone produces: till the beautiful eyes come rejoicing which weeping made me come to you, you may sit or go among them" (27:133–138). In the repetition of the imperative to behold ("*vedi ... vedi*"), Virgil invokes at once the paradisal environment that Dante beheld in dream and is now about

---

15. I am indebted to Singleton's comments on *Purgatorio* 27:106 for this idea (II [ii], 660).

to encounter at the summit of his journey. At the same time Virgil's proclamation culminates in a promise of the divine vision toward which that journey has been moving. The vision is appropriately conceived through the synecdoche of eyes ("*occhi belli*"), a synecdoche that both recalls the reasons that impelled Virgil to undertake the journey and alludes to the options that now confront Dante in the fulfillment of his quest.

It is at this point in the narrative that Dante finds himself in the terrestrial paradise. Delineated in canto 28, this discovery brings to closure the first division of the tripartite sequence outlined above. With its emphasis upon the elements of pastoral, this canto prepares us for the grand vision that is to follow. The canto itself is fundamentally heuristic: it provides the means by which Dante's emerging awareness of himself and his surroundings after the trials of his long journey is given expression. This process of realization is signaled in the action of the canto. Beginning with a childlike eagerness ("*vaga*") to "search [*cercar*] within and round about the divine forest [*divina foresta*] green and dense" (28:1–2), it proceeds to a series of discoveries, each more wonderful and delightful than the next. In a triumph of synesthesia the forest comes alive with a sensuous display of fragrance, motion, and sound that draws the pilgrim, step by step, progressively into its confines.

Moving slowly but deliberately through the ancient wood ("*selva antica*"), Dante is given access to its wonders: its undergrowth, its trees and flowers, its birds, and rivulets (28:3–33). In the fragrant and gentle darkness that envelops him he is made aware of his return to a time of pastoral innocence and joy. Unlike the wild, rugged, and harsh "dark wood" ("*selva oscura*") in which he awakens at the outset of the *Inferno* (1:1–6), the *selva antica* of the *Purgatorio* is a place of pleasure rather than of fear. The darkness of this *locus amoenus* is paradoxically an invitation to more discovery, a clarifying of vision as an anticipation of the more profound sights that are to come. For this reason Dante's eyes, which begin in darkness as the canto opens, are given the power of greater sight as the poet moves through the *divina foresta* in his eagerness to behold what is there.

This process of discovery culminates in the figure of the "*donna soletta*" who, in a moment of illumination, suddenly appears to Dante on the other side of the stream (28:34–42). Later identified as Matelda (33:119), she is beheld singing and culling flowers like the Leah of Dante's dream.[16] Whatever else is implicit in her identity and demeanor, she represents a stage in the continuing enlightenment of the poet. The nature of the enlightenment that she provides is appropriately symbolized by that gesture which encompasses all others in the act of divine disclosure. Responding to Dante's desire to know who and what she is, she bestows upon him "the gift of lifting her eyes [*di levar li occhi suoi me fece dono*]", an act that prompts the poet to exclaim: "I do not believe that so great a light shone forth under the eyelids of Venus, transfixed by her son against all his custom" (28:65–66).[17] A further reflection of the amatory dimension of Dante's quest, this moment of illumination serves to intensify his desire to realize the ultimate union he seeks.

As a lover admitted into the *hortus conclusus* of his own lost innocence, he encounters in this pastoral landscape the possibility of recovering a world denied all those unable to attain so profound a height. Having attained this height, Dante is prepared to be instructed by Matelda in the ways of God, so that he, like the Psalmist, may proclaim, "For thou hast given me, O Lord, a delight in thy doings: and in the works of thy hands I shall rejoice [*quia delectasti me Domine in factura tua et in operibus manuum tuarum exultabo*" (Ps. 91:5–6 [92:4–5]). Invoked by Matelda in her allusion to the *Delectasti* of the Psalmist (28:80), this idea of celebrating the handiwork of God concludes the process of enlightenment that Dante undergoes in this canto. So enlightened, Dante learns not only the nature and operation of the terrestrial paradise but its identity as that paradisal realm described by the pagan poets but in fact "historically" delineated by the biblical account. It is this Edenic world to which Dante has returned and to which Matelda alludes in her final pronouncement: "Here the root of mankind was innocent; here is always spring, and every fruit; this is the nectar of which each tells" (28:138–144). With that declaration the canto concludes, and the pastoral underpinnings of the first of the tripartite division finds resolution.

16. Although there have been many attempts to discover who Matelda represents as a historical personage (assuming that one was intended), the precise identity of this character has not been determined. See Singleton, II [ii], 823.

17. Compare the account of Cupid's accidental wounding of Venus, who then falls in love with the mortal, Adonis. Ovid's *Metamorphoses* (10:525–532).

III

At this juncture the second division (cantos 29–31) of the narrative commences. Essentially apocalyptic in focus, that division encompasses the procession of the triumphal chariot, the encounter with Beatrice, and the immersion in the waters of Lethe. Because of the complexity of the details surrounding the description of the procession, an account of its appearance and structure might be in order before proceeding further. As if proclaiming the arrival of the procession, a sudden brightness of increasing intensity floods the forest on all sides, accompanied by a sweet melody that permeates the luminous air. Facing east to behold the source of this phenomenon, Dante, in turn, is "all enrapt [*tutto sospeso*]" by the experience and "still desirous of more joys" (29:16–32). Enveloped by the light, he is able to discern the form of the procession as it makes its way toward him. Calling upon Helicon to pour forth its waters of inspiration, he invokes the Heavenly Muse Urania to aid him in finding a means to express the inexpressible (29:41–42).

As he describes it, the procession approaches first with what initially appear to be seven trees of gold but are in fact seven lighted candlesticks, accompanied with the chant of "Hosanna." The flames of the candlesticks, in turn, streak the sky with the colors of a rainbow, which is spread like a canopy over the entire procession (29:42–78).[18] Conceived as the banners of a great army, the flames of these candlesticks are followed by the main body of the procession, itself divisible into three units: the vanguard (29:61–87), the center (29:88–132), and the rearguard (29:133–150).[19] The vanguard is composed of twenty-four elders clothed in white raiment and crowned with lilies. The elders move in pairs while singing a variation of the benediction of Gabriel to Mary concerning the advent of Christ (Luke 1:28): "Blessed art thou among the daughters of Adam, and blessed forever be thy beauties."

Following the elders there appears the second division of the

18. The outer bands of the rainbow are described as being ten paces apart (29:81). The symbolism suggests the idea of perfection, as well as the Ten Commandments.

19. This tripartite division is indebted in part to the analysis of Moore, *Studies in Dante*, pp. 181–183, whose own interpretation is influenced by such early interpreters as Jacopo della Lana (fourteenth century). Of comparable interest in the ordering of the vision is Carroll, *Prisoners of Hope*, pp. 390–393, and esp. the diagram between pp. 392 and 393.

main body of the procession, that is, the center of the army. There, one finds the "triumphal chariot on two wheels [*un carro, in su due rote, trïunfale*]," drawn by a griffin with two wings stretched upward between the bands. Surrounding the chariot are "four living creatures [*quattro animali*]," each "crowned with green leaves" and each "plumed with six wings, [and] the plumes full of eyes." Dancing in a round at the right wheel of the chariot are three ladies, one of whom is red like fire, the next green like emerald, and the third white like snow. Correspondingly, at the left wheel of the chariot are four ladies clothed in purple, three of whom are led by the fourth who has three eyes in her head. After the center of the army, finally, comes the rearguard, which is made up first of two old men "venerable and grave," second of four of "lowly aspect," and third of an old man "coming alone, asleep, with keen visage." These seven are attired like those figures that constitute the vanguard, except that their heads are encircled by roses and other red flowers rather than lilies. Such, in brief, is the procession that Dante beholds. Its description, which unfolds in as orderly and elaborate a manner as the procession itself, concludes with a thunderclap when the chariot arrives at a point opposite the poet (29:151–154).

Speculation on the allegorical significance of the various details of the procession extends back to the earliest expositors.[20] There

20. See, for example, Jacopo della Lana (fourteenth century), *Comedia di Dante Degli Allagherii col Commento di Jacopo della Lana Bolognese*, 3 vols. in 2 (Bologna: Tipografia Regia, 1866), I, 344–389; Benvenuto Rambaldi da Imola (1331–1380), *Illustrato nella Vita e Nelle Opere e di Lui Commento Latino sulla Divina Commedia di Dante Allighieri*, 3 vols. (Imola: Tipografia Galeati, 1855–1856), II, 566–578; Pietro di Dante (d. 1364), *Pietri Alleghierii super Dantis ipsius Genitoris Comoedian Commentarium* (Florence: Guilielmum Piatti, 1845), 502–515; and Francesco di Bartola da Buti (1324–1406), *Commento di Francesco da Buti sopra la Divina Comedia di Dante Allighieri*, 3 vols. (Pisa: Fratelli Nistri, 1858–1862), 706–723.

In our own time, see, among others, Moore, *Studies in Dante*, pp. 178–219; Carroll, *Prisoners of Hope*, pp. 389–430; Lizette Andrewes Fisher, *The Mystic Vision in the Grail Legend and in The Divine Comedy* (New York: Columbia University Press, 1917); H. Flanders Dunbar, *Symbolism in Medieval Thought and Its Consummation in the Divine Comedy* (New Haven: Yale University Press, 1929), pp. 316–330; J. P. Tatlock, "The Last Cantos of the *Purgatorio*," *MP* 32 (1934): 113–123; Colin Hardie, "Beatrice's chariot in Dante's earthly paradise," *Deutsches Dante-Jahrbuch* 39 (1961): 137–172; Charles S. Singleton's crucial *Dante Studies I: Commedia, Elements of Structure* (1949) (Baltimore: Johns Hopkins University Press, 1977), hereafter referred to as *Elements of Structure*; and *Dante Studies 2: Journey to Beatrice* (1958) (Baltimore: Johns Hopkins University Press, 1977); and the studies of Peter Dronke, esp. "*Purgatorio* XXIX: The Procession," *Cambridge Readings in Dante's Comedy*, ed. Kenelm Foster and Patrick Boyde (Cambridge: Cambridge University Press, 1981), pp. 114–137; *Dante and Medieval Latin Traditions*, pp. 55–81; and "L'Apocalisse negli ultimi canti del is general but not universal consensus, for example, that the seven candlesticks with rainbow bands represent the seven spirits of God or gifts of the Holy Ghost (cf. Isa. 11:12; Rev. 1:4, 12–13); that, as an emblem of the covenant, the rainbow is a symbol of the New Dispensation; that the chant of the "Hosanna" recalls the cry of the crowds celebrating Jesus' entry into Jerusalem (Matt. 21:9); that, within the vanguard, the twenty-four elders accord with the books of the Old Testament, and that their attire signifies the faith in the Redeemer who is to come; that, within the center of the army, the chariot is a symbol of the Church Militant and that its two wheels are either the active and contemplative lives, the Old and New Testaments, or a combination of the two; that the griffin is Christ in his two natures; that the four beasts are the evangelists; that the three ladies dancing by the right wheel symbolize the theological and the four by the left the cardinal virtues; that, in the rearguard, the two old men are the authors of the book of Acts and the Pauline epistles, the four lowlier figures the authors of the general epistles, and the last the seer of the Apocalypse.

These readings have much to recommend them, especially as they bear upon the significance of the procession as a whole. Of particular interest are those interpretations that place the procession in a liturgical setting. According to Lizette Andrews Fisher, for example, the characteristics of the procession bear a "marked resemblance to the procession of Corpus Christi day, which at the time the *Purgatory* was written, had but lately been advanced from a matter of tradition and custom to one of official authorization." This day of festal celebration of the eucharist "included not only the officiating clergy but the monks, the boys with their master, and the friars." Advancing two by two, they were "accompanied by banners, crucifixes, lighted candles, censers, and two subdeacons carrying texts of the gospels." In the midst of the procession was the *feretrum* or bier containing the host. "At the antiphon, *Hosanna, filio David, benedictus qui venus in nomine Domini, Hosanna in excelsi*, all bowed the knee." In response to the next antiphon, *Ave, rex noster*, "the bearers of the *feretrum* took up their burden, and the procession went on through the city, the people bending the knee as the host passed in front of them."[21]

Purgatorio," in *Dante e la Bibbia* (Atti del Convegno Internazionale Promosso da "Biblia," Florence, 26–28 September 1986), ed. Giovanni Barblan (Florence: Leo S. Olschki, 1988), pp. 81–94.

21. Fisher, *The Mystic Vision*, pp. 92–96. Signaling the appearance of Beatrice in *Pur-*

Reinforcing this dimension, H. Flanders Dunbar has suggested the analogy of the Mass, "the supreme drama of the church," an idea corroborated by J. P. Tatlock.[22] According to Tatlock, the Mass was conceived in a manner that involved an episcopal procession representing "Christ's advent and the founding and operation of the church." Accompanying the procession, "seven acolytes in the van with candlesticks represent[ed] the scribes, and their lights the seven gifts of the Holy Ghost," after which "seven subdeacons with books of the gospels represent[ed] the *sapientes*, seven deacons the prophets, twelve higher clergy the apostles, three acolytes with thuribles the Magi; the book of the gospels borne next convey[ed] the teaching of Christ." Last in procession came the bishop, supported by two clergy representing the Old and New Testaments. A symbol of Christ, the bishop advanced "*quasi in curru vectus*," transported as in a chariot, itself a symbol of the *currus Dei*. The deacons standing behind the bishop on the left and on the right were the active and contemplative lives, and the subdeacons represented the parts of Scripture. Corresponding symbolism found its way into other aspects of the procession of the Mass.[23] Whether conceived in terms of the feast of Corpus Christi or the celebration of the Mass, the procession focused upon the *currus Dei* as a manifestation of godhead and as an ecclesiastical institution. As one familiar with the rituals through which the holiest occasions of the church were celebrated, Dante might well have incorporated elements of these rituals into his formulation of the procession dramatized at the summit of the purgatorial mount.

Fascinating as such an approach appears to be, it only begins to suggest the kinds of readings that Dante's procession has elicited. These readings are cited not to argue on behalf of one-to-one relationships but to underscore the complexity of the procession as a whole. What Dante envisions is as much a procession of

---

gatorio 30:19, the *Benedictus qui venit* and the *Ave, rex noster* find their source in Christ's entry into Jerusalem on Palm Sunday (Matt. 21:4–9; John 12:12–15). For an account of the Corpus Christi procession, see the *New Catholic Encyclopedia*, ed. by Staff at The Catholic University of America, 16 vols. (New York: McGraw-Hill, 1967), IV, 345–347.

22. Dunbar, *Symbolism in Medieval Thought*, pp. 315–319; and Tatlock, "The Last Cantos," passim.

23. Tatlock, "The Last Cantos," pp. 114–115. The principal source of Tatlock's analogies is the *Gemma animae* of Honorius Augustodunensis, called of Autun, or more likely of Augsburg (d. 1152). An entire section concerning the chariot of God (entitled "*De curru Dei*") can be found in the *Gemma* (I.6), *PL*, CLXXII, 545–546.

meanings as a procession of images, liturgical or otherwise. As a work that is essentially multivalent or polysemous, the *Commedia* assumes a particular complexity at moments of heightened vision such as that portrayed in the procession. Nor should the attempt to understand the meanings latent in the various images resolve itself simply into an exercise in cryptography. Dante's own reaction to what he beholds should represent a cue to the reader: "I turned round full of wonder [*ammirazion*] to the good Virgil, and he answered me with a look no less charged with amazement [*stupor*]" (29:55–57).

Such *ammirazion* and *stupor* should be the means by which readers determine their response to the text, so that the fundamental mystery of what Dante beholds is not undermined by the paraphernalia of learned exegesis. Such an "anti-interpretive" point of view suggests the need for a reading that is apophatic rather than cataphatic, that relies upon the wonder and amazement generated by the poetic mysteries underlying Dante's "mystical theology" rather than upon the elucidations of a categorical *allegoresis* to disclose meaning at every point. Not that such an *allegoresis* is out of order or contrary to individual moments in the procession: it is just that this approach must be constantly aware of the dangers latent in its own methodology and sensitive to the mysteries it seeks to elucidate.

In his analysis of the procession Peter Dronke adopts the notion of the "hidden comparison [*collatio occulta*]" to suggest how the scene of the procession is to be read. According to this notion the poetic text generates "a new, wondrously ingrafted transplantation, where something assumes its place so surely in the design as if it were born of the theme itself—yet it is taken from elsewhere, though it seems to be from there."[24] It is this sense of the "new, wondrously ingrafted transplantation" that distinguishes the multivalent, indeed, polysemous, dimensions of the text in which the divine procession is portrayed. As an attempt to understand the procession from the perspective of the *collatio occulta*, we shall focus specifically upon what Charles S. Singleton calls "the pattern at the center."[25] For our purposes, that pattern will be seen to

24. See Dronke's "*Purgatorio* XXIX," p. 115. As Dronke makes clear, the concept of the *collatio occulta* comes from the *Poetria Nova* (247–253) of Geoffrey of Vinsauf, the finest of the thirteenth-century theorists. Compare Dronke's discussion of similar issues in *Dante and Medieval Latin Traditions*, pp. 36–37.

25. The reference is to the chapter title in *Elements of Structure*, pp. 45–60.

encompass the chariot and its defining characteristics as a kind of generative source of interpretive insight. Approaching the chariot as focal point, we shall attend not only to the image itself but to the milieu that defines it.

The nature of this milieu is made clear in the matter that prefaces the description of the chariot. There, we are introduced to the four living creatures ("*quattro animali*"). Although preceding the chariot in the order of description, these creatures actually surround it, as it emerges from "the space within the four of them [*Lo spazio dentro a lor quattro*]" (29:106). Conceived in this manner, the creatures provide a framework, a *spazio*, as it were, for understanding the chariot itself. From that perspective Dante is careful to establish the contexts through which not simply the creatures but the vision as a whole is delineated. Foremost among those contexts are the visions beheld by Ezekiel, on the one hand, and Saint John the Divine, on the other. In his delineation of the creatures, then, Dante addresses the reader in the following terms:

> A descriver lor forme piu non spargo
>   rime, lettor; ch'altra spesa mi strigne,
>   tanto ch'a questa non posso esser largo;
> ma leggi Ezechïel, che li dipigne
>   come li vide da la fredda parte
>   venir con vento e con nube e con igne;
> e quali i troverai ne le sue carte,
>   tali eran quivi, salvo ch'a le penne
>   Giovanni è meco e da lui si diparte. (29:96–105)
> [To describe their forms, reader, I do not lay out [lit. scatter] more rhymes, for other spending constrains me so that I cannot be lavish in this; but read Ezekiel who depicts them as he saw them come from the cold parts, with wind and cloud and fire; and such as you shall find them on his pages, such were they here, except that, as to the wings, John is with me, and differs from him.]

The address is remarkable for a number of reasons, not the least of which is the tone in which it is expressed. That tone is almost dismissive: it suggests that, because of other constraints ("*ch'altra spesa mi strigne*"), Dante lacks both the time and possibly the inclination to be "lavish [*largo*]" in his description. Accordingly, he directs the reader to Ezekiel and Saint John the Divine for further detail and corroboration of what he beholds.

Something more is going on here than meets the eye. To be

aware that this is so, we need only recall how Dante, in the letter
to Can Grande, reinforces his notion of the visionary by invoking
the overwhelming experience Ezekiel as the culminating prooftext
of his account. The tone of reverence he adopts there (in connection with his other citations) should suggest the importance
that Ezekiel held for him. What, then, is to be made of the dismissive tone that Dante adopts in the present context? The answer,
I think, lies in a fine irony that underscores the reference. Fully
aware of both the awesomeness of the experience that Ezekiel
undergoes and the inability of any individual, no matter what the
extent of his poetic powers, to do it justice, Dante underscores
the nature of the *collatio occulta* through which it is to be conceived
by adopting a tone that is apparently dismissive but in its very
dismissiveness is paradoxically reverential. To dismiss it in this
manner is in fact to acknowledge Dante's own reverence toward
it, as that which should be encountered not through the poet's
rhymes but through the very words of the prophet who first
underwent that experience on the shores of the Chebar, as he
beheld the living creatures approaching "from the cold parts, with
wind and cloud and fire."

Even in this respect, however, Dante alters the experience by
suggesting that the wings of the creatures he beholds are in agreement with those depicted by Saint John the Divine (that is, six),
as opposed to those described by Ezekiel (that is, four).[26] The
change is notable not only because it aligns Dante in this instance
with the seer of the Apocalypse but because it further complicates
the implications of what Dante says and the way he says it. From
the first point of view the alteration no doubt emphasizes what is
essentially the New Testament perspective embodied in Dante's
poem, a perspective for which the seer of the Apocalypse is understandably invoked as ultimate authority. From the second point
of view one is made aware that in the very act of acknowledging
the significance of Ezekiel by paradoxically adopting a tone that
is dismissive of the precise details of the prophet's vision, Dante
refocuses or indeed "corrects" Ezekiel to accord with this new
perspective. In the process Dante thereby has it both ways: demonstrating his allegiance to Ezekiel by appearing not to attend to
the multiple complexities of his vision, the poet asserts his own

26. The idea of a six-winged creature, as opposed to a four-winged creature, is, of
course, indebted to the seraphim of Isaiah (6:2).

authority through recourse to the New Testament seer. This act of transumption rearticulates what we have seen to be a fundamental characteristic of Ezekiel's own *visio Dei* as a phenomenon constantly undergoing metamorphosis both in the very act of its articulation and in the hands of those later visionaries and exegetes who rearticulate it in their own terms. Dante is no exception: adopting Saint John the Divine's reformulation of the vision, he does not hesitate to reconceive that vision in a new form.

If the foregoing suggests some of the implications of Dante's address to the reader at this stage of his narrative, there are others as well. Not the least of these is that which is implied by what is finally the remarkable statement "*ma leggi Ezechïel.*" In the very process of delineating a vision that is distinctly the product of his own experience, Dante situates that experience not obliquely or by indirection but pointedly and directly in the biblical text. "If you would know what is *happening* to me," he implies, "go to the source and *read* it there." Event becomes text, and, by implication, text event. The experience of an event is synonymous with the reading of a text, and vice versa. As a result of this transformation and interchange, Dante the mystic is at once Dante the poet and Dante the hermeneut. At the height of the visionary experience the two are synonymous. To see the divine is to read the divine as that which unfolds before the poet not only in the form of the books of Scripture marshaled in orderly procession but in the experience of individual events the source of which assumes canonical authority, *is*, in fact, canonized in the body of the poem.[27]

If the "matter" of the mystical event recounted in the text of the poet is grounded in that of the originary event recounted in the text of the prophet, that grounding amounts to a veritable identification. What happens to Dante is not *like* that which happens to Ezekiel: it *is* what happens to Ezekiel, except that what happens to Dante assumes its own form and its own meaning within the context of his poem. In that assumption, the poet not only refashions the "original" but reads or interprets it in a manner that bestows upon the new version all the authority of the old, an

---

27. Compare, in this regard, the comments of Singleton in *Elements of Structure*. Citing Saint Bonaventure's discussion of the cosmic dimensions of Scripture in the prologue to the *Breviloquium* (a text we have discussed in depth in Chapter 7), Singleton observes that the procession is one in which Scripture "literally" unfolds before Dante (*Elements of Structure*, p. 49). It is the *textuality* of the experience that is at issue here.

authority that is as much hermeneutical as it is poetic. Addressing the concept of authority in the *Convivio*, Dante maintains that "authority," as "worthy of faith and of obedience," is consistent with the notion of "poet" as *auctor* (IV.6). No less is true of the present context, one in which the poet assumes an authority tantamount to that bestowed upon the prophet as he beholds his *visio Dei* on the shores of the Chebar. In the new text of that event, which is concurrently a reenactment and an exegesis of it, the poet establishes his own framework by which his particular experience is to be understood.

As an experience that both recreates and reinterprets that which Ezekiel undergoes, Dante's vision at the summit of the purgatorial mount represents his version of the encounter with the *merkabah*.[28] It is this encounter that the description of the living creatures anticipates and frames, as the "triumphal chariot" emerges from the *spazio* encompassed by the *quatro animali*. This *spazio* is at once the physical ground and the interpretive site of that emergence. As Dante envisions the *carro*, it immediately conforms to the two-wheeled vehicle employed by the ancient Romans during war and as the centerpiece of triumphal processions. Establishing this context, Dante observes that not even Rome "gladden[ed] an Africanus or an Augustus with a chariot so splendid" (29:115–116).[29] Reinforcing the classical dimensions of the chariot, Dante alludes to the myth of Phaëthon's ill-fated journey on the chariot of the Sun, "which, going astray, was consumed at devout Earth's prayer, when Jove in his secrecy was just [*quando fu Giove arcanamente giusto*]" (29:117–120).

This and the earlier allusion are interesting for a number of reasons. Comparing the chariot of his vision to those of the classical world, Dante suggests that his *carro* outdoes anything the ancients might have to offer in their portrayal of chariots either in history or in myth, human or divine. The distinctions implicit in both allusions signify the superiority of the Dantean chariot to those of the past. As triumphal vehicles, the chariots of Africanus

28. As far as I can determine, it was Fisher who first called attention to this dimension, only to dismiss it (*The Mystic Vision*, pp. 103–104, n. 4).

29. The references here are to Publius Scipio Aemilianus Africanus Numantinus, known as Scipio the Younger (ca. 185–125 B.C.) and to Gaius Julius Caesar Octavianus, Augustus Caesar (63 B.C.–A.D. 14), the first Roman emperor. Defeating Carthage, Scipio the Younger was honored with a triumph at Rome and with the surname Africanus. Augustus's triumphs are recorded by Virgil (*Aeneid* [8:714–715]) and Suetonius (*De vita Caesarum* [II.xxii.1]). See Singleton, II (ii), 719–720.

and Augustus suggest the pomp attendant upon success in war and the glorification of those who prevailed. The centerpiece of the divine procession that Dante beholds, his *carro* reflects the grandeur and magnificence of a triumph in comparison to which all others pale.

The allusion to the chariot, in turn, carries with it additional connotations. Implied in the reference to this vehicle is not only the splendor that distinguishes it but the element of danger that surrounds the appropriation of its forces by those incapable of controlling them. It is here that the allusion becomes particularly interesting, for underlying the presumption of Phaëthon in thinking himself qualified to undertake a task reserved for the gods is the idea that anyone who would presume to take control of that which so far transcends one's abilities faces the prospect of complete devastation. In this act of devastation we are made aware of the mystery (*arcano*) of the chariot and the secret ways of that God to whose unsearchable nature the chariot is a testament. The allusion, in short, places us directly within the context of the *merkabah* as a phenomenon that carries with it the possibility of great danger and even devastation.

Whether or not the allusion points directly to this idea, there is little doubt that Dante has taken the occasion to refashion the *merkabah* in his own terms. A *yored merkabah* of the first magnitude, Dante has penetrated the world of *pardes*, sustained its dangers, been purified by its fires, and overcome its obstacles in his quest to attain to the realm of the *merkabah*.[30] Having achieved that realm, he integrates it into his own point of view. This point of view is fully delineated in the remaining cantos. There, it assumes a decidely apocalyptic bearing, one reinforced by the realization that, until the thirtieth canto, the chariot is *empty*.[31] It requires the revelation of Beatrice to fulfill the apocalyptic expectations to which the thirtieth canto gives rise from the very outset.

With all eyes focused on the chariot, those expectations are dramatically enhanced and solemnized by the song of welcome to

30. Cf. not only the accounts given in the earlier *hekhalot* literature but that described in the *Zohar* (*Vayaqhel* 209a–212a) concerning the ascent of the soul through the firmaments in order to appear before the divine throne. There, we recall, the soul in Eden undergoes an act of penance by passing through the fires that purge it of its impurities.

31. This idea is given particular cogency by Charles Singleton in his apocalyptic reading in *Elements of Structure*, p. 50.

the bride who is to be glorified: "*Veni, sponsa de Libano* [Come from Libanus, my spouse, come from Libanus, come: thou shalt be crowned]" (Song of Songs 4:8), an anticipation of that apocalyptic moment when Saint John the Divine beholds "the new Jerusalem, coming down out of heaven from God, prepared as a bride adorned for her husband" (Rev. 21:2; see 30:11–12). In keeping with the tenor of this moment, Dante proclaims:

> Quali i beati al novissimo band
>   surgeran presti ognun di sua caverna,
>   la revestita voce alleluiando,
> cotali in su la divina basterna
>   si levar cento, ad vocem tanti senis,
>   ministri e messagier di vita etterna.
> Tutti dicean: "Benedictus qui venis!"
>   e fior gittando e di sopra e dintorno,
>   "Manibus, *oh*, date lilïa plenis!" (30:13–21)

[As the blessed at the last Trump will rise ready each from his tomb, singing Hallelujah with reclad voice, so upon the divine chariot, *ad vocem tanti senis*, rose up a hundred ministers and messengers of life eternal, who all cried, "*Benedictus qui venis*" and, scattering flowers up and around, "*Manibus, oh, date lilias plenis*."]

The rising of the angelic "*ministri e messagior di vita etterna*" upon the chariot as "*basterna* [covered vehicle]" to celebrate the advent of Beatrice assumes an apocalyptic aspect in the trope that projects this moment into the future when the "*beati*" will rise from their sepulchres to sing Hallelujah with a voice "reclad [*revestita*]."[32] A symbol of the "reclothing" of the risen soul in its flesh, the act of adorning at this supreme moment is implicit the very voices that commemorate the event.

The language in which they commemorate that event ("*Benedictus qui venis*"), of course, recalls Christ's own triumphal entry into Jerusalem: "And the multitudes that went before and that followed, cried, saying: *Hosanna to the son of David: Blessed is he that cometh in the name of the Lord: Hosanna in the highest*" (Matt. 21:9; cf. Ps. 117:26). The Hosanna that celebrates the triumphal advent of the procession (*Purg.* 29:51), then, culminates in the *Benedictus*

---

32. For a discussion of the particular significance of the concept concerning the advent of Beatrice, see Singleton, *Dante Studies 2: Journey to Beatrice*, pp. 72–85, hereafter referred to as *Journey to Beatrice*.

that celebrates the advent of Beatrice.[33] Welcomed with the words that greet Christ himself in his entry into Jerusalem, Beatrice assumes the supreme Christocentric role, that of triumphator. Just as the multitude "cut boughs from the trees, and strewed them in the way" (Matt. 21:8), moreover, the angels "scatter flowers" all about. Their gesture, in turn, is accompanied by the words of Anchises to Aeneas in the underworld of the *Aeneid*: "*manibus date lilia plenis* [Give me lilies with full hands]" (6:883). Used there to commemorate the great Romans who would descend from Aeneas' stock, among whom would be the young Marcellus, these words at once herald the generation of the *beati* made possible through the advent of Beatrice and acknowledge Virgil's own role in providing the occasion through which that advent is made possible at this point in the poem. In some respects, finally, it is as much a gesture of valediction to indicate the imminent departure of Virgil (30:49) as it is a gesture of benediction to herald the arrival of Beatrice.

With the arrival of this figure Dante undergoes a visionary experience of profound significance. Conceived through a copiousness of rhetorical exuberance, Beatrice is welcomed with an elaborate simile that graces her like the attire that at once conceals and reveals her presence. Carrying through the concept of adornment that permeates the language of her advent, Dante recalls that

> Io vidi già nel cominciar del giorno
> la parte orïental tutta rosata,
> e l'artro ciel di bel sereno addorno;
> e la faccia del sol nascere ombrata,
> sì che per temperanca di vapori
> l'occhio la sostenea lunga fïata:
> così dentro una nuvola di fiori

---

33. As Singleton points out, Beatrice is welcomed not with "*Benedicta quae venis*" but with "*Benedictus qui venis*." In this way the masculine form of the greeting underscores the association that Dante draws between the advent of Beatrice and the advent of Christ. Not that we are to assume a one-to-one relationship: rather, once again, the allegory is seen to operate on a number of levels (*Elements of Structure*, p. 51). From the liturgical perspective explored earlier, we recall that the *Benedictus* was intoned as part of the Corpus Christi ceremony; it was also sung by the assistants before the Canon of the Mass to indicate the expectation of the bodily advent of Christ. Singleton, citing Tatlock, observes that the *Benedictus* was correspondingly used as "a cry of ceremonial welcome to great personages on earth; as to a Lombard king coming for his coronation at Milan," and so forth (II [ii], 734).

che da le mani angeliche saliva
e ricadeva in giu dentro e di fori,
sovra candido vel cinta d'uliva
donna m'apparve, sotto verde manto
vestita di color di fiamma viva. (30:22–33)

[Sometimes I have seen at the beginning of the day the eastern region all rosy, while the rest of the heaven was adorned with fair clear sky, and the face of the sun rise shaded, so that through the tempering of the vapors the eye sustained it a long while: so within a cloud of flowers, which rose from the angelic hands and fell down again within and without, olive-crowned over a white veil a lady appeared to me, clad, under a green mantle, with hue of living flame.]

The description, of course, is both highly personal and elaborately symbolical. Recalling Dante's references to the sun upon entering the terrestrial paradise at the point of dawn (29:4), the association of the advent of Beatrice with the rising of the sun is a fulfillment of expectations engendered earlier. Here, at the beginning of the day, Dante's own consciousness awakens to the vision that will afford him new enlightenment.

Such illumination is enhanced by the symbolism that underscores the event. At the core of the symbolism is the rising sun itself: an established emblem for the coming of Christ, the figure reenacts the idea that, as an expression of God's mercy, we who sit in darkness are enlightened by "the Orient from on high [*oriens ex alto*]" (Luke 1:78–79; cf. Isa. 9:2).[34] Because of the brilliance of the illumination that emanates from this being, however, its presence must be tempered. Accordingly, Dante envisions the sun as shaded in a manner that will allow the eye to become accustomed to the intensity of its light. As the vehicle of the simile invoked to delineate the advent of Beatrice, this idea finds its tenor in the tempering of her brilliance by the "cloud of flowers [*nuvola di fiori*]" that "rose from the angelic hands and fell down again within and

34. My observations on this central passage are heavily indebted to Singleton's commentary on the *Purgatorio*, II [ii], 376–379. As Singleton observes in *Elements of Structure*, "the image of a rising sun . . . bring[s] with it, out of a long traditional usage, an established burden of symbolic meaning. A rising sun was the image for Christ, the established image for the coming of Christ. Later, in Paradise, we may even see the confirmation of this. For there, where Christ comes in what is truly His triumph, He comes as a sun [*Par.* 23:29]" (p. 51).

without."[35] Bestowing upon Beatrice that sign of reverence and devotion implied by the *"Manibus date lilia plenis,"* the floral benediction of the angelic forms is correspondingly and paradoxically an acknowledgment of the innate splendor that graces the *donna* herself.

At once a gesture of adornment and occultation, the scattering of flowers, in turn, is complemented by the nature of Beatrice's own "appearance": "olive-crowned over a white veil a lady appeared to me, clad, under a green mantle, with hue of living flame." The description is replete with symbolic meanings that resonate throughout the procession. Attired in the three dominant colors of the procession (white, green, and red), she is the consummate expression of the theological virtues, portrayed as ladies that dance in a round at the right wheel of the chariot (29:121–129).[36] At the same time the green of her crown replicates the green leaves with which the *quatro animali* are crowned (29:93). As a symbol of hope, green is her dominant color: it not only distinguishes her crown and mantle but is the very color of her eyes (cf. 31:116). In its association with the tree of Minerva, moreover, the olive crown suggests that aspect of Beatrice's presence symbolized by the figure of Wisdom or Sapientia. From the biblical perspective we recall the extravagant praise bestowed upon this figure as one who is "more beautiful than the sun, and above all the order of the stars: being compared with the light, she is found before it" (Wisdom 7:29). These are only a few of the many associations suggested by the depiction of Beatrice as "olive-crowned."

Complementing such associations are those that reinforce the sense of mystery surrounding Beatrice, who appears before Dante

35. As Singleton reminds us, Christ in His ascension rose in a cloud (Acts 1:9). In the *Vita Nuova* (23:25) Beatrice "is seen to ascend as a little cloud, to the cry of hosanna." As Christ is to return "with the clouds, and every eye shall see him" (Rev. 1:7), so Beatrice returns at this point in the *Commedia*. "The analogy Beatrice-Christ continues to be the controlling pattern of the imagery" (II [ii], 737).

36. White is traditionally the color of faith, green of hope, and red of charity. The color red, moreover, suggests the cardinal virtues as well. Reflected in the purple of the ladies that dance at the left wheel of the chariot (29:130–132), deep red in the Middle Ages was associated with purple. "Dante's use of that color here symbolizes the fact that these are the cardinal virtues that partake of charity, hence are the *infused* cardinal virtues, as distinguished from the *acquired* cardinal virtues, which bear the same names and were known and accessible to the pagans" (Singleton, II [ii], 723).

at this point as a yet-unnamed (and therefore "unknown") *donna*.[37]
In that capacity she is beheld as one who is veiled. So adorned,
she nonetheless represents the reincarnation of her former self,
whom Dante in *La Vita Nuova* had imagined as a being occluded
by a veil in her death.[38] Although once again shrouded in such a
manner, she nonetheless represents the promise of a new life. As
the fulfillment of that promise, she is veiled in white. Beatrice's
veil is an emblem of the reclamation of the purity that Eve for-
feited by her disobedience, an event that had earlier prompted
Dante to reprove "Eve's daring that, there where earth and heaven
were obedient, a woman, alone and but then formed, did not bear
to remain under any veil [*non sofferse di star sotto alcun velo*]" (29:24–
27). Arrayed here in her white veil, Beatrice symbolizes not only
purity but the faith of all those whose attire is a sign of their
uncompromising allegiance to the sanctity of Christ, an idea already sounded in the description of the white robes of the elders
in the procession (29:64–66; cf. Rev. 3:4–5, 18; 4:4; 7:9–14).

As one who is veiled, moreover, the *donna* is a figure whose
appearance is in accord with the mysteries that she embodies.[39]
She herself is the *adytum* into which the high priest must penetrate
in order to understand God's unknowability. An idea that we have
already seen in the earlier traditions of the ascent, it is reasserted
here in the form of the veiled *donna* through whom the divine
mysteries are at once occluded and revealed. As such, her veiled
face is reminiscent of that prophet of prophets who "put a veil
upon his face" to render the brilliance of his own aspect bearable
after his experience of beholding God in the mount (Exod. 34:29–
35; cf. Matt. 17:1–7; 2 Cor. 3:7–18). Such is the aura that surrounds Beatrice as she stands before Dante both metaphorically
"veiled under the angelic festival" and adorned with a "veil that
fell from her head, encircled with Minerva's leaves" (30:65–68).

The adornment through which Beatrice is at once occluded and

37. She reveals her identity only later in the canto: "*Guardaci ben! Ben son, ben son Beatrice*
[Look at me well: indeed I am, indeed I am Beatrice!" (30:73).
38. Cf. *La Vita Nuova* (23:62–65): "*Lo imaginar fallace / Mi condusse a veder madonna morta;
/ E quand'io l'avea scorta, / Vedea che donne la covrian d'un velo; / Ed avea seco umiltà verace, /
Che parea che dicesse: —Io sono in pace* [My wild illusions / Led me to see my lady (Beatrice)
lying dead, / And as I looked at her / I saw that ladies hid her with a cloth. / Such was the
joyful resignation on her face, / It was as if she said: —I am in peace]"; trans. Mark Musa
(Bloomington: Indiana University Press, 1965).
39. From the sacramental point of view, she recalls the Host that is veiled as part of
the ritual of the Mass, an aspect discussed above.

revealed, finally, culminates in the realization that this is a figure
"*vestita di color di fiamma viva* [clad with the hue of living flame]."
The implications of such an idea are manifold. Having passed
through the *fiamma* that is preparatory to the entrance into the
terrestrial paradise, Dante is well aware of what fires of this sort
signify. It is this recognition that prompts him to exclaim upon
seeing Beatrice: " '*Men che dramma | di sangue m'è rimaso che non
tremi: | conosco i segni de l'antica fiamma*' ['Not a drop of blood is
left in me that does not tremble: I know the tokens of the ancient
flame']" (30:46–48). Embodying the force of the *antica fiamma*, the
fiamma viva is the means by which the ancient flame is resuscitated
once the passage through the purificatory fires has been accomplished. The *fiama viva* in which Beatrice is clad suggests other
readings as well, ones that recall the fact that the procession itself
is, as it were, encompassed with flames as it moves into Dante's line
of vision (29:52, 73).

The procession as a whole reenacts that sense of awesomeness
associated with Ezekiel's own *visio Dei* as that which appears to the
prophet not only with "a fire infolding it" and brightness all about
it but is consummated in that Enthroned Figure enveloped by
fire: "From his loins and upward, and from his loins downward,"
proclaims Ezekiel, "I saw as it were the resemblance of fire shining
round about" (1:4, 27). Reflected in the *fiamma viva* that emanates
from Beatrice as a counterpart to the Enthroned Figure that the
prophet beholds in his fiery vision, the living flame in which the
donna is clad at once recalls these earlier contexts and imbues them
with renewed meaning. As this flame radiates from the attire of
Beatrice, it suggests that profound love through which the quest
of the *viator* will ultimately be fulfilled.

Whatever the sources of Dante's depiction of Beatrice, the beau-
tifully and elaborately adorned *donna* upon her chariot represents
a most striking figure, one that finds its correspondence in a host
of analogues. In her own way Beatrice here suggests her counterpart in the Judaic traditions. We recall in particular the Zoharic
rendering of the *Shekhinah* upon her *merkabah*. Attired as a queen,
the *Shekhinah* or *Matrona*, as she is variously designated, represents, we recall, the feminine element in God. It is this queenly
figure that the *yored merkabah* of later Judaic lore beholds in his
progressive ascent to the throne-world in order to encounter in
the highest reaches the King Himself within His *merkabah*. As such
a *Shekhinah* upon her own chariot, Beatrice, too, has all those

qualities through which Dante as *yored merkabah* has access to the divine. She, too, embodies what might be called the feminine element in God, that aspect through which the seer finds his way to a full understanding of godhead. As we have seen, the idea is hardly foreign to the Christian traditions. Already present in such figures as Saint Bernard, it early assumed its own form within the traditions of patristic commentary. Appropriating such traditions and refashioning them, Dante assimilates the idea of the feminine dimension of godhead into his vision of Beatrice, who stands magnificently attired before the seer as the object of his visionary quest within the terrestrial paradise.

Before this quest can be fulfilled, however, Dante must first become accountable for the sins of his past life. That is, he must first undergo the reproaches of Beatrice (30:73–31:69).[40] Having endured judgment and confessed his sins in a state of contrition, Dante experiences a penance of self-reproach and suffering that culminates in the absolution afforded by his baptismal immersion in Lethe. This event, in turn, is accompanied by the *"Asperges me"* (Ps. 50:9) that testifies to his cleansing (31:91–108). So purified, he finds himself on the other side of the stream prepared to consummate that beatific vision made manifest in the figure of Beatrice. The nature of this experience is signaled by *"le quattro belle* [the four fair ones]," that is, the cardinal virtues, who, as handmaids, encircle Dante and make him part of their dance (31:103–108). In that festive moment they declare to the cleansed *viator*: *"Merrenti a li occhi suoi; ma nel giocondo / lume ch'è dentro aguzzeranno i tuoi / le tre di là, che miran piu profondo* [We will bring you to her eyes; but in the joyous light which is within them the three on the other side, who look deeper, shall quicken yours]" (31:109–111). The declaration suggests that progressive clarification and intensification of vision implicit in the movement from the cardinal virtues, dancing on the left side of the chariot, to the theological virtues, dancing on the right. Whereas the cardinal virtues move Dante to the point of vision, the theological virtues become the means by which his ability to see is brought fully into play. Before the eyes of Beatrice, Dante is finally able to see.

This experience is enacted as a divine visionary drama, one in

---

40. For an enlightening discussion of this aspect, see Moore, *Studies in Dante*, pp. 221–252. Moore discusses the nature of the reproaches leveled at Dante and what those reproaches imply about his former life.

which the eyes of Beatrice are the central point of focus. Within this drama the setting is arranged such that Dante as seer is first led to a position facing the griffin at the front of the chariot (31:113). As the object of vision, Beatrice, in turn, at once faces Dante and focuses her eyes upon the griffin (31:114). She is both the seer and the seen. The drama itself is divided into two acts, each of which represents a stage in Dante's emerging perception. The first act is orchestrated by the cardinal virtues; the second, by the theological virtues. As a signal for the first act to begin, the cardinal virtues address Dante: "*Disser: 'Fa che le viste non risparmi; / posto t'avem dinanzi a li smeraldi / ond' Amor già ti trasse le sue armi'* ['See that you spare not your gaze,' they said, 'we have placed you before the emeralds from which Love once shot his darts at you']" (31:115–117). Recalling the initial experience of love that infuses *La Vita Nuova*, the reappearance of Beatrice as the embodiment of Amor in its most exalted form is centered within the emerald eyes that at once transfix with their gaze and brilliantly reflect what they themselves behold.

In response to so profound and complex a moment of seeing, Dante exclaims: "*Mille disiri piu che fiamma caldi / strinsermi li occhi a li occhi rilucenti, / che pur sopra 'l grifone stavan saldi* [A thousand desires hotter than flame held my eyes on the shining eyes that remained ever fixed on the griffin]" (31:118–120). The *fiamma viva* that emanates from Beatrice is rearticulated in the experience of those desires that hold Dante's eyes on the *occhi rilucenti*. Undergoing that experience, Dante is, in a sense, able to see as he has never seen before: "*Come in lo specchio il sol, non altrimenti / la doppia fiera dentro vi raggiava, / or con altri, or con altri reggimenti* [As the sun in a mirror, so was the twofold animal gleaming therewithin, now with the one, now with the other bearing]" (31:121–123). The effect of such an event causes Dante to marvel ("*mi maravigliava*") in the reflected vision of a creature "stand[ing] still in itself [*in sé star queta*], and in its image changing [*trasmutava*]" (31:124–126). Speculation on the significance of this visionary event provides insight into the multiplicity of its meanings.

As a fulfillment of the emphasis upon seeing made apparent as early as Dante's dream of Leah and Rachel, the revelation of Beatrice commences, as indicated, with the vision of her eyes. Dante is led not just to Beatrice but "*a li occhi suoi*" as the emblems of the visionary experience. That experience is one of being inspired by the flames of love, on the one hand, and of achieving a

new level of perception, on the other. The first is suggested by
the light that springs forth from the eyes that are beheld as they
transfix the eyes of the beholder. So transfixed, the beholder's
eyes are consumed with the desires of renewed love. The second
is suggested by the image reflected within the eyes that are beheld
as they in turn focus upon another object. With the head of an
eagle and the body of a lion, this other object is the griffin, the
mysterious animal that, as Dante conceives it, is in itself unchang-
ing but in its reflected image is constantly undergoing a transformation from one state to another.

Whatever is to be made of this creature both in itself and in its
transformation as reflected in the eyes of Beatrice, it is clear that
Dante beholds revealed to him at this moment mysteries of the
profoundest sort.[41] The precise meaning of those mysteries is not
at issue. What is significant is the dynamic quality implicit in the
vision: forever changing and yet constantly the same, that which
is reflected in the eyes of Beatrice *"come in lo specchio il sol* [as the
sun in a mirror]" embodies that sense of dynamism (*trasmutava*)
so essential to the visionary mode. Underlying this dynamism is
the realization that what Dante beholds must be interpreted apophatically as a reflection of the *collatio occulta* implied by the vision
as a whole. Fundamental to the disclosure of meaning is the ability
not to know. Like the source from which the visionary mode springs,
the vision that is beheld knows more than the beholder who sees.
So it is with Dante at this moment: what he sees remains, by virtue
of the nature through which it is revealed, that very mystery its
dynamism discloses. The proper response to this event is indicated
by Dante's own reaction: I "marveled" at what I saw. He stands
at once "full of amazement [*stupore*] and gladness [*lieta*]" (31:127).

Even this state, however, is preparatory to a higher and more
profound one, for, although Dante is sustained by what he sees,

---

41. The commonly accepted interpretation of the griffin is that it symbolizes Christ as
He is manifested in His divine and human natures. The transformation that the reflected
image of the griffin is seen to undergo within the mirror of Beatrice's eyes is looked upon
as the alternation from one nature to next as a reflection of the reciprocity implicit in the
hypostatical union (Singleton, II [ii], 718, 776). Indebted to what is supposed to have been
(but may in fact be a misreading of) Isidore of Seville's interpretation in the *Etymologiarum
sive Originum libri XX* (XII. ii.17), the identification of the griffin with Christ has been
called into doubt by Colin Hardie, "The Symbol of the Gryphon in *Purgatorio* xxix.108
and Following Cantos," *Centenary Essays on Dante* (Oxford: Clarendon Press, 1965), pp. 103–
131. In its theriomorphic form as part eagle and part lion, Dante's griffin shares characteristics with the four animal forms that surround the chariot.

"that food [*cibo*]," which is "sating of itself [*saziando di sé*]," likewise "causes hunger for itself [*di sé asseta*]" (31:128–129), a fact that inaugurates the second act of the visionary drama in which the seer participates. If the first act is orchestrated by the cardinal virtues, the second is orchestrated by the theological virtues. Revealing themselves by their bearing to be of a "higher order [*alto tribo*]" than their counterparts, the theological virtues come forward "dancing to their angelic roundelay [*danzando al loro angelico caribo*]."

It is this festive dance into which Dante is taken as the theological virtues address Beatrice in their song:

> "Volgi, Beatrice, volgi li occhi santi,"
>   era la sua canzone, "al tuo fedele
>   che, per vederti, ha mossi passi tanti!
> Per grazia fa noi grazia che disvele
>   a lui la bocca tua, sì che discerna
>   la seconda bellezza che tu cele." (31:133–138)

["Turn, Beatrice, turn your holy eyes upon your faithful one," was their song, "who has moved so many steps to see you. For grace do us the grace to unveil to him your mouth, that he may discern the second beauty which you conceal."]

Two activities are implied by this appeal: whereas the first involves a movement of the eyes from an oblique line of vision to a direct line of vision, the second involves a removal of all impediments to a direct encounter with the face in its entirety. In both gestures the seer is made fully aware not only of the visionary but of the oracular. With this awareness he experiences the effects of a complete unveiling or *revelatio* as anticipated in the first act of the visionary drama and as fulfilled in the second act.

Exclaiming "*O isplendor di viva luce etterna* [O splendor of living light eternal!]" in response to this revelatory disclosure, Dante at first acknowledges the glory of what he beholds and then immediately attests to his inability to render that glory by means of any poetic depiction (31:138–145).[42] This attestation is tantamount to an acknowledgment of the apophatic approach that

42. The revelation of Beatrice through the laying aside of her veil is anticipated by its profane counterpart in the rending of the siren's garments to disclose her ugliness and filth in Dante's second dream during his journey up the purgatorial mount (19:7–33). Whereas Beatrice's *revelatio* is that of divinity, the siren's is that of its opposite.

Dante adopts both as poet and as interpreter of his own visionary experience: as one undergoes that experience through the effects of a progressive revelation, one becomes increasingly aware of one's inability to *know*, that is, to conceptualize that which finally transcends the knowable and conceptual. Such is Dante's state of mind at this moment, one that represents a pivotal point in the drama through which the visionary mode unfolds at the summit of the purgatorial mount. This event brings to a close the thirty-first canto and, with it, the second division of the tripartite delineation of what might be called Dante's encounter with the *merkabah* in the concluding cantos of the *Purgatorio*.

IV

As indicated earlier, the final two cantos represent the dramatization of the apocalyptic in the form of prophetic history. This involves a series of seven visions, accompanied by a series of transformations that the chariot undergoes, a commentary on the meaning of those visions culminating in an enigmatic announcement of the eschaton, followed by Dante's immersion in the waters of Eunoe as a fulfillment of the process begun by his immersion in the waters of Lethe. As recounted in the thirty-second canto, the series of seven visions assumes the form of a visionary pageant populated by its own fantastic creatures that participate in the masque witnessed by Dante before the *albero* or tree to which the pole of the chariot has been bound by the griffin (32:37–160).

In the unfolding of the masque the visions are depicted in the following manner: First, an eagle swoops down through the branches of the tree, rending its foliage, after which it smites the chariot with all its force (32:112–117). Next, the chariot is invaded by a lean and hungry fox that is driven away by Beatrice (32:118–123). After this the eagle descends once again and leaves the chariot covered with its feathers (32:124–139). Following these events a dragon issues from the earth between the chariot wheels, drives its tail upward through the floor of the chariot, and drags away part of it (32:136–141). Thereafter, the chariot undergoes a transformation whereby it puts forth seven heads, three on its pole and one on each of its corners. Whereas the first three of the seven heads have two horns, each of the others has one (32:142–147). Finally, there appears on the transformed chariot a shameless whore, accompanied by a giant standing on the ground beside the *carro*. Although the whore and the giant kiss one another repeatedly, the giant takes offense because she attempts to flirt with Dante. As a result the giant beats the whore mercilessly, after which he loosens the chariot, now become a monster, and draws what remains of the vehicle, occupied by the whore, through the wood and out of sight (32:148–160). Such in brief is the masque of the seven visions witnessed by Dante before the *albero*.

As an expression of topical allegory, each of these visions has received detailed commentary centered on the *status ecclesiae* or ages of the church from the earliest times to those contemporary with Dante. Thus, the first is seen to represent the series of persecutions suffered by the church under the early Roman emperors; the second, the early heresies that were suppressed through the authority of the church; the third, the acquisition of temporal wealth as a result of the Donation of Constantine; the fourth, those great schisms (such as Mohammedanism) through which the fabric of the church was rent; the fifth, the ecclesiastical accession of temporal possessions (among them, the Donations of Pepin and Charles the Great); the sixth, the further corruptions of the church manifested in such events as the appointment of the seven Electors of the Empire; and the seventh, the Avignon captivity.[43]

How accurate these and corresponding readings are need not concern us here. What is of significance is the distinctly apocalyptic basis of the visions, one that derives its primary impetus from the book of Revelation itself, particularly those chapters that recount the opening of the seven seals (Revelation 6–8). With the apocalyptic bearing suggested through such contexts, the portrayal of the *status ecclesiae* extends into history the institutional dimensions of the vision that first appeared to Dante in processional form upon his arrival in the terrestrial paradise. In this respect the *status ecclesiae* is a procession as well.

Whereas the first procession might be looked upon as "history"

43. This account is indebted to Edward Moore's *Studies in Dante*, pp. 201–209. See also Singleton, II [ii], 789–807, which reiterates, as well as elaborates, Moore's analysis. Especially illuminating are the studies of Kaske, "Dante's *Purgatorio* XXXII and XXXIII: A Survey of Christian History," *UTQ* 43 (1974): 196–211; and "The Seven *Status Ecclesiae* in *Purgatorio* XXXII and XXXIII," *Dante, Petrarch, Boccaccio: Studies in the Italian Trecento in Honor of Charles S. Singleton*, ed. Aldo S. Bernardo and Anthony Pellegrini (Binghamton, N.Y.: Medieval and Renaissance Texts and Studies, 1983), pp. 89–113.

as it exists in "the mind of God," the second is history as it is allowed to work itself out in a "material universe." As R. E. Kaske observes,

> the Procession of Scripture—unearthly, severely ordered, and using as its major symbols the Books that are themselves the word of God —is history seen, as it were, *sub specie aeternitatis*; the historical survey of Cantos XXXII and XXXIII, allegorical though it is, presents with greater liveliness and variety the vicissitudes and ultimate triumph of this divinely ordained drama when it is put into production on the imperfect stage of earth.[44]

Conceived in this manner, the events surrounding the emergence of the procession as it is first beheld *sub specie aeternitatis* find their counterpart in those surrounding the emergence of the procession as it is thereafter beheld *sub specie temporis*. What is true of the first procession is no less true of the second: the chariot is at the very center of the drama. Particularly with respect to that which occurs *sub specie temporis*, the account of the *status ecclesiae* reformulates in apocalyptic terms the fate of the chariot, a fate that, as we have seen, causes it to undergo a multitude of transformations in the working out of history.

Whether in the form of the smiting and subsequent adorning of the chariot by the eagle, the invading of the chariot by the fox, the desecration of the chariot by the dragon, or the monstrous metamorphosis through which the chariot puts forth seven heads with horns, one discovers how crucial the transformative nature of this vehicle is to an understanding of its significance. Underlying the Dantean delineation of the *carro* as central symbol is that transformative impulse so consistent with the corresponding impulse through which the *merkabah* is made known from its point of origin in the biblical text to the Judaic and Christian hermeneutical traditions that reformulate it and recreate it in their own terms. For Dante, the transformative impulse, of course, assumes a distinctly ecclesiastical bearing. As depicted in the working out of history in the final two cantos of the *Purgatorio*, the Dantean *carro* is tantamount to the Church Militant.

Accepting this as a given, we can see that what makes the trans-

---

44. "Dante's *Purgatorio*," p. 211. Kaske quite properly sees the visions extending into the thirty-third canto with the prophecy of the DXV or *"cinquecento diece e cinque* [five hundred, ten, and five]" (33:43–45).

formations so interesting are the ties that Dante establishes between the *carro* as a vehicle with its origins in Old Testament
prophecy ("*ma leggi Ezechïel*") and the *carro* as a vehicle with its
reformulation in New Testament apocalyptic ("*Giovanni è meco e
da lui si diparte*"), an act that moves the site (*spàzio*) of interpretation
from Ezekiel to Saint John the Divine. In that movement the *carro*
itself is radically transformed. Having already suggested the possibility of that movement in the twenty-ninth canto (96–105),
Dante reintroduces it here as an event in his reassimilation of
Ezekiel's *visio Dei* into the fantastic panorama that underlies the
apocalyptic working out of history made apparent in the visions
of Saint John the Divine. Inspired by this apocalyptic point of
view, Dante gives us the new *merkabah* as that which undergoes
the transformative and ultimately destructive fate of the *carro*
buffeted by the adversities of that which transpires within the
context of history conceived *sub specie temporis*.

Beset by forces it can no longer control, the *carro* becomes a
vehicle for shameless whores, instead of divine maidens, as that
which, once the sublimest of entities, is now a monster of horren-
dous aspect:

> et vidi mulierem sedentem super bestiam coccineam plenam nomi-
> nibus blasphemiae habentem capita septem et cornua decem et mu-
> lier erat circumdata purpura et coccino et inaurata auro et lapide
> pretioso et margaritis habens poculum aureum in manu sua plenum
> abominationum et inmunditia fornicationis eius. (Rev. 17:3–4)
> [And I saw a woman sitting upon a scarlet coloured beast, full of
> names of blasphemy, having seven heads and ten horns. And the
> woman was clothed round about with purple and scarlet, and gilt
> with gold, and precious stones and pearls, having a golden cup in
> her hand, full of the abomination and filthiness of her fornication].

Such is the fate of both the chariot and the charioteer in the
apocalyptic working out of history that the *carro* undergoes in the
final two cantos of the *Purgatorio*.

With the demise of the chariot, a new vision takes its place, a
new understanding of what it means to ascend to the divine
realms. As a result of that ascent, we are presented with a uniquely
Dantean refashioning of the traditions that underlie the formulation of the *merkabah* as a phenomenon of crucial importance to
the visionary point of view. In its expression of that point of view
Dante's *carro* emerges as a vehicle that embodies its own dynamics

and its own distinguishing characteristics. With intimate ties to
the kind of outlook through which the *merkabah* assumed a position of profound significance to the traditions that trace their
origins to Ezekiel's *visio Dei*, Dante's *carro* is nonetheless *sui generis*.
Portraying it as coming forth in grand procession at the summit
of the Purgatorial mount, Dante bestows on it a life and a history
of its own. This is a chariot with a history, with a beginning and
an end. Moving from the grandeur of eternal vision, it is subsumed
into the temporal flux of alteration, of transformation, and finally
of desecration. As grand as it is, it cannot survive Dante's ultimate
visionary experience. This is what Dante the pilgrim comes to
learn in the final two cantos, as his *carro* gives way to a totally new
perspective.

Already implicit in the earlier cantos, that perspective is one
that is bestowed upon Dante as a result of his encounter with
prophetic history in the final two cantos of the *Purgatorio*. Having
explored something of the nature and meaning of that encounter
in the foregoing discussion, we shall conclude with a glance at the
way that encounter is dramatized. That is, by attending to certain
aspects of the experience that Dante undergoes, we shall be concerned with the manner in which his encounter with prophetic
history is delineated as a dramatic event. For that purpose we shall
return to the contexts established at the point at which the face
of Beatrice is fully revealed, a disclosure, we recall, that culminates
the thirty-first canto. There, Beatrice reveals herself not only
through her eyes but through her mouth. In this revelation she
becomes an emblem of both the visionary and the oracular. It is
in particular these dimensions that come into play in the final two
cantos. Whereas the thirty-second canto depicts in visionary form
the procession through which the fate of the church is disclosed
(32:37–160), the thirty-third canto portrays in oracular form Beatrice's commentary on that procession and her prophecy of the
eschaton (33:34–78).

From the dramatic perspective that underlies these disclosures,
the experience that Dante himself undergoes accords with the
tenor of what he beholds and hears. In both respects Dante is
made ready for the experience by falling into a deep sleep, the
nature of which is depicted in visionary and transfigurational
terms. Although impossible to describe, the kind of sleep that
Dante falls into corresponds in intensity, as he observes, to that
experienced by the hundred-eyed guardian of Io, Argus, who was

put to sleep by Mercury's song of the nymph Syrinx, loved by Pan (32:64–66). Recalling that the sleeping guardian was then slain by Mercury, Dante makes a point of focusing upon what he terms Argus's "pitiless eyes [*occhi spietate*]," those eyes whose "long vigil" cost Argus so dear ("*li occhi a cui pur vegghiar costò sì caro*"). The allusion calls to mind not only the myth of Argus in the *Metamorphoses* (1.567–747) but Dante's earlier incorporation of that myth to underscore the multi-eyed nature of the *animali* surrounding the chariot. Specifically associating the eyes of the *animali* with those of Argus, Dante comments: "*Ognuno era pennuto di sei ali; / le penne piene d'occhi; e li occhi d'Argo, / se fosser vivi, sarebber cotali* [and each of them was plumed with six wings, the plumes full of eyes, and the eyes of Argus, were they alive, would be such]" (29:94–96).[45] Considering the power latent in these *occhi spietate*, the idea of closing them in sleep is not without significance. In his association of himself with this experience, Dante implies not only that the *animali* that surround the chariot are in some very real sense a manifestation of his own visionary faculties but that in the closing off of those faculties through slumber, something of momentous import is about to commence.

This fact is underscored by the allusion through which Dante describes the nature of his awakening. Maintaining that a "*splendor*" rends the "*velo*" of his sleep, he hears a voice call, "*Surgi* [Arise]," an exclamation that immediately brings to mind the "*Surgite*" that the disciples hear after they have witnessed the Transfiguration of Christ (Matt. 17:1–8). As Dante is overpowered and then returned to consciousness,

> Pietro e Giovanni e Iacopo condotti
>   e vinti, ritornaro a la parola
>   da la qual furon maggior sonni rotti,
> e videro scemata loro scuola
>   così di Moïsè come d'Elia,
>   e al maestro suo cangiata stola
> tal torna' io. (32:76–82)
> [Peter and John and James were overpowered, and came to themselves again at the word by which deeper slumbers were broken,

45. The emphasis upon the eyes of the creatures embedded in the wings is conceptualized both biblically as a characteristic of the visions of Ezekiel (1:12) and Saint John the Divine (4:6) and mythologically as a dimension of that "all-seeing" one Argus, surnamed Panoptes, an idea already enunciated as early as Jerome: *Commentariorum in Hiezechielem* (I.18.465–75).

and saw their company diminished alike by Moses and Elias, and their Master's raiment changed, so I came to myself].

The act of coming to oneself after sleep is placed squarely within the context of those who were correspondingly overcome and then brought back to life on the occasion of the Transfiguration. These are the disciples, who are led up to a high mountain to behold Jesus transfigured before them, "as his face shone as the sun" and "his garments became white as snow," and as he conversed with the prophets Moses and Elijah. Something of this sort, the allusion suggests, characterizes the experience of Dante as he, too, is overcome and then returned to life. At the center of his experience in these final cantos is a transfiguration of the greatest moment. In that transfiguration all that exists *sub specie temporis* will be destroyed, so that that which exists *sub specie aeternitatis* may endure (cf. Heb. 12:27–28).

What endures is the renewed sense of the significance of the eschaton. As Beatrice makes clear in the final canto of the *Purgatorio*, this significance is intimately tied to the fate of the chariot, that "vessel [*vaso*]" which once existed but is now destroyed ("*fu e non è*) as a result of the ravages it suffered under the dragon ("*serpente*") (33:34–36). Recalling once again the apocalyptic beast that bears the whore in Revelation 17, the implied allusion is made even more compelling in the eschatological declaration that climaxes Beatrice's discourse:

> Non sarà tutto tempo sanza reda
>   l'aguglia che lasciò le penne al carro,
>   per che divenne mostro e poscia preda;
> ch'io veggio certamente, e però il narro,
>   a darne tempo già stelle propinque,
>   secure d'ogn' intoppo e d'ogne sbarro,
> nel quale un cinquecento diece e cinque,
>   messo di Dio, anciderà la fuia
>   con quel gigante che con lei delinque. (33:37–45)

[Not for all time shall be without an heir the eagle that left its feathers on the chariot, whereby it became a monster and then a prey: for I see surely, and therefore I tell of it, stars already close at hand, secure from all check and hindrance, that shall bring us a time wherein a Five Hundred, Ten, and Five, sent by God, shall slay the thievish woman, with that giant who sins with her.]

Whatever the precise meaning of the *gematria* embedded in the reference to the eschaton as *"cinquecento diece e cinque,"* one fact regarding this *"enigma forte* [hard enigma]" (33:50) is evident: the advent of this mysterious figure is one that fully takes into account the transformations suffered by the *carro* in the working out of human history.[46]

In the apocalyptic formulation of that idea, the site (*spàzio*) of interpretation is once again consistent with the movement from Ezekiel to Saint John the Divine. One thinks of Rev. 19:11–13: *"et vidi caelum apertum et ecce equus albus et qui sedebat super eum vocabatur Fidelis et Verax vocatur et iustitia iudicat et pugnat oculi autem eius sicut flamma ignis et in capite eius diademata multa habens nomen scriptum quod nemo novit nisi ipse et vestitus erat vestem aspersam sanguine et vocatur nomen eius Verbum Dei* [And I saw heaven opened, and behold a white horse; and he that sat upon him was called faithful and true, and with justice doth he judge and fight. And his eyes were as a flame of fire, and on his head were many diadems, and he had a name written, which no man knoweth but himself. And he was clothed with a garment sprinked with blood; and his name is called, the Word of God"]. As one who "had a name written, which no man knoweth but himself," this mysterious emissary of divine vengeance becomes the means by which the forces that wreaked havoc on the *carro* would be undermined. So is "the great harlot which corrupted the earth with her fornication" overcome (Rev. 1: 2) and the beast, along with its armies, cast down (Rev. 19: 19–20). As a result of these events, the pollutions suffered by the *carro* will be removed.

Reflecting the apocalyptic perspective that Dante establishes in the announcement of the eschaton, the adoption of the *enigma forte* to proclaim such occurrences reinforces at once the occlusive

46. There has been a great deal of debate over the meaning of the *cinquecento diece e cinque*. See the entry "Cinquecento diece e cinque" in the *Enciclopedia dantesca*, ed. Umberto Bosco, 6 vols. (Rome: Instituto della Enciclopedia Italiana, 1970–1981), s.v., as well as Singleton, II (ii), 813–814, for summaries and appropriate references. The suggestion of the *cinquecento diece e cinque* as a *gematria* is consistent with Grandgent's reference to "the Kabbalistic method" prominent in the thirteenth and fourteenth centuries: *La Divina Commedia di Dante Alighieri*, ed. Charles H. Grandgent (Boston: D. C. Heath, 1933), p. 635. Dante's specific indebtedness to such a kabbalistic formulation is, of course, impossible to determine. As Grandgent notes, however, the idea was a commonplace of medieval numerology. For an illuminating recent analysis of the philosophical backgrounds underlying the *cinquecento diece e cinque*, see Antonio C. Mastrobuono, "The Powerful Enigma," *Lectura Dantis Newberryana*, ed. Paolo Cherchi and Antonio C. Mastrobuono (Evanston: Northwestern University Press, 1988), pp. 153–198.

and revelatory nature of the final cantos. Although acknowledging that her prophecy is as obscure as those of Themis and Sphinx, Beatrice offers the prospect of ultimate clarification (33:46–51). Until that time, Dante, like those who accompany him on his journey, must remain content to read apophatically, that is, to approach the matter of divine revelation with an awareness that the nature of its meaning resides in its denial of ultimate disclosure. It is from the willingness not to know that true knowledge emerges. Having attained the summit of this awareness, Dante embarks upon the passage through the "good knowledge" represented by the waters of Eunoe and comes forth from those holy waters *"rifatto sì come piante novelle / rinovellate di novella fronda, puro e disposto a salire a le stelle* [renovated even as new trees renewed with new foliage, pure and ready to rise to the stars]" (33:142–145).

As the foregoing discussion of Dante's experience at the summit of the Purgatorial mount has attempted to demonstrate, the concept of the *merkabah* that was of such crucial importance to the traditions of the visionary mode is reenacted in *The Divine Comedy*. Drawing upon his understanding of that concept, Dante portrays a chariot of his own devising, a portrayal that bestows upon his *carro* not only a unique significance but a complex history that traces the course of its development from the very beginnings of Christianity to Dante's own time. In the process of placing this chariot in a prophetic and an apocalyptic setting, Dante formulates a poetics that reasserts the visionary implications of the biblical original and refashions those implications in a new form. That new form is one in which poetics and hermeneutics become intimately related and indeed complementary activities. As a result of these activities, the visionary mode is defined and redefined not only through an attempt to understand the forces that gave rise to an orginary event in which the *visio Dei* is first communicated but to reconceptualize that event in a manner consistent with the outlook that the later transcriber is seen to reflect. Such is the nature of Dante's *carro* as the profound expression of the visionary sensibility through which the *Purgatorio* culminates. Such is the nature of the visionary mode as the expression of one who is at once a poet and a hermeneut of the highest order.

Conclusion

In Patrick White's well-hewn novel *Riders in the Chariot,* a character appropriately named Mordecai Himmelfarb is discovered one evening by his wife Reha as he sits alone in his room drawing pictures. Surrounding him are newly acquired books and manuscripts of a decidedly esoteric cast. The dialogue that follows this discovery might well suggest the nature of what has transpired in the foregoing study of the visionary mode:

> As the wind her nightdress made in passing stirred the papers uppermost on her husband's desk, she could not resist asking, "What is that, Mordecai? I did not know you could draw."
>
> "I was scribbling," he said. "This, it appears, is the Chariot."
>
> "Ah," she exclaimed, softly, withdrawing her glance; she could have lost interest. "Which chariot?" she did certainly ask, but now it might have been to humour him.
>
> "That, I am not sure," he replied. "It is difficult to distinguish. Just when I think I have understood, I discover some fresh form— so many—streaming with implications. There is the Throne of God, for instance. That is obvious enough—all gold, and chrysoprase, and jasper. Then there is the Chariot of Redemption, much more shadowy, poignant, personal. And the faces of the riders. I cannot begin to see the expression of the faces."[1]

It is notable that in his attempt to understand the Chariot, Mordecai is moved to render it visibly, to imagine it as form. For it is this impulse to visualize the unvisualizable that is the distinguishing characteristic of the visionary as *Urerlebnis.* Of no phenomenon does this hold greater cogency than the *merkabah,* which we have

---

1. *Riders in the Chariot* (New York: Viking Press, 1961), p. 142. For a brief but illuminating study of this novel, see Frederick W. Dillistone, *Patrick White's "Riders in the Chariot"* (New York: Seabury Press, 1967).

witnessed undergoing the process of inscription and reinscription from the moment of its inception as biblical event to its multiple articulations in the centuries of interpretations that followed upon its initial appearance. Streaming with implications, it has been seen to undergo a series of metamorphoses that have confirmed throughout not only its essentially polysemous nature but its dynamic propensity for change.

At the heart of the *merkabah* is this transformative spirit: "*Gestaltung, Umgestaltung, / Des ewigen Sinnes ewige Unterhaltung.*" Jung knew precisely what he was about in adopting these lines as the guiding principle of his formulation of the visionary mode. It has been our guiding principle as well. Conceived in its various forms as an apocalyptic event, as a means of ascent, as a theology of utterance, as an interpretive paradigm, as a heuristic enterprise, as an embodiment of typology, as a key to the powers of theurgy and gnosis, as a form of numeration, as a process of cognition, as a pictograph of the divine, as a symbol of proceation, as a form of cultic enactment, as a source of angelology, as a psycho-vehicle, as a poetic trope, the *merkabah* has been seen to undergo that acculturation attendant upon the transmission of the *Urerlebnis* from one generation to the next.

Tracing the process of this acculturation, we have had occasion to examine the hermeneutic and poetic career of the *merkabah*. "We demand commentaries and explanations," declares Jung. For the *merkabah* there is no lack of them. Visionary history is interpretive history: to attend to one is to attend to the other. Such attention has brought into focus the immensely rich possibilities associated with a willingness to view the *merkabah* as a cross-cultural event. With its grounding in Hebrew Scriptures, it finds itself at the very center of Judaic discourse. As the foregoing study has attempted to demonstrate, there is what might likewise be called a Christocentric *merkabah*. This notion is already canonized in the New Testament and receives elaborate treatment in the Christian exegetical traditions that follow in its wake. In this regard the *merkabah* may be viewed as both a Judaic and Christocentric phenomenon, one that reinforces our understanding of what might be called the Judeo-Christian perspective. Adopting such a perspective throughout our investigation, we have sought to provide a renewed understanding of the visionary mode as a source of cross-fertilization and interdependency.

With the acculturation of the visionary, however, our greatest source of understanding comes not from an awareness of the various systems of thought that the *Urerlebnis* inspires. True knowledge of that experience is derived from a sensitivity to the transformative nature of its bearing. At the very core of its conception the *Urerlebnis* defines itself through its propensity to assume new forms. "Just when we think we have understood," we exclaim with Himmelfarb, we discover a new delineation, "some fresh form," in fact, many forms "streaming with implications." It is this act of discovery that has underscored our investigation throughout. Attempting to formulate some notion of the Chariot, we, like Himmelfarb, have sought to sensitize ourselves to its propensity to redefine itself as every turn. As it enfolds itself within itself, the *merkabah* constantly generates new meanings, new modes of perception, that are forever multiplying, wheel within wheel, a hermeneutics of transformation and visionary reenactment. As such, the *Urerlebnis* is essentially an event, a dynamic repository of ever-changing meanings that are inscribed and reinscribed in that circle of reciprocity that occurs between hermeneut and text.

As we have seen, it is the nature of the visionary mode to question that reciprocity as much as it is to endorse it. What begins with the proclamation that the prophet as seer beholds the "visions of God" concludes with an awareness that it is not the prophet who beholds the vision so much as it is the vision that beholds him. The prophet discovers that he is in the paradoxical situation of one who is seen by his own vision. In this reversal of roles the vision becomes the seer, the visionary the seen. So it is with the hermeneut who participates in the originary interchange that transpires between seer and visionary event. In the text through which the hermeneut seeks to interpret that event, the vision remains ultimately impenetrable. Defying all attempts at a hermeneutic, the text distinguishes itself by virtue of its "otherness." In its remoteness it refuses to disclose its meanings. It will not allow the act of interpretation to compromise its indeterminacy. On the contrary, it obliges the hermeneut to reveal himself instead. In the hermeneutical circle that defines the visionary mode, the act of interpretation is finally not reciprocal at all. Attempting to impose his will upon the text, the hermeneut discloses himself. Such is the nature of the relationship between vision and seer, text and interpreter that defines the originary experience we have termed the visionary mode.

Our history of the acculturation of this phenomenon from the point of its inception in the biblical text to its reenvisioning in the later Middle Ages is not meant to be exhaustive. Surveying some of the major documents through which the visionary mode finds expression, we have sought to provide a sense of the shape that this particular form of visionary history assumes in its larger cultural contexts. Adopting Ezekiel's *visio Dei* as the originary moment of all enactment, we have sought, that is, to trace what Amos Wilder calls "the progressive culturizing of the initial vision."

Implicit in this progressive culturizing is a sense of historicity. The acculturation of the visionary may be seen to assume a certain shape, a particular form. It has a career rather like the Chariot itself as it moves from one point to the next. There is indeed what Joseph Anthony Wittreich, Jr., terms a "line of vision," one in which the numinous undergoes a series of transformations that can be categorized. Although the nature of these transformations defies ultimate categorization, it also invites such an activity. At the very point that the inaugural vision frustrates all attempts at localization, it cries out for the bestowal of a name. It spawns a history, a progressive culturizing.

In the process the vision assumes those forms through which it may be said to have a local habitation and a name. To this end it is classifiable: it prompts a nomenclature. The nomenclature that this study has seen fit to bestow (*phenomenology, hermeneutics, esoterics,* and the like) has been descriptive rather than prescriptive. By means of this nomenclature the study has sought to suggest the multiple dimensions of the visionary as it set about its transformative career from the moment of its initial enactment to its acculturation in the later Middle Ages. It is the history of this acculturation that this study of the visionary mode has attempted to undertake in its discourse on the nature of biblical prophecy, hermeneutics, and cultural change.

Index

Abraham, 11, 47, 55–56, 83, 180, 214
Abraham ben Samuel Abulafia, 126n, 128, 155n
Acher (Elisha ben Abuyah), 101, 102, 205
Akiba, Rabbi, 60–61, 64n, 101, 102, 105–6, 137
Aletheia, 207–8
Altmann, Alexander, 59n, 64n, 65n, 114, 127n, 138n, 210n
Ancient of Days, 97
Angelic hierarchies: Bernard of Clairvaux on, 278–79; in *III Enoch*, 78, 79; Eriugena on, 272–74; Gregory of Nyssa on, 225–27; Pseudo-Dionysius on, 242, 243, 246–48
Anti-*merkabah*, concept of, 205
Apocalypse of Abraham, 55, 56–59, 222n
Apocalypse of Paul, 190, 201–4
Apocalyptic, genre of, 48
Apocalypticism, 46n, 47–48
Aquinas, Thomas, 316n, 317n
Aristotle, 119
Ark of covenant, 29–31, 34; Richard of Saint Victor on, 287, 292–96
Ark of Noah, Hugh of Saint Victor on, 287, 289–91
Artistic creation, modes of, 2
Ascension of Isaiah, 190–201, 202; ascent in, 192–99; descent of Christ in, 198; emphasis on occultation in, 199–200; motifs in, 192, 199; structure of, 191, 200
Ascent, 64n; in *Ascension of Isaiah*, 192–99; Bernard of Clairvaux on, 279, 282; Bonaventure on, 304; of Christ, 251; in *Divine Comedy*, 345; of Enoch, 49–50; in *II Enoch*, 53–54; Eriugena on, 266, 269–70; of gnostic, 210–12; in *Hekhalot Rabbati*, 65; Hugh of Saint Victor on, 290; of Rabbi Ishmael, 73–74; of Saint John the Divine, 181–90; of Moses, 223, 224–27, 226; motif of, 60–65; of Paul, 180–81; Pseudo-Dionysius on, 234–35; Rich-

ard of Saint Victor on, 294; in *Sefer ha-Zohar*, 166–67
Augustine, Saint, 254n, 309, 310n

Baba Mezi'a, 9
Babylonian Talmud, 9, 86, 98n, 99n
Bahir. See Sefer ha-Bahir
Baptism, 177, 221, 251
Beatrice, in *Divine Comedy*, 313, 315, 317, 322, 331–41, 346, 348, 350
Ben Azzai, 101, 102, 105, 126
Ben Sira, Book of (Ecclesiasticus), 32, 90
Ben Zoma, 101, 102
Bernard of Clairvaux, 276–77, 309, 310n, 338
Bible: Acts, 179, 183, 192–93, 202, 234; 1 Chronicles, 29, 130n; 2 Chronicles, 82; Colossians, 25, 229; 1 Corinthians, 203, 261, 316; 2 Corinthians, 179, 180, 181, 201, 286, 308, 336; Daniel, 37, 51, 80, 96, 97, 115, 184, 187, 189, 239, 244, 247, 248, 274; Deuteronomy, 82, 89, 90; Ecclesiastes, 279; Ephesians, 279; Exodus, 28, 29, 30, 33, 67, 77, 82, 137, 153, 167, 189, 193, 202, 219, 223, 224, 287, 294, 336; Ezekiel, 15–20, 21–22, 24–26, 31, 32, 34, 37, 42, 56, 87, 94, 95, 97, 105, 131, 143, 145, 147, 164, 179, 181, 183, 184, 185, 187–89, 202, 216, 225, 244, 245, 247, 251, 253, 254, 261, 272, 273, 274, 288, 293, 295, 308, 309, 347n; Galatians, 179; Genesis, 28, 35, 36, 43, 49, 53, 55, 65, 82, 87, 89, 106, 137, 167, 183, 184, 193, 214, 252, 259n, 260, 287, 288, 314, 317, 318; Habakkuk, 28; Haggai, 99n; Hebrews, 191n, 225, 251, 272; Hosea, 99n; Isaiah, 28, 51, 54, 80, 82, 89, 90, 91, 92, 96, 97, 105, 185n, 191, 273, 274, 290, 324, 334; James, 238; Jeremiah, 19; John, 189, 248, 251, 280, 286; Joshua, 30, 287; Judges, 33, 193; 1 Kings, 28, 31, 89, 99n, 106, 184; 2 Kings, 28, 33, 75,

Bible: Acts, (*cont.*)
    244, 246, 248; Leviticus, 87*n*; Luke,
    178*n*, 244, 248, 251, 259, 317, 322, 334;
    Mark, 178*n*, 187, 248, 254; Matthew,
    178*n*, 183, 199, 202, 230, 241, 244, 248,
    251, 254, 258, 279, 286, 309, 314, 315,
    324, 332, 333, 336, 347; Micah, 290;
    Numbers, 30, 106, 109, 219; 1 Peter,
    189, 229, 230, 232; Philippians, 195,
    199, 279; Proverbs, 47; Psalms, 28, 29,
    30, 39, 80, 89–90, 99, 104, 109, 151,
    167, 232, 248, 251, 290, 321, 338; Reve-
    lation, 182, 183, 185*n*, 187*n*, 188*n*, 193,
    196, 202, 203–4, 239, 242, 246, 247,
    254, 324, 336, 343, 348, 349; Romans,
    238; Ruth, 75; 1 Samuel, 28, 40*n*; 2
    Samuel, 34; Song of Songs, 94, 95, 97,
    107, 114, 136, 252, 277*n*, 282, 283, 285,
    288, 332; Zechariah, 189, 239, 246, 248
Bloom, Harold, 128*n*, 132, 307*n*
Bonaventure, Saint, 263, 296–305, 314,
    329*n*
Bowker, J. W., 177*n*, 178–79
Bride/Bridegroom: Bernard of Clairvaux
    on, 282, 284–86*n*; Dante on, 331–32

Can Grande della Scala, 307–8, 311–12,
    328
Cassirer, Ernst, 32*n*, 36–37
Celestial mysteries, Bernard of Clairvaux
    on, 278
Celestial spheres, *Hagigah* on, 88–90
Celestial tabernacle, Gregory of Nyssa on,
    224–27
Chariot: in *Apocalypse* of Abraham, 58;
    Bernard of Clairvaux on, 281–82; in
    Divine Comedy, 313, 323, 324, 327, 330–
    32, 342, 344, 345, 347; in *III Enoch*, 79;
    Eriugena on, 274, 275–76; in Ezekiel's
    visio Dei, 16; of God, 325; Hugh of
    Saint Victor on, 288; Rabbi Jacob on,
    152, 153–54; Jerome on, 253; in *Life of
    Moses*, 221; Macarius the Egyptian on,
    228–29, 231–33; in *Midrash Rabbah*,
    105–8; as Near Eastern concept, 26–27;
    Rabbi Nehunya on, 66; in *Phaedrus*,
    222; Pseudo-Dionysius on, 248; in *Sefer
    ha-Bahir*, 148, 149–50; in *Sefer ha-Zohar*,
    159–60, 164–65, 168; in *Sefer Yetsirah*,
    142–43
Christ: ascension of, 335*n*; birth of, 200;
    as the charioteer of God, 251; Dante on
    entry of into Jerusalem, 332–33; de-
    scent of, 198–99; four mysteries of,
    260; griffin as symbol of, 340*n*; Hugh
    of Saint Victor on, 289–91; Origen on
    events of the life of, 251. *See also* Jesus
Christian spirituality, traditions of, 12

Circle, Eriugena on concept of, 266, 267–
    69
Circularity, sense of, in *Sefer Yetsirah*, 143
Circumcision, 70–71
Cistercian Order, 276–77*n*
Clement of Alexandria, 204*n*, 205, 213,
    214, 216, 218, 220
Collective unconscious, 5
Color symbolism: in *Divine Comedy*, 335–
    37, 349; Eleazar of Worms on, 116;
    Hugh of Saint Victor on, 287; Pseudo-
    Dionysius on, 247
Contemplation: Bernard on, 277*n*; Bon-
    aventure on, 304–5; Richard of Saint
    Victor on, 294–95, 296
corpus symbolicum, Torah as, 156–57
Creation: Bonaventure on, 303; Eriugena
    on, 265–66; *Hagigah* on, 88; in *Sefer ha-
    Zohar*, 162–63; in *Sefer Yetsirah*, 141–42,
    144
Creation account, symbolism of, 35–36
Crucifixion, 251, 260
Cultural mythology, and visionary mode,
    6

Dante Alighieri, 12, 259*n*, 307–50; as *yo-
    red merkabah*, 338
Deification, Eriugena on, 270–71
Deity: nature of, and the kabbalists, 129;
    Pseudo-Dionysius on deconceptualizing,
    237–38
Denial, theology of, as center of Pseudo-
    Dionysian viewpoint, 236
Deus absconditus, nature of, 152
Dionysius the Areopagite, 12, 227, 234–
    49, 249, 264, 273–74, 275*n*, 276, 297
Divine anger, *merkabah* as symbol of, 96
Divine names, 82, 248–49*n*
Divine science, Maimonides on, 120–21,
    122
Dronke, Peter, 313*n*, 323*n*, 326
Dunbar, H. Flanders, 316*n*, 323*n*, 325
Dürr, Lorenz, 26–27

Eagle, 96; in *Apocalypse* of Abraham, 58;
    in *Divine Comedy*, 342, 344; Eriugena
    on, 274–75; in Ezekiel's *visio Dei*, 16, 38;
    Jerome on, 254; in *Midrash Tehilim*, 104;
    Pseudo-Dionysius on, 246; in *Sefer ha-
    Zohar*, 161–62
Egyptian monasticism, 227–28
Eichrodt, Walther, 19*n*, 31
Eleazar ben Arak, 98, 100
Eleazar ben Jehuda of Worms, 113–17,
    282*n*
Eliezer ben Hyrkanos, 9–10, 112*n*, 119*n*
Eliezer ben Jacob, 105
Elijah, 17, 47
Enoch, 11, 47, 180; ascension of, 49–50;

in *Ascension of Isaiah* and *Apocalypse of Paul*, 202; enthronement of, 76–77; as scribe, 80*n*; transformation of, 75–76

I Enoch (Ethiopic Enoch), 48–49, 52, 182, 184, 187

II Enoch (Book of the Secrets of Enoch), 52–53, 55, 73, 76

III Enoch (Hebrew Book of Enoch), 71–84; angelic hierarchies in, 78, 79; ascent and exaltation in, 78; genre of, 72; "romance" in, 72; as self-conscious literary enterprise, 73; significance of, 71–72; structure of, 72–73

Enoch-Metatron, 77–78

Enoch pseudepigrapha, 58, 75, 76

Enthroned Figure: in *Apocalypse of Paul*, 203; in ascent of Enoch, 51; in *III Enoch*, 73; Eriugena on, 274; in Ezekiel's *visio Dei*, 35, 95, 96, 97; Gregory the Great on, 260–61; in *Hagigah*, 90, 91; in *hekhalot* texts, 63; Hugh of Saint Victor on, 291; Jerome on, 253; of Saint John the Divine, 183, 186; Maimonides on, 122; Rabbi Nehunya on, 66; as the Only-Begotten, 261–62; Origen on, 251; in *Sefer ha-Bahir*, 147–48; in *Sefer ha-Zohar*, 167–68; in *Shi'ur Komah*, 137–38

Eriugena, Johannes Scotus, 263–76, 297, 305

Eschaton, significance of, 348–49

Esoteric dimensions of visionary mode, 168–69

Etiology, of vision, 15–41

Evil, domain of, in *Sefer ha-Zohar*, 160

Exegesis: dimensions of, 217; fourfold method of interpretation common to, 133–34; patristic, 217–18

Ezekiel: book of, as poorly preserved, 17; calling of, 25*n*; commissioning of, 24–25; inconsistencies and contradictions in, 17–19; instability of text of, 23; literary appraisal of, 23; as poet, 306; prophecy of, 1, 33, 37, 188, 217; Pseudo-Dionysius on, 245; as seer, 40; self-authentication of, 24

Ezekiel's *visio Dei*, 1, 10, 15–20, 26, 27–28, 31, 42, 136, 182, 226, 242, 255, 354; arrangement of, 34–35; balance in, 35; bipartite sense of division in, 34–36; Bonaventure on, 299; cherubim-chariot of, 229–30; cohesiveness of, 35; concretization of, 33–34; Dante on, 327–29; Enthroned Figure in, 35; as formative experience in Jewish mysticism, 43; fourfold creatures of, 245–47; Gregory the Great on, 257–62; Hugh of Saint Victor on, 288; importance of, 249; interpretive dimensions of, 256; Jerome

on, 252–58; as literary event, 40–41; Macarius the Egyptian on, 228–33; as manifestation of *Urerlebnis*, 42; as "model vision," 42; Pseudo-Dionysius on, 239–42; quadripartite sense in, 36–37; in *Sefer ha-Zohar*, 157–59, 162; symbolism in, 35; symmetry in, 35; throne-chariot in, 142–43; transformative dimension of, 231; visionary mode as grounded in, 103; visionary temple of, 203

IV Ezra, 59

Fire: in *Apocalypse* of Abraham, 58; in ascent of Enoch, 49–50, 51; in *Celestial Hierarchy*, 244–45; in *Divine Comedy*, 314–16, 322; in Ezekiel's *visio Dei*, 16, 37; Pseudo-Dionysius on, 244–45, 247–48; in *Sefer ha-Zohar*, 161; in *Sefer Yetsirah*, 143–44

Fishbane, Michael, 1, 20*n*, 25*n*, 134*n*

Forbidden Relations, 87*n*

Fourfold creatures: Bernard of Clairvaux on, 278*n*, 280; Dante on, 323, 324, 327; in *Divine Comedy*, 323, 324; Eleazar of Worms on, 114–15, 116; Eriugena on, 272–75; in Ezekiel's *visio Dei*, 16, 20, 34–35, 37, 38, 39; Gregory the Great on, 258–62; Jerome on, 253–56; in Saint John the Divine's vision, 185–86; Macarius the Egyptian on, 228; Pseudo-Dionysius on, 246–47; Richard of Saint Victor on, 295–96. *See also ḥayyot*; Quaternary form

Fourfold method of interpretation, 133–34

Fox, in *Divine Comedy*, 342, 344

Francis, Saint, Bonaventure on, 302–3

Franciscans, 296–97

Gardner, Edmund G., 310*n*, 311–12

Gemara, 44*n*, 86, 87

Gender distinctions: Eleazar of Worms on, 116; in *Sefer ha-Zohar*, 167–68

Gnosis, of vision, 173–215

Gnostic, description of, 213–14

Gnosticism: Christian, 174–75, 213; church fathers on, 204*n*; as class-concept, 175–77; emergence of, 11; heretical, 205, 210–11, 212, 213, 214; incipient, 176*n*; New Testament, 176*n*; origins of, 174–75*n*; pagan opposition to, 204*n*; as term, 174–75; transformative dimension of, 176

Gnostic power, 269

God: Bernard of Clairvaux on, 279–81; as *deus absconditus*, 129; Eriugena on, 265, 266, 267, 269–70, 275; as *ha-Ein-Sof*,

God: Bernard of Clairvaux on, (*cont.*)
  129; in *Shi'ur Komah*, 138–39; visions of,
  40; will of, and motion, 123
Goethe, Johann Wolfgang von, 3, 4*n*, 5, 71
Greenberg, Moshe, 21–22, 32*n*, 34, 35*n*
Gregory of Nyssa, 12, 219–27, 232, 234,
  235, 249, 264*n*
Gregory the Great, 12, 249–50, 257–62,
  292
Griffin, in *Divine Comedy*, 340*n*, 342
Gruenwald, Ithamar, 44*n*, 46*n*, 47*n*, 49*n*,
  51, 56*n*, 59*n*, 61*n*, 62*n*, 64*n*, 65*n*, 74*n*,
  173–74*n*, 182*n*, 190*n*, 191*n*, 194*n*, 203

Ḥagigah, 85–87, 94; on celestial spheres,
  88–90; on creation, 88; *ma'aseh bere'shit*
  in, 87; *ma'aseh merkabah* in, 92; reforma-
  tion of inaugural vision of Ezekiel in,
  91–92; structure of, 91
Hai Gaon, 101–2
Halperin, David, 44*n*, 46*n*, 49*n*, 51*n*, 57*n*,
  61*n*, 62*n*, 64*n*, 66*n*, 70, 86*n*, 98*n*, 103*n*,
  107*n*, 108*n*, 109*n*, 111*n*, 118*n*, 178*n*,
  205, 219*n*, 250*n*, 283*n*
Hananiah ben Hezekiah, 17
ḥashmal, 95
ḥayyot (fourfold creatures), 70–71, 96; in
  Apocalypse of Abraham, 57–58; Eleazar
  of Worms on, 115, in *III Enoch*, 79, 80,
  81; in Ezekiel's *visio Dei*, 19–20, 34–35,
  37; Gregory of Nyssa on, 226; Jerome
  on, 253–56; in Saint John the Divine's
  vision, 185–86; Macarius the Egyptian
  on, 228; Maimonides on, 122; in *Midrash Rabbah*, 107–8; in *Midrash Tehilim*,
  104; as Near Eastern concept, 27; Rabbi
  Nehunya on, 69–70, 71; Pseudo-
  Dionysius on, 246–47; Richard of Saint
  Victor on, 295–96; in *Sefer ha-Zohar*,
  167; in *Sefer Yetsirah*, 143–44. *See also*
  Fourfold creatures; Quaternary form
Hearing: Gregory of Nyssa on, 223;
  Pseudo-Dionysius on, 245
Hebrew letters: foundation of, 144–45;
  pictorial significance of, 150–55
hekhalot literature, 11; literary dimensions
  of, 62*n*
Hekhalot Rabbati (Greater *Hekhalot*), 60–61,
  70–71, 76, 222*n*; *piyyutim* in, 203–4;
  pseudo-historical nature of setting, 65;
  as technical guide, 64–65
Hekhalot Zutarti, 60–61, 70
Hermeneutics, 7–8; of kabbalistic inter-
  pretation, 133–34; of vision, 8, 85–126
Hidden comparison (*collatio occulta*), 326–
  27, 328, 340
Horse, Pseudo-Dionysius on, 246–47
Hugh of Saint Victor, 286, 287–92, 297*n*
Human figure, Rabbi Jacob on, 152

Humaniform, Eriugena on, 274–75

Idel, Moshe, 128*n*, 155*n*, 247*n*, 283*n*
Inaugural vision, transformative nature
  of, 42
Incarnation, 251, 260
Irenaeus, 204, 205–7, 208, 211*n*, 212–13,
  216, 254*n*
Isaac, Rabbi, 95
Isaiah, 47, 225; in *Ascension of Isaiah*, 192–
  98; vision of, 97, 226, 242, 291, 303; as
  yored merkabah, 243
Ishmael, Rabbi, 61, 64, 65–66, 73–75, 82,
  83, 137–38

Jacob ben Jacob ha-Kohen, 150–55
Jehudah 'the Saint,' 86*n*
Jerome, Saint, 12, 249–50, 252–58, 260*n*,
  347*n*
Jesus: as paradigm of *yored merkabah*, 176–
  77; transfiguration of, 348. *See also*
  Christ
Jewish gnosticism, 173–75
Jewish mysticism, 42–43
Jewish thought, analysis of *merkabah* in,
  43–44
Jochanan ben Zakkai, 44, 62, 98, 112*n*
John the Divine, Saint, 178, 327, 328,
  329, 347*n*; Apocalypse of, 187–88; on
  ma'aseh merkabah, 181–90; New Jerusa-
  lem of, 203; *trisagion* of, 203; vision of,
  188, 332, 345
Jonas, Hans, 174–76, 214
Joseph, Rabbi, 94, 95
Joseph ben Judah, 126
Josephus, 17
Joshua, Rabbi, 10
Judah, Rabbi, 85, 88
Judeo-Christian perspective, 352
Jung, Carl Gustav, 2–6, 7, 10*n*, 71, 169,
  352

kabbalah: definition of, 127–28; flourishing
  of, 168; and *ma'aseh merkabah*, 127, 128;
  as speculative phenomenon, 129; as
  writing theory, 132
Kabbalistic interpretation: hermeneutics
  of, 133–34; of Torah, 133
Kabbalistic phenomenon, *sefirot* as, 129–32
Kinetics, 122–23
Kiss, Bernard of Clairvaux on concept of
  divine, 283–84

Language, importance of in the Marcosian system, 207
Latif, Isaac ibn, 126*n*, 128
Leah, in *Divine Comedy*, 313, 316–17, 318,
  339

Lectio divina, 298; Bonaventure on, 299, 302; Hugh of Saint Victor on, 287, 288

Letter mysticism, 150–55, 155*n*

Letter to Paulinus, 252*n*, 254–55

Lion, 96; in *Apocalypse* of Abraham, 57; Eriugena on, 274; in Ezekiel's *visio Dei*, 16, 38; Jerome on, 254; in *Midrash Tehilim*, 104; Pseudo-Dionysius on, 246; in *Sefer ha-Zohar*, 161, 162

Logoi, in *Sefer ha-Bahir*, 147–48

Lossky, Vladimir, 218, 227*n*, 228*n*, 234*n*

Louth, Andrew, 218, 219*n*, 227*n*, 236*n*

ma'aseh bere'shit (Work of Creation), 32, 33, 34, 43, 65, 87, 88, 89, 92, 94, 96, 99, 104, 117*n*, 119*n*, 121, 141

ma'aseh merkabah (Work of the Chariot), 43, 45, 52, 59, 60*n*, 61, 63, 64, 65, 68, 71, 86*n*, 87, 88, 92, 93, 94, 97, 98, 99, 103, 104, 105, 106, 108, 111, 114, 117*n*, 118, 119, 120*n*, 121, 122, 123, 124, 134, 146, 150, 162, 173, 178, 179, 180, 181, 182, 185, 186, 189, 190, 209, 210, 241, 243, 249, 250, 251, 257, 288. *See also merkabah*

Macarian corpus, provenance and dating of, 227*n*

Macarius of Alexandria, 227–28

Macarius the Egyptian, 227–33, 249; influence of Gregory of Nyssa on, 227*n*; spirituality of, 228

Maimonides, Moses, 11, 113, 117–26

Man: in *Apocalypse* of Abraham, 57; Eriugena on, 275; in Ezekiel's *visio Dei*, 16, 38; image of, in *Sefer ha-Zohar*, 161, 162

Marcus, 205–8

Martha: in *Divine Comedy*, 317; Gregory the Great on, 259

Mary: in *Divine Comedy*, 317; Gregory the Great on, 259; vision of, 199–200

Mass, analogy of in *Divine Comedy*, 325

Matelda, in *Divine Comedy*, 313, 317, 321

Menstruating woman, as impure, 68*n*

merkabah: analysis of, in Jewish thought, 43–44; in *Apocalypse* of Abraham, 58–59; in *Apocalypse of Paul*, 204; apocalyptic, 44–60, 89, 91; appreciation of, 125–26; attempt to categorize, 45; biblical motifs associated with, 51–52; Christocentric, 11, 173–74, 176–77, 178, 352; consummation of, 63–64, 124; as cosmic entity, 108–9; creating atmosphere of, 100; cult of, 57; in Dante, 331, 345–46, 350, 351–52, 353; dark side of, 57*n*, 205; delineation of, 94; Eleazar of Worms on, 114, 116; in *III Enoch*, 80, 81–82; Eriugena on, 276; eschatological reformulation of, 105; esoteric, 44, 85, 145; essential goal of, 103; as first-person

testimony, 46; as gnostic phenomenon, 11, 176, 204; in *Hagigah*, 92; hermeneutics of, 105; Jerome on, 257; and *kabbalah*, 127, 128; liturgy of, 64; Maimonides on, 117–26; metaphysical identity of, 125; mystical, 44–71, 89, 91; Origen on, 251–52; precosmogonic vision of, 104; Pseudo-Dionysius on, 241; as rabbinical enterprise, 99–100; relationship between *ma'aseh bere'shit* and, 92–94, 104; in *Sefer ha-Bahir*, 147; in *Sefer ha-Zohar*, 167–68; in *Sefer Yetsirah*, 143–44; Song of Songs as crucial in delineation of, 107; special properties of, 140–41; speculative, 44, 85–126; as symbol of divine anger, 96; as talmudic enterprise, 93, 94, 97–98; as theosophical phenomenon, 154–55; as visionary enterprise, 103; visionary event, 95, 103, 124; visionary substratum of, 145

merkabah mysticism, 44; language of, 180–81

Metatron, 73, 74, 83, 111, 165

Methurgeman, 93–94

Midrash Rabbah, 105–8, 160; interpretation of firmament in, 106; interpretation of numbers in, 106–7; presence of *merkabah* in, 106

Midrash Tanhuma, 104–5

Midrash Tehilim, 104

Mishnah, 85, 86*n*, 124

Moore, Edward, 313*n*, 322*n*, 323*n*, 338*n*, 343*n*

Moses, 29–30, 47, 83; access of, to white fire, 158; ascent of, 214, 220, 221, 223, 224–27; of Gregory of Nyssa, 235; life of, 219–20; *visio Dei* of, 220, 221; as *yored merkabah*, 220, 222*n*

Moses ben Jacob Cordovero, 128

Moses ben Maimon. *See* Maimonides, Moses

Moses ben Shem Tob de León, 126*n*, 128, 154–55, 157

Motion: tension between, and stasis, 38; and will of God, 123

Mysticism, 217–18

Nathan, Rabbi, 137

Nativity, of Christ, 251

Natural science, Maimonides on, 119, 120–21

Nehunya ben Hakkanah, 65–71, 146

Neoplatonism, 129

Neusner, Jacob, 98*n*, 177*n*

Neuss, Wilhelm, 217*n*, 250*n*, 254*n*

New Dispensation, 184

Numbers, interpretation of, in *Midrash Rabbah*, 106–7

Occultatio Dei: profundity surrounding the, 209; understanding nature of, 209
Occultation, emphasis on in *Ascension of Isaiah*, 199–200
Omnipresent One, in *III Enoch*, 82–83
Ophites, 210–11
Origen, 204, 205, 208–13, 216, 218–19*n*, 250–52, 259*n*
'otiot: foundation of, 144–45; in *Sefer ha-Bahir*, 150–55
Otto, Rudolf, 7
Ovid, 321*n*, 347
Ox, 96; in *Apocalypse* of Abraham, 57; Eriugena on, 274; in Ezekiel's *visio Dei*, 16, 20, 38; Jerome on, 254; Pseudo-Dionysius on, 246; in *Sefer ha-Zohar*, 161, 162

pardes, 101, 103, 105, 106, 114, 134, 180, 202, 205, 331
pargod, in *III Enoch*, 83
Parrot, André, 27
Paul (apostle): Bernard of Clairvaux on, 284; as émigré, 178–79; vision of, 178–81, 201–4, 225
Pauline ascent, 214; Bernard of Clairvaux on, 278; Dante on, 308, 309; Eriugena on, 271; Pauline conversion, 179–80; Richard of Saint Victor on, 296
Phaedran myth, chariot of, 232–33
Phenomenology of vision, 42–84
Philo, 220, 221*n*, 226*n*, 232*n*
Pirke de Rabbi Eliezer, 112*n*
piyyutim, in *Hekhalot Rabbati*, 203–4
Plato, 119, 121, 214, 222, 256
Poetics of vision, 306–50
Power: *Hekhalot Rabbati* as text of, 65; in *Sefer ha-Zohar*, 159–60
Procession, in *Divine Comedy*, 324–27, 343–44
Prophet as *nabi*, 25*n*
Pseudo-Dionysius. *See* Dionysius the Areopagite
Psychocosmogram, Hugh of Saint Victor on, 289–91
Psychological mode, 2–3
Purification: in *Divine Comedy*, 314–16, 338; Origen on, 251; Pseudo-Dionysius on, 235, 241–42; rituals of, 221, 222–23

Quadripartite form, 36–37
Quaternary form, 291*n*; Bernard of Clairvaux on, 281–82; Bonaventure on, 298–99, 300, 301, 305; in *Divine Comedy*, 335; Richard of Saint Victor on, 292, 293. *See also* Fourfold creatures; *hayyot*

Rachel, in *Divine Comedy*, 313, 316–17, 318–19, 339

Redactionist approach, 18, 22–23
Re'iyyot Yehezk'el, 108–12, 194*n*
Resurrection, 178, 251, 260
Return, Eriugena on concept of, 271
Revelation, modes of, in Bible, 240
Richard of Saint Victor, 286, 287, 292–96, 309, 310*n*
Ritual purity, 9
Romance: mythos of, 72; term of, in *III Enoch*, 72
rota in *rota*, Jerome on, 256–57
Rowland, Christopher, 51*n*, 98*n*, 99*n*, 101*n*, 177*n*, 178*n*, 179*n*, 181, 182
Running, Eriugena on act of, 267–68

Sandalfon, 96
Sapientia, figure of, in *Divine Comedy*, 335
Schäfer, Peter, 45*n*, 46*n*, 60*n*, 61*n*, 64*n*, 69*n*, 70*n*, 180–81*n*
Scholem, Gershom, 42–44, 46, 60–71, 77*n*, 85, 86*n*, 103, 113*n*, 127*n*, 129, 131*n*, 132–33, 134–35, 136*n*, 138*n*, 140*n*, 141, 146, 147*n*, 150*n*, 155*n*, 156*n*, 157, 168*n*, 173–74, 177*n*, 180–81*n*, 207*n*, 252*n*, 264*n*
Science of the nut, Eleazar of Worms on, 114–16
Scroll, of Saint John the Divine, 187–88
Scroll of Torah, 115
Second Coming of Christ, 230
Seeing: in *Divine Comedy*, 316, 318–19, 321, 338–42; Eriugena on, 266–67, 268; Gregory of Nyssa on, 223–24; Pseudo-Dionysius on, 245
Sefer ha-Bahir (Book of Brightness), 128; chariot in, 148, 149–50; as earliest work of kabbalistic literature, 145; God of, 146–47; rearticulation of *'otiot* in, 150–55; *sefirot* in, 146–49; symbolic dimensions of, 146; theosophical foundations of, 149; wheel in, 148
Sefer ha-Zohar (Book of Splendor), 11, 155–69; account of *merkabah* in, 167–68; ascent in, 166–67; chariot in, 164–65, 168; on concept of power, 159–60; concern with feminine/masculine dimension, 168*n*; creation in, 162–63; domain of evil in, 160; eagle in, 161–62; fire in, 161; gender distinctions in, 167–68; *hayyot* in, 160–64, 167; interpretation of Ezekiel's vision, 162; as kabbalistic commentary on Torah, 156–57; kabbalistic framework established in, 165–66; lion in, 161, 162; man in, 161, 162; multilayered interpretive structure of, 162; outlook reflected in, 168; ox in, 161, 162; portrayal of *Shekhinah* in, 168; *sefirot* in, 165–66; vision of Ezekiel in, 157–59
Sefer Hekhalot. See III Enoch

Sefer Yetsirah (Book of Formation), 11,
135, 141–45; categories in, 142–43; creation in, 141–42, 144; fire in, 143;
hayyot in, 143–44; importance of, 141;
on paths of wisdom, 141–42; reconception of *merkabah* in, 143–44; *sefirot* in,
142–44; sense of circularity in, 143; terminology, 146; versions of, 141*n*; wheel
in, 145
sefirot: categories of, 142–43; cosmic dimensions of, 131; emanative quality of,
131; images associated with, 130–33; as
kabbalistic phenomenon, 129–32; linguistic dimension of, 131–32; number
of, 129–30; in *Sefer ha-Bahir*, 146–49; in
Sefer ha-Zohar, 165–66; in *Sefer Yetsirah*,
143–44
Self-adornment, in *Divine Comedy*, 318–19
Seraphim: Eriugena on, 273–74; Gregory
of Nyssa on, 226; Richard of Saint Victor on, 295
Shekhinah, 161; in *Sefer ha-Zohar*, 168;
splendor of, 108
Shi'ur Komah, 11, 135, 136–41; controversy generated by, 138; designation in,
139–40; liberalization of trope in, 139,
140; as magic text, 140–41; numeration
in, 139; original function of, 140
Sieve, concept of open as sexual, 70–71
Simeon ben Yochai, 98*n*, 156, 158
Sinai theophany, 220–21
Singleton, Charles, 307*n*, 316*n*, 319*n*,
323*n*, 326, 329*n*, 331*n*, 333*n*, 334*n*,
335*n*, 340*n*
Sixfold nature, Bonaventure on, 303–4
Six-winged creature, Dante on, 328*n*
Sleep, symbolism of in *Divine Comedy*,
346–48
Smend, Rudolf, 18
Smith, Morton, 64*n*, 68*n*, 177–78
Solomon's temple, Eriugena on, 272
Song of the Ark, 30
Spirituality of vision, 216–62
Stasis, tension between motion and, 38
Sun, symbolism of, in *Divine Comedy*, 334–
35
Sun-wheel, 6–7
Symbolism, in *Divine Comedy*, 317–18,
334–35

Tanur shel 'Aknai ('Aknai Oven), 9
Technology of vision, 123
Temple, 58; Richard of Saint Victor on,
293–94
Terrestrial, relationship between celestial
and, 36
Tetragrammaton, 56
Thaumaturgus, Gregory, 261*n*

Theology: affirmative or cataphatic, 237,
238; negative or apophatic, 236–37, 238
Theosis: Bernard of Clairvaux on, 279–
80; Bonaventure on, 305; Eriugena on,
270–73; of vision, 263–305
Throne, in ascent of Enoch, 50–51
Throne-chariot: embodiment in temple,
29; as expression of natural phenomena, 28–29; Ezekiel's description of,
142–43
Throne-mysticism, 43
Throne of Glory, 107
Throne-room, Saint John the Divine on,
183–85
Torah: conflicts between Ezekiel and, 17;
as *corpus symbolicum*, 156–57; hidden
meanings of, 132; kabbalistic attitude
toward, 133; sacred laws of, 115; *Sefer
ha-Zohar* as kabbalistic commentary on,
156–57
Transfiguration, 177, 348; Dante on, 308,
309
Triadic form: Bernard of Clairvaux on,
285–86; Bonaventure on, 300–301, 302,
304; of Isaiah's vision, 291*n*

Unio mystica, dimensions of, 282–83*n*
Universal Church, vision of, 260–61
Upper realm: bipartite quality, 35–36; division from lower, 35–36
Urerlebnis, 3, 4–5, 7–8, 10, 41, 351, 352,
353; as archetypal phenomenon, 15–20;
Christocentric contexts of, 173; circumstances surrounding, 49–50; Ezekiel's
visio Dei as manifestation of, 42; transformative quality of, 6; visionary implications of, 50

Valentinians, 175, 205*n*
Victorines, 276, 286
Virgil, 256–57; in *Divine Comedy*, 314–15,
319–20, 326, 330*n*, 333
visio Dei, 9, 15; in *Divine Comedy*, 315; as
Near Eastern concept, 26–28; transformative nature of, 263
Vision: esoterics of, 11, 127–69; etiology
of, 15–41; gnosis of, 11, 173–215; hermeneutics of, 11, 85–126; internal coherence of, 35; as literary event, 40–41;
phenomenology of, 11, 42–84; poetics
of, 11, 306–50; as self-generating and
self-moving, 37–38; spirituality of, 11,
216–62; theophanic, 1; theosis of, 11,
263–305
Visionary: as complex phenomenon, 7; as
seer and prophet, 4
Visionary experience, Maimonides on nature of, 123
Visionary hermeneutics, 8

Visionary metaphysics, 247
Visionary mode, 1–2, 3–5; biblical and Judaic dimensions of, 10; Christocentric
dimensions of, 10; as conducive to reformulations, 42; and cultural mythology, 6; esoteric dimensions of, 168–69;
gnostic formulations of, 12; Judaic renderings of, 11; as phenomenon of ascent, 47–48; primacy of, in Victorine
thought, 286–87, 290; psychological dimensions of, 2; transformative dimension, 5–6
Visionary poetics, 306–7
Visionary process, Neoplatonic formulation of, 110
Visionary realm, quadripartite nature of,
35
Visionary seeing, 50

Wheel(s): in *Apocalypse* of Abraham, 58;
Bonaventure on, 299, 300–301; in *Divine Comedy*, 323, 324; in Eleazar of
Worms, 115–16; in *III Enoch*, 79; Eriugena on, 267–69, 274, 275; in Ezekiel's

visio Dei, 16, 20, 34, 37–38, 263; Gre-
gory the Great on, 260; Macarius the
Egyptian on, 228; Maimonides on, 123;
in *Sefer ha-Bahir*, 148; in *Sefer ha-Zohar*,
162–63; in *Sefer Yetsirah*, 145
White, Patrick, 351
Wilder, Amos, 6–7, 41, 354
Wittreich, Joseph Anthony, Jr., 8, 306–7,
354
Work of Creation. *See ma'aseh bere'shit*
(Work of Creation)
Work of the Chariot. *See ma'aseh merkabah*
(Work of the Chariot)

yordei merkabah (descenders to the *merkabah*), 61, 62, 78, 92, 101, 102, 114, 149–
50, 164, 177, 178, 180, 183, 189, 192,
196, 197, 199, 201n, 206, 212, 220, 222,
243, 281, 331
Yotser Bere'shit, 136, 141

Zakkai, Jochanan ben, 178
Zimmerli, Walther, 18–21, 37n
Zohar. See Sefer ha-Zohar

Library of Congress Cataloging-in-Publication Data,

Lieb, Michael, 1940–
    The visionary mode : biblical prophecy, hermeneutics, and
cultural change / Michael Lieb.
        p.   cm.
    Includes bibliographical references and index.
    ISBN 0-8014-2273-6 (cloth : alk. paper)
    1. Visions in the Bible.   2. Bible.   O.T.—Criticism,
interpretation, etc., Jewish—History.   3. Bible—Criticism,
interpretation, etc.—History.   I. Title.
BS680.V57L54   1991
221.6'01—dc20
                                                            91-9439